KU-369-739

HARPER & ROW SERIES IN ACCOUNTING AND FINANCE

Consulting Editor: Michael J. Sherer

The aim of this series is to publish lively and readable textbooks for university, polytechnic and professional students, and important, up-to-date reference books for researchers, managers and practising accountants. All the authors have been commissioned because of their specialist knowledge of their subjects and their established reputations as lecturers and researchers. All the major topics in accounting and finance will be included, and the series will give special emphasis to recent developments in the field and to issues of continuing debate and controversy.

CONSOLIDATED FINANCIAL STATEMENTS: CONCEPTS, ISSUES AND TECHNIQUES

CONSOLIDATED FINANCIAL STATEMENTS: CONCEPTS, ISSUES AND TECHNIQUES

P. A. TAYLOR
Lancaster University

Harper & Row, Publishers
London

Cambridge
Mexico City
New York
Philadelphia

San Francisco
São Paulo
Singapore
Sydney

Copyright © 1987 P. A. Taylor
All rights reserved

First published 1987

Harper & Row Ltd
28 Tavistock Street
London WC2E 7PN

No part of this book may be reproduced in any manner whatsoever
without written permission except in the case of brief quotations embodied
in critical articles or reviews.

British Library Cataloguing in Publication Data

Taylor, P.A.
  Consolidated financial statements:
  concepts, issues and techniques.
  1. Financial statements, Consolidated
  I. Title
  657'.3   HF5681.B2

ISBN 0-06-318372-2

Typeset by Burns & Smith, Derby
Printed and bound by Redwood Burn Ltd, Trowbridge

To the students I teach. May we always understand that teaching and learning take place in both directions.

Contents

Series Editor's Foreword

Whenever companies take over or merge with other companies, and whenever they set up separate companies for new ventures, it is necessary to prepare financial statements for the group as a whole as well as for the individual companies within the group. Most companies of any reasonable size are in fact groups of companies where the parent company has an equity stake in one or more other companies. Depending upon the precise equity stake and voting power of the parent company, these companies are defined, by both company law and accounting practice, as subsidiaries, associates or investments. Even companies with a divisionalized organization structure may choose to retain the separate legal identity of their subsidiaries within a division.

It is therefore almost impossible to analyse and interpret the financial statements of modern companies without a thorough knowledge of the principles and techniques of the various types of group accounts. That is why the study of group accounts is such a major part of the syllabuses of accounting degree courses and professional examinations. However, the enthusiasm of many students for the subject area is not always equal to its importance. This is due partly to the inability of most writers to bring the subject to life and partly to the lack of depth and breadth given to group accounts in most financial accounting textbooks.

Paul Taylor's *Consolidated Financial Statements* provides a thoroughly researched analysis of all the main areas of group accounts and is written in a light and entertaining style which will appeal to both degree and professional students. The book includes a discussion of consolidated funds statements, segment reporting and the rationale for consolidated accounts, in addition to the more conventional consolidated balance sheet and profit and loss account. Each new principle and technique is illustrated with worked examples which, as with the rest of the book, have been thoroughly tested in the lecture room. Students will find *Consolidated Financial Statements* a very comprehensive and approachable textbook on the subject of group accounts. It is a valuable addition to the Harper & Row Accounting and Finance Series.

Michael Sherer

Preface and Acknowledgements

The objective of this book is to facilitate an understanding of the technical processes underlying consolidation and group financial reporting within the context of contemporary accounting theory and practice. As such, the book integrates technical procedures, theoretical debates and current practice. It discusses intuitive rationales for consolidation techniques within the context of historical cost accounting, using clearly developed illustrations, worked examples and problem sets. Each of the major financial statements is examined in turn (including the funds statement) and their interrelationships are clarified. Controversial areas and debates (e.g. acquisition and merger accounting, goodwill, foreign currency translation and segmental reporting) are examined from the standpoint of modern accounting theory and empirical research. The numerous accounting standards and pronouncements in this area are also analysed.

Consolidated financial reporting is the most intellectually challenging and central technical area to be covered after the first course in accounting. It is the major new technical area to be mastered, but is often relegated to relative obscurity in advanced accounting courses as a necessary evil, a series of hard techniques to be mastered, with little theoretical merit. Inflation accounting (which has far less practical application) is often given far more prominence. Probably this state of affairs has persisted because of the lack of suitable materials. What is available is mostly a collection of professionally oriented texts which focus on technique and institutional detail, with rather less conceptual analysis. The author's experience is that when such techniques are integrated with theory and issues, students find the area stimulating, relevant, and a concrete and accessible entrée to many issues affecting modern accounting theory. The blend of calculation and discussion generates interest and has a synergistic effect – calculations illustrating theoretical controversies, theoretical controversies clarifying technical procedures.

The text is aimed at second and third year undergraduates at universities and polytechnics, and also at professional examination candidates, both in clarifying and developing their understanding of consolidation procedures (the why as well as the how) and in dealing with the increasing emphasis on discussion questions on issues of principle, accounting standards and theory. Its approach is particularly relevant for the new syllabuses and objective testing (which allows more probing questions about standards and matters of principle). The book has also been used to provide core material for areas within Masters' courses in financial accounting. The prerequisite knowledge assumed is a first course in accounting covering double entry bookkeeping. Throughout the text, debit entries are shown as positive numbers and credit entries as negative numbers. Such a convention prevents confusion in switching from one area to another. Taxation aspects are not covered.

Particular features of the book include: group accounting issues set into a historical and comparative context (particularly with the USA); the use of side-by-side numerical examples and diagrams to compare and contrast acquisition with merger accounting, equity accounting with consolidation alternatives, and also foreign currency translation approaches; integrating frameworks for viewing consolidation adjustments, linking the consolidated profit and loss account with the balance sheet and for preparing and evaluating consolidated funds statements; critical analyses of SSAPs 1, 6, 10, 14, 20, 22, 23; a discussion of the usefulness of consolidated statements and the impact of the wider economic and political environment on their structure.

The book emphasizes and reinforces the basic consolidation processes underlying each financial statement at a reasonable technical level, taking great care not to obscure principles with unnecessarily complex calculations, many of which are dealt with separately in a later chapter, after a well grounded overview has been obtained.

It has been used as the basis for a course on consolidation accounting and its relationship to accounting theory and current practice. It can be used in a variety of ways, emphasizing particular themes as required. Chapters are mainly self-contained so that the book can easily be used if desired over two years (for example Chapters 1, 2, 3, 4 and 6 in year 1 (basic mainstream) and 5, 7, 8, 9 and 10 (more advanced techniques, other statements and controversies) in year 2). The author's experience is that a block on consolidated financial statements including concepts and issues has sufficient variety, depth and illustrative material to form a substantial area of advanced financial accounting and accounting theory courses. At Lancaster University it is a very popular option in its own right, mirroring and reinforcing themes from other courses, and is motivationally very attractive to students in developing their accounting skills whilst also focusing on much broader accounting issues. Other possible approaches to the area are as follows:

Approach	Major emphases (by chapter)
Technical focus	Technical areas of 1, 3–9 and concluding questions
Mainstream introduction	1–6 and 8
Group accounting issues	A selection of technical areas plus discussion areas of 1–4, 7, 9–11 (and selected articles)
Accounting standards/institutional	Technical sections plus institutional discussions in 1–4 and 6–9

The book contains problems sets, graded in function and order of difficulty, and includes a selection of professional examination questions at the end. A teachers' manual is available with solutions to problems, and suggestions for using the text.

Acknowledgements

I wish to express my gratitude to the following people who through their comments, suggestions and encouragement assisted in the preparation of this book: Cliff Taylor (who read innumerable drafts and made numerous helpful suggestions); Robert Ashton of Nottingham University; Simon Archer, David Brown, Pelham Gore, T. S. Ho, Michael Mumford and Ken Peasnell of Lancaster University; A. A. Ibrahim, Robert Yansah and Marcus Milne, formerly of the MA class at Lancaster; Tony Steele of Warwick University; past undergraduates on the 301 and 311 courses who endured many of the errors in drafts and who provided the stimulus for the book; Ian Lough and Jim Reid of ICI; Derek Wilson of Cadbury Schweppes; Peter Holgate, Deloitte, Haskins and Sells; David Tweedie of KMG Thomson McLintock and Visiting Professor at the International Centre for Research in Accounting, University of Lancaster; J. B. Bowers, Peat Marwick & Mitchell; Marianne Lagrange, Catherine McLaren and the readers of Harper and Row. I am also grateful to Val Goulding, Elaine Voyle and Rosemary Timperley for administrative assistance in correcting and copying drafts. The Accounting Standards Committee, the American Institute of Certified Accountants and the Financial Accounting Standards Board for permission to quote from their pronouncements. The Institute of Chartered Accountants in England and Wales and the Chartered Association of Certified Accountants for permission to quote past examination questions. Of course any errors remaining are my own responsibility.

Having now been through the ordeal of writing a first book, I know why people express gratitude to their spouses. It is a real trial of patience and tolerance for those close to you. I'm grateful to Trish my wife for helping me keep my sense of perspective, by kind words, often by patience and sometimes by firm words spoken in kindness.

PART I

FUNDAMENTALS OF
GROUP ACCOUNTING

1 Introduction

Group accounting (with consolidation) is the most important technical area in financial accounting after a first accounting course. It includes numerous challenging technical and conceptual issues not easily resolvable by current accounting theory (which is often concerned with simpler and more abstract issues). This book has two aims – to facilitate the development of technical skills, and to provide a framework for understanding conceptual issues. The first section of this chapter briefly outlines historical developments in group accounting; the second examines interactions between organizational structures of complex entities and financial statement preparation.

THE DEVELOPMENT OF GROUP ACCOUNTING

The twentieth century has been characterized by accelerating technological advance, societal change and increasing complexity in business organization. A single multinational corporation today might be involved in mining, manufacturing and marketing a wide range of products incorporating vastly different technologies in a number of different countries. A marked trend towards conducting business through groups of companies controlled by a single holding company has occurred, the holding company usually exercising its control over its subsidiaries via its voting power. At first most subsidiaries were wholly owned, but by the 1920s and 1930s majority holdings became more common.

In the UK until the 1940s, holding company shareholders usually only received individual company accounts which were not very informative. Investments were stated at cost, and if a profit and loss account was provided at all, only dividends due from subsidiaries were shown. No information was given about the total assets and liabilities controlled by the group as a whole, or details of the profitability of subsidiaries – as if the holding company was walled in as shown by Figure 1.1.

The amount of disclosure depended on the corporate form adopted. Using a divisional or departmental structure within a single legal entity would require disclosure of all the assets, liabilities and profits of the complete entity. Similar companies might carry on the same business via subsidiaries, legally separate companies controlled by the holding company. Because at that time accounts were *legal entity* based, these companies would disclose only the assets and liabilities of the *holding company* and the dividends due from investments (in subsidiaries). It was not surprising then that disclosure-shy managements usually opted for the holding company–subsidiary corporate format.

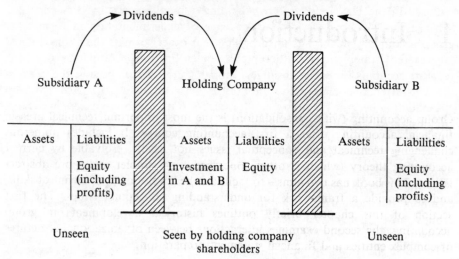

Figure 1.1   Effects of holding company accounting

The first holding company was formed in the USA in 1832, though it took until the 1890s for the first consolidated accounts to be published. US Steel set the standard in its 1900 accounts, producing consolidated accounts by aggregating the component assets and liabilities of the holding company and its subsidiaries. Effectively, the investment at cost in the holding company's own accounts was expanded into the component assets and liabilities of the subsidiaries. Further, US Steel disclosed *profits earned* by the subsidiaries rather than just dividends received – the latter being open to easy manipulation by management. Such consolidated accounts narrowed disclosure differences between divisional and holding company–subsidiary formats. By the 1920s consolidation was generally accepted practice in the USA and such consolidated statements were viewed as improvements on and substitutes for holding company statements.[1]

Edwards and Webb (1984) found the earliest example of consolidated statements in the UK to be Pearson and Knowles Coal and Iron Co. Ltd in 1910, but such reporting was not widely adopted. An early and influential advocate of consolidation was Sir Gilbert Garnsey who published a book on the subject in 1923, but the publication of consolidated accounts by Dunlop Rubber in 1933 was still a newsworthy event. Edwards and Webb suggest a number of plausible explanations for this slow takeup including the inherent conservatism of the UK accounting profession, its possible lack of expertise in the area, a predisposition of UK managements towards secrecy (and the use of 'secret reserves' prior to the *Royal Mail* case) and the influence of contemporary company law which required disclosure of individual company information. Because of these company law antecedents, consolidation and group accounts have subsequently been viewed in the UK as *supplementary to* holding company reports and not substitutes for them.

The state of Victoria in Australia in 1938 became the first place in the world to require consolidated accounts by law. Not until 1947 were group accounts required in the UK, *in addition to* holding company accounts. Prior to this, Edwards and Webb (1984) found evidence of experimentation in format for group accounts. Thus it was unsurprising that other formats than consolidated (aggregated) statements were acceptable under the 1947 Companies Act, e.g. separate accounts for each subsidiary, though consolidation became the norm in the UK after that date. Not until 1978 with the issue of SSAP 14, did consolidation become the *prescribed* format for group accounts except in defined circumstances. In Europe developments were even slower. Nobes and Parker (1985) comment that German companies were not obliged to consolidate until 1965, and as late as 1967 only twenty-two French companies published consolidated balance sheets.

By the 1930s majority (less than 100 per cent) interests in subsidiaries were common, and accounting for minority interests was widely discussed. Since 1947, groups have increasingly acquired substantially but not majority owned companies. Accounting for such related/associated companies was only agreed in 1971 when the first UK accounting standard required the 'equity' method, midway between the cost approach and full consolidation. Walker (1978a) and Edwards and Webb (1984) found that such an approach had been used for subsidiaries as early as the 1920s as an alternative to consolidation, but had fallen out of favour. Particularly in the USA, a vehement debate raged in the 1960s and 1970s over the best way to account for business combinations. At present in the UK there are no fewer than five accounting standards dealing specifically with group accounts, an area of growing importance as corporate structures grow ever more complex and diverse. Recently the EEC has published its Seventh Directive dealing with group accounts, due to be enacted into British law by 1990.

Some argue that accounting technique has not kept pace with such environmental change, and that many of the proposals around now are merely recycled versions of debates which took place as early as the 1920s. As will be demonstrated, accounting for complex corporate structures is not at all straightforward. At times aggregate information is less helpful than a detailed breakdown by segments. However, it is still true to say that consolidation has stood the test of time as the most widely used and accepted approach to accounting for complex groups, and most financial ratio analyses use the consolidated accounts.

THE ORGANIZATION OF COMPLEX CORPORATE STRUCTURES

Most corporations are set up as limited liability companies. Large companies deal with the problems caused by size by organizing on a divisional basis or via subsidiaries or by some combination of the two. In the former, the divisions are subsets of a single legal entity. In the latter, a group comprises a number of separate legal entities. Non-corporate entities are usually legally constituted and accounted for as partnerships, whose accounting problems are not examined in this book.

Divisional corporate structures

Divisionalization has legal advantages over the holding company–subsidiary format. Certain legal expenses are reduced since, in a group of separate legal entities, each company is required to publish its own accounts which are to be separately audited. Only one audit is required in a divisional structure. There can be taxation advantages.

There are many possibilities for accounting systems in a divisionalized company. At one end of the spectrum, accounting records can be centralized at head office (often termed *departmental accounting*). Financial statements are produced for each 'department' and overheads centrally allocated, etc. At the other end of the spectrum, the division keeps its own financial records, linked to the head office records via a set of interlinking 'control' accounts (such an alternative often being termed *branch accounting*). The division produces its own financial statements which at the end of the period are combined with those of other divisions and head office by a process analogous to the consolidation of the financial statements of legally separate entities. Profits are usually transferred to head office at the end of each period.

Example 1.1   Branch accounting

Hub Ltd has the following balance sheet at 1 January 1986:

Balance sheet at 1 January 1986 (£000)

Fixed assets	900	Loan	300
Stock	500	Share capital	1,000
Cash	1,000	Reserves	1,100
	2,400		2,400

On this date, Hub forms two divisions. Head office will administer both divisions and market bicycle hubs. The newly formed Spoke division will market bicycle spokes and rims, and will keep its own accounting records. On 2 January head office sends £500,000 to establish Spoke division. During the year, the following transactions take place:

Head office
1. Stocks costing £300,000 were sold for £600,000 in cash.
2. Depreciation of £50,000 was charged for the year.
3. Administrative costs for the group were £300,000.
4. A management charge of £100,000 was made to Spoke division to cover its share of administration costs.

Spoke division
5. Purchases of stocks (all for cash) totalled £300,000.
6. £200,000 of goods were sold for £500,000 in cash.
7. Spoke sent head office a remittance covering the year's management fee.

The bookkeeping entries are shown in the form of 'T' accounts below:

Head office records (£000)   **Branch records (£000)**

Cash					Cash			
b/f	1,000	** Set up	500	** Set up	500	5 Stock	300
1 Sales	600	3 Admin	300	6 Sales	500	7 Remittance	100
7 Remittance	100						

Fixed assets			
b/f	900	2 Depn	50

Stock					Stock			
b/f	500	1 COGS	300	5 Stock	300	6 COGS	200

Loan			
		b/f	300

Share capital			
		b/f	1,000

Reserves (incl. P & L)					P & L			
1 COGS	300	b/f	1,100	4 Mgt fee	100	6 Sales	500
2 Depn	50	1 Sales	600	6 COGS	200		
3 Admin	300	4 Mgt fee	100	* To H/O	200		
		*Spoke profits	200	profits			

Branch A/C					Head office A/C			
** Set up	500	7 Remittance	100	7 Remittance	100	** Set up	500
4 Mgt fee	100					4 Mgt fee	100
* Spoke profits	200					* H/O profits	200

The vital feature of *branch accounting* is the interlocking control accounts. Consider their entries – first, the set up of the branch (marked ** in the accounts). £500,000 is transferred from head office. Thus the branch has a debit balance in head office's books and head office has a credit balance in the branch's books. Cash decreases at head office and increases at the branch. When a transaction involves an interdivisional transfer it is a *fourfold* entry, two extra components recording the interdivisional indebtedness.

The management fee is treated as a contribution towards head office administration expenses. The fourfold entry affects the profit and loss accounts of both together with the control accounts. A similar fourfold entry occurs when profit is transferred to head office (marked * in the accounts). Note the *payment* of the management fee is a separate transaction from its accrual. At each stage, the control accounts should be mirror images of each other. Consider the accounts of each division and also those of the company:

Balance sheets at 31 December 1986

	Head office (£000)	Spoke division (£000)	Company (£000)
Fixed assets	850		850
Stock	200	100	300
Cash	900	600	1,500
Branch accounts	700	(700)	—
Loan	(300)		(300)
Share capital	(1,000)		(1,000)
Reserves	(1,350)		(1,350)

The branch control accounts cancel out when divisions are combined since they reflect purely *internal* indebtedness whereas the accounts of the company as a whole reflect its external relationships. *Cancellation of internal balances is central to all consolidation procedures.* Note that head office equity incorporates the branch on a 'profits earned' basis.

Holding company–subsidiary structure

Now 'divisions' become legally separate entities. Despite the statutory expenses incurred, there are advantages of this form of structure (but *not* the avoidance of disclosure as in pre-consolidation days). Acquisitions and disposals of subsidiaries are easier to effect than divisions, since they are legally self-contained, and it is possible to deal in fractional interests, whereas divisions are always wholly owned. A legally incorporated subsidiary may be necessary in a foreign country in order to benefit from taxation concessions. Also, in theory each company has separate limited liability, and is protected against the insolvency of the others, whereas if a division were liquidated other divisions would be liable for its debts. In practice the use of such a device would significantly harm the creditworthiness of other group companies. However, a group's legal structure may only reflect the manner of its corporate acquisitions, rather than having any deeper meaning.

Consider the following example of a 100 per cent holding company–subsidiary relationship which is designed to be as similar as possible to Example 1.1.

Example 1.2   Consolidation accounting

Suppose Hub plc has the same balance sheet at 1 January 1986 as before, but on 2 January sets up a *subsidiary,* Spoke Ltd, by purchasing 500,000 £1 shares of Spoke for £500,000 in cash. Immediately after the transaction, Spoke's balance sheet would be as follows:

Spoke Ltd – balance sheet at 2 January 1986 (£000)

Cash	500	Share capital	500

On 2 January, assuming no other trading, Hub's balance sheet would become:

Hub plc – balance sheet at 2 January 1986 (£000)

Fixed assets	900	Loan	300
Investment	500	Share capital	1,000
Stock	500	Reserves	1,100
Cash	500		
	2,400		2,400

The individual company and consolidated balance sheets would be as follows:

Balance sheets at 2 January 1986

	Hub	Spoke	Elimination	Consolidated
Fixed assets	900	—	—	900
Investment	500	—	(500)	—
Stock	500	—	—	500
Cash	500	500	—	1,000
Loan	(300)	—	—	(300)
Share capital	(1,000)	(500)	500	(1,000)
Reserves	(1,100)	—	—	(1,100)

The investment has been cancelled against the share capital of Spoke. In Example 1.1 £500,000 was advanced directly to Spoke division. In this case £500,000 was introduced into Spoke by issuing shares for cash. The head office account in Spoke's records in the branch accounting example is analogous to its share capital in this case – both representing the holding company's stake. Previously Hub could remove its stake at any time since the divisional arrangement was purely for internal convenience. Now, since Spoke is a registered company, it would have to undertake the full legal process of liquidation to remove its funds (or else to sell its shares). The investment account in Hub's books is analogous to the branch account, thus the cancellation.

Suppose the year's transactions, shown below, were the same as in Example 1.1, except that just before its year-end Spoke Ltd declared a dividend of £100,000. Transaction recording is similar to the branch account case except for the following differences: the capital transaction setting up the company (marked ** in the accounts) is segregated from trading transactions and shown as investment and share capital; trading transactions are passed through intra-group debtor and creditor accounts which function like the branch accounts of the previous section. By law the companies are regarded as separate legal entities and each is bound not to distribute its contributed capital. The *profits* of the subsidiary are not automatically transferred to the holding company as in branch accounting. As with other investments, only *dividends* declared by the subsidiary are recorded in the holding company's accounts (marked * in the accounts), as shown in Figure 1.1

Bookkeeping entries – holding company/subsidiary (£000)

Hub plc   **Spoke Ltd**

Cash (Hub plc)

b/f	1,000	** Investment	500
1 Sales	600	3 Admin	300
7 Mgt fee	100		

Cash (Spoke Ltd)

** Share issue	500	5 Stock	300
6 Sales	500	7 Mgt fee	100

Fixed assets

b/f	900	2 Depn	50

Stock (Hub plc)

b/f	500	1 COGS	300

Stock (Spoke Ltd)

5 Stock	300	6 COGS	200

Loan

		b/f	300

Hub share capital

		b/f	1,000

Reserves (incl. P & L)

1 COGS	300	b/f	1,100
2 Depn	50	1 Sales	600
3 Admin	300	4 Mgt fee	100
		* Dividend	100

P & L a/c (Spoke)

4 Mgt fee	100	6 Sales	500
6 COGS	200		
* Dividend	100		

Investment in Spoke

** Shares	500		

Spoke share capital

		** Issue	500

Spoke – group debtor

4 Mgt fee	100	7 Mgt fee	100
* Dividend	100		

Hub – group creditor

7 Mgt fee	100	4 Mgt fee	100
		* Dividend	100

Consider now the individual company and group consolidated financial statements (£000). Note the cancellation of intercompany indebtedness.

Balance sheets at 31 December 1986

	Hub	Spoke	Elimination	Consolidated
Fixed assets	850	—	—	850
Investment	500	—	(500)	—
Stock	200	100	—	300
Debtors – Spoke	100	—	(100)	—
Cash	900	600	—	1,500
Creditors – Hub	—	(100)	100	—
Loan	(300)	—	—	(300)
Share capital	(1,000)	(500)	500	(1,000)
Reserves	(1,250)	(100)	—	(1,350)

Under UK company law, Hub plc must disclose both its own balance sheet *and* the group's consolidated balance sheet. In the divisional case only the company balance sheet is required, which in these examples would be the same as the consolidated balance sheet in the group case. Consider the profit and loss accounts of the companies and the group.

Profit and loss accounts – year ended 31 December 1986 (£000)

	Hub	*Spoke*	*Consolidated*
Sales	600	500	1,100
COGS	(300)	(200)	(500)
Depreciation	(50)	—	(50)
Administration	(300)	—	(300)
Management fee	100	(100)	—
Profit before dividends	50	200	250
Intra-group dividends	100	(100)	—
Retained earnings	150	100	250

Under UK company law, Hub is required to publish only a consolidated profit and loss account. A separate holding company profit and loss account is not required provided it states how much of its own profits are included therein. In branch accounting, Hub would merely disclose its company profit and loss account (which in these examples is the same as its consolidated profit and loss account in the group case).

The aggregate accounts under both branch and consolidation accounting are identical in these simple examples, illustrating that the processes of aggregation are essentially the same. However, the analogue of the head office accounts is not holding company accounts. The head office accounts include the branch's profits earned, whereas the holding company accounts include the subsidiary's dividends receivable. In the latter, the difference between the holding company's and consolidated retained earnings is the subsidiary's undistributed retained earnings of £100,000. Later it will be shown that the analogy in group accounting is the equity approach – the assets and liabilities of the 'associate' being excluded, and income being recognized on a profits earned basis.

The rest of the book focuses on accounting for groups of companies within the holding company–subsidiary relationship since this is by far the most common form of organization for complex entities in the UK. Most of the techniques discussed have counterparts in branch accounting (e.g. foreign branches, alignment adjustments, etc.).

Exercise

1.1   In the Hub/Spoke examples:

(a)   Suppose in *the divisional structure case* that the transactions for 1987 were as follows:

Head office

1.   Stock purchases (all for cash) were £400,000.

2. Cash sales of £800,000 of stocks costing £300,000 were made to outsiders. Further non-cash sales of £200,000 of stocks costing £100,000 were made to Spoke division.
3. Depreciation of £50,000 was charged for the year.
4. Administration costs for the company were £400,000.
5. A management charge of £125,000 was made to Spoke division.

Spoke division

1. Purchases of stocks totalled £400,000 for cash and £200,000 on credit from head office.
2. £800,000 of goods were sold (including all the goods purchased from head office) whose cost was £400,000.
3. Spoke sent head office a remittance to cover its management fee, its stock purchases for the year and an additional £100,000.

Required   Enter the above transactions in 'T' accounts, paying particular attention to the transactions which affect the interlocking accounts. Prepare divisional balance sheets for both companies at 31 December 1987 and a company balance sheet.

(b) Assume that a *holding company–subsidiary* relationship exists and that the transactions are the same except that the additional £100,000 above relates to the payment of last year's dividend, and the dividend declared for this year is £200,000.

Required   Prepare individual company balance sheets for both companies and a consolidated balance sheet for the Hub–Spoke group. (If you wish, prepare 'T' accounts, but they are not essential.)

(c) Compare the balance sheets in (a) and (b).

SUMMARY

The chapter has reviewed the historical development of group accounting in the UK, discussing the drawbacks of accounting for holding companies purely on a legal entity basis. Only dividends due from subsidiaries are recorded, giving rise to a great temptation to smooth holding company profits, and the underlying assets and liabilities under the control of the group are not disclosed. The difference between accounting for divisionalized companies (departmental and branch accounting) and group structures (consolidation accounting) was examined, and the process of consolidation as a means of achieving some comparability in disclosure was discussed. In consolidated accounts, subsidiaries' results are accounted for on a profits earned basis, which in principle allows less scope for manipulation of results via dividend policies of subsidiaries.

NOTES

1. Holding company financial statements are not usually included in the annual reports of US groups, but US registered companies have to include such statements in filings with the SEC.

FURTHER READING

Historical development

Edwards, J. R. and Webb, K. M. (1984) The development of group accounting in the United Kingdom to 1933, *The Accounting Historians Journal,* Vol. 11, No. 1, pp. 31–61.
Walker, R. G. (1978) *Consolidated Statements: A History and Analysis,* Arno Press, New York.

Entity organizational structures

Deloitte, Haskins & Sells (1983) *Corporate Structure – Subsidiaries or Divisions?,* Deloitte, Haskins & Sells, London.

2 The Nature of Group Accounts

Modern group accounts constitute a highly complex package of financial statements. For some groups they are prepared from a database incorporating more than a hundred subsidiaries in more than a score of currencies. They involve complex accounting issues and group structures, and become manageable only through the use of computer packages. As a prelude to examining these areas, this chapter reviews in broad outline the legal and institutional context of group accounts in the UK, which shapes their content and scope. It examines purported objectives for group accounts, the criteria for when group accounts are to be prepared, and the form such accounts should take.

Group accounts are normally presented in consolidated form, aggregating the accounts of the holding company and subsidiaries after adjustment, to produce a single set of accounts. The term 'group accounts' is wider than 'consolidated accounts' since it is possible to provide alternative formats (e.g. consolidated accounts for some subsidiaries and separate statements for others which are dissimilar, or producing separate statements for each subsidiary). Group accounts also include accounting entries relating to substantially but not majority owned affiliates (called under UK law 'related companies'), information about business segments of the group and holdings and indebtedness in and with subsidiaries and affiliates.

The criteria for when group accounts are to be prepared lead to the somewhat controversial area of what constitutes a group for accounting purposes. In the UK, USA and Australia definitions focus on *legally enforceable rights* (e.g. of share ownership or ability to appoint directors), the so-called *de jure* approach. In Germany, and in the initial draft of the EEC directive on group accounts, definitions focus on the *fact* of economic control, on the existence of central and unified management irrespective of potential control via legal rights – the *de facto* approach. Such differences reflect differing viewpoints as to the objectives of group accounts.

In the UK, consolidation is usual for all subsidiaries, subject to defined exclusion criteria where it is deemed misleading or inappropriate. Legislation or standards usually prescribe alternative disclosures for excluded subsidiaries, which are thus included in the group accounts, but not in the main consolidation.

THE OBJECTIVES OF GROUP ACCOUNTS

Few studies have examined the extent to which the objectives of group accounts are distinct from those of individual company accounting statements. Very little is known about user needs in this area. Walker (1978a) analyses often overlapping hypotheses in the accounting literature and what follows draws on his analysis, with some modifications. A basic controversy is the extent to which a group exists as a reporting 'entity' in its own right, distinct from the holding company.

One view is that group accounts, mere memorandum statements, are prepared for the proprietors of the holding company, the primary entity, to amplify information in holding company accounts. Consolidation is then only one possible format for this amplification, another being, for example, separate financial statements for subsidiaries. Even if agreeing with this perspective, others grant greater importance to consolidation, as a group's legal structure as holding company and subsidiaries is often a result of historical accident as to the sequence of acquisitions or for taxation or other reasons. In this case consolidated accounts would be of primary importance.

Some view the group as an entity in its own right, distinct from the shareholders of the holding company, arguing that the focus of consolidated reports should be wider than this narrow group, and that a wider set of users have 'a reasonable right to information arising from the public accountability of the entity' (ASSC, *Corporate Report*, 1975, p. 77). This leads to a definition in terms of concentrations of economic power over resources – the *actual* exercise of control, rather than shareholder rights. The EEC Seventh Directive supported such a definition in its early drafts. It also required a European subconsolidation of subsidiaries of multinationals, suggesting the focus of such accounts was wider than ultimate holding company shareholders. However, in its final form (to be embodied into UK law by 1990), the subconsolidation requirement was dropped and the Directive's core definitions moved towards a definition based on shareholder control, but optional clauses allow member states to embrace the *de facto* definition. It requires consolidated accounts in addition to those of the parent undertaking.

UK company law tends to amplification and proprietary viewpoints. Group accounts are produced by the holding company *in addition to* its own company accounts, in contrast to the USA where consolidated accounts are often the only published financial statements in annual reports (see Chapter 1, note 1). The Companies Act 1985 (section 230(2)) states that 'Group accounts shall give a true and fair view . . . so far as concerns members of the [holding] company' and gives directors the option to use alternative formats to consolidated accounts. In the UK *companies* are legal entities, not groups. Groups cannot enter into contracts or enforce them. Indeed, in the Companies Act the definition of a group is only implicit, deducible from the definition of holding company–subsidiary relationship, the primary use of which is to determine the scope of group accounts. UK and US group definitions are both shareholder based. SSAP 14 constrains the flexibility given by the Companies Acts. It refers to the 'usual practice' of preparing group accounts as if they were the financial statements of a single entity, and *requires* consolidation except in certain specified cases.

Walker (1978a) cites other objectives including that consolidated accounts facilitate the assessment of firms' abilities to meet their debts (see Chapter 4). He contends that writers cite particular objectives but produce proposals inconsistent with those objectives, a theme examined later in the book.

DEFINING A GROUP

The Companies Act 1985, section 229, states that group accounts should be prepared if at the *end* of the year a company has subsidiaries. However, these are not required if the company is itself at the end of the year a *wholly owned* subsidiary of another company incorporated in the UK. The term 'group' here refers to the focus of group accounts. The current UK group definition, originating from the Companies Act 1947, is soon to be modified as a result of incorporating the EEC Seventh Directive into UK legislation by 1990. The current UK position is discussed first, and its boundaries clarified by comparing it with current US and German positions. Then the changes as a result of the EEC Seventh Directive are examined.

The current UK position

In the UK a group is implicitly defined as a holding company and its subsidiaries. Under the Companies Act 1985 (section 736),

> a company is deemed to be the subsidiary of another if (but only if)
> (a)   that other either:
>   (i) is a member of it and controls the composition of its board of directors, or
>   (ii) holds more than half in nominal value of its equity share capital, or
> (b)   the first mentioned company is a subsidiary of any company which is that other's subsidiary.

Subsection (a)(i) requires *membership and legally effective control*. Subsection (a)(ii) requires majority *participation* (though not necessarily voting control, as all equity may not carry equal voting rights). Subsection (b) recognizes that 'control' can be exercised through a vertical chain of 'controlled' subsidiaries. Nobes (1986, p. 5) points out that 'ownership is a sufficient condition whereas control is neither necessary nor sufficient [since membership is also required]'.

Shaw (1976, p. 71) comments that the 1947 Cohen Committee (whose report formed the basis of the Companies Act 1947 which first incorporated the above definition) appeared to emphasize the concept of 'control' but not the requirement of membership, which was introduced at a subsequent stage. The concept of an equity majority was referred to merely as an example of circumstances of possible control. However, rather than treating it as a rebuttable presumption the Act introduced it as an equal requirement, making it possible for one company to be the subsidiary of two holding companies as shown in Example 2.1. Shaw provides other examples of where no 'group' exists under the current definition, such as where the ultimate holding entity is not a limited company or where control is exercised other than by membership.

Example 2.1   One company as the subsidiary of two holding companies

Doublespeak Ltd has 'A' and 'B' classes of ordinary shares, for which total nominal amounts are £1 million and £2 million respectively. Only 'A' shares carry voting rights. Votecontroller plc holds 51 per cent of the 'A' shares and 49 per cent of the 'B' shares. Participator plc holds 51 per cent of the 'B' shares and 49 per cent of the 'A' shares. Votecontroller appoints the majority of the board of directors of Doublespeak by virtue of its voting rights.

Doublespeak is a subsidiary of Votecontroller which is a *member* of it and *controls* the composition of its board of directors (criterion (a)(i)), but also of Participator which *owns* more than half the nominal amount of its *equity* capital (49 per cent of £1 million plus 51 per cent of £2 million) (criterion (a)(ii)). Prior to SSAP 14, both companies could consolidate Doublespeak. SSAP 14 changed this by requiring exclusion from consolidation where a company owns a majority of equity but not of votes. Without modifying the legal definition of a subsidiary (details of excluded subsidiaries are disclosed in *group* accounts), SSAP 14 used the flexibility in formats allowed by the Companies Act to ensure only voting controlled subsidiaries are *consolidated*.

However, a marginal change in the holdings so that each company owns 50 per cent each of the 'A' and 'B' shares would mean (provided neither could appoint the majority of directors) that Doublespeak is a subsidiary of *neither*! This minor incremental change could have a great threshold effect on the group financial statements and ratio analyses, since the equity method would probably be used, not full consolidation (see Chapter 4).

Limitations and boundaries of the UK definition – the 'true and fair view'

It is worth considering briefly a couple of cases, one in the UK and one in the USA, which are important in considering how far the UK definition can be modified and what form such modifications can take to disclose a 'true and fair view'.

Example 2.2   The date group existence is determined (The Argyll Foods case)

Section 229 of the Companies Act states that group accounts should be prepared if at the *end* of the year a company has subsidiaries. The *Argyll Foods* case (see for example Bird, 1982) decided that it is not permissible to restate the scope of consolidation to include subsidiaries acquired subsequent to the end of the period, even if the motive is to show a 'true and fair view' via clearer presentation.

This case and its subsequent interpretation have resulted in a continuing and vigorous debate over the ways it is permissible to adjust accounts to disclose a true and fair view (see e.g. ICAEW, 1985, and Law Society, 1986). However, only aspects particularly relating to group accounts are discussed here. The

Companies Act has changed since the case, focusing some of the issues. Section 228(3) of the 1985 Act states that the requirement to show 'a true and fair view' overrides provisions elsewhere in the Act as regards matters to be included in group accounts. Sections 228(4) and (5) state that if the accounts do not give a 'true and fair view', this requirement is to be satisfied firstly by giving *additional* information (to that resulting from straight compliance) in the financial statements or notes, and only where a true and fair view does not result even from giving this additional information can departures from strict compliance be permitted.

However, a Department of Trade and Industry statement (1982) on the *Argyll* case expressed the view that, in relation to subsidiaries acquired since the year-end, the alternative of restating the accounts would not be available, since section 229 which defines subsidiaries to be included is 'not a requirement as to matters to be included in the accounts, but a definition of group accounts and the companies they must deal with'.

The statement went on to say that

> where it is necessary in order to give a true and fair view of the financial position of [group companies defined according to the Companies Act] to include in the accounts information about [another] company which is neither the holding company nor a subsidiary, that information must be given in accordance with the provisions [discussed above].

Thus there would have been no problem if Argyll had included as supplementary information the accounts of the subsidiary acquired after the year-end, rather than including it in the main consolidation *as if* it had been a subsidiary at the year-end.

Example 2.3   A controlling financial interest without membership (a real case)

An interesting example which helps in an examination of the above problems is the *Digilog* case in the USA. A US company, Digilog Inc. (Digilog), wished to enter the high-risk microcomputer market. Rather than acquire an existing company, it decided to incorporate Digilog Business Systems (DBS) with a former vice-president of the systems division of Commodore Business Machines as its chief executive. The agreement between Digilog and DBS was contingent amongst other things on receipt of an opinion by Coopers and Lybrand that DBS would not have to be consolidated in Digilog's financial statements. In entering a new market, DBS made considerable losses in its early years which were not consolidated in Digilog's statements.

Digilog provided 90 per cent of DBS's opening working capital in exchange for notes convertible at will into 90 per cent of DBS's common stock (shares). The agreement also specified that DBS would continue to employ the current chief executive or another person satisfactory to Digilog, and that DBS could not merge or sell its assets without Digilog's consent (which could not be unreasonably withheld). The agreement also included a financing plan in which Digilog would lend amounts to DBS provided it met certain financial targets, a business plan which amongst other things specified the sales director, the support services director and certain organizational characteristics of DBS, and a distribution plan limiting DBS's actions.

Under US provisions Digilog did not possess a 'controlling financial interest' in terms of more than half the votes. Further, regulation S–X of the Securities and Exchange Commission (SEC) states that a subsidiary which is not majority owned should not be consolidated. However, the SEC in its Opinion and Order (SEC, 1984) commented that APB Statement No. 4's requirement of 'substance over form' (the US counterpart of a 'true and fair view') overrode the specific definition and stated that 'consolidation may be required in the absence of majority ownership where one entity in substance achieves the same effect as majority ownership, through control by contract or otherwise'.

In the UK, if the DTI's statement on the *Argyll* case is taken as correct, a plausible application of its principles might suggest that it would be illegal to consolidate DBS since the 'true and fair view' requirement in the Act is subservient to requirements stating which subsidiaries should be consolidated. Digilog is not a member of DBS, and so DBS would not be a subsidiary under a strict interpretation of the UK definition. However, if further information about DBS (which is not a member of the legally defined group) is not given *in addition to* the group accounts, then (according to the DTI's interpretation) these accounts may not disclose a true and fair view for the legally defined group itself, and so might be contrary to the Companies Act provisions.

This case stands at the limit of a current vigorous debate involving the professional accounting bodies, the Law Society and the DTI over how far transactions should be recorded to reflect their substance rather than their form. For example, it could be argued that DBS's assets and liabilities should be included in the group accounts because they are in substance assets and liabilities relating to an off-balance-sheet financing arrangement of a member of the group, rather than the attempted consolidation of a 'subsidiary'. This debate is considered further in Chapter 11. Technically the UK definition of a group is not altered by such treatment, but under either alternative above, the 'true and fair' requirement may ameliorate extreme consequences of a *de jure* definition.

The US and German definitions – antecedents of the EEC Seventh Directive

To set the current definition into context, and to appreciate the changes proposed by the EEC Seventh Directive, it is helpful to compare it with the current US and German positions. Both were formative in preparing the Directive and provide insights into the nature of its proposals.

As in the UK, the US definition is based on legally enforceable rights (*de jure*). The inclusion criterion is where one enterprise *directly or indirectly* has a *controlling financial interest* in other enterprises. ARB No. 51 states that the *usual* condition for such a controlling financial interest is direct or indirect ownership of over 50 per cent of the outstanding *voting* shares. Though a *de jure* criterion, this definition is quite different from the UK one, based on voting rights not total equity holdings.

Unlike the USA and the UK, in Germany the definition of a group is based on an economic concept of control, on whether or not there is a *centralized and unified management,* irrespective of holdings or legal powers, even irrespective of whether there is a holding company (i.e. on the economic *fact* of a group, rather than the potentiality of power). A group is regarded as a legal entity. Group accounts are viewed as reports on economic concentrations of control for wider purposes, particularly as consolidated accounts are required in addition for 'groups' not headed by limited companies (e.g. individuals and partnerships). Only domestic subsidiaries are consolidated.

Impending changes to the UK definition by the EEC Seventh Directive

This Directive, binding on the UK and due to be enacted into UK law by 1990, will change the UK definition of a group. Early drafts followed the German *de facto* criterion of central and unified management and required certain groups not headed by limited companies to be consolidated. However, this was not acceptable to the majority and would have caused sweeping changes in national laws, because of complex legal interactions. It was suggested that the Church of England might have to produce consolidated accounts!

The final version tries to accommodate the wide divergences in practice in the EEC. The core compulsory definition is now *de jure.* Consolidated accounts are only compulsory for groups headed by limited liability companies but *non-incorporated subsidiaries* must be included. Certain optional criteria of a *de facto* nature can be introduced by member states (mainly to preserve the basis of their own national approach), but it is unlikely that the UK will do so. For example, Germany will probably require consolidation where subsidiaries are managed on a unified basis, and also where groups are headed by non-limited liability parents.

The core definition requires consolidation (subject to exclusion criteria to be discussed later) where the parent undertaking:
(a) has a majority of voting rights; or
(b) is a member and has the right to appoint a majority of the board of directors; or
(c) has a right to exercise a dominant influence as the result of a 'control contract'; or
(d) is a member and as the result of an agreement with other shareholders in the subsidiary, has the right to control alone a majority of voting rights.

Voting rights include those held by the parent *and* by subsidiaries or nominees, and article 3 states that a subsidiary of a subsidiary shall by that fact be treated as a subsidiary of the parent company.

This compulsory definition will modify the UK definition slightly. The current requirement of the majority of *equity* rights will need to be changed to *voting* rights (which will now include *indirect* holdings as in the USA). The clause on 'control contracts' is unlikely to affect the UK, since such contracts are rare outside Germany. However, depending on how such a clause is defined it could cover cases like Digilog. Clause (d) will allow minority control under certain circumstances. The UK has the right to determine the forms of agreement which will satisfy (d), and it is likely these will be restricted to lasting and legally enforceable ones.

None of the *options* in this area is likely to be adopted by the UK. However, these are interesting in terms of previous discussions. Consolidation *may* be required by individual member states where a parent:

(a) *has* appointed the majority of the board of directors, solely as a result of its voting rights;
(b) actually exercises a dominant influence over a subsidiary;
(c) manages itself and the subsidiary on a unified basis.

A sceptic might feel that the Directive narrows very little the differences in countries with group accounting requirements. However countries which at present have no such requirements (e.g. France and Italy) are now required to have them. The Directive also extends the UK exemption for wholly owned subsidiaries from producing group accounts to at least 90 per cent owned subsidiaries of EEC registered companies, where the minority agrees. The UK has until 2000 to implement this change! The international accounting standard – IAS No. 3, 'Consolidated financial statements', published in 1976 – adds little. Its basic criterion is a majority of voting rights held directly or indirectly, but it has option clauses which broadly cover the UK and German positions.

'Group' accounts also include the results of substantially but not majority owned companies (related/associated companies). The definition and accounting treatment of these is discussed in Chapter 4.

The link between objectives and group concepts

Walker (1978a) shows that problems over group definition have a pedigree of over fifty years. He tries to link proposals with the functional objectives for consolidation suggested in the literature, illustrating that differences stem from disagreements over fundamental objectives. Table 2.1 lists objectives for consolidation gleaned from Walker's historical analysis of the literature and his deduction of the area of consolidation and the form of group accounts corresponding to these.

The first two objectives define the scope of consolidation in terms of the holding company's interest, and the third in terms of creditors' interests. The last two view the group itself as an entity, the former in terms of managerial (*de facto*) control, whereas the latter narrows this to consolidate only a homogeneous subset of economic activities. The current UK position hovers uneasily between objectives 1 and 2, whereas the USA tends to 1. The initial EEC position would be consistent with 4. However, as Walker (1978b) points out, most proposals are compromise affairs (e.g. the exclusion of dissimilar lines of business allowed by the Companies Act incorporates something of 5). Walker's table provides a useful framework for discussion. Later, reasons for the compromise nature of current practice will be examined. Whether it is because of confused theory (as suggested by Walker) or deeper political and behavioural factors underlying the accounting environment, will be considered.

Status and supposed function	Possible area of consolidation
1. Primary documents – to depict the financial position and performance of *holding companies*	Holding company and substantially owned subsidiaries
2. Supplementary reports – to *amplify* the financial statements of holding companies	Substantially owned subsidiaries only, excluding holding company, *or* A series of group statements each covering those subsidiaries engaged in particular line of business, *or* A series of group statements each covering domestic subsidiaries, foreign subsidiaries *or* Holding company and all 'material' subsidiaries
3. Supplementary reports – to facilitate *assessments* of the ability of firms to meet their *debts*	Holding company and all 'controlled' subsidiaries, *or* All companies which have guaranteed the indebtedness of other companies, plus the companies subject to those guarantees, *or* Some other combination – depending on the pattern of intercompany loans
4. Supplementary statements – to depict position and performance of *'group entities'*	All corporations (or unincorporated associations) subject to (actually exercised) control (NB: tests of control might be based on voting power or contractual rights)
5. Supplementary statements to depict position and performance of *'economic entities'*	All 'controlled' corporations (or unincorporated associations) engaged in specified business activity or activities

Source: Exhibit 1 in Walker (1978b) (emphases added).

Table 2.1   The link between objectives and the area of consolidation

Consolidated accounts	Balance sheet, profit and loss, funds statement, general notes
Holding company balance sheet	Shows investments and indebtedness
Group structure notes	Details on excluded subsidiaries Details of investments in (a) subsidiaries (b) affiliates (c) others Details of ultimate holding company
Segmental data	Details of turnover and profit by lines of business Details of turnover by geographical area

Table 2.2   The normal format of UK group accounts

THE FORMAT OF GROUP ACCOUNTS

The usual format for UK group accounts is shown in Table 2.2, and each item will be discussed in turn.

Consolidated accounts

The Companies Act 1985 (as did its predecessors) treats consolidation as the norm, but allows directors to use alternative formats (e.g. separate sets of accounts for each subsidiary, subconsolidations for different parts of the group, or notes about subsidiaries to amplify holding company statements), if *they* consider that these are better for presenting the same or equivalent information to the holding company shareholders. SSAP 14, 'Group accounts', narrows these options and *requires* consolidated accounts for all subsidiaries unless specific exclusion criteria (to be discussed later) are met. Thus, group accounts normally comprise a single set of consolidated accounts, plus further information about non-consolidated subsidiaries.

Consolidated balance sheets and profit and loss accounts are required by law, and a consolidated funds statement by SSAP 10, 'Statements of source and application of funds'. The Companies Act also lays down the usual disclosure and valuation criteria for such accounts, and also specific provisions relating to group accounts *per se*. Only the latter are discussed in this book.

SSAP 14 requires *uniform accounting policies* to be applied for group accounts purposes, either directly or by consolidation adjustments. Certain disclosures have to be made if this is not possible. It also requires (where practicable) that financial statements of subsidiaries should be prepared to the *same accounting date* and for the same accounting period as the parent, or DTI permission be sought to use interim accounts for that purpose. If not, adjustments should be made for any abnormal transactions in the intervening period, noting subsidiaries so treated.

In individual company accounts, investments are generally accounted for at cost. In consolidated accounts, their treatment is usually a three-tier affair depending on the level of ownership:

(a) less than 20 per cent – trade investments – at cost;
(b) 20–50 per cent – related (i.e. associated) companies – cost plus attributable profit, one line consolidation;
(c) over 50 per cent – subsidiaries – full line by line consolidation.

As the degree of ownership increases, so the accounting approach gets more sophisticated. Non-substantially owned investments are included at cost. Substantially owned affiliates, called by the Act 'related companies' and by SSAP 1 'associated companies', are incorporated by an abbreviated form of consolidation called the equity approach. Majority owned investments (subsidiaries) are consolidated, i.e. each item in their accounts is added line by line to the same caption for other subsidiaries, subject to certain adjustments. This area is discussed in Chapter 4.

Holding company accounts

Only the holding company *balance sheet* is required in addition to the full set of consolidated accounts. Section 258(5) exempts the holding company from publishing its profit and loss account, provided a consolidated profit and loss account is prepared showing (by way of note) 'how much of the consolidated profit or loss for the financial year is dealt with in the [holding] company's [own] accounts'. SSAP 10 does not require the holding company to produce an individual funds statement.

The usefulness of holding company accounts is limited by the fact that group structures vary so much. In some groups, the holding company comprises just investments in group companies. In others it might comprise for example all UK operations, with a separate subsidiary running operations in each foreign market. The 'size' of the holding company often depends on the path of acquisitions and taxation considerations. However, the holding company balance sheet does contain certain information not disclosed by the consolidated balance sheet in relation to the following items 'lost' in the cancellation process:

(a) details of the cost of investments in subsidiaries and in related companies (both of which are required to be disclosed separately under fixed assets and as appropriate under current assets); and

(b) details of debt relationships between the holding company and the rest of the group;

(c) details of realized and unrealized reserves of the company (companies make distributions in the UK, not groups).

Details of indebtedness

Since a group is not regarded in the UK as a legal entity with contractual rights, creditors must look to individual companies in the group for debt repayment. Hence the pattern of intra-group indebtedness between group companies (which cancels out on consolidation) is very important. The Companies Act 1985 requires in the long-term sections of the holding company's balance sheet the separate disclosure of long-term loans to group companies and related companies and, within the current sections, separate headings for amounts owed *by* group companies and by related companies under debtors, and amounts owed *to* group companies and to related companies under creditors.

However, these are only totals and do not show either the debt pattern between individual group companies or the pattern of indebtedness between fellow subsidiaries. In subsidiaries' own accounts, loans to/from the holding company are distinguished from those to/from fellow subsidiaries, but again these are *aggregates* of a number of subsidiaries. This area and its problems are discussed in more depth in Chapter 4.

Nobes (1986b, p. 10) in a useful discussion of the area, questions the information content of holding company accounts and suggests that any potentially useful information (e.g. on distributable profits) might be better provided in note form.

Group structure notes

Excluded subsidiaries

The accounting treatment of excluded subsidiaries is discussed in Chapter 4. Here only the exclusion criteria are reviewed. Group accounts or consolidation are not required (section 229(2)) if a company with subsidiaries is the wholly owned subsidiary of a UK incorporated company. In addition to this overall exemption, both the Companies Act 1985 and SSAP 14 give exclusion criteria, in the former case from *group* accounts and in the latter from *consolidation*. These are summarized in Table 2.3.

Criteria	Companies Act	SSAP 14
Impractical	•	
Insignificant amounts involved	•	
Costs outweigh benefits to members	•	
Harmful to business of holding company	•	
Result misleading	•	
Businesses too dissimilar to add	•	•
Owns half equity but not half votes		•
Restriction on power to appoint directors		•
Subsidiary operates under severe restrictions		•
Control only intended to be temporary		•

Table 2.3   Criteria for excluding subsidiaries

The first three are administrative. The next is mainly commercial. The following two, 'result misleading' and 'businesses too dissimilar', relate to the consolidation process itself, namely that under certain circumstances the 'averaging' implied by consolidation produces a meaningless result, a triffid produced by averaging a plant and an animal (discussed in Chapter 5). The last four criteria relate to the meaning of effective control. The last two in particular ameliorate extreme consequences of a *de jure* definition in a *de facto* direction – has effective control *in fact* been exercised? The requirements on voting rights and ability to appoint a board majority effectively narrow the area of *consolidation* from the Companies Act definition of the scope of *group* accounts. Exclusion because disclosure is harmful to the holding company or differences in business requires Department of Trade and Industry approval. SSAP 14 outlines specific treatments when its exclusion criteria operate.

The Survey of Published Accounts 1985/6 (Skerratt and Tonkin, 1986) indicates that 97 per cent of the 200 listed companies surveyed had no exclusions from consolidation, and for the 100 large unlisted companies surveyed, the corresponding figure for those with subsidiaries is 89 per cent. The main reason for non-consolidation was insignificance! This suggests that for the vast majority of groups, consolidation of all members is the norm. In the previous year the main reason for exclusion was dissimilar activities, but this was not repeated. Whilst it is possible that some companies exclude to massage, e.g. group gearing ratios, the Survey figures suggest that this is not widespread. Whether groups should exclude more subsidiaries is examined in later chapters.

The EEC Seventh Directive will not alter significantly the UK criteria. Certain criteria now enforced by accounting standard will be incorporated into statute. Member states are given an *option* to exempt groups below a certain size (a medium-sized company as defined in the Fourth Directive) from having to produce group accounts. It will no longer be possible to exclude subsidiaries from consolidation because of harm to the holding company's business, and the first three criteria in Table 2.3 are effectively subsumed under 'negligible importance' of the subsidiary. The exemption on wholly owned subsidiaries producing group accounts will be extended to greater than 90 per cent owned subsidiaries of EEC incorporated companies provided the outstanding minority agree to non-publication.

Details of investments

Consolidated accounts do not deal with components of the group. The average of a set of data gives some information about typical size, but little about, for example, variation. UK requirements tackle this problem in a rather superficial way; by disaggregating consolidated results to show how *segments* of the business have performed, and by giving limited information about investments and indebtedness with subsidiaries.

The Companies Act 1985 requires a list of *subsidiaries* (which may be truncated to principal subsidiaries if the list is excessive) showing for each its name, its country of registration or incorporation, its principal country of operation (the last being a Stock Exchange requirement for listed companies), the classes of shares held and the *proportions* held, directly and indirectly. SSAP 1 requires similar information about associated companies (usually 20–50 per cent investments). The Companies Act requires similar information (excepting country of operation) of more than 10 per cent owned investments. However the 10 per cent requirement is measured only in terms of a *direct* stake. SSAP 14 requires the nature of the business of the principal subsidiaries to be disclosed.

.However, such information does not indicate the relative size of each investment, but merely *proportionate* holdings. An investor would have to try to glean some of this information from details of acquisitions in the previous funds statements. The Act requires the holding company's balance sheet to disclose investments in group, related and other companies, but these are *total* amounts and are not broken down further.

Segmental data

Consolidation can be viewed as adding accounts of *legal* entities to produce a single set of accounts *as if* of a super entity. Segmental reporting disaggregates consolidated information into *economic* segments, for example by line of business or geographical location. These differ from the original source data since, for example, a single company may operate in multiple lines of business, or a number of companies may comprise a single geographical segment. Chapter 10 examines this area in more detail, and there is evidence that financial analysts find such disaggregation useful.

Requirements for segmental reporting are extremely rudimentary compared to the USA. The Companies Act 1985 (Schedule 4 paragraph 55) requires that if a company (group) carries on a number of classes of business it shall disclose, in respect of each class, its turnover and its profit or loss before tax. Further, if a group has supplied different geographical markets, it should disclose the turnover attributable to each location. However, directors do not have to disclose such information if *they* consider such disclosures are seriously prejudicial to the interests of the company, indicating only that it has not been published – a broad let-out clause! The Stock Exchange requires listed companies to disclose in addition profit before tax by geographical area, but allows non-disclosure unless contribution from a particular area is 'abnormal'. In the USA, far more is disclosed. Even the normally bland international accounting standards (IAS No. 14) exceed current UK requirements.

SUMMARY

Differing views exist as to *objectives* of group accounts, whether they should *amplify* holding company accounts as memorandum statements, or whether the group 'entity' is primary and consolidated accounts the *principal* accounts. Differences arise as to whether a group is characterized by holding company shareholdings or according to concentrations of economic power. The definition of a *group* is *wider than* the area of consolidation since the latter is only one possible alternative allowed by the Companies Act. However, SSAP 14 now requires consolidated accounts, unless specified exclusion criteria are met.

The UK *de jure* definition of a subsidiary is a mixture – participation in equity, membership and power to appoint, or indirect control via controlled subsidiaries. The USA definition depends on majority *voting* power whereas the German definition depends on *de facto* control – the existence of centralized and unified management. The EEC Seventh Directive has a *de jure* compulsory core, but allows member states the option of introducing *de facto* criteria. It will alter the UK definition to include *voting power* rather than total equity stake.

The group accounting package in the UK normally includes a consolidated balance sheet, profit and loss account and funds statement, but only a holding company balance sheet. The holding company statement shows certain balances which are cancelled out on consolidation. Other details regarding group investment holdings and non-consolidated subsidiaries are included together with segmental information.

Exercises

2.1   Consider the following group structures (assuming all proportions refer to voting rights):

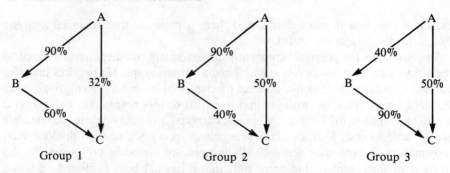

Group 1   Group 2   Group 3

Required
(a) In each case calculate the direct and indirect proportionate share A owns in C, and assess whether C should be treated as a subsidiary of A in group accounts.
(b) Suppose in addition to the above information D owned the remaining shares in C and through contractual arrangements with A controlled the composition of its board of directors. How would this affect your answer in (a). Is C a subsidiary of D in each case?
(c) Suppose the situation is as in (b) except that D owns no shares in C. Contrast this situation.

In answering this question contrast the current UK group definition with your own intuitions as to the best form of group definition.

2.2   Compare and contrast the advantages and disadvantages of *de jure* and *de facto* definitions of a group from the perspective of (a) holding company shareholders (b) group auditors (c) governmental agencies.

2.3   Compare the current UK definition of a group to the German definition (incorporated in the first draft of the Seventh Directive) on the grounds of (a) relevance (b) practicality.

2.4   How far do the EEC Seventh Directive's provisions improve the current UK definition of a group for accounting purposes?

2.5   Assess the extent to which additional information is necessary to supplement consolidated accounts in a typical group to provide a 'true and fair view' of the group's operations and financial position.

FURTHER READING

Accounting Standards Committee (1978) *SSAP 14 – Group Accounts*, paras. 1–22, ASC, London.

Nobes, C. W. (1986) *Some Practical and Theoretical Problems of Group Accounting*, pp. 5–11, Deloitte, Haskins & Sells, London.

Shaw, J. (1976) Criteria for consolidation, *Accounting & Business Research*, Winter, pp. 71–8.

Walker, R. G. (1978) International accounting compromises – the case of consolidation accounting, *Abacus*, Vol. 14, No. 2 (December), pp. 98–106.

Willott, R. (1985) *Current Accounting Law and Practice 1985*, Quinta Publishing, London.

A number of the large accounting firms publish book(let)s assessing the effects of the EEC Seventh Directive.

3 Accounting for Business Combinations

Prior to 1950, the vast majority of business combinations were accounted for as purchases. At that time the American Institute of Certified Public Accountants (AICPA) issued a research bulletin which distinguished between two different types of business combination, a purchase and a pooling of interests (now termed acquisition and merger respectively in the UK). Since that time, particularly in the USA, the area has become a focus for such issues as the relevance of historical cost accounting, the determination of distributable profits, and the size of reported profits of groups.

Critics of the merger accounting (pooling) approach have blamed it for encouraging the sleazier side of the conglomerate merger boom in the USA in the 1960s and 1970s, accusing excessively profit-conscious managements of using the most favourable accounting treatment to massage results. Doubts as to its legality under UK company law caused the acquisition approach to dominate in the UK. However, the 1981 Companies Act legalized merger accounting under specified conditions and thus reopened the debate. Here the term 'business combination' is used to encompass all situations in which two or more firms are combined under common ownership, and the terms 'merger' and 'acquisition' refer to types of combinations.

ACQUISITIONS AND MERGERS: AN INTUITIVE ANALYSIS

This book does not examine the financial, strategic or legal implications of acquiring other companies, but focuses only on problems of accounting for such combinations. Other books (see for example Cooke, 1986) provide in-depth analyses of these areas. However, within the present context, it is important to note that combinations can take a variety of forms.
1. The assets and liabilities of a company can be acquired directly or control over these assets and liabilities can be obtained indirectly by the acquisition of its equity.
2. Consideration offered can take a variety of forms, e.g. voting shares, cash,

some combination of the two, or even a more complex package which might include non-voting shares and loan stocks.

3. The corporate structure may be altered, e.g. a third company – a holding company – may be created which issues new shares and from its resources obtains the voting share capital of the existing companies.

4. Either or both of the parties to the transaction may be liquidated or may continue unchanged.

Just as there are many ways of *effecting* business combinations, there are many ways of *accounting* for them, of aggregating company financial statements. The two most common are the acquisition (purchase) approach and the merger (pooling of interests) approach. *The choice of accounting approach is in principle independent of the method of effecting the combination.* Under a particular approach, which individual company records the combination (e.g. issue of shares and the investment in other companies arising from it) will differ according to the structure chosen, as described above. However, adjusting entries usually ensure that the group results under a particular approach are not dependent on whatever legal structure is used internally.

In the UK legalistic requirements classify which accounting technique may be used in which set of economic circumstances and try to prevent a choice of treatment purely on cosmetic grounds. The term 'merger' or 'acquisition' is used loosely in the accounting literature to refer to any of three different levels – economic description, legalistic definition or accounting approach – and it is important for the reader to establish which level is being referred to. Differences between an acquisition and a merger are now examined informally, at the three levels discussed above.

The intuitive level

Carl Gustav Jung, the celebrated psychoanalyst, talked of archetypes, subconscious images or symbols which influence our everyday perceptions but underlie them. Gut notions of 'acquisition' and 'merger' can be viewed in this way. The term 'acquisition' is used to describe a combination where one company 'dominates' the other. The holding company is the controller and the subsidiary the satellite or appendage. The term 'merger' is used where the combination results in a 'confederation' of companies, each constituent preserving its own identity/automony – a pooling rather than domination. When Britain joined the EEC in 1971, was it a merger or an acquisition?

The accounting approaches

Differences between accounting approaches are shown in Table 3.1.

Under the merger approach, all mergee profits contribute to group profits in the combined statements, whereas under acquisition accounting the acquiree contributes to group profits only subsequent to the combination. In the USA it was argued that companies artificially boosted profits by adding extra pre-acquisition profits using the merger approach. The fact that the investment by the

Item	Acquisition	Merger
Investment amount in combinor's records	Market value	Nominal value*
Pre-combination profits of combinee	Excluded from group reserves	Included in group reserves if possible
Combinee's assets and liabilities	Revalued at acquisition	Not revalued

*Some companies in the USA record the investment at the net book amount of the net assets acquired. This approach effectively includes the mergee's earnings in the holding company's own accounts (making its earnings equal to consolidated earnings – akin to the equity approach to be discussed in Chapter 4). Such a treatment is not used in the UK. However, this difference at an individual company level is removed on consolidation, giving the same consolidated balance sheet as discussed in this chapter. Other companies in the USA use the nominal value approach, as described here.

Table 3.1 Differences between the acquisition and merger approaches

holding company is recorded at nominal value and that assets and liabilities of the combinee are not revalued at combination was also criticized, for example:

> Pooling of interests as a device for cost suppression occurred in Union Carbide's acquisition of Visking. At the time of acquisition, the book value of Visking was $25 million. The market value was considerably higher, for Carbide gave up $97 million in stock to acquire the firm. Because pooling accounting was used, only the book value of Visking was counted. The $72 million difference between market value and recorded value disappeared from view. The potential distortion arising from such treatment can be seen in a hypothetical case. If Carbide sold Visking for $50 million in cash, the receipts would be compared to the $25 million book value, and a profit of $25 million would accrue, even though the value received was nearly $50 million less than the original purchase price paid.[1]

Because of revaluation under the acquisition approach, resultant higher write-offs of revalued assets and goodwill decrease subsequent profits, giving managements further incentive to use the merger accounting approach. Many of these problems disappear under current cost accounting.

Classifying reality: defining acquisitions and mergers

With such apparent advantages resulting from indiscriminate use of the merger approach, accounting bodies took steps to curb the excesses; first, the classification of combinations for accounting purposes was tightened to prevent inappropriate usage; second, improved disclosure provisions were added to prevent wilder excesses of 'creative' accounting, by making clearer the effects of differences caused by choice of approach. The criterion for a 'good' definition oscillated between relevance and non-manipulability, with the latter taking primacy over intuitive notions.

There is great controversy whether the distinction between acquisition and merger is merely one of accounting technique, or whether and to what extent there are essential economic differences in the nature of business combinations which justify different accounting treatments. Some writers consider that a real-world difference dictates the accounting technique but others consider that availability of techniques and a desire to massage profits lead to justifying a difference which does not really exist. Still others argue that although a real difference exists real mergers are very rare, and merger accounting should be used much more sparingly than has been the case, particularly in the USA. The next section assumes (for pedagogic reasons) a 'real-world' difference, which is examined in an intuitive sense, a definitional sense and in an accounting technique sense. Later the alternative viewpoint is examined.

ACQUISITION AND MERGER ACCOUNTING: THE APPROACHES CONTRASTED

In a consolidated balance sheet, assets and liabilities are normally, item by item, the sum of their individual counterparts. This simple additivity holds under both acquisition and merger accounting. However, aggregation of the *equity* section follows a different pattern under each approach. It is helpful to think of a company's profits for each year as being its 'memory' of performance for that year. The equity section in the balance sheet can thus be thought of as a storehouse of past 'memories', past profits, past capital inputs.

Merger accounting

It is as if the complete memories of the separate companies are merged into a single common memory in the consolidated balance sheet. As far as possible consolidated share capital, share premium and reserves are each constrained to equal the sum of their individual counterparts. Consolidated profit and loss accounts too represent the sum of results for the merged companies, regardless of when during the year the merger took place.

   An implicit assumption is that the consolidated accounts represent merely a change in the *scope of the accounts,* showing the combined results of the companies, as if separate streams were put side by side and taken together, nothing added and nothing taken away. A merger can be viewed as analogous to a change in the *ownership rights* of the shareholders of the two companies rather than the purchase of one entity by another. Thus, it is not deemed necessary to establish new historical costs at combination, so assets and liabilities of the mergee are not revalued.

Acquisition accounting

In this case, the acquiror is considered to have purchased the acquiree, buying out its shareholders, often establishing a holding company–subsidiary relationship. The consolidated accounts are prepared from the point of view of the shareholders of the holding company, the subsidiary contributing to the group only *after* combination. It is as if the memory banks from a used computer were wiped clean on being added to the main computer, providing new storage capacity only from the time they were added on.

An acquisition, the purchase of a company, is sometimes compared by analogy to the purchase of its assets, liabilities and goodwill *as separate items*, though in fact they were purchased as a complete package by acquiring its equity. Its results are included only post-combination since, if the components had been purchased separately, they would only contribute since purchase. Likewise, historical costs would have been determined at that date, so the assets and liabilities of the subsidiary should be revalued at takeover to reflect these 'new' historical costs. The former shareholders of the combinee do not lose out by exclusion of pre-combination profits since they have been bought out.

The merger approach stresses *continuity* of ownership (the reorganization of ownership interests among continuing owners) and the acquisition approach *discontinuity* of ownership (the severing of ownership rights in exchange for the purchase consideration). Accounting approaches stress opposites, continuity versus discontinuity, whereas in reality some interests have continued whereas others have not. We are asked to fit black or white to varying shades of grey! Much depends on intentions of parties to the combination transaction, which are difficult to ascertain and may change rapidly during negotiations and afterwards.

Figure 3.1 shows the effects of the approaches on reported profits.

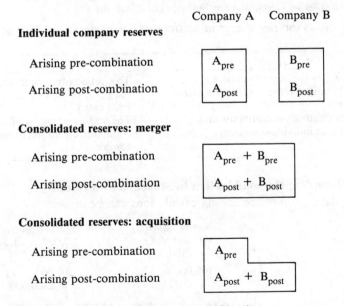

Figure 3.1 Consolidated reserves in a business combination

A numerical example is now used to illustrate the foregoing and to introduce the mechanics of acquisition and merger accounting. To keep matters simple, only the purchase of shares in a holding company–subsidiary relationship is examined here. The purchase of separate assets and liabilities is alluded to in

Chapter 4. SSAP 23's requirements as to when each approach is to be used are ignored here so that main features of the two approaches can be contrasted using the same basic data. These conditions are discussed later in the chapter.

Example 3.1   The Student–Union group

The condensed balance sheets of Student plc and Union Ltd at 31 March 1986 prior to the combination were as follows:

	Student (£000)	Union (£000)
Miscellaneous assets	570	330
Miscellaneous liabilities	(70)	(30)
Share capital	(400)	(200)
Other reserves	(60)	(80)
Retained earnings	(40)	(20)

The companies combined on 31 March, Student issuing new shares and exchanging them for the share capital of Union. The details were:
1. Percentage of share capital acquired – 100.
2. Nominal value of shares – Student £2;   Union £1.
3. Market value of shares – Student £3;   Union £1.50.
4. Offer terms – 1 for 2.

Table 3.2   Stages in accounting for business combinations

Table 3.2 shows the *two stages* in accounting for business combinations.

Stage	Details	Purpose
1	*Recording* the consideration for the combination in the combinor's *own* records	This reflects the combination from the point of view of the individual legal entity
2	*Consolidating* the combinor and combinee individual accounts	The stage 1 accounts of the combinor are added to those of the combinee

Stage 1: Recording the combination in Student's own records
From the data given the following calculations can be made:

	Shares issued	Shares acquired
Market values	100,000 × £3 = £300,000	200,000 × £1.50 = £300,000
Nominal values	100,000 × £2 = £200,000	200,000 × £1 = £200,000

Book value of net assets acquired = £330,000 – £30,000 = £300,000.

The individual company balance sheet of Student plc showing the share issue to effect the investment is shown below under the merger approach (nominal amount) and acquisition approach (fair value).

Student plc – company balance sheet (showing combination) at 31 March 1986 (£000)

	Acquisition approach		Merger approach	
	New bals	Acq'n entry	New bals	Merger entry
Assets	570		570	
Investment in Union	300	300	200	200
Liabilities	(70)		(70)	
Share capital	(600)	(200)	(600)	(200)
Other reserves[2]	(160)	(100)	(60)	
Retained earnings	(40)		(40)	

The difference between the approaches is merely the increase in the 'Investment in Union' and in 'Other reserves' by £100,000 under acquisition accounting. Note that the above balance sheet is an *individual company* balance sheet and this recording of the combination is done *prior to* consolidation. If the investment had been made for cash, a credit entry would have been made for £300,000 against 'Assets' (cash).

Stage 2: Consolidating the individual balance sheets
The consolidation of the two companies' balance sheets uses Student's balance sheet after recording the combination (Stage 1). Revaluation issues are ignored in this initial example.

Merger accounting
Merger accounting stresses continuity of ownership. Its basic aim is to make each consolidated equity component the sum of corresponding individual balance sheet equity components prior to the combination (*as if* it had never taken place). This equality is termed here 'perfect additivity'. Thus collective 'memories' of the mergee are preserved in the consolidated balance sheet. The consolidated equity would be (£000):

Equity component	Student	+	Union	=	Consolidated
Share capital	(400)		(200)		(600)
Other reserves	(60)		(80)		(140)
Retained earnings	(40)		(20)		(60)
Total	(500)		(300)		(800)

The cancellation process to achieve this result is shown below:

Student Union group – merger consolidation at 31 March 1986 (£000)

	Student	Union	Elimination	Consolidated
Assets	570	330		900
Investment in Union	200	—	(200)	—
Liabilities	(70)	(30)		(100)
Share capital	(600)	(200)	200	(600)
Other reserves	(60)	(80)		(140)
Retained earnings	(40)	(20)		(60)

Assets and liabilities are added item by item to get consolidated amounts. The elimination entry removes the entry effecting the combination, thus attaining the sum of individual company amounts 'as if the combination had not taken place'. Another way of viewing the elimination entry is that, since the consolidated balance sheet shows resources and claims of the group as a whole, the investment should be eliminated since its object is internal to the *group*. Analogously, share capital of Union should be eliminated since it is held by parties internal to the group.

Acquisition accounting

Under acquisition accounting, the aim is to eliminate pre-acquisition equity (i.e. share capital, other reserves and retained earnings) of the subsidiary so that it only contributes to consolidated reserves after acquisition. This is achieved in cancellation by grouping these equity items of Union into a *single* amount – pre-acquisition equity. The cancellation process is shown below:

Student Union group – acquisition consolidation at 31 March 1986 (£000)

	Student	Union	Pre-acq. equity	Elimination	Consolidated
Assets	570	330			900
Investment in Union	300			(300)	—
Liabilities	(70)	(30)			(100)
Share capital	(600)	(200)	200		(600)
Other reserves	(160)	(80)	80		(160)
Retained earnings	(40)	(20)	20		(40)
Pre-acquisition equity			(300)	300	—

To emphasize discontinuity of ownership, the column 'Pre-acq. equity' lumps all such equity of Union into a single figure. The investment is then cancelled against this. Equity components in the consolidated balance sheet are thus merely those of the holding company. The reader can verify that (assuming assets and liabilities are correctly stated at 31 March) the result is the same as if Student had purchased Union's separate assets (£330,000) less liabilities (£30,000) instead of an indirect share in its equity – hence the analogy proposed for acquisition accounting. This aspect is explored further in Chapter 4.

Comparing acquisition and merger balance sheets

Consider now *consolidated* balance sheets under the two approaches.

Student Union group – consolidated balance sheet – 31 March 1986 (£000)

	Acquisition approach	Merger approach	Note
Assets	900	900	
Liabilities	(100)	(100)	
Share capital	(600)	(600)	1
Other reserves	(160)	(140)	2
Retained earnings	(40)	(60)	3

Notes on comparison
1. Share capital (i.e. nominal value) is the same under both methods, the *externally* held share capital of the group.

2. Though other reserves are approximately equal under both approaches, their interpretation is quite different. Under acquisition accounting, the credit balance of £160,000 relates to *one* company, Student. Union's other reserves are eliminated. Under merger accounting, the balance of £140,000 is the sum of other reserves for *two* companies. Why should other reserves for one company be larger than for two? Under the acquisition approach the fact that the investment is recorded at *market* value adds £100,000 to Student's original other reserves of £60,000. This is larger than Union's other reserves of £80,000.

3. Under acquisition accounting, group retained earnings *at acquisition* is only Student's (Union's being eliminated). Under merger accounting, it is the sum of retained earnings of the two companies.

One year later

Suppose information on post-combination results from 1 April to 31 December 1986, the financial year-end of Student plc, were available.

In the nine months to 31 December 1986, Student's and Union's assets increased by £100,000 and £50,000 respectively, and liabilities by £30,000 and £10,000. Neither company made share issues since combination.

Check that, had there been no combination, the individual balance sheets of the two companies at 31 December 1986 would have been:

Individual company balance sheets at 31 December 1986 – no combination (£000)

	Student	Union
Assets	670	380
Liabilities	(100)	(40)
Share capital	(400)	(200)
Other reserves	(60)	(80)
Retained earnings	(110)	(60)

Assets and liabilities are increased from the 31 March balances by the increments above, and retained earnings changes by the net difference since there are no share issues. With the combination included in Student's balance sheet (Stage 1), the above balance sheets become:

Individual company balance sheets at 31 December 1986 – showing combination (£000)

	Student		Union
	Acquisition	Merger	
Miscellaneous assets	670	670	380
Investment in Union	300	200	
Miscellaneous liabilities	(100)	(100)	(40)
Share capital	(600)	(600)	(200)
Other reserves	(160)	(60)	(80)
Retained earnings	(110)	(110)	(60)

Under *merger* accounting, the consolidation is:

Merger consolidation nine months after combination at 31 December 1986 (£000)

	Student	Union	Elimination	Consolidated
Assets	670	380		1,050
Investment in Union	200		(200)	—
Liabilities	(100)	(40)		(140)
Share capital	(600)	(200)	200	(600)
Other reserves	(60)	(80)		(140)
Retained earnings	(110)	(60)		(170)

And under *acquisition* accounting, it becomes:

Acquisition consolidation nine months after combination at 31 December 1986 (£000)

	Student	Union	Pre-acq.	Elimination	Consolidated
Assets	670	380			1,050
Investment in Union	300			(300)	—
Liabilities	(100)	(40)			(140)
Share capital	(600)	(200)	200		(600)
Other reserves	(160)	(80)	80		(160)
Retained earnings	(110)	(60)	20		(150)
Pre-acquisition equity			(300)	300	—

Pre-acquisition equity is eliminated as before, ensuring the subsidiary only contributes post-acquisition, (40) being added to Student's retained earnings to obtain group retained earnings. Relationships in Figure 3.1 can now be verified:
1. *Merger* – group retained earnings = (170), made up of:

	Student		Union
Pre	(40)	+	(20)
Post	(70)	+	(40)

2. *Acquisition* – group retained earnings = (150), made up of:

	Student		Union
Pre	(40)		Nil
Post	(70)	+	(40)

Exercises

3.1 Compare the equity components in the consolidated balance sheets at 31 December under both approaches, along the lines of the analysis on pages 36–7. How is the figure of £150,000 for consolidated reserves under acquisition accounting constituted?

3.2 Wholla plc acquires a 100 per cent interest in Bitta on 31 December 1985. The balance sheets of the two companies at that date, before the combination was reflected were as follows:

	Wholla (£000)	Bitta (£000)
Miscellaneous assets	280	160
Miscellaneous liabilities	(100)	(80)
Share capital (£1 shares)	(60)	(50)
Other reserves	(20)	(10)
Retained earnings	(100)	(20)

A one for one share swop was made to effect the combination. At that time the stock market quotation of the two companies was £1.60 for Wholla and £1.50 for Bitta.

Prepare a consolidated balance sheet for the Wholla Bitta group at 31 December 1985 under both merger and acquisition approaches (using the two-stage approach described earlier).

3.3   Over the year to 31 December 1986, the reserves of Wholla increased by £40,000 and Bitta by £20,000. For both companies, the change in assets was twice that of liabilities.

Prepare group balance sheets at 31 December 1986 under both methods.

3.4   Using the financial statements prepared in either 3.2 or 3.3, explain in your own words the intuitive principles of the two cancellation processes examined.

Example 3.2 Changing the offer conditions – the investment amount

Some of the simplifications used in Example 3.1 are now relaxed as follows:
1.   Percentage of share capital acquired – 100.
2.   Nominal value of shares – Student £2; Union £1.
3.   Market value of shares – Student £3.50; Union £2.50.
4.   Offer terms (all consideration in the form of shares):
     (a)   3 for 5;
     (b)   2 for 5;
     (c)   5 for 5.

Over the rest of the year to 31 December 1986 (as before) assets of Student and Union increased by £100,000 and £50,000 and liabilities by £30,000 and £10,000 respectively. No share issues were made post-combination.

Three different sets of offer terms are examined – (a), (b) and (c) – to illustrate the main features of acquisition and merger cancellation processes. The amount of the investment in the subsidiary changes from case to case. Consolidation at the combination date is ignored here (see Exercise 3.5) and the focus is on consolidation at 31 December 1986, nine months after the combination. In this example assets, liabilities and results from 31 March to 31 December are identical to Example 3.1. The company balance sheets prior to recording the combination are as previously, and are repeated here for convenience.

Individual company balance sheets at 31 December 1986 – no combination (£000)

	Student	Union
Assets	670	380
Liabilities	(100)	(40)
Share capital	(400)	(200)
Other reserves	(60)	(80)
Retained earnings	(110)	(60)

Student purchases 200,000 shares with a nominal value as before of £200,000. The investment can be valued under each case.

Shares issued   *Nominal amount*

(a)   3 for 5   200,000 × 3/5 × £2 = £240,000
(b)   2 for 5   200,000 × 2/5 × £2 = £160,000
(c)   5 for 5   200,000 × 5/5 × £2 = £400,000

     Market value

(a)   3 for 5   200,000 × 3/5 × £3.50 = £420,000
(b)   2 for 5   200,000 × 2/5 × £3.50 = £280,000
(c)   5 for 5   200,000 × 5/5 × £3.50 = £700,000

Note that the nominal amounts issued are in each case different from each other and from the nominal amount acquired. In combinations, there is no reason at all why in practice the nominal amount issued should even be close to that acquired. Their relationship is merely a residual calculation after the terms of the offer (which depend on the mix of consideration given and its estimated *market* value) have been agreed by the parties. The relationship between nominal and market amounts in individual companies is often a historical accident, the former usually being used only to determine the number of shares in issue. Company balance sheets for Student at 31 December 1986 under each case, after recording the combination are as follows:

Individual company balance sheets of Student at 31 December showing combination

	Merger			Acquisition			Union
	(a)	(b)	(c)	(a)	(b)	(c)	
Assets	670	670	670	670	670	670	380
Investment	240	160	400	420	280	700	—
Liabilities	(100)	(100)	(100)	(100)	(100)	(100)	(40)
Share capital	(640)	(560)	(800)	(640)	(560)	(800)	(200)
Other reserves	(60)	(60)	(60)	(240)	(180)	(360)	(80)
Retained earnings	(110)	(110)	(110)	(110)	(110)	(110)	(60)

These reflect the differing investment amounts under the offer assumptions. Other reserves under acquisition accounting are increased from £60,000 by the excess of market value of the investment over nominal value. So in case (c), market value is £700,000, nominal value £400,000, and so other reserves are 60,000 + (700,000 − 400,000) = £360,000.

Merger accounting

Consider case (a). The most intuitively appealing result (unfortunately incorrect) would appear to be as follows:

Incorrect merger consolidation – case (a) (£000)

	Student	Union	Elimination	Consolidated
Assets	670	380		1,050
Investment	240		(240)	—
Liabilities	(100)	(40)		(140)
Share capital	(640)	(200)	240	(600)
Other reserves	(60)	(80)		(140)
Retained earnings	(110)	(60)		(170)

As can be seen by adding the 'individual balance sheets – no combination' – above, this (incorrect) consolidated balance sheet is the sum of the individual balance sheets prior to recording the combination (perfect additivity). However, the group *as a whole* has an issued share capital of £640,000 held by *external* parties (Union's share capital being held internally). That this should appear in the consolidated balance sheet overrides the 'perfect additivity' principle discussed earlier. To allow this, only £200,000 of the investment can be cancelled against the £200,000 equity of Union at the combination date (i.e. to remove it and no more). Group share capital would then be £640,000.

What of the remaining uncancelled £40,000? In the 1930s some argued it should be left in the balance sheet as a debit balance (akin to but different from goodwill under the acquisition approach since it would be based on nominal amounts). This approach preserved perfect additivity of other reserves and retained earnings, but only at the price of a debit balance appearing in the balance sheet.

Progressive cancellation

The debit balance solution has not been regarded as acceptable since the 1930s. Current practice is to cancel excess nominal value against reserves, including retained earnings (SSAP 23, paragraph 20). There is some disagreement whether certain reserves of the subsidiary at the combination date are unavailable for such cancellation (e.g. its share premium account or revaluation reserves). Paragraph 61 of Schedule 4 to the Companies Act 1985 allows in the preparation of consolidated accounts 'such adjustments (if any) as the directors of the holding company think necessary'. The next paragraph states that 'the consolidated accounts shall, in giving the information required by paragraph 61, comply in so far as is practicable with ... the other requirements of this Act as if they were the accounts of an actual company'. Does paragraph 62 prevent the group from using its share premium account or valuation reserves for progressive cancellation, since the use of share premium and revaluation reserves is so restricted for individual companies, or is the cancellation process covered by paragraph 61 in that it is a consolidation adjustment?

In the author's opinion, since all reserves are removed under acquisition accounting, the argument that some cannot be removed under merger accounting seems weak. Further, Holgate (1986b, p. 18) argues that in his opinion merger cancellation is not covered by paragraph 62 as there is no counterpart in accounting for individual companies. Therefore, in the text it is assumed that all reserves and retained earnings of the subsidiary are available for cancellation under merger accounting.

The question then is which reserves should be used for the cancellation of this debit, this excess nominal amount. The choice depends on one's priority as to the reserves one wishes to preserve perfect additivity for. If, for example, one wishes to preserve additivity of, say, revaluation reserves, then the excess would be cancelled first against all other reserves/retained earnings, leaving revaluation reserves as a last resort. However, the convention taken here is to cancel the excess progressively, first against the equity component with *most restricted* uses, then against the next most restricted, and so on (if necessary) to the *least restricted*. This implicitly gives priority to preserving the additivity of retained earnings and leaves it least affected. This area is further discussed in Chapter 11. In the USA, the existence of 'no par value' shares often allows companies to define nominal amount issued as equal to that acquired, thus bypassing this problem, but this is not possible in the UK.

In this example excess nominal value is £40,000 (i.e. £240,000 investment less the £200,000 share capital of Union, all internally held), and the equity components available for progressive cancellation are 'other reserves' (which would include share premium accounts) and 'retained earnings'. Share premium is more restricted than any other reserve by section 130 of the 1985 Companies Act. It is assumed here that 'other reserves' are more restricted than 'retained earnings' which are unrestricted as to their uses. So the excess is cancelled *progressively,* first against other reserves *at combination* and, if greater, versus retained earnings. In this example the excess (£40,000) is less than other reserves and so no cancellation is necessary versus retained earnings.

Correct merger consolidation – case (a) (£000)

	Student	Union	Elimination	Consolidated
Assets	670	380		1,050
Investment	240		(240)	—
Liabilities	(100)	(40)		(140)
Share capital	(640)	(200)	200	(640)
Other reserves	(60)	(80)	40	(100)
Retained earnings	(110)	(60)		(170)

Perfect additivity has been sacrificed to ensure that externally held share capital is correct. Thus, if we compare the progressive cancellation statement with the incorrect perfectly additive statement, balance sheet share capital is 'overstated' by £40,000 as compared to perfect additivity, and other reserves 'understated' by the same amount. Effectively £40,000 of other reserves has been 'capitalized'.

Consider the other cases. The elimination entries and consolidated figures are shown in abbreviated form only for share capital, other reserves and retained earnings. Consolidated assets and liabilities are the same as in case (a) just discussed (£000):

	Case (a)		Case (b)		Case (c)	
	Elimination	Consolidated	Elim.	Cons.	Elim.	Cons.
Investment	(240)	—	(160)	—	(400)	—
Share capital	200	(640)	200	(560)	200	(800)
Other reserves	40	(100)	—	(140)	140	—
Retained earnings	—	(170)	—	(170)	60	(110)
Consolidation reserve	—	—	(40)	(40)	—	—

In case (b), shares issued have a *lower* nominal value than shares acquired. The share capital of Union has to be completely removed to ensure that the group accounts only show externally held share capital of the group, and so an extra credit of £40,000 arises, shown in the consolidated balance sheet as 'other reserves arising on consolidation'.

In case (c), excess nominal value of shares issued over shares acquired is greater than 'other reserves' of the *mergee*. It is not completely clear in the UK whether progressive cancellation should be against reserves of the mergee only, or against the combined totals for holding company *and* subsidiary. In the USA, APB Opinion No. 16 states unambiguously that *combined* figures should be used. However, if cancellation is against combined holding company and subsidiary's other reserves, some of the *holding company's* other reserves will not appear in the consolidated balance sheet; so, for example, it is conceivable that consolidated share premium (an element of other reserves) could be less than holding company share premium as a result of the merger. There is some doubt as to whether or not this is legal under the Companies Acts, and the same interpretative difficulties arise over the meaning of paragraphs 61 and 62 of Schedule 4 to the Act as have already been discussed.

It is the author's opinion that UK company law may not preclude such a cancellation against combined reserves for the reasons outlined above by Holgate (1986b). However, whereas the argument was used before to support cancellation to no greater extent than under acquisition cancellation, similar reasoning applied here potentially takes merger cancellation into new and uncharted territories, to the holding company's reserves themselves, and for this reason many groups may be wary of taking such a step. However, it seems that the real question should be whether or not such a cancellation is *useful*. Is it more useful, say, to ensure that group share premium is at least that of the holding company or alternatively to preserve as far as possible the perfect additivity of retained earnings? Alas, there are no easy answers. The interpretation and functions of consolidated equity are complex issues, discussed further in Chapter 11. Only the technical features of progressive cancellation are examined here.

If cancellation against combined reserves were carried out in case (c), excess nominal value of £200,000 (i.e. £400,000 − £200,000) is greater than *combined* 'other reserves' accounts of £140,000 (£80,000 + £60,000), thus the remaining excess of £60,000 is cancelled against retained earnings. Compared to 'perfect additivity', group share capital is now 'overstated' by £200,000, and consolidated 'other reserves' and 'retained earnings' 'understated' (i.e. effectively 'capitalized') by £140,000 and £60,000 respectively. If the cancellations were made against *mergee* equity components only, the £200,000 excess nominal value would have been cancelled as to £80,000 (maximum) against 'other reserves' and £60,000 against 'retained earnings', leaving a £60,000 debit amount remaining on consolidation. This is not the same in nature as 'goodwill' under acquisition accounting (below) as it is based on the nominal amount of the investment, whereas the former is based on 'fair' values. The treatment of goodwill is discussed in Chapter 4.

As a general comment, the merger cancellation approach is affected by the nominal amount of shares issued and acquired. The market values have no effect.

Acquisition accounting

Consider again case (a) first. The consolidation process is (£000):

	Student	Union	Pre-acq. equity	Elimination	Consolidated
Assets	670	380			1,050
Investment	420			(420)	—
Liabilities	(100)	(40)			(140)
Share capital	(640)	(200)	200		(640)
Other reserves	(240)	(80)	80		(240)
Retained earnings	(110)	(60)	20		(150)
Pre-acquisition equity/ Goodwill			(300)	420	120

The only difference between this example and the original case is that the investment has changed from £300,000 to £420,000 with consequent changes to Student's own share capital and other reserves. The pre-acquisition equity 'lumping together' is identical. Because the investment is larger than equity acquired (= net assets acquired £330,000 − £30,000) an excess arises on consolidation (£120,000) called 'goodwill' or more accurately 'excess on consolidation' shown as a consolidated asset. SSAP 22, the current accounting standard on goodwill, recommends that it is written off immediately against reserves, or second best, written off over its estimated useful life. This write-off is ignored here. *Post*-acquisition reserves of Union are added to the group retained earnings.

Thus, changes in the market value of the consideration given for the combination affect the acquisition approach. Changes in the nominal amount (assuming unchanged market values) have no effect.

In both the other cases, the removal of pre-acquisition equity is identical. Also, consolidated retained earnings remain at £150,000 – Student's plus Union's earnings since acquisition. The change is in the amount of the investment cancelled against pre-acquisition equity of £300,000. The excess/(deficit) is as follows (a deficit usually being included in other reserves):

Case (a)   420,000 − 300,000 = 120,000
Case (b)   280,000 − 300,000 = (20,000)
Case (c)   700,000 − 300,000 = 400,000

A medical analogy may help. Acquisition accounting can be likened to major or radical surgery, where an organ may be completely removed to prevent the growth of a tumour, while merger accounting can be likened to progressive surgery, where the aim is only to remove the diseased portions of the organ.

Exercise

3.5 Assume in Exercise 3.3 a 3 for 2 share swop and produce a consolidated balance sheet at 31 December 1986.

Example 3.3 Group profit and loss accounts for the year of the combination

Thus far the two approaches have been contrasted in terms of the balance sheet. Now their respective consolidated profit and loss accounts are contrasted. Suppose the profit and loss accounts for the two companies for the year ended 31 December 1986 had been:

	Student	Union		
	12 months	3 months to comb.	9 months since comb.	Total for year
Sales	500,000	50,000	80,000	130,000
Cost of sales	(250,000)	(20,000)	(40,000)	(60,000)
Depreciation	(60,000)	(2,000)	(6,000)	(8,000)
Other expenses	(120,000)	(5,000)	(14,000)	(19,000)
Net profit	70,000	23,000	20,000	43,000

Under merger accounting, the consolidated profit and loss account for the year ended 31 December 1986 would be the sum of the first and last columns above, the two separate streams being merged into one. Comparative figures for preceding years would be restated as if the two companies had already been combined (i.e. two streams as if always together). Under acquisition accounting, Union only contributes since acquisition, and so the consolidated profit and loss account is the Student column plus the '9 month' column of Union. Comparative figures would not be restated (see Holgate (1986b) for a discussion of the implications of the treatment of comparatives). If goodwill arising under acquisition accounting were written off over a twenty-year life, the group profit and loss account under the two approaches becomes:

Student–Union consolidated profit and loss account – year ended 31 December 1986

	Acquisition	Merger
Sales	580,000	630,000
Cost of sales	(290,000)	(310,000)
Depreciation	(66,000)	(68,000)
Other expenses	(134,000)	(139,000)
Goodwill	(6,750)	—
Consolidated net profit	83,250	113,000

The more conservative acquisition approach requires:

(a) revaluation of assets of the combinee at acquisition, thus increasing the base on which cost of sales and depreciation are calculated;

(b) only post-acquisition profits (and hence revenues and expenses) of the combinee to be consolidated;

(c) if the gradual amortization approach is adopted, any goodwill at acquisition to be progressively amortized.

Thus, it is not surprising that merger accounting has obvious attractions to those seeking to maximize profits, particularly in the year of acquisition.

Example 3.4   Acquisition and merger accounting contrasted – a more complex case

In this final example, the offer by Student for Union is made using both shares *and* cash, and now Student only obtains a 90 per cent interest, leaving a 10 per cent minority (outside) interest in Union. Assume balance sheets of the two companies are the same as before at 31 March and 31 December 1986. Details of the combination are as follows:

1. Percentage of share capital acquired – 90.
2. Nominal values of shares – Student £2;   Union £1.
3. Market values of shares – Student £3.50;   Union £2.50.
4. Offer terms – 3 shares plus 50p in cash for each 5 shares of Union.

Thus Student will now acquire 90 per cent of 200,000 = 180,000 shares in Union whose nominal value is £180,000 and whose market value is 180,000 × £2.50 = £450,000. Consider the investment under both approaches:

1. Nominal value of investment:

Shares	180,000 × 3/5 × £2.00	=	£216,000
+ Cash	180,000/5 × 0.50	=	£18,000
Total		=	£234,000

2. Market value of investment:

Shares	180,000 × 3/5 × £3.50	=	£378,000
+ Cash	180,000/5 × 0.50	=	£18,000
Total		=	£396,000

Again, consolidation at the date of combination is ignored, and the focus here is on consolidation at 31 December 1986. The starting point again is the balance sheets at 31 December prior to recording the combination. If we record the investment at the above amounts (Stage 1), the company balance sheets at 31 December 1986 are:

Individual company balance sheets showing combination – 31 December 1986 (£000)

	Merger		Student Acquisition		Union
	Merging entry	Merger Balance sheet	Acquisition entry	Acquisition Balance sheet	
Assets	(18)	652	(18)	652	380
Investment	234	234	396	396	—
Liabilities		(100)		(100)	(40)
Share capital	(216)	(616)	(216)	(616)	(200)
Other reserves		(60)	(162)	(222)	(80)
Retained earnings		(110)		(110)	(60)

Share capital increases by £216,000 nominal to £616,000 under both approaches. Under the acquisition approach other reserves are increased by £396,000 − £234,000 = £162,000 to £222,000. Cash decreases by £18,000.

Merger approach
The merger consolidation process can be illustrated as follows:

Student Union group – merger consolidation (90% interest) at 31 December 1986 (£000)

	Student	Union	Minority	Elimination	Consolidated
Assets	652	380			1,032
Investment	234	—		(234)	—
Liabilities	(100)	(40)			(140)
Share capital	(616)	(200)	20	180	(616)
Other reserves	(60)	(80)	8	54	(78)
Retained earnings	(110)	(60)	6		(164)
Minority interest	—	—	(34)	—	(34)

Since Student has only acquired a 90 per cent stake in Union, the remaining 10 per cent, called the minority interest, is shown separately as a single figure in the consolidated balance sheet (i.e. 10 per cent of (200 + 80 + 60) = 34). This is effected by means of a separate column. So under merger accounting, group retained earnings are Student's plus 90 per cent of Union's, i.e. 110 + 90 per cent of 60 = 164. Progressive cancellation still applies.

The majority shareholders have direct interests in the holding company, and hence an indirect interest in the rest of the group, a 90 per cent holding in Union. Minority shareholders have direct interests in other group companies (here a 10 per cent interest in Union) and at most an indirect interest in *part* of the group. In group accounts the two classes are distinguished, minimal disclosure being given to the minority.

Merger accounting cancellation table
In more complicated examples, it is clumsy to write out the whole balance sheet of each company and to do consolidation in columnar form. A shorthand form is

a cancellation table in which items are only included if they require adjustment in moving from the individual company balance sheets to the consolidated balance sheet, as follows:

Merger accounting cancellation table (£000)

	Student	Union	Progressive cancellation	Consolidated
Investment	234		(234)	—
Share capital	(616)	(180)	180	(616)
Other reserves	(60)	(72)	54	(78)
Retained earnings	(110)	(54)		(164)
Minority interest	—	(34)		(34)

There is now no minority interest vertical column as the minority interest is analysed immediately. In the full columnar consolidation, Union's share capital, other reserves and retained earnings are written down as 200, 80 and 60 respectively. In the minority interest column, 20, 8 and 6 are removed giving a figure of 34. In the abbreviated table, the majority share capital, other reserves and retained earnings are analysed directly at 90 per cent of the component figures and the minority of 34 is immediately 10 per cent of the *total*.

Here no excess nominal value is remaining after cancellation against other reserves. In theory, perfect additivity of retained earnings is preserved. Consider whether this is so. Minority retained earnings has to be included, viz. (£000):

Retained earnings as if
no merger had taken place   = (110) Student + (60) Union = (170)

Consolidated retained
earnings   = (164) Majority + (6) Minority = (170)

Finally, the consolidated balance sheet can be easily obtained from the abbreviated cancellation table. All items not included in the table are obtained by simply adding together individual balance sheet amounts. The cancellation table method is purely a labour saving device.

Acquisition approach

Under acquisition accounting, the consolidation process becomes:

Student Union group – acquisition accounting (90% interest) at 31 December 1986 (£000)

	Student	Union	Minority	Pre-acq.	Elimination	Consolidated
Assets	652	380				1,032
Investment	396				(396)	—
Liabilities	(100)	(40)				(140)
Share capital	(616)	(200)	20	180		(616)
Other reserves	(222)	(80)	8	72		(222)
Retained earnings	(110)	(60)	6	18		(146)
Pre-acq./Goodwill				(270)	396	126
Minority interest		(34)				(34)

Again a new column, that of minority interest, has been introduced, identical to the corresponding column under merger accounting. The pre-acquisition equity column is slightly modified in that the group's share is now 90 per cent of share capital, other reserves and retained earnings of Union at acquisition, i.e. 90 per cent of 200,000, 80,000 and 20,000 respectively. The investment at £396,000 is bigger than the *holding company's* share of equity at acquisition (90 per cent of (200,000 + 80,000 + 20,000) = 270,000) and so a 'goodwill' figure of £126,000 arises, the treatment of which will be discussed in Chapter 4. It is also possible to abbreviate the acquisition cancellation table, but this too is deferred until the next chapter. Minority interests are identical under both approaches in this example. Where differential write-offs of goodwill and revaluation of assets occur under the acquisition approach, the two differ accordingly.

Exercises

3.6   For the student union example discussed on pages 46–9:
(a)   Compare and contrast the equity components.
(b)   Analyse the change from 'perfect additivity' under merger accounting by first analysing the minority equity components and adding them to the consolidated components.

3.7   In the Wholla Bitta example, outlined in Exercises 3.2 and 3.3, assume Wholla acquires a 90 per cent interest in Bitta by means of a 3 for 2 share swop. Otherwise the facts of the case remain unchanged.

Prepare a consolidated balance sheet for the Wholla Bitta group at 31 December *1986* under both merger and acquisition approaches.

3.8   The following balance sheets at 30 November 1986 are taken from the draft financial statements of Acquisator plc and Mergee Ltd.

	Acquisator	Mergee
Assets:		
Cash	10,000	5,000
Investment in Mergee (note 1)	75,000	—
Other assets	225,000	150,000
	£310,000	£155,000
Liabilities:		
Miscellaneous liabilities	100,000	60,000
Equities:		
Ordinary shares	60,000	20,000
Share premium	70,000	30,000
Retained earnings (note 2)	80,000	45,000
	£310,000	£155,000

Notes
1.   Acquisator made an offer of 2 £1 ordinary shares plus 16⅔p in cash for each £1 ordinary share in Mergee on 28 February 1986. The offer was accepted by 90 per cent of the shareholders in Mergee. At the time of the combination, the market values of the shares in Acquisator and Mergee were £2 and £3.50 respectively per share.

2.   At the date of the combination, 28 February 1986, retained earnings of the two companies were £50,000 for Acquisator and £30,000 for Mergee.

Using the above financial statements to calculate relevant figures, explain to the chief accountant of Acquisator, the main difference between the 'purchase' and 'pooling' approaches and comment why he might prefer one to the other, using your calculations for illustrative purposes.

SSAP 23, 'ACCOUNTING FOR ACQUISITIONS AND MERGERS' – AN ANALYSIS

Merger accounting has never been widely practised in the UK. The 1969–70 and 1970–1 Surveys of Published Accounts refer to six combinations treated as mergers in each year. Famous names practising merger accounting around this time included Bass Charrington, British Leyland, Rowntree Mackintosh, Cadbury Schweppes and Trust House Forte. ED3, 'Accounting for Acquisitions and Mergers', was issued in 1971 in an attempt to standardize extant practice. It never became an accounting standard.

The main reason was a suggestion that merger accounting might be contrary to section 56 of the Companies Act 1948 which required that whenever shares are issued at a premium, the excess over nominal value should be credited to a share premium account. Sufficient doubts were raised to cause ED3 to remain 'on ice'. In 1980 a minor taxation case, *Shearer* v. *Bercain Ltd*, appeared to clarify and crystallize the position, stating pre-acquisition profits of a subsidiary were not distributable to the holding company. This decision left companies who had practised merger accounting ten years earlier in an embarrassing position!

In the 1981 Companies Act, the government legalized merger accounting where 'an issuing company has by an arrangement including the exchange of shares, secured at least a 90 per cent holding in another company', stating that 'section 56 of the Companies Act 1948 shall not apply to the premium on any shares which are included in the consideration given'. Also the Act gave retrospective relief to combinations previously treated as mergers and to group reconstructions. This led to ED31 in 1982, and the subsequent accounting standard, SSAP 23, in 1985.

In the USA, merger accounting has always been legal and the reticence which characterized the UK debate has been noticeably absent. The intensity of the debate was examined earlier and its implications for setting UK standards will be examined later in this section.

Standard practice in SSAP 23 is quite short. Broadly, it deals with three areas; the classification of business combinations, the accounting treatment of acquisitions and mergers, and disclosures required for business combinations in individual company accounts. Guidance for the latter is given in an appendix which does not form part of the SSAP.

Accounting treatment

For acquisition accounting consideration must be stated at 'fair value'. Separable net assets should be restated to fair value, and any excess of the fair value consideration over fair value net assets represents goodwill, discussed in the next chapter.

Under merger accounting, shares issued are to be recorded at nominal values, though other consideration (e.g. cash) is to be included at 'fair value'. If the carrying value of the investment is less than the nominal value of shares acquired, the difference is to be treated as a reserve (see case (b) in Example 3.2). If it is greater, progressive cancellation effectively capitalizes some of the reserves (though which are not specified). Assets and liabilities of the subsidiary are not revalued except to achieve uniformity of accounting policies within the group. Profit and loss accounts are to include the results of the subsidiaries for the whole period in the year of the combination, and comparative figures are to be restated as if the companies had been combined at the start of the period.

Definition

SSAP 23 defines the conditions under which merger accounting *may* be used, *allowing* acquisition accounting to be used if the conditions are met, but *requiring* acquisition accounting to be used if they are not. This was a significant change from ED 31 which did not allow acquisition and merger accounting to be used as alternatives for the same combination, defining when each was required. Further, the choice of one approach now does not preclude the other approach being chosen (when the conditions are met) for future combinations.

The basis for distinguishing between an acquisition and a merger for accounting purposes is whether or not the combination is based principally on a share for share exchange and consequently on whether or not significant resources leave the combining companies (paragraph 3). Merger accounting is to be used where 'two groups of shareholders continue, or are in a position to continue their shareholdings as before but on a combined basis'. The term 'offeror' includes fellow subsidiaries.

Paragraph 17 states:

A business combination may be accounted for as a *merger* if all of the following conditions are met:
(a) the business combination results from an offer to the holders of all equity shares and the holders of all voting shares which are not already held by the offeror; and
(b) the offeror has secured, as a result of the offer, a holding of (i) at least 90 per cent of all equity shares (taking each class of equity separately) and (ii) the shares carrying at least 90 per cent of the votes of the offeree; and
(c) immediately prior to the offer, the offeror does not hold (i) 20 per cent or more of all equity shares of the offeree (taking each class of equity separately) or (ii) shares carrying 20 per cent or more of the votes of the offeree; and
(d) not less than 90 per cent of the fair value of the total consideration given for the equity share capital (including that given for the shares already held) is in the form

of equity capital; not less than 90 per cent of the fair value of the consideration given for voting non-equity share capital (including that given for shares already held) is in the form of equity and/or voting non-equity share capital.

These requirements are more restrictive than the conditions for not recording a share premium in the Companies Act 1985, which merely requires a greater than 90 per cent takeover involving some shares. Criterion (c) specifies the maximum permissible starting stake, (b) the minimum permissible ending stake, and (d) the minimum *final* offer proportion of shares to non-shares. The proposed EEC Seventh Directive on group accounts, to be enacted into UK company law by 1990, will narrow the definition of a merger even further, only allowing merger accounting where less than 10 per cent of the consideration in terms of *nominal* amount is in the form of cash. SSAP 23 is based on 'fair value'. Holgate (1986b, p. 35) points out that there are difficulties in interpreting the EEC definition, and that in fact there may be wider differences between it and SSAP 23's merger definitions, in that the Directive stipulates not more than 10 per cent 'cash' *nominal* amount whereas SSAP 23 talks of non-equity proportions of fair values (he speculates whether, for example, loan stock may be acceptable under the Directive but not under SSAP 23), and according to Holgate the Directive's 90 per cent mix requirement seems to relate to the final transaction reaching over the 90 per cent ownership threshold rather than the total consideration involved as in SSAP 23. The interactions between SSAP 23 and the Seventh Directive are therefore complex, but it is likely that some combinations now qualifying for the merger option will be restricted to acquisition accounting when the Directive is enacted into UK law.

As will be shown in the next chapter, greater than 20 per cent owned subsidiaries are accounted for by a modified form of acquisition accounting called the equity method. Criterion (c) is presumably to prevent investments which were formerly accounted for by an acquisition-based approach changing to merger accounting.

The reasons stated by the SSAP 23 working party for making merger accounting optional include the fact that relatively few people in the UK were strongly in favour of merger accounting being mandatory, some feeling that acquisition accounting was the benchmark; that the method was relatively new in the UK; that related statutory provisions permit rather than require a particular treatment; and that some companies may see themselves as making acquisitions where the use of shares as the form of consideration was merely incidental. The uneasy compromise embodied in the change in treatment between ED and SSAP is examined later.

Disclosure

SSAP 23 requires details of the companies, shares issued, whether acquisition or merger accounting has been used, and details of significant accounting adjustments to achieve consistency of accounting policies between companies. Under acquisition accounting, sufficient other information must be given for shareholders to appreciate the effect on consolidated results of subsidiaries acquired in the year, including effective acquisition dates. Additional disclosures are required for mergers, presumably to help prevent cosmetic accounting, as shown in Table 3.3.

	Previous year	Profits	
		Current year	
		Pre-combination	Post-combination
Before extraordinary items	•	•	••
Extraordinary items	•••	•	•

Key
• Figures to be analysed between holding company and subsidiary.
•• Figure only to be disclosed in total (i.e. aggregated).
••• No disclosure required.

Table 3.3   Additional disclosure requirements on mergers

Also the fair value of consideration given by the issuing company must be disclosed. These additional disclosures go some way to enable an analyst to determine the differential effects of accounting for a combination as a merger rather than an acquisition. However, a significant piece of information, the revalued amount of the subsidiary's net assets, is missing. Further, if a subsidiary (or a substantial part of its business) were disposed of in the year *subsequent* to the combination, no special disclosures would be required.

The relationship between group accounts and holding company accounts

This section can be omitted without loss of continuity. As stated earlier, under UK company law, a holding company must present its own accounts *and* a set of consolidated accounts. Company law in the area of business combinations mainly deals with the accounts of the *holding company,* and SSAP 23 deals with *group accounts.* The interaction between the two is dealt with in an appendix to SSAP 23 which is for guidance only, and discusses such matters as the accounting treatment of investments, dividends received from subsidiaries, etc. in the holding company's *own* accounts. The treatment of the investment (Stage 1) is examined here. In the examples of acquisition accounting, the investment was recorded at fair value and the excess over nominal value was credited to 'other reserves'. Consider now the nature of this credit.

UK company law (section 130 Companies Act 1985) requires an investment in another company to be stated at fair value, and the excess over nominal amount to be credited to a 'share premium account', unless the merger relief provisions of section 131 of the Act are satisfied. Where a company acquires at least a 90 per cent stake in another company and the consideration includes some equity, the requirement for a share premium account is dispensed with. Under these circumstances, the company has the *option* of recording the investment either at nominal amount or at fair value. If the latter is chosen the excess over nominal amount is credited to a discretionary (unrealized) reserve, usually termed a 'merger reserve'. The share premium account is restricted by law to such matters as bonus issues of shares, but the discretionary reserve is less restricted.

The Companies Act provisions apply to the accounts of the holding company, and the 'merger relief' provisions therein only affect the treatment of the investment and have nothing to do with group accounts. The qualifying conditions for the *option* of merger accounting in group accounts are tighter than those of section 131. Thus, some companies meeting section 131 (allowing the option of 'merger relief' provisions in the *holding company* accounts) will not meet the merger requirements of SSAP 23 (allowing the option of merger accounting in the *group* accounts). But all firms meeting SSAP 23's merger requirements will meet section 131.

The interaction is considered in the non-mandatory appendix of SSAP 23, in which guidelines are issued as to the treatment of the investment in the accounts of the holding company to try to provide some consistency between the two sets of accounts. Broadly, they recommend the following.

If a company uses *acquisition* accounting, the investment should be recorded at *fair* value and the excess over nominal amount be credited to a share premium account if the requirements of section 131 are not met, or to a discretionary (unrealized) reserve if they are. If the merger requirements of SSAP 23 are met and the company chooses the *merger* accounting option in group accounts, the investment should be recorded at *nominal* amount in holding company accounts.

SSAP 23's recommendations ensure consistency between the treatment of the investment in holding company accounts, and the consolidation approach adopted. However, these are not requirements and companies are able to choose the other Companies Acts options in their own accounts. For example, a company entitled to merger relief (section 131) could, in accordance with SSAP 23 and the law (though not SSAP 23's guidance), record the investment at *nominal* amount and (either by requirement or choice) use *acquisition* accounting in consolidated accounts. Both Ladbroke Group plc and Pleasurama plc have used variants on this treatment prior to the introduction of SSAP 23.[3] It is fairly straightforward to design consolidation adjustments to get from a nominal amount investment to an acquisition accounting consolidated balance sheet, but this is not considered here.

DEFINING A MERGER: CONTROVERSIES AND ISSUES

Since, under historical cost, acquisition and merger accounting have such radically different effects on such matters as valuation of assets, distributability of profits and calculation of goodwill, the search for a workable definition of a merger is highly controversial. To prevent abuse, a major concern has been to define a merger as tightly as possible.

Early attempts to define a merger

The first attempt at defining a merger for accounting purposes was made in the USA in 1950 by Accounting Research Bulletin No. 40. The criteria (none of

which was conclusive by itself) were:
1. Voting shares should be the basic medium of exchange.
2. Ownership interests in predecessor corporations should continue in substantially the same proportions in surviving or new company.
3. Relative sizes of constituent companies should not be too disproportionate.
4. Managements of all constituents should continue as influential in the management of surviving or new company.
5. Business activities of constituents should be similar or complementary.
6. No substantial minority interest should exist post-combination.

A quick comparison with paragraph 17 of SSAP 23 (above) reveals that few criteria of ARB 40 survive the thirty or so years between the two! If anything, the criteria of ARB 40 seem to correspond more to the intuitive idea of a merger than SSAP 23's. For example, if relative sizes were too different, it is difficult to see how one company would not dominate another in the new group. The reasons for the changes are now examined.

In the years following ARB 40, a vigorous debate ensued over whether a merger (pooling) required continuity of ownership interests, continuity of management interests or even continuity in existing business activities. Parker (1966) argued that the most important question was asset valuation. To justify the carry forward of 'old' historical costs under merger accounting, there had to be continuity in business activity. Otherwise it was incorrect to match costs to current revenues of what was in essence a different entity. He argued that day-to-day changes in ownership claims in companies are ignored for accounting purposes, the entity being regarded as independent of its owners. Thus, continuity of *ownership* was not vital. Despite these arguments, continuity of ownership became generally accepted in the US. Complementarity of businesses was dropped subsequently and other criteria were more tightly defined.

Is there such a thing as a merger?

The 1960s and 1970s were characterized by a boom in combination activities in the USA, and by attempts to erode the criteria for merger accounting to apply it more widely for cosmetic purposes. Controversial research reports prepared for the Accounting Principles Board by Wyatt (1963) and Catlett and Olsen (1968), concluded that no theoretical basis existed at all for pooling of interests (merger) accounting, on the grounds that all combinations involved the acquisition of one entity by another; that the medium of consideration was irrelevant. Foster (1974, p. 17) later echoed their conclusion. The idea of 'pooling as a transaction between separate groups of stockholders' is

> a flight of fantasy. One almost expects a wink when this rationale is advanced. We know that corporate officers negotiate the transaction from end to end. Indeed, we know that many corporations employ personnel for the purpose of identifying likely acquisition candidates. And potential acquisitions are reviewed by the corporation to determine if the purchase or pooling method will look better.

Such radical conclusions were unacceptable to the APB. Instead one observes gradual attempts to fill in the cracks that were appearing rather than proscribe one approach altogether. Consequently criteria became more legalistic. When the APB issued the current US standard APB Opinion No. 16 in 1970, the definition of a pooling had become extremely tortuous.

ED 3 – the first UK pronouncement

In 1971 the ASSC issued ED 3 on acquisitions and mergers, which remained 'exposed' for ten years before being finally discarded. Its criteria for a merger were:

(a)   the substance of the main business of the constituent companies continues in the amalgamated undertaking; and

(b)   the equity voting rights of the amalgamated undertaking to be held by the shareholders of any one of the constituent companies are not more than three times the equity voting rights to be held by the shareholders of any of the other constituent companies; and

(c)   the amalgamation results from an offer to equity shareholders and not less than 90 per cent in value of the offer is in the form of equity capital with rights identical with the equity voting capital rights of the offeree company or companies already in issue . . .

(d)   the offer is approved by the voting shareholders of the company making the offer and is accepted by shareholders representing at least 90 per cent of the total equity capital (voting and non-voting) of the company or companies receiving the offer.

Much is common with ARB 40 issued twenty years previously, except an attempt has been made to quantify certain criteria, e.g. the minimum share content in the offer mix (90 per cent), the maximum size of the minority interest remaining (10 per cent) and relative sizes. Continuation of management and complementarity provisions have been replaced by continuity of the substance of the main business. Requirement (c) stringently defines continuity of identical voting rights of the offeree company or companies. The complementarity of businesses criterion has been dropped.

SSAP 23 – a cropped definition

SSAP 23's criteria are shorter and more clear cut. The relative size criterion and continuation of the substance of the main business have been dropped. Instead, deciding criteria are size of minority remaining and that the combination is effected essentially by a share for share exchange without significant resources leaving the combining companies 'so that the two groups of shareholders continue, or are in a position to continue their shareholdings as before but on a combined basis' (paragraph 3). Wider criteria additional to continuity of ownership interest have been gradually eroded and now seem to disappear. Has the intuitive concept of a merger changed or have pragmatic considerations alone prevailed?

Criteria for accounting measures

Ijiri (1975) emphasizes an important feature of external reporting – that of conflict of interest – discussing the concept of the 'hardness' of accounting measures. A 'hard' measure is one constructed so that it is difficult to bend the rules. To do this it must be verifiable, well specified, and the number of justifiable alternatives must be restricted.

Ijiri (1975) comments that the criterion of 'decision relevance' ignores conflict of interest. Where conflicts exist, relevant measures can be manipulated if they do not also exhibit 'hardness'. Even 'objectivity' in the sense of consensus between trained measurers assumes that there is no attempt to 'bend the rules'. He concludes that in a conflictual environment 'hardness' may well be the most important criterion analogous to rules of a game which must be clearly specified to prevent disastrous consequences. The ASC seems to have gone for a 'hard' definition. Given American experience, this is not surprising.

Vendor rights and vendor placings

Given SSAP 23's apparently 'hard' criteria for when merger accounting may be applied, do these accord with intuitive concepts of a merger or is what is defined something other than a 'merger'? The News section of *Accountancy* for March 1985 draws attention on page 4 to devices such as 'vendor rights' and 'vendor placings' by UK companies such as System Designers International to satisfy the letter of SSAP 23's definition whilst, it is claimed, blatantly contravening the spirit of a 'merger'.

Under 'vendor rights' the offering company's shares are offered to the offeree's shareholders, who sell the shares for cash to an intermediary who itself offers them back to the offeror's shareholders as a rights issue. The 'letter of the law' is complied with. Shares have been offered for shares. However, the substance seems difficult to distinguish from the offeror making a rights issue to its shareholders and from the proceeds offering cash (under SSAP 23 requiring acquisition accounting!). In 'vendor placing' the intermediary places the offeror's shares with outsiders rather than offering them back to the offeror's shareholders.

Holgate (1986b, p. 25) comments:

A different sequence of transactions has taken place [under vendor placings]. The criticism appears to be based on the view that for merger accounting to be appropriate, the previous shareholders in [both companies] should continue to be shareholders in the combined group. That may be one way of defining when merger accounting may be used, but it is not the way used by SSAP 23. Rather the standard focuses on whether or not material resources leave the combining companies. In vendor placing they do not and so merger accounting may be used.

Certainly this viewpoint is technically correct. A share for share exchange has taken place within the 'boundaries' of the group. Further cash received by the offeree's shareholders is replenished in vendor rights by the offeror's shareholders and in vendor placings by outsiders. However, it seems to the author to be a serious matter that such a trivial nicety over whether cash is input into the group before passing to the offeror's shareholders, or whether shares are offered and the cash input and passing on is done just outside the borders of the group in such a premeditated and linked way, should have such drastically different effects on the accounting treatment – especially when the transaction is entered into solely for the purpose of manipulating the accounting treatment. Indeed in a recent Institute examination question (July 1986), reproduced in Chapter 12 as Question 12.12, a large part of an answer might have been to advise management how to do this! This viewpoint will be contrasted later with the continuity of ownership perspective.

APB Opinion No. 16 – the US solution compared

The US standard implicitly stresses continuity of ownership rights. It only allows pooling (merger) accounting when the offer for voting shares is made completely in shares (cf. the mix provisions of both ED 3 and SSAP 23). Further, the rights of shares issued have to be identical with those in issue of the offeror company (rather than the offeree company as in ED 3), and voting rights of shareholders in a combining company shall not change *vis-à-vis* other shareholders in the same company. These conditions try to ensure continuity of the combinee shareholders' rights in the group. As with SSAP 23 there is no 'size' criterion.

Because of the rumbustious experience of the 1960s and 1970s, and to prevent the 'continuity of ownership' principle being circumvented, the US standard contains a detailed list of 'anti-avoidance' clauses, e.g.:

Each of the combining companies . . . has not been a subsidiary or division of another corporation within two years before the plan of combination is initiated.

The combination is effected in a single transaction or in accordance with a specific plan within one year.

The combination is resolved at the date the plan is consummated and no provisions of the plan . . . are pending.

The combined corporation does not agree directly or indirectly to . . . reacquire all or part of the common stock [shares] issued to effect the combination.

The combined corporation does not intend or plan to dispose of a significant part of the assets of the combining companies within two years.

None of the combining companies changes the equity interest of the voting common stock in contemplation of effecting the combination.

The fourth is clearly designed to prevent vendor rights and placings. These would also have prevented British Syphon Industries accounting for its acquisition of Marshall's Universal as a merger.[4] On 7 November 1985 it acquired 25 per cent of Marshall's ordinary shares, and on 7 April 1986 it disposed of 12 per cent to its financial advisers, the day before making its offer which in itself satisfied SSAP 23's criteria. This disposal reduced its starting stake below the 20 per cent maximum starting stake specified by SSAP 23 for merger accounting. Leo (1984) also points out that it would be extremely easy under the UK definition for the mergee to distribute cash prior to the combination. It has further been suggested that, since under SSAP 23 most preference shares are excluded from the definition of equity, if the combinee issued preference shares just before the takeover, and the combinor paid a large amount of cash for these, issuing a trivial amount of shares for the remaining equity, this would qualify as a merger.[5]

Assessing the definitions from a continuity of ownership perspective

It is difficult to compare definitions. In the author's view, a helpful framework for comparison is the continuity of ownership perspective. Even if one accepts this perspective as *the* basis, a major difficulty is in discerning managements' and owners' intentions. One can view the definitions as providing pragmatic means for assessing such intentions. Table 3.4 views definitions from this perspective and arranges their criteria into three classes: externally verifiable signs of *ownership* continuity; circumstantial evidence of *ownership* continuity; and anti-avoidance clauses to ensure 'continuity' is not just cosmetic.

Verifiable signs	Offer mix
	Final proportional stake
	Voting rights etc. continue
Circumstantial evidence	Managements continue
	Relative sizes not too unequal
	Substance of business continues
	Complementarity of businesses
Exclusion clauses	No linked prior ownership
	Offer is part of a single plan
	No linked transactions
	No sudden large disposals

Table 3.4   Merger definitions from a continuity of ownership perspective

SSAP 23 focuses purely on externally verifiable signs. However, vendor placings and rights show it is possible to manipulate such signs. APB Opinion No. 16 illustrates anti-avoidance clauses, omitted from SSAP 23. Continuity of management, relative size, continuity of business substance, and even complementarity of businesses can be viewed from this perspective not as substantive criteria in themselves, but as circumstantial evidence of continuity of *ownership*. For example, if one business is wound up, it is possible that this is decided by the *joint* owners but this is very unlikely, particularly if relative sizes are very different. The circumstantial evidence grouping has been quietly dropped over time. From the continuity of ownership perspective they are not necessary conditions. They may be better seen as rebuttable presumptions in a definition, i.e. factors presumed to be present, and managements must show why merger accounting is appropriate when they are not. However, Foster (1974) might argue that even the mode of consideration itself is only circumstantial!

Other perspectives

Not all authors agree on the continuity of ownership criterion. Edey (1985) argues (following Parker, discussed earlier) that a limited company should be viewed as an 'anonymous society' separate from its members. He argues that the 'no significant resources leaving the group' criterion and the consequent accounting basis adopted in SSAP 23 are consistent with the intent of the Companies Act 1981 to recognize a *business need* to lift the share premium requirement in share for share exchanges. His main criterion is based on continued protection of creditors and shareholders (a major concern of company law), arguing that protection is not diminished if significant resources do not leave the group. Such a viewpoint implicitly treats a share swop as if it is a transaction in the secondary market. However, whether a 'business need' provides sufficient justification for defining the use of a controversial treatment is debatable.

The Canadian standard recognizes no significant resources leaving the group as a necessary but not sufficient reason for departure from the purchase (acquisition) method, *also* emphasizing that it should not be possible to identify an acquiror. Application of pooling of interests is deemed to be a rare occurrence.

Summary

The debate is difficult to resolve. Some do not agree with the continuity of ownership perspective. Even if this is accepted, discerning when such a continuity is deemed to occur (i.e. determining intentions) is not easy. It will be interesting to see how the UK definition of a merger evolves – to include anti-avoidance clauses suggesting continuity of ownership, or to continue to support a criterion consistent with the protection of shareholders and creditors. Evidence of 'loopholes' (discussed earlier) is already apparent. Wilkins (1986) in an early survey does not find a rush in the UK to use merger accounting, though this might merely reflect lack of experience!

THE FUNCTIONAL OBJECTIVES OF
ACCOUNTING FOR BUSINESS COMBINATIONS

A great deal of energy has been expended over the correct characterization of a merger or an acquisition. This section examines various theoretical objectives proposed by different authors for accounting for business combinations, and whether these are mutually compatible. Possible objectives include the following.

To preserve the integrity of the underlying valuation system

Both acquisition and merger approaches are consistent with either a historical or a current cost accounting system. Under the former, the difference in valuation arises because the accounting entity itself is characterized differently. The key question is 'When is the combined entity deemed to come into being?' Under the merger approach, the combinee is deemed to be a part of the combined entity from the outset. Hence its own historical costs become those of the group. Under the acquisition approach, the combinee is deemed to become a part only from acquisition. Hence, its historical costs are re-established at that date. Under current cost accounting, both would value assets at current price and so valuations would be identical (see Ketz, 1984). The *new entity* approach, to combinations recognized in the IASC's Exposure Draft E 22 (and mentioned in ED 31 though dropped in SSAP 23) in which assets and liabilities of both combining companies are restated to fair values at combination and in other respects merger accounting is used, does not seem to be so easy to rationalize under this objective as the 'pure' merger and acquisition alternatives.

To allow distributability of the combinee's pre-acquisition profits

Historically the acquisition approach has been characterized as freezing pre-combination profits of the combinee, and the merger approach as one which allows these to be distributed. Recent changes in company law now embodied in the Companies Act 1985 remove this simple distinction.

Usually discussions are couched in terms of potential distributability. For actual distributions, the combinee's profits have to be physically transferred to the combinor as dividends, which become profits of the *combinor*. This transfer does not affect total group profits, but merely their location. The combinor then pays dividends from its own profits. Only profits located at the holding company can be distributed to its shareholders. The sections in the Companies Acts dealing with distributions apply to companies not to groups.

Prior to the Companies Act 1981 pre-acquisition profits of the combinee could never be treated as profits of the holding company, hence merger accounting was illegal. The 1981 Act, in addition to introducing the 'merger relief' provisions, made minor wording amendments to earlier Acts. One of these removed a general restriction on inclusion of pre-acquisition profits of the subsidiary by the holding company. The current position now views distributability of holding company profits purely from a *holding company* perspective, ignoring the pre-/post-acquisition split in the group accounts. Restrictions on distributions now just depend on generally accepted accounting principles for fixed asset accounting – their statement at cost unless there is a *permanent* diminution in value.

Thus, SSAP 23's non-mandatory appendix states that such dividends from pre-acquisition profits can be regarded as holding company profits except 'to the extent that it is necessary to provide for a diminution in value of the investment in the subsidiary in the accounts of the [holding] company' (paragraph 3). If the investment is recorded at nominal amount in the *holding company* (i.e. merger relief is available), the standard for distributions will be lower than at market value. However, as discussed on pages 53–4, the valuation of the investment is not necessarily related to the consolidation approach, so distributability of pre-acquisition profits is not necessarily dependent on choice of acquisition or merger accounting in group accounts. It is even possible that companies which qualify for merger relief and follow SSAP 23's guidance to value the investment at fair value if they use acquisition accounting, will lose out. The appendix is unsure whether the standard for distributions in this case is the stiffer *market* value even where they have *voluntarily* rejected recording the investment at nominal amount.

Thus, a traditional distinguishing feature between the approaches no longer necessarily holds. Many of the ramifications of this are quite complex and are beyond the scope of this book, including the determination of diminution in value. Some will be dealt with in the next chapter. Whether group accounts should assist holding company shareholders in assessing potentially distributable profits is an interesting question which is examined in Chapter 11.

To enhance the predictive ability of the group financial statements

Snavely (1975) argues that the business combinations debate has gone off on the wrong track – that the main purpose of group financial statements is to aid prediction. He argues that merger accounting is superior for all combinations on the grounds that comparatives are restated and the track record of the companies of the group can be better compared over time prior to and post-combination.

He argues that it is easy to boost the size of group profits under acquisition accounting since the subsidiary is only included from acquisition; comparative figures from the previous period will not include assets or liabilities of the companies acquired, giving a misleading impression of growth in size and profit. Whittaker and Cooke (1983) argue, however, that where there are great size differences, economic changes in the running of the smaller business will make pre-/post-combination comparisons meaningless.

It is not universally accepted that the prime purpose of historical cost accounts should be to aid prediction. Snavely's (1975) argument is also consistent with an objective for accounting for business combinations of preserving relationships in the original accounts. Both of these will be reconsidered in the chapter on foreign currency translation.

To remove goodwill from the financial statements

Intimately interwoven with the debate is the treatment of goodwill examined in Chapter 4. Many practitioners and theorists are unhappy about its inclusion in financial statements as a result of business combinations (purchased goodwill) because firms in a similar position which have expanded from internal resources do not record goodwill. Further, it is inseparable from the firm as a whole and therefore extremely difficult to find a defensible amortization policy. Merger accounting has been viewed as a means of keeping goodwill off the balance sheet. However, a more favoured recent approach in the UK is to use acquisition accounting, and then to write off goodwill immediately versus reserves.

Comparing the balance sheet effects of the two alternatives, merger accounting tends to show larger retained earnings (because of progressive cancellation), whereas acquisition accounting with immediate write-off usually tends to show larger group share premium and a smaller group retained earnings (because of removal of pre-acquisition profits and goodwill write-off versus reserves).

The section has revealed that merger and acquisition accounting are not 'pure' alternatives. Wilkins (1979) shows that over the years prior to SSAP 14 and SSAP 23, a whole variety of hybrids were practised (including acquisition accounting without revaluation at acquisition). The range of permissible alternatives has been reduced by SSAPs 14 and 23, though discussions in this chapter and the next illustrate the significant diversity in practice. Some authors suggest other alternatives, e.g. Wyatt (1963) suggests that in many combinations, neither company continues and so in the new entity, assets should be revalued and pre-acquisition profits of *both* constituents should be removed, calling this 'fair value pooling', and the 'new entity' approach was outlined on page 61. Such alternatives are not discussed further here.

THE WIDER CONTEXT

Thus far, accounting for business combinations has been considered in terms of refining the merger and acquisition concepts, or in deducing an accounting treatment from desired theoretical objectives. Two further areas of research examined here probe the context of the debate and suggest that an understanding of its nature may be more correctly centred in the realm of political and economic consequences and not merely in a conceptual dimension.

Accounting concepts as rationalizations/excuses

In the 1970s an increasing awareness of the 'economic consequences' of accounting proposals became apparent as a constraint on policy-making (see for example Zeff, 1978). Watts and Zimmerman (1979), in a seminal paper, went a stage further to argue that accounting theories are produced in response to a demand from vested interests for 'excuses' to legitimate their own interests, rather than being judged according to their 'truth'. They argued that managements have an incentive to search out theories which accord with their own interests. Investors are aware of such managerial behaviour and will discount share prices accordingly. Academics and theoreticians do not deliberately compromise their integrity, but Watts and Zimmerman argue that they are naturally drawn to areas where research funds are available and are drawn to positions which will enhance their professional reputations. Certain institutional and empirical developments are now considered in this light.

It could be argued that inertia in changing the UK merger definition could be due to vested interests in keeping open the avenue of vendor rights and placing schemes. Further, the change between ED 31 and SSAP 23 in making merger accounting optional, not required, suggests political posturing rather than a conceptually based solution. SSAP 22 on goodwill will also be seen in Chapter 4 to have this same flavour. Consider also the evolution to no size test in APB Opinion No. 16 in the USA. Its original exposure draft included a size test of three to one. In the period leading up to the standard, after vehement debate, this was watered down to a nine to one test before being finally dropped as 'arbitrary' in the standard itself. This debate seems a political rather than a theoretical one (see for example Rayburn, 1979).

How far was this definition weakened by pressure groups? An empirical study prior to the introduction of APB 16 by Gagnon (1971) tests the 'income maximization hypothesis'. This states that the approach to accounting for business combinations will be chosen to maximize subsequently reported income – firms where the market value of the investment exceeded book value of the firm acquired would use pooling to avoid future goodwill write-offs. He found weak evidence of this, whereas results were inconclusive where the investment was less than book value. Copeland and Wojdack (1969) replicated the study for the period immediately after APB 16 when the definition of a merger had supposedly been tightened. Somewhat surprisingly, they found evidence which continued to support the 'income maximization hypothesis', suggesting that managements may have found ways to meet 'pooling' criteria when it suited them, and accordingly wished to keep APB No. 16's criteria as vague as possible.

Are users fooled by cosmetic choice of accounting treatments?

Professor Abraham J. Briloff, a leading proponent of the case against the misuse of merger (pooling) accounting, has provided a number of case studies illustrating such abuses – e.g. asset stripping, showing high profits by comparing current revenues versus the old costs introduced via the combinee, thus boosting 'tired' P/E ratios, enhancing group earnings by merging with companies near or even after the year-end so that a complete year's earnings are included (for example, Briloff, 1972, chs. 3 and 4; 1976, ch. 8). Such cases assume that investors are somewhat naïve and that managements can fool them through choice of accounting methods. A recent body of research into the behaviour of stock markets and their reaction to accounting data, called 'efficient markets research' has questioned this view of investors.

Efficient markets researchers argue, based on a wide body of empirical evidence, that capital markets are semi-strong efficient, (i.e. that the market price reflects all *publicly* available information instantaneously and accurately for each share). They also argue that such research shows the market can see through 'cosmetic' changes in accounting numbers, reacting only to those changes which have a real impact on future cash flows. This implies that one should not assume the stock market will view the choice between accounting proposals as important unless it feels any change has a direct effect on future cash flows. But, the market can *only* see through cosmetic changes if it has enough information to form a judgement.

Hong, Kaplan and Mandelker (1978) used efficient markets methodology to examine whether higher earnings resulting from merger (pooling of interests) accounting have any effect on share prices of the firms concerned (i.e. are investors fooled by 'cosmetic' changes in earnings which have no effect on future cash flows?). They examined over two hundred US business combinations over the period 1954–64 (i.e. prior to APB 16 when the option of approach was still easily available to management), hypothesizing that the New York Stock Exchange could distinguish between higher earnings caused by the merger approach and higher earnings caused by real economic events. Using a 'market model' for share prices, they found no evidence (i.e. no market reaction) that the merger approach raises share prices of acquiring firms around the time of the combination. Investors were not 'fooled' by the choice of the accounting convention.

However, Hines (1984) cautions against reading too much into 'non-reaction' results, commenting that if firms' motivations for changes are heterogeneous and if investors' interpretations of such actions are also heterogeneous, any micro (company level) reactions are likely to be averaged away when efficient markets tests (which examine aggregate reactions) are performed.

If the market is efficient (i.e. investors are sophisticated), maybe extra disclosure about the combination event is more useful than debating accounting alternatives. The investor can make a relevant assessment of the effect of the combination. It is interesting that SSAP 23 contains extra disclosure requirements where merger accounting is adopted to enable an investor to make a rudimentary comparison with acquisition accounting. In efficient markets terms, it could be argued that if these disclosures were detailed enough, the choice of method would be irrelevant. However, current disclosures, whilst attempting to prevent the abuses cited by Briloff, do not allow full reconciliation. Also, increased disclosure has its costs and it should be noted that efficient markets tests do not consider *social* costs and benefits of alternatives – investors may reap the benefits but not bear the costs.

Efficient markets research examines aggregate level reactions to changes in accounting methods. In contrast, Gaertner (1979) used a small-scale laboratory study to see whether individuals are 'fooled' by the choice of approach over combinations. His results are difficult to interpret because the test did not examine a straight choice between acquisition and merger accounting. Broadly his study found that the investment decisions were not affected by differing approaches, except 'investors' tended to shy away from companies with large amounts of goodwill in their balance sheets. Gaertner recognized difficulties in generalizing such studies because of the artificial environment, and because 'investors' in this study, business studies students, were not experts, and were not investing real money.

The analysis of the previous sections suggests that choice of approach and circumstances of use involve complex issues which touch at the heart of the standard-setting difficulties. It illustrates why it is important to study the context of the debate as well as its technical content. The reader is left to form her or his own judgement as to the 'best' way of accounting for business combinations!

Discussion questions

3.9 Explain in your own words the analogies used to justify acquisition and merger accounting. How far do you consider them to be appropriate justifications for such accounting treatments?

3.10   Discuss whether or not you feel merger accounting should be abolished, giving reasons.

3.11   Formulate what you consider to be an improvement on SSAP 23's definition of when merger accounting may be used. Discuss the criteria you have used.

See also professional question 12 in Chapter 12.

SUMMARY

The *acquisition* (purchase) approach generally records the investment in the holding company's records at *fair value*. Pre-acquisition profits of the combinee are *excluded* from group results, and its assets and liabilities are *revalued* at acquisition to establish new historical costs. The *merger* (pooling of interests) approach records the investment at *nominal* amount, *includes* pre-acquisition results of the combinee as far as possible, and does *not revalue* assets and liabilities of the combinee at acquisition. The accounting approach was found in principle to be independent of the mechanism for effecting the combination (e.g. creating a new holding company or not).

The acquisition approach stresses *discontinuity* of ownership, and characterizes the acquisition of a business analogously to the purchase of its separate components which contribute since purchase. The merger approach stresses *continuity* of ownership, and uses the analogy of an adjustment of the ownership rights of the two companies.

The distinction between recording the combination in holding company and in consolidated accounts was stressed. Technically, the aim in acquisition accounting is to *eliminate* (in one lump) pre-acquisition *equity* of the subsidiary. In merger accounting, *progressive* cancellation is used. The approaches were contrasted at the date of the combination and subsequently, and the treatment of minority interests was examined.

SSAP 23 was examined, with its relationship to UK company law and US accounting standards. It covers three main areas; accounting treatment, definition of when merger accounting is allowable, and disclosure. Its non-mandatory appendix dealing with the investment in holding company accounts was examined. Problems in merger *definition* were considered to illustrate conflicts in setting accounting standards in the area. Finally, the *purposes* of accounting for business combinations were reviewed, in a technical/functional sense and in a wider context.

NOTES

1.   *Economic Report on Mergers*. Staff Report of the Federal Trade Commission, quoted in McLean (1972), p. 32.

2. The term 'other reserves' is used to prevent the distinction between a share premium account and a merger reserve being used at such an early stage in the chapter. The distinction is discussed later.
3. See Holgate, P. (1986) SSAP 23 – an emerging issue, *Accountancy,* July, pp. 26–7.
4. See 'British Syphon finds SSAP 23 loophole', in Reports and Accounts, *Accountancy,* July 1986, p. 31.
5. See 'No Minister! SSAP 23 will not do', *Accountancy Age,* January 1987, p. 19.

FURTHER READING

Accounting Principles Board (1970) *Opinion No. 16 – Business Combinations,* APB, New York.

Accounting Standards Committee (1985) *SSAP 23 – Accounting for acquisitions and mergers,* ASC, London.

Holgate, P. A. (1986) *A Guide to Accounting Standards – SSAP 23 'Accounting for acquisitions and mergers',* Accountants Digest No. 189, Institute of Chartered Accountants in England and Wales, London.

Leo, K. J. (1984) *Accounting for Business Combinations,* Discussion Paper No. 8, Australian Accounting Research Foundation, Melbourne.

Watts, R. and Zimmerman, J. (1979) The demand for and supply of accounting theories: the market for excuses, *The Accounting Review,* Vol. LIV, No. 2, pp. 273–305.

Wilkins, R. M. (1986) Takeovers, in L. Skerratt and D. Tonkin (eds.) *Financial Reporting 1985/6,* Institute of Chartered Accountants in England and Wales, London.

PART II

CONSOLIDATING THE
MAJOR FINANCIAL STATEMENTS

4 The Consolidated Balance Sheet under Acquisition Accounting

This is the first of four chapters to examine the consolidation of specific financial statements, in this case the consolidated balance sheet. These chapters focus on the *acquisition* approach since it is by far the most widely used approach in the UK. However, many of the issues examined also arise under merger accounting. The first section reinforces the conventional consolidation process; the second locates conventional consolidation as one alternative in a spectrum of possible approaches for accounting for trade investments, another important element being the equity approach; the third examines the accounting treatment of goodwill. Each section considers and evaluates relevant professional pronouncements.

CONVENTIONAL CONSOLIDATION

The acquisition cancellation process

The key element in acquisition accounting is how the *equity* of the holding company is combined with that of the subsidiary. The acquisition cancellation process removes pre-acquisition equity of the subsidiary (major surgery) so that the subsidiary contributes to the group only *after* acquisition. This process necessitates a reclassification of equity balances of the two companies. Consider where a less than a 100 per cent holding in a subsidiary is acquired (i.e. with a minority interest), shown schematically in Figure 4.1.

The top section shows individual company reserves of holding company and subsidiary, split for convenience into pre- and post-acquisition amounts. The subsidiary's reserves are further subdivided in each period to show majority and minority interests. The bottom section shows consolidated amounts evolving from the individual company balances. On the left is *consolidated* reserves. The group (majority) holding in the subsidiary contributes to group retained earnings only *after* acquisition. On the right, the minority share in the subsidiary is an ongoing one including pre-acquisition retained earnings.

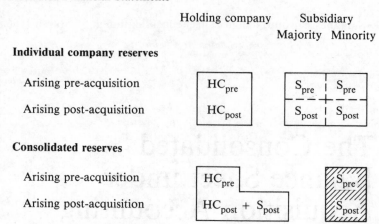

Figure 4.1   *Group reserves under acquisition accounting*

Example 4.1   Largesse/Smallnesse – acquisition accounting

Largesse plc acquires 80 per cent of the shares in Smallnesse Ltd on 31 March 1983 when the reserves of the two companies were respectively £80,000 and £30,000. The balance sheets of the two companies at 31 March 1986 were:

Individual company balance sheets at 31 March 1986 (£000)

	Largesse	Smallnesse
Land	40	20
Investment in Smallnesse	80	—
Stocks	50	30
Other assets	250	60
Liabilities	(100)	(20)
Share capital	(130)	(35)
Share premium	(70)	(15)
Retained earnings	(120)	(40)

Date of acquisition

SSAP 14 (paragraph 32) defines the effective date for accounting for acquisitions or disposals as the earlier of:

(a) the date on which consideration passes; or

(b) the date on which an offer becomes or is declared unconditional.

This is even if the acquiring company has a right to share in the acquired business's profits from an earlier date. Here this is assumed to be 31 March 1983.

Note the combination has *already* been recorded in Largesse's records at *market* value in accordance with SSAP 23 (80 per cent combination), and the acquisition approach should be used. No information is given suggesting a revaluation of the subsidiary's assets and liabilities at acquisition is necessary, so the problems of revaluation are ignored here. Try the consolidation before referring to the following solution.

Largesse–Smallnesse group: balance sheet consolidation at 31 March 1986 (£000)

	Largesse	Smallnesse	Minority	Pre-acq.	Elim.	Consol.
Land	40	20				60
Investment	80	—			(80)	—
Stock	50	30				80
Other assets	250	60				310
Liabilities	(100)	(20)				(120)
Share capital	(130)	(35)	7	28		(130)
Share premium	(70)	(15)	3	12		(70)
Retained earnings	(120)	(40)	8	24		(128)
Pre-acq./goodwill				(64)	80	16
Minority interests			(18)			(18)

The minority's share of retained earnings is 20 per cent of £40, but the pre-acquisition removal is 80 per cent of £30, (*pre*-acquisition retained earnings). Thus the majority's share of *post*-acquisition earnings of the subsidiary is included in consolidated reserves, i.e. £120 + 80% × £10 = £128.

The abbreviated cancellation table

Writing out full balance sheets each time a consolidation is performed is cumbersome in more complex examples. An abbreviated format is now discussed and is used throughout the remainder of the book. Table 4.1 is in vertical format since in more complex examples most people find it easier to analyse balances line by line going down the page rather than across, column by column.

	Investment	Share capital	Share premium	Retained earnings	Goodwill	Minority
Largesse	80	(130)	(70)	(120)	—	—
Smallnesse						
– at acquisition					(64)	(16)
– post-acquisition				(8)	—	(2)
Elimination	(80)				80	
Consolidated amounts	—	(130)	(70)	(128)	16	(18)

Table 4.1   Abbreviated acquisition cancellation table in vertical form

Steps in completing the abbreviated table

1. Only balances requiring adjustment in going from individual company to consolidated balance sheets are included (i.e. not land, stocks, assets or liabilities here).
2. Holding company balances are filled in item by item.
3. The subsidiary's equity balances are directly analysed as they are entered, each component being reformatted as used in consolidation. First the total equity of (35 + 15 + 40 = 90) is split into equity at acquisition (80), and movement in equity since acquisition (10). Then these aggregates are divided between majority and minority, the former between 'goodwill' and

'minority' columns, and the latter between '[consolidated] retained earnings' and 'minority', both 80:20. This procedure reflects the disjunction in treatment of the majority, whereas the minority share is ongoing.

4. The investment is then cancelled against the pre-acquisition amount to determine goodwill.

Exercises

4.1 For Example 4.1:
(a) interpret intuitively the change in consolidated reserves and minority interests since acquisition;
(b) discuss the breakdown of the minority interest figure into components;
(c) explain why under acquisition accounting the share capital and share premium of the group are equal to those of the holding company.

4.2 Redraft the balance sheet consolidation for Student plc and Union Ltd on page 48, into abbreviated form, checking your solution below:

	Investment	Share cap.	Other res.	Retained earnings	Goodwill	Minor. ints.
Student	396	(616)	(222)	(110)		
Union:						
– pre-acq.					(270)	(30)
– post-acq.				(36)		(4)
Cancellation	(396)				396	
Consolidated	—	(616)	(222)	(146)	126	(34)

4.3 You are presented with the summarized financial statements of Bigfry plc and its subsidiary Smallfry Ltd shown in Table 4.2.

Note that:
1. Bigfry acquired a 60 per cent stake in Smallfry on 31 May 1986, when the retained earnings of Smallfry were £50,000.
2. Bigfry acquired an 18 per cent interest in Tinyfry on 30 November 1985. This should be accounted for at cost in the consolidated statement.

Required Prepare a consolidated balance sheet for the Bigfry group at 30 November 1986, using the abbreviated acquisition cancellation table.

GROUP MEASUREMENT AND DISCLOSURE CONCEPTS

This section examines alternatives for accounting for investments in other companies under acquisition accounting, the name for a *family of techniques* centred on a single measurement basis but differing in the extent of disclosures provided. Conventional consolidation is shown to be part of an extended spectrum of alternatives. Each characterizes the group and its ownership in different ways, some giving prominence to minority interests, others completely

	Bigfry (£000)			Smallfry (£000)	
Assets employed:					
Land		40		20	
Buildings		60		20	
Plant and equipment		360		100	
		460		140	
Investment in Smallfry		72			
Investment in Tinyfry		20			
Current assets:					
Stocks	50			15	
Debtors	30			10	
Cash	5			2	
	85			27	
Current liabilities:					
Creditors	(25)			(23)	
Dividends payable	(10)			—	
	(35)	50		(23)	4
Long-term loans		(200)			(30)
		402			114
Financed by:					
Ordinary share capital	60			20	
Share premium	50			30	
Retained earnings	292			64	
		402			114

Table 4.2 Bigfry and Smallfry balance sheets at 30 November 1986

excluding them. 'Theories' underlying accounting for investments, minorities and groups are discussed after technical alternatives have been examined. In the UK, in group accounts different treatments correspond approximately to differing degrees of ownership. Broadly 0–20 per cent owned investments are accounted for at cost, 21–50 per cent investments by equity accounting, and 51–100 per cent by consolidation. In the holding company's own accounts investments (including subsidiaries) are all recorded at cost.

A similar family of techniques is deducible under merger accounting, but is not widely used since merger accounting only tends to be used for nearly wholly owned investments where only consolidation is deemed appropriate. Therefore the corresponding merger spectrum is not discussed in this book. The acquisition 'family' of techniques is used in consolidated accounts for a wide spectrum of 20–100 per cent investments.

Approaches to accounting for trade investments under historical cost

The cost basis

In individual company accounts, an investment in another company is treated either as a current or a long-term asset. The normal historical cost basis of 'valuation' of such assets is, if current, the lower of cost and net realizable value; if long-term, at cost unless there is a *permanent* decline in value in which case it is written down (implicitly assuming temporary fluctuations will reverse themselves over the life of the asset and so should be ignored). A few investments, e.g. 'investment properties', are often valued at market value but are outside the scope of the text, as is the valuation of investments under current value systems.

Income from such investments is normally recognized on a dividends receivable basis, and such investments remain anchored at cost, viz.:

> Dr. Dividends receivable   Cr. Profit and loss (P & L a/c)

and when the cash is received

> Dr. Cash   Cr. Dividends receivable

Though unexceptionable in historical cost terms, difficulties arose with this approach as early as the turn of the century as group structures were more widely used to conduct operations. It starved investors of disclosure and, whilst 'objective' in principle, in practice was anything but. Controlled subsidiaries declared increasing dividends (which was all holding company shareholders saw) whilst underlying profits might be fluctuating wildly. Directors could 'prudently' build up 'secret reserves' in subsidiaries or be downright unscrupulous!

Increasing pressure for different disclosure and measurement alternatives for investments in substantially owned and controlled companies was inevitable. One route to be taken could have been the increasing use of current (or market) value accounting with increased subsidiary disclosures. This was nipped in the bud by the great economic crises in the 1920s and 1930s. The less radical alternative of modifying and expanding the historical cost treatment (in the UK via supplementary group accounts) whilst still attempting to remain broadly within the historical cost system's tenets, is the route that was taken.

Within this historical cost context, this chapter examines first the simplest *measurement* alternative for overcoming the defects with the cost basis, and then the increasingly detailed ·*disclosure* alternatives which are possible. Full consolidation is only one possible way of enhancing the basic information, and as we shall see, full consolidation itself has many varieties! In the UK today, the holding company is required to produce its own company balance sheet (in which investments in group companies are accounted for at *cost*), and another for the group (using various techniques for enhancing the measurement and disclosure of these investments) usually called the consolidated accounts.

Accounting for substantially owned investments – the equity method

Cost plus attributable profit basis   Designed to overcome measurement problems discussed above, an objective of the approach is to disclose as income the *profits* of the company underlying the investment, so that dividend-based manipulations are not possible. Effectively, the way this has been handled is as follows:

Dr. Investment   Cr. P & L a/c

with the group's share, i.e. *attributable profits* of the investee *since the acquisition of the investment*. Thus the profit and loss account discloses *profits* of the investee. Profit realization for the group is now on an 'earned' rather than a 'dividends declared' basis. Such a treatment is only used in the UK in the *group accounts*, where the investment is no longer stated at cost, but at cost plus attributable profit. Consider now in more detail this cost 'plus profit' basis.

The treatments of dividends   Before, if a dividend were declared, the entry would be:

Dr. Dividends receivable   Cr. P & L a/c

Here if this were done, we would be double counting income on both an earned and on a receivable basis. Under the equity approach, dividends are treated as follows:

Dr. Dividends receivable   Cr. Investment

Thus, the investment strictly is stated at 'cost plus attributable *retained earnings*' of the investee. It is debited with attributable profits and credited with dividends receivable.

The bookkeeping for the cost and equity approaches

1. Cost basis

Dividends receivable		Investment		P & L a/c	
1 Div		Cost			1 Div

2. Equity approach

Dividends receivable		Investment		P & L a/c	
2 Div		Cost 1 Profit	2 Div		1 Profit

In comparison with the cost approach, both the investment and the profit and loss account are increased under the equity approach by attributable retained earnings, the latter through the increase from dividends to attributable profits.

Full consolidation viewed as an expansion of the equity approach

Various degrees of expanded disclosure of the 'equity' approach are possible. All involve expanding the investment into the individual assets, liabilities and goodwill comprising it and then adding these exploded components item by item to those of the holding company. Consider how this expansion works assuming an 80 per cent takeover.

At acquisition   At acquisition, since goodwill is the excess of the investment over the majority share of the equity (= net assets) acquired,

Investment at cost = Goodwill + 80% × (Assets − Liabilities)

Later than acquisition   It will now be demonstrated that, at *any time* later than acquisition,

$$\text{Investment at cost } plus \text{ attributable retained earnings} = \text{Goodwill} + 80\% \times (\text{Assets} - \text{Liabilities})$$

If this is true, we can *at any time* replace the 'equitized' investment by its component assets and liabilities. The first (more obvious) relationship is just a special case of the second, at the time of acquisition. But, *why* the second more general relationship holds is not immediately apparent and is examined further.

Let A = assets at acquisition, ΔA = the change in assets since acquisition, G = goodwill at acquisition, etc. Then at acquisition,

$$I = G + 0.8 \times (A - L) \tag{4.1}$$

Since acquisition, as the change in equity of the investee is equal to the change in its net assets (the fundamental balance sheet relationship), it follows that (provided there are no share issues):

$$\Delta RE = \Delta A - \Delta L$$

and so

$$0.8 \Delta RE = 0.8 (\Delta A - \Delta L)$$

Adding this to equation 4.1, we get:

$$I + 0.8 \Delta \text{RE} = G + 0.8 [(A + \Delta A) - (L - \Delta L)] \tag{4.2}$$

The left-hand side comprises investment at cost plus attributable retained earnings since acquisition, i.e. the 'equitized' investment now. The right-hand side comprises goodwill (ignoring any write-offs at this stage) plus majority assets and liabilities currently. If any revaluations of assets, etc. were made and related to the period subsequent to acquisition, the asset values on the right would include them, and 80 per cent of the revaluation reserve would be included in the update of the investment. If they were made prior to acquisition, they would be included in the computation of goodwill.

Hence, the equitized investment can be broken down into component assets, liabilities and goodwill at *any* date.

In the UK, the equity method is only used in *group* accounts for 20–50 per cent holdings. In the USA it is used in some *holding company* accounts for associates and subsidiaries as well as in *group* accounts for associates. In an earlier version of SSAP 1, 'Accounting for associated companies', the investment was to be stated at 'cost plus attributable profit'. The current version discussed later requires a breakdown of the equitized amount between 'goodwill' and 'attributable net assets'. Equation 4.2 demonstrates why the same figure can be broken down in two different ways. In what follows, since the purpose is merely to illustrate technique, the 80 per cent investment in Example 4.1 will be 'equitized', though this would not be its normal treatment in practice. Figure 4.2 shows a spectrum of possible expansions arising from the basic equity method.

	Cost plus breakdown	Component breakdown	Proportional consolidation	Conventional consolidation	Entity consolidation
			Goodwill	Goodwill	$Goodwill_{100}$
			$0.8\,A_1$	A_1	A_1
			$0.8\,A_2$	A_2	A_2
			$0.8\,A_3$	A_3	A_3
			$\vdots$	$\vdots$	$\vdots$
	Cost	Goodwill	$0.8\,A_n$	A_n	A_n
Investment	$0.8\,RE$	$0.8\,(A - L)$	$0.8\,L_1$	L_1	L_1
			$0.8\,L_2$	L_2	L_2
			$0.8\,L_3$	L_3	L_3
			$\vdots$	$\vdots$	$\vdots$
			$0.8\,L_m$	L_m	L_m
				Minority	$Minority_{100}$

Figure 4.2   Expansions of the equitized investment

Each column from left to right in Figure 4.2 progressively expands the 'equitized' investment, using equation 4.2. Column 1 shows cost and attributable retained earnings since acquisition. Column 2 gives the complementary breakdown into goodwill and the *majority* (80 per cent) proportion of *aggregate* net assets at the *current* date. Column 3 breaks down this aggregate into the *majority portion* (80 per cent) of *each* asset and each liability of the investee, the basis for proportional consolidation discussed later. Column 4 shows goodwill plus 100 per cent of each asset and liability of the subsidiary, less a deduction of

20 per cent of their aggregate, the minority interest. It forms the basis for conventional consolidation. Note each expansion has the same total – that of the equitized investment.

Column 5 forms the basis of entity consolidation, and is included here for completeness. Under conventional consolidation, goodwill is computed on the majority (80 per cent) interest only. Entity consolidation computes *total* (i.e. 100 per cent) goodwill at acquisition, including minority goodwill. The implied entry for the 'new' 20 per cent is to Dr. Goodwill and Cr. Minority. Hence, goodwill is denoted 'Goodwill$_{100}$' and the augmented minority as 'Minority$_{100}$'.

Consolidation as equitization and expansion
Starting with the investment *at cost*, consolidation *under any approach* is characterized in Table 4.3 as a two-stage process.

Equitization	The investment at cost in the individual company accounts is augmented by the entry: Dr. Investment Cr. Group retained earnings with the majority share of subsidiary/investee retained earnings since acquisition.
Expansion	The single figure of the equitized investment is expanded into individual components to be added item by item to the same components of the holding company.

Table 4.3   The twofold aspect of consolidation

The cost approach is *before* equitization and expansion. The equity approach is *after* equitization but *before* expansion. Conventional consolidation is one possible expansion of the equitized investment.

The recommended disclosure for associated companies under SSAP 1 requiring the breakdown into two figures, *aggregate* net assets and goodwill, is a limited form of expansion, rather than under conventional consolidation where the net asset *components* are aggregated item by item with the holding company's component balances. Different forms of 'consolidation' under acquisition accounting can thus be seen as different expansions of the equitized investment. Here too can be seen the basis for the intuitive analogy for acquisition accounting discussed in Chapter 3 – the purchase of the subsidiary's assets, liabilities and goodwill. Here too, consolidated reserves are the *same* under the equity approach and *all* consolidation (i.e. expansion) approaches. Hence the equity approach without expansion is termed 'one line consolidation'.

Table 4.3 is a useful way of conceptualizing consolidation in principle and reconciling it to a cost basis. The acquisition cancellation table is a *means* of achieving this. The cancellation of majority pre-acquisition profits against the investment to determine goodwill, calculation of minorities, and adding post-acquisition retained earnings to the group's, are just computationally effective ways of achieving the end result of the two-stage process of equitization plus expansion. In the USA where parent companies use the *equity* approach in their own accounts, the consolidation process is akin to *expansion* (of the already equitized investment). Where they use cost, consolidation is cancellation-based.

Largesse–Smallnesse: a numerical illustration

Consider again Example 4.1 to illustrate the above. Figure 4.3 is an expansion table of the equitized investment, using the example data. Credits are bracketed.

Stage 1: calculation of equitized investment Post-acquisition retained earnings of Smallnesse are 40 − 30 = 10. The majority share is 80% × 10 = 8. Consolidated reserves calculated below can be checked with the cancellation table, Table 4.1.

Equitized investment = Cost + attributable retained earnings since acquisition = 80 + 8 = 88.

Consolidated reserves under *all* approaches = 120 + 8 = 128.

Stage 2: expansions of the equitized amount Check carefully the derivation of the figures in Figure 4.3 and how to distinguish between the expansions. Work through the calculations for the equitized investment and its two complementary expansions. This basic equitizing equation in both its forms is used extensively in accounting for associated companies under SSAP 1, and also for accounting for disposals of subsidiaries in Chapter 6. Before more complex situations are encountered, it is very important that the basic equitizing equations and their calculations are fully understood.

Stage 3: replacement of equitized investment by its expansion The group balance sheets under the various approaches, shown in Table 4.4, are obtained from the original parent company balance sheet (shown at the beginning of Example 4.1), by adding the expansions in Figure 4.3.

In Table 4.4 the first three columns show the conversion of the individual company balance sheet to an equitized group basis by equitizing the investment. Note that group retained earnings for all other consolidation approaches are identical to that in column 3. The remaining columns are obtained by removing the single figure equitized investment (hence the term 'one line consolidation' for the basic equity approach) and replacing it with the relevant expansion from Figure 4.3. The different consolidation approaches correspond merely to different expansions.

The conventional consolidation group balance sheet obtained here by equitization and expansion is *identical* to that obtained earlier by using the cancellation table (see page 73). The equitization and expansion approach is useful in understanding the *nature* of consolidation and the relationship between approaches. The cancellation table approach is the *means* of obtaining the desired result in a computationally efficient manner.

	Cost plus breakdown	Component breakdown	Proportional consolidation	Conventional consolidation	Entity consolidation
	80 Cost	16 Goodwill	16 Goodwill	16 Goodwill	20 100% Goodwill
88 Investment			16 80% Land	20 100% Land	20 100% Land
			24 80% Stocks	30 100% Stocks	30 100% Stocks
	8 Attributable retained earnings	72* 80% Net assets	48 80% Other	60 100% Other	60 100% Other
			(16) 80% Liabilities	(20) 100% Liabilities	(20) 100% Liabilities
				(18)† Minority	(22)‡ Minority (incl. goodwill)

Notes
* 80% of net assets of Smallnesse, $80\% \times (20 + 30 + 60 - 20) = 72$. In more complex examples it is easier to calculate as 80% of equity, $80\% \times (35 + 15 + 40) = 72$.
† 20% of net assets of Smallnesse now, i.e. one quarter of the above, also 20% of equity *now*, viz. $= 20\% \times (35 + 15 + 40)$.
‡ Goodwill is grossed up to $100/80 \times 16 = 20$, the (imputed) minority share of which is $20 - 16 = 4$ (which can be calculated directly as $20/80 \times 16$). The minority stake is increased by 4 from 18 to 22 to include this imputed goodwill.

Figure 4.3   Expansions of equitized investment: Example 4.1

	Company	Equitizing entry	Equity	Proportional	Conventional	Entity
Goodwill				16	16	20
Land	40		40	56	60	60
Investment	80	8	88	—	—	—
Stocks	50		50	74	80	80
Other assets	250		250	298	310	310
Liabilities	(100)		(100)	(116)	(120)	(120)
Minority	—		—	—	(18)	(22)
Share capital	(130)		(130)	(130)	(130)	(130)
Share premium	(70)		(70)	(70)	(70)	(70)
Retained earnings	(120)	(8)	(128)	(128)	(128)	(128)

Table 4.4   Balance sheets of the Largesse group at 31 March 1986 under various consolidation approaches

The treatment of minority interests in group accounts

Baxter and Spinney (1975) try to examine 'theories' underlying various consolidation approaches. They distinguish a continuum of four consolidation theories; proprietary, parent, parent company extension and entity theories. Each justifies a particular consolidation approach and treatment of minority interest. The parent company extension is discussed in the next chapter, the other three being examined briefly here.

The proprietary approach

Baxter and Spinney (1975) argue that this approach views the group through the eyes of its ultimate owners only. Since minority interests are not ultimate owners of the group, their share of net assets (equity) is disregarded. Such a 'theory' has been used to justify proportional consolidation for all subsidiaries. A recent supporter of proportional consolidation is Rubin in Rosenfield and Rubin (1986). He argues that it better represents the substance of the acquisition transaction rather than its form, that one way for a company to acquire say 80 per cent of another's results would be to purchase a package of 80 per cent of its separate assets and liabilities, and that this is equivalent to acquiring 80 per cent of its equity. Proportional consolidation also excludes the 'nondescript amount' minority interests.

The parent company concept

This approach argues that the ultimate owners have a joint claim with a secondary set of owners – minority interests – to the *undivided* assets and liabilities of the subsidiary, and that it is meaningless to aggregate fractional assets, etc. Since the minority are not important to the group as a whole, their share is summarized, usually as one figure. A weakness of the approach is that the status of the minority interest is ill-defined – is it a part of equity, or a liability or as a separate class of ownership altogether? What is its nature? Rosenfield and Rubin (1986) give examples of conflicting proposals in the literature.

The entity concept

This approach, popularised by Moonitz (1951), regards consolidated assets, liabilities and equities as being those of a group entity. The majority and minority are given equal prominence as co-equal owners. From this perspective it can be argued that measurement and disclosure principles for both should be identical, and so minority goodwill should be revalued at acquisition (since majority goodwill is recognized). The single figure minority could be expanded into its components and these could be given equal prominence with those of the holding company. Thus there is potentially a measurement difference (goodwill) and a disclosure difference. Consider the contrast with conventional consolidation shown in Table 4.5.

	Conventional	Entity
Share capital:		
– Holding co.	(130)	(130)
– Minority	—	(7)
Share premium:		
– Holding co	(70)	(70)
– Minority	—	(3)
Retained earnings:		
– Holding co.	(128)	(128)
– Minority – other	—	(8)
– goodwill		(4)
Minority interests	(18)	—

Table 4.5   Conventional and entity consolidation contrasted

However, Rosenfield in Rosenfield and Rubin (1986), whilst supporting an entity-based report, suggests that any numerical breakdown of residual equity between classes serves no useful purpose. He argues that as a historical document showing how equity arose, or as a guide to restrictions on distributions, it is inefficient. He argues that all that should be presented is a residual, the excess of assets over liabilities, and matters of distributability and claims (e.g. of the minority) should be reported as memorandum notes. Note that the use of the term 'entity' here is different from Chapter 2 when the *de facto* definition of a group was considered. There it referred to concentrations of economic power (often by *management*). Here it refers to *all* ownership claims, not just those of the holding company.

It can be seen that the differing approaches are not clearly or unambiguously defined regarding the treatment of the elements of consolidated equity. One might be excused for viewing them as rationalizations for particular technical alternatives, rather than fundamental concepts which dictate the alternatives.

Exercise

4.4

(a)   Using the Bigfry–Smallfry example (Exercise 4.3), calculate the amount of the investment in Smallfry at 30 November 1986 under the equity approach.

(b)   Show numerically the different possible expansions of this figure (using as an example Figure 4.3).

(c)   Prepare a consolidated balance sheet under each approach (using as an example Table 4.4).

(d)   Why are consolidated reserves equal under each approach?

GROUP MEASUREMENT AND DISCLOSURE CONCEPTS – UK PRACTICE

Current UK practice adopts a tiered approach (brings tiers to your eyes!) to accounting for long-term investments in group accounts:

(a)   less than 20 per cent – trade investments – at cost;
(b)   20–50 per cent – associated companies – the equity approach;
(c)   over 50 per cent – subsidiaries – full consolidation.

Associated companies – definition

SSAP 1, 'Accounting for associated companies', was issued in 1971 and revised in 1982. Prior to 1971, company law only recognized either the cost basis or full consolidation in group accounts, and so SSAP 1 had a major impact. The term 'related company' (similar to the definition of associated company in SSAP 1) and 'equity' method were used and recognized in law for the first time in the Companies Act 1981.

SSAP 1 requires associated companies to be accounted for using the equity method. A simple 20 per cent plus criterion for such companies would allow cosmetic accounting. Consider the case of the Bendix Corporation in the USA (Greene, 1980). Bendix acquired a marginally less than 20 per cent interest in ASARCO, a metals producer, which allowed it under US accounting rules (APB Opinion No. 18) to account for its investment at cost. When conditions in the metals market improved in 1978, it increased its holding to 21 per cent which allowed it to use the equity method and to bring in for the first time ASARCO's (improved) profits which made a significant difference to Bendix's consolidated results.

To try to prevent such cosmetic reporting, SSAP 1 currently uses a qualitative criterion with a quantitative back-up. Paragraph 13 sets out the criterion for an associated company:

> the interest of the investing group is for the *long term and is substantial* and, having regard to the disposition of the other shareholdings, the investing group or company is *in a position to exercise a significant influence* over the company in which the investment is made [emphasis added]. ...significant influence over a company essentially involves participation in the financial and operating decisions of that company (including dividend policy) but not necessarily control of those policies.

Paragraphs 14 and 15 state that a holding of 20 per cent of the equity voting rights or more leads to the rebuttable presumption that the qualitative criterion is met, and less than 20 per cent leads to the rebuttable presumption that the criterion is not met. In theory such a wording should make it more difficult for a company to keep changing its treatment by marginally adjusting holdings around the 20 per cent mark, though it is difficult for auditors to discern managerial intentions. In fact the Bendix case occurred despite similar wording in the US standard!

The Companies Act term 'related company' is defined slightly differently, as a long-term voting equity interest to secure a contribution by the exercise of *control or influence* arising from that interest. A 20 per cent interest is presumptive, but *not* rebuttable in this context. The Act requires in the holding company's own accounts separate disclosure of long-term investments in group companies, *related* companies and others. It is possible to have a related but not associated company (the presumptions of SSAP 1 being rebutted), or an associated but not related company. There is interaction in that some related company disclosure provisions are obviated by the use of the equity method.

SSAP 1 also defines joint ventures and consortial partnerships as associated companies where a significant influence is exercisable. The 20 per cent rebuttable presumptions are not applied in this case. Such cases will be referred to later in this section.

Not all authors agree that equity accounting is 'equitable', arguing that equity accounting leads to the same profits being counted in the associate's own statements and in the accounts of the parent. Others argue that since the holding company does not hold a controlling share in the associate, it may not be able to get hold of the associate's reported earnings for distribution to its own shareholders. Finally, it has been argued that the equity approach records profits of associates, but gives little indication of their debt structure for evaluating group gearing.

Associated companies – balance sheet disclosure

The revised standard requires disclosure of proportionate net assets and, separately, goodwill comprising the equitized investment (which includes both goodwill arising in the associate's own accounts plus goodwill on acquisition). This goodwill total is not required to be added to consolidated goodwill, but is included in the total investment amount in the consolidated balance sheet. Ma and Parker (1983, p. 121) outline the use of a slight variation in Australia, the 'pure equity' approach where goodwill is severed from the 'investment' and is included in consolidated goodwill, leaving the investment reported at net asset amount, but this is different from SSAP 1's treatment.

In addition the attributable post-acquisition reserves of the associate should be disclosed (i.e. breakdown 1 in addition to breakdown 2 on page 79). It also requires details of the associate's business, separate disclosure of loans to and from associates, and greater disclosure of trading balances and a breakdown of associate assets and liabilities if 'material in the context of the financial statements of the investing group'.

This last requirement is presumably included to try to prevent Leasco-type peculiarities (Briloff, 1980). In 1979, the Reliance group in the USA sold off Leasco, a computer leasing subsidiary to its *own* shareholders. In conventional accounting terms, Leasco was now an independent company. Later, Leasco bought 3.2 per cent of Reliance's share capital. It argued that although the proportion was so small, it could use the equity approach since the two companies were under common management. Though proportionally small, Leasco's shareholding in the much larger Reliance dwarfed its other income. The additional disclosures above would in principle have required disclosure of more information about Reliance to Leasco's own shareholders (who were by now different from those of Reliance) than the minimal disclosures normally required of associates. This case illustrates how easy it is to circumvent the 20 per cent plus general rule for associates. Briloff (1980) argues that common management should not have been the determining criterion as there is little evidence that

Reliance's policies would be affected *because of* the 3.2 per cent interest of Leasco, and so Leasco did not possess a significant interest.

Parker (1977) shows that European practice differs in the treatment of 'associates'. Consolidation is not compulsory in France but many companies follow the National Accounting Council's recommendations, and *'mise en equivalence'* is used for substantial holdings but not majority holdings in 'open' companies. Broadly this is the same as breakdown 2 on page 79. In Germany, no distinction is made between associates and subsidiaries.

Associated companies – treatment in the cancellation table.

Initially, an associated company is included in the investment column in the cancellation table at cost. Two adjustments are made:

1. The investment at cost is 'equitized' by adding attributable retained earnings to the investment column, and a corresponding credit (negative) is made to the retained earnings column.
2. Any goodwill write-off reduces the *investment* column, and the corresponding debit (positive) is made to the retained earnings column.

The first adjustment 'equitizes' the investment, which as discussed earlier, equals proportionate net assets plus goodwill of the associate. The second entry allows the write-off of this goodwill element and is discussed later. If a group includes both subsidiaries and associates, the investment column will include both cancellation entries for subsidiaries, and equitizing entries for associates. After the consolidation process is complete, only associates and trade investments will be left in the investment column. Example 4.2 includes Smallnesse as if it were an associate. Goodwill was calculated in Example 4.1 at £16,000, and for this example we will assume it is written off at 10 per cent per annum (£1,600) over the three years since acquisition.

Example 4.2   Extracts from acquisition cancellation table

	Investment	Retained earnings
Subtotal of other entries		(120,000)
Investment in associate – cost	80,000	
(a) Attributable retained earnings	8,000	(8,000)
(b) Goodwill write-off	(4,800)	4,800
Consolidated amounts	83,200	(123,200)

Associated companies – joint ventures

SSAP 1 requires joint ventures and other consortial arrangements to be treated as associates, where significant influence is exercisable. It allows but does not require proportional consolidation to be applied to 'partnerships or non-corporate joint ventures where such arrangements have features which justify [it]' (paragraph 18). Proportional consolidation is a common treatment in France for such arrangements.

Rio Tinto Zinc uses proportional consolidation for subsidiaries and associates as a supplement to conventional consolidated accounts. It argues that this approach is designed to cope with 'the very specific problems of a multinational natural resource group which has varying percentage stakes in a huge range of companies';[1] that the proportional approach gives a more realistic estimate of debt–equity ratios for the group when minority interests are removed.

Subsidiaries – consolidation

The legal definition of a subsidiary was examined in Chapter 2. It was found to depend on either equity share ownership or on 'control'. SSAP 14 defines consolidated financial statements as 'present[ing] the information contained in the separate financial statements of the holding company and its subsidiaries *as if* they were the financial statements of a single entity'. Later it states that minority interests 'should be shown as a separate amount [i.e. singular] in the consolidated balance sheet and should *not be shown as part of the shareholders' funds*' (paragraph 34, emphasis added), implying the parent rather than entity concept of consolidation.

Subsidiaries – other approaches

In Chapter 2 reasons for excluding subsidiaries from consolidation were examined. Table 4.6 summarizes the accounting treatment for excluded subsidiaries required by SSAP 14, 'Group accounts'.

Reason for exclusion	Accounting treatment
Dissimilar activities	Equity method and in addition separate individual company statements
Lack of effective control	Equity method per SSAP 1 unless the lack of control is severe, if so at cost
Severe restrictions	Equity method curtailed at the date the restrictions came into force
Intended temporary control	Lower of cost and net realizable value as a current asset

Table 4.6   SSAP 14 accounting treatment for excluded subsidiaries

It is interesting that the equity approach is required in three out of four cases, reinforcing the idea that the basis for accounting is broadly based on degree of effective control. The severe restrictions criterion is consistent with the substantial influence to the date of restrictions (equity method), and then minor influence thereafter (establishing the investment at a pseudo 'cost'). A good example of the 'lack of effective control' criterion is that of Trust House Forte's investment in the Savoy Hotel Group, in which it holds 69 per cent of the equity, but only 42 per cent of the voting shares, and where its influence on management and representation on the board of directors is consistently thwarted.[2] In previous years this investment was accounted for at cost, but in the 1985 accounts it is measured as an associate.

The Companies Act 1985 requires certain particulars where holdings in another company exceed 10 per cent of issued equity shares or of total assets.

Overview

Cost and equity approaches, proportional and parent consolidation are all used in specific circumstances, suggesting that a single concept does not explain group accounts adequately, either because practice is not based on theory, or because the theories themselves are too simplistic to express realities within which multinational groups operate. This theme will be returned to in later chapters.

Exercise

4.5 Assume the facts are as Exercise 4.3 except that Bigfry now has a 25 per cent interest in Tinyfry (not 18 per cent) and is able to exercise significant influence. When the investment was purchased, Tinyfry's retained earnings were £31,000. The draft balance sheet of Tinyfry plc at 30 November 1986 is shown in Table 4.7.

		£
Land		29,000
Buildings		15,000
Plant and equipment		40,000
		84,000
Current assets:		
Stocks	25,000	
Debtors	12,000	
Cash	10,000	
	47,000	
Current liabilities – creditors	30,000	17,000
Long-term loan		(17,000)
		84,000
Capital and reserves:		
Ordinary share capital	15,000	
Share premium	14,000	
Retained earnings	55,000	
		84,000

4.7 Tinyfry balance sheet at 30 November 1986

Required Prepare a consolidated balance sheet at 30 November 1986 for the Bigfry–Smallfry group complying with SSAP 1 and SSAP 14.

ACCOUNTING FOR GOODWILL

Accounting for goodwill is one of the most problematic areas in financial accounting, occurring at the uneasy seam between transaction-based accounting and financial economics. Even with the advent of SSAP 22, 'Accounting for goodwill', a profusion of differing practices exist. This section examines the problem of accounting for consolidated goodwill, and the wider issues in measuring and recording goodwill are only examined in so far as they are necessary to this aim.

The nature of goodwill

Hughes provides a useful historical survey of the area, and offers a 'working definition' of the concept of goodwill as 'the differential ability of one business, in comparison with another or an assumed average firm, to make a profit' (Hughes, 1982, p. 7). Often characterized as arising from such factors as superior management, business contacts, good relations with employees, etc., it has been suggested that goodwill can be measured as the capitalized 'super-profits' of a firm. However, this 'concept' is extremely difficult to operationalize, since 'normal' profits of a firm is a somewhat vague concept in itself. Normally in conventional financial reporting this 'concept' is merely used as a justification for a particular accounting treatment, rather than as a serious attempt to measure goodwill as an asset.

In accounting, the term 'goodwill' is used slightly differently as the difference between the value of an entity as a whole and the imputed value of its component parts, necessitating the valuation of the firm as a whole, but not the measurement of 'normal' returns. Earlier writers (e.g. Gynther, 1969) saw the valuation of goodwill as part of a schema to include more relevant and even economic values into financial reports. However, the academic literature (e.g. Peasnell, 1979, and Barton, 1974) now generally accepts that accountants do not have comparative advantage in themselves providing valuations of companies as a whole. It is not feasible even apart from objectivity problems.

Usually conventional transaction-based accounting manages to avoid this area by excluding proprietorial activity from financial statements. However, when one entity purchases another there is no way to avoid valuations of a firm as a whole entering the transaction-based accounting equation. The oddity in this case is that the transaction as a whole is verifiable, but once a *hypothetical* breakdown of this whole is made, the problem of accounting for this excess arises – for example in group accounting where a company is purchased and then disclosed as separable assets and liabilities on consolidation.

Reconciling the whole with the parts

Some of the reasons why a valuation as a whole differs from a component perspective may be summarized as:

1. Component tangible assets and liabilities valued individually.
2. Specified intangible assets, etc.
3. Items not measured in conventional accounting (e.g. human resources).
4. Other items reflected causing excess earnings in current use.
5. Other items causing excess incremental earnings as a result of combination (e.g. synergy effects caused by combinor's plans).

In basic economic theory with perfect information, frictionless markets, etc., one might ask why a package of items should not have the same value as its contents. In practice, with lack of information, divergences in beliefs, transaction costs and availability of finance, and with inertia, etc., it is not difficult to rationalize the discrepancy. Further, conventional accounting only encompasses assets purchased for valuable consideration so, for example, human resources are not included in financial statments. The first three categories together might be seen in principle as corresponding to 'normal' returns. The fourth is miscellaneous factors resulting in 'super-profits', and the fifth shows, as Woolf (1985) points out, the valuation of purchased goodwill may differ from non-purchased. The acquiror may have different plans for that firm (e.g. merging financial assets, rationalizing overlapping product lines, merging complementary technical know-how), and so may assess a different valuation for its purposes (alternative use) than for current use.

The allocation problem

Thomas, in a number of research studies (see for example the short summary in Thomas, 1975), has shown that the allocation of a total value arising from interacting inputs among those inputs is incorrigible (i.e. arbitrary). One way is no less defensible than another. Combined inputs produce a greater output together than as separate units (e.g. the combined product of man interacting with a machine is more than the sum of the products of the man with no machine and the machine with no man). How is the increment caused by the interacting components to be allocated? Which component is responsible? Without either the extra product would not be produced. Should it be incorporated in the value of one, the other, 50:50, 25:75, 75:25? There is no way to decide unambiguously.

It therefore is not possible to break down a valuation as a whole unambiguously into component valuations. Under conventional accounting this problem is skirted by using individual market prices for separable assets and liabilities, calling the remainder 'goodwill'. But is it meaningful to talk of this difference as an 'asset', and to give it an economic life? The problem here is not one of measurement, but of meaning.

The accounting treatment of goodwill

Goodwill has been treated in many colourful ways throughout its chequered history. Hughes (1982) notes that even at the turn of the century the professional literature contained arguments supporting three alternative treatments; permanent retention as an asset, gradual amortization of the asset and immediate write-off versus reserves.

Determining the amount of purchased goodwill

After the 'Great Crash' of 1929, the debate centred on *purchased* goodwill. Backdoor ways of incorporating non-purchased goodwill such as capitalizing advertising expenditures or early losses were frowned upon. Cooke (1986, p. 3) points out that in the USA, APB Opinion No. 17's conditions for capitalizing intangible assets generally preclude capitalizing expenditures on developing, maintaining or restoring inherent (non-purchased) goodwill. SSAP 22 explicitly excludes it. In principle the determination of purchased goodwill is easy under transaction-based accounting. SSAP 14 requires under acquisition accounting a revaluation of assets and liabilities to 'fair value' at the time of acquisition, goodwill being the difference from the total paid.

However, in share for share exchanges, it is difficult to determine values. The market capitalization of consideration given by the *acquiring* firm is often used as a surrogate (since it is this firm's planned use of the assets and liabilities which is important). However, the quoted share price at acquisition usually reflects transactions in small, marginal parcels of shares. Also share prices fluctuate wildly around acquisition dates. An ASC working party is looking into this area. Pragmatically one might use the quoted price immediately prior to the offer announcement.

Subsequent accounting treatment

This area is controversial since proposals reflect widely differing perspectives on the purpose of financial statements and the nature of assets and liabilities. The Companies Act 1985 and the EEC Seventh Directive on group accounts narrow permissible treatments in requiring that goodwill should be amortized if shown as an asset. Immediate write-off is acceptable because goodwill is never recorded as an asset.

Permanent retention as an asset

It is possible to argue that goodwill should be capitalized even if other intangibles, e.g. research and development expenditures (R & D) are not. In some ways goodwill is even more nebulous than R & D. However, whereas the 'recoverability' of R & D is related to the success of a product line, that of goodwill relates to the future of the whole firm.

Many early writers commented that in a successful business goodwill did not decline, being continuously renewed. However, opponents of this view argued that if it is accepted that only purchased goodwill should be reported, it should not remain permanently as an asset, because such goodwill is being continually replaced by non-purchased goodwill generated since acquisition.

Gradual amortization

Purchased goodwill is viewed as an asset to be amortized against revenues. APB Opinion No. 17, supporting this view, weakly suggests straight line amortization over its 'economic life' or a maximum of forty years. It is argued that the write-off of purchased goodwill will reduce future 'abnormal' returns expected from the purchase by the allocated cost of acquiring these returns. The consequent normalized returns are a test of a good bargain and may still be higher than that of similar firms if so. However, such arguments are difficult to verify because of subsequent changes in economic conditions and the allocation problem.

It can be argued that double counting occurs in that both expenditures to replace declining purchased goodwill (as non-purchased goodwill) and amortization of current purchased goodwill are made simultaneously.

Immediate write-off

Arguments have ranged from inherent conservatism, through the desire to achieve comparability between purchased and non-purchased goodwill, to the idea that financial statements should include only separable economic resources of the firm. Knortz, quoted in McLean (1972, p. 48), seeing problems with introducing and fixing goodwill at an amount determined at an arbitrary date, that of acquisition, comments: 'One may well ask whether it will make sense forty years from now [towards the end of its arbitrary write-off period] to have the earnings of the year 2010 affected by the fact that Vice-President [of the USA] Agnew made a speech which affected the stock market in 1970.'

Purchased goodwill may be extremely large in a particular year, and the location of the write-off is not a trivial decision. Possibilities include current year profit and loss, extraordinary items in the profit and loss account, realized reserves or unrealized reserves. Each reflects decreasing immediacy in reported profits and distributable profits. Traditional wisdom emphasizes the importance of the bottom line – profit. Efficient markets research has questioned whether location is significant provided investors are given enough information to reconcile alternatives. This area is explored later.

Immediate write-off treats purchased and non-purchased goodwill comparably by removing them both, which may be helpful when comparing two similar firms, one of which has grown by acquisition (i.e. with a great deal of purchased goodwill) and another by internal growth. Accounting Research Study No. 10, 'Accounting for goodwill', by Catlett and Olson (1968), commissioned by the US Accounting Principles Board, advocated immediate write-off for many of the reasons discussed above. It was discarded in producing APB Opinion No. 17 in 1970.

The 'dangling debit'

This treatment shows goodwill as a permanent deduction from the subtotal of equity. The difference between this treatment and immediate write-off is that the 'dangling debit' is never cancelled against a particular reserve, goodwill being shown at its original amount. This is rather a fudge, combining features of permanent retention (i.e. the debit never being reduced) with immediate write-off (i.e. the 'asset' is shown as a deduction from equity). It is now prohibited by the

Companies Act 1985, which prohibits the permanent retention of goodwill. However, it will be discussed later how some companies have circumvented this prohibition by using a 'negative reserve'.

Negative goodwill

Occasionally the valuation as a whole is exceeded by component valuation. Sometimes it is argued that such negative goodwill arises from outlays to preserve future profitability. However, SSAP 22 views this case as liabilities (provisions) being understated, not negative goodwill. However, the possibility of a genuine bargain purchase (e.g because of different tax positions of acquiror and acquired) exists, in which case it is reasonable to view negative goodwill as a form of gain. SSAP 22 comes nearer than APB No. 17 to a mirror image treatment of negative goodwill, and its requirements will be discussed later. The US standard requires that any negative goodwill should be apportioned amongst the assets and liabilities acquired to determine their 'true' values, assuming the component valuation is necessarily overstated.

So, the accounting treatment depends on one's view of the purpose of published financial statments. Should they be considered as a set of financial statistics upon which investors base future decisions (in which case comparability would seem to be important and 'historical' goodwill irrelevant), or are they a stewardship report to proprietors (in which case the matching of particular transaction costs may be relevant for that purpose), or even a valuation report (including non-purchased goodwill)?

SSAP 22, 'ACCOUNTING FOR GOODWILL' – AN ANALYSIS

Accounting for goodwill has been a controversial issue since the turn of the century. By the 1940s there was general agreement on the cost basis, although subsequent treatment remained controversial. Early UK recommendations observed that goodwill did not depreciate through use in the business, and if amortized should be disclosed separately in the profit and loss account. However, surveys of published accounts showed a significant movement towards immediate write-off in the late 1970s.

The EEC Fourth Directive in the late 1970s concentrated minds. In initial draft versions it allowed a maximum life for goodwill in company accounts of five years. Later drafts, whose provisions were included in the Companies Act 1981, gave member states the option to extend this period up to its economic life. Thus, permanent retention and dangling debit were proscribed. Not until 1980 did the ASC issue a discussion paper which opted for gradual amortization. In 1982, ED 30 was issued, allowing immediate write-off or gradual amortization, the latter over a maximum period of twenty years. SSAP 22 was issued in 1984, proscribing permanent retention, preferring immediate write-off, and tolerating gradual amortization! No maximum life was included.

In the USA an earlier debate moved towards gradual amortization. Immediate write-off was first prohibited by (non-mandatory) ARB No. 43 in 1953, except in cases of permanent diminution in value. It allowed both permanent retention and amortization. The ARB acquired the status of a standard when the Accounting Principles Board was set up in 1959. In 1970, APB Opinion No. 17 banned permanent retention, requiring gradual amortization over a maximum period of forty years as the only treatment, reaffirming ARB's allowing immediate write-offs to the income statement only if diminution of value had occurred. Some argue that such prohibitions fuelled the widespread adoption of pooling (merger) accounting in the 1960s and 1970s in the USA. Though the debate moved in different directions, the tolerance of gradual amortization in SSAP 22 allows UK multinationals to meet current US requirements, though it is not preferred UK treatment.

The nature of goodwill

The nature of goodwill is not discussed in SSAP 22, but is to be calculated as 'the difference between the fair value of the consideration given and the aggregate of the fair values of the separable assets acquired' (paragraph 29). It is characterized in the explanatory foreword as 'by definition' (!) being incapable of realization separately from the business as a whole. The explanatory foreword then lists other characteristics including having no predictable relationship to costs; its component parts cannot be separately identified; its value fluctuates widely over relatively short periods of time; and its value is highly subjective.

Only purchased goodwill is to be recognized, including goodwill in associates. The technical release accompanying SSAP 22 states that when a debit balance arises under merger accounting (see page 44), this is not goodwill under the SSAP because it is not based on fair values. SSAP 22 states (paragraph 5) that there is no difference between purchased and non-purchased goodwill and suggests (paragraph 18) that because the fair value of the shares acquired will normally equal that of the shares issued, no purchased goodwill will arise in the accounts of the holding company. Would an inequality result from alternative use plans versus existing use discussed on page 91? However, Campbell and Patient (1985) suggest that value to the *purchaser* of shares acquired always equals consideration given.

Subsequent accounting treatment

Following the EEC Fourth Directive, SSAP 22 prohibits permanent retention and dangling debits. It is unique amongst accounting standards, expressing (for *positive* goodwill) a preference for one treatment, immediate write-off against reserves, but allowing another, gradual amortization via the profit and loss account. *Negative* goodwill should be written off immediately against reserves – not the mirror image of positive goodwill (unlike ED 30). Companies can choose afresh their treatment with each acquisition, with no requirement for consistency (again unlike ED 30 which required companies to use one approach for all future acquisitions).

Note that if immediate write-off is chosen for associated companies, then such investments are effectively stated at *net asset* value (see page 78), the accounting entry being:

Dr. Reserves   Cr. Investment in associate

Where gradual amortization is used, positive goodwill should be eliminated 'in arriving at profit or loss on ordinary activities on a systematic basis over its *useful economic life*'. It should not be revalued subsequently, though should be written down immediately if there is a permanent diminution in value. Useful economic life (for which no maximum is stated, unlike ED 30 which specified a maximum of twenty years) should be estimated at acquisition. The effects of subsequent expenditures should not be used in determining this life, which may subsequently be shortened but not increased.

The ASC was squeezed. Extant UK practice gave overwhelming support for immediate write-off. APB No. 17 (which bound many multinationals) requires gradual amortization over a maximum period of forty years. Possibly as the best it could do, via SSAP 22, the ASC argued the benefits of one treatment, but met its practical obligations through an escape clause.

SSAP 22 emphasizes that immediate write-off is recommended as a matter of accounting policy, and not because of a diminution in value. Its main criterion is comparability between purchased and non-purchased goodwill. Immediate write-off against *reserves* is recommended so that current year profit is not adversely affected by a large lump sum, since the cause was not a diminution in value. APB No. 17 deduced exactly the opposite conclusion from similar data, banning discretionary write-offs and requiring amortization! It is instructive to ask whether immediate write-off was chosen for theoretical reasons or for expedient ones (since most UK firms already use it).

Allowing free choice of approach at each acquisition was apparently to encourage the maximum use of immediate write-off.[3] Companies might be reluctant to choose immediate write-off if they are bound by a single treatment, in case in future acquisitions their reserves might be insufficient to absorb *future* immediate write-offs. SSAP 22 erects no such obstacle. Not specifying a maximum life was designed to discourage the use of such a maximum as a norm (most firms using forty years as standard in the USA!). But is the purpose of accounting standards to persuade or mandate? The approach illustrates the ASC's decline in confidence since the inflation accounting debacle. It also raises the criticism that you adopt one treatment if you have enough profits/reserves and another if you have not. The policital context discussed in Chapter 3 is very relevant here.

Recent experience[4] suggests a plethora of treatments of immediate write-offs, with little evidence of standardization. The Department of Trade and Industry has indicated (DTI, 1986) it considers revaluation reserves and share premium accounts are not available for the immediate write-off of goodwill because Companies Act restrictions on the use of these accounts, without further court approval, apply to group accounts as well as to individual company accounts. Unlike under merger cancellation (see pages 41–2), consolidated goodwill write-off does have a counterpart in the accounts of individual companies, so individual company restrictions seem to apply. However, although 'dangling debits' (discussed above) are illegal, a surprisingly similar treatment has been invented, setting up a zero reserve and writing off goodwill against it. This *debit* balance is apparently legal only because it is called a (negative) reserve and not goodwill!

A number of companies, including Guinness/Bells, Burtons/Debenhams and Dixons/Curry's have (as discussed in Chapter 3) met the merger relief criteria (a 90 per cent takeover with shares included in the consideration) and have elected for acquisition accounting. They have then written off goodwill against the merger reserve, effectively removing from the accounts some of the 'premium' on the share issue. Other companies not meeting merger relief criteria have sought court approval to write off existing goodwill against their share premium accounts. Although these latter treatments preserve the main features of acquisition accounting (cancellation of pre-acquisition profits and asset revaluation), some differences from merger accounting (goodwill recording and write-off, and the recording of a 'premium' on the issue of shares) disappear. Now the clarity of two distinct treatments for combinations seems in practice to have shaded into a spectrum of alternatives.

Disclosure

SSAP 22 requries the following disclosures: the accounting policies followed; the amount of goodwill recognized as a result of any acquisitions during the year (with separate amounts for each acquisition if material); where the amortization approach is adopted, purchased goodwill should be disclosed in the balance sheet, also its movements, showing cost, accumulated amortization, and net book value at the beginning and end of the year, and the amount amortized, together with the period of amortization for each acquisition.

Distributable profits: holding company versus group accounts

The non-mandatory appendix of SSAP 22 deals with the write-off of goodwill in the accounts of *companies*, not groups. It is a masterly example of casuistic reasoning. It tries to attain parity in *distributable* profits (i.e. *realized* reserves) between immediate write-off and gradual amortization. In the accounts of companies, the immediate write-off of goodwill can be made against *unrealized* reserves because it is a decision of accounting policy and not a diminution in value. Then, over the goodwill's useful economic life, an amount equivalent to the amount under gradual amortization (which had that approach been adopted would have reduced realized reserves in the form of retained earnings) can be transferred from unrealized to realized reserves. This may be tortuous, but it is certainly an ingenious way to ensure parity of realized reserves between treatments. However, it does not deal with consolidated reserves or write-off of consolidated goodwill.

The proper relationship between holding company and group reserves is a difficult issue, particularly as regards congruence in write-offs between the two sets of accounts. For example, paragraph 18 of the explanatory foreword of SSAP 22 'does not require an adjustment to be made in the holding company's accounts [to the investment] in respect of any consolidation goodwill written off in the group accounts . . . except to the extent that [there is] a permanent diminution in value'. Holgate (1986b) suggests that write-offs of consolidated goodwill in the group accounts have no effect on distributable profits whereas, if the investment is correspondingly written down in the holding company's accounts (known as 'push down' accounting – reflecting consolidated adjustments in the individual accounts), this could affect distributable profits of the holding company over a period.

Whether group accounts should assist shareholders of the holding company in assessing *potential* distributable profits is controversial. Strictly, as SSAP 22's appendix points out, companies make distributions – not groups. However, because of immediate write-offs of consolidated goodwill (which do not have to be made in holding company accounts), group reserves can be significantly less than holding company reserves, and there is evidence of a great variety in choice of reserves for such write-offs. These issues are examined further in Chapter 11.

Discussion questions

4.6   An engineering company has a 50 per cent investment in an affiliated company which operates in the retail trade. It has no other affiliates. The investment at cost forms 30 per cent of the assets in the latest holding company balance sheet. The finance director is contemplating purchasing a further 2 per cent of the voting shares in the affiliate. Advise him of the accounting effects of such a purchase on the group accounts including possible effects on the financial ratios calculated therefrom.

4.7   Assess the validity of the argument that goodwill should be removed from group accounts.

4.8   Discuss the extent to which SSAP 22 has improved the quality of accounting for goodwill in UK consolidated accounts.

Note   Calculation questions dealing with accounting for goodwill are included in Chapter 5.

SUMMARY

The acquisition cancellation approach removes the holding company's share of *pre-acquisition equity* of the subsidiary. The subsidiary only contributes to consolidated results *after* acquisition. However, the minority's share is an *ongoing* one.

Conventional consolidation is one point on a spectrum of ways of accounting for investments. *Equitization* updates an investment from a cost–dividends receivable basis, to a cost plus profits earned basis. The equitized investment always equals the proportionate net assets of the other company, plus goodwill.

Consolidation can be characterized as *equitization plus expansion*, and the different consolidation approaches correspond to different degrees of expansion, from the equity approach to the entity approach. Conventional consolidation (the parent approach) lies in the middle. Quasi-theoretical concepts correspond with the expansions.

In the UK less than 20 per cent investments are accounted for as trade investments at cost, 20–50 per cent investments as associated companies (SSAP 1) using a form of the equity approach, and over 50 per cent investments as subsidiaries (SSAP 14) subject to full consolidation, using either the acquisition or merger approach (SSAP 23) if the requisite merger conditions are met and that option chosen. SSAP 14 provides criteria of when to *exclude* subsidiaries from consolidation and prescribes alternative treatments.

Goodwill arises because of the wish to split a holistic transaction into components. Non-purchased goodwill is excluded from financial statements. Purchased goodwill can be dealt with in a number of ways, the most common being *immediate write-off* against reserves, or *gradual amortization* to the profit and loss account. SSAP 22 prefers the former but tolerates the latter. In the USA only the latter is allowed. The relationship between holding company and group reserves is unresolved.

NOTES

1. See 'How a multinational presents its accounts', Report of the Week in *Accountancy Age*, 1984.
2. See 'THF faces an equity accounting quandary, by Stuart Mansell in News Extra, *Accountancy Age*, 30 January 1986.
3. See 'The standard ways of getting rid of goodwill', by Peter Holgate in Technical Analysis, *Accountancy Age*, 15 August 1985.
4. See, for example, 'Companies find holes in goodwill', in Reports and Accounts, *Accountancy*, August 1986, p. 24, and 'Much goodwill – little standardization', by R. Hickinbotham in Accounting Issues, *Accountancy*, June 1986, pp. 24–5.

FURTHER READING

The spectrum of approaches

Accounting Standards Committee (1982) *SSAP 1 – Accounting for Associated Companies*, ASC, London.
Accounting Standards Committee (1978) *SSAP 14 – Group Accounts*, ASC, London.
Baxter, G. C. and Spinney, J. C. (1975) A closer look at consolidated financial theory, *CA Magazine*, January 1975, pp. 31–5.
Parker, R. (1977) Concepts of consolidation in the EEC, *Accountancy*, Vol. 88, No. 1002 (February) pp. 72–5.

Accounting for goodwill

Accounting Standards Committee (1984) *SSAP 22 – Accounting for Goodwill*, ASC, London.

Holgate, P. A. (1986) *A Guide to Accounting Standards — Accounting for Goodwill*, Accountants Digest No. 178, Institute of Chartered Accountants in England and Wales, London.

Hughes, H. P. (1982) *Goodwill in Accounting: A History of the Issues and Problems*, Georgia State University, USA.

Thomas, A. (1975) The FASB and the allocation fallacy, *Journal of Accountancy*, November 1975, pp. 65–8.

Wilkins, R. M. (1986) Takeovers, in L. Skerratt and D. Tonkin (eds.) *Financial Reporting 1985/6*, Institute of Chartered Accountants in England and Wales, London.

5 The Consolidated Balance Sheet under Acquisition Accounting II: Alignment Problems

Measurement problems arise on consolidation because, for example, realization and matching conventions now apply to the 'super' entity, the group. The first section examines adjustments necessary to reflect this change in scope, suggesting a framework for considering such adjustments, and discussing controversies which arise over the choice of approach; the second reviews the usefulness of the consolidated balance sheet.

ALIGNMENT PROBLEMS IN CONSOLIDATED ACCOUNTS

When pieces of wood are assembled to make a chair, each piece is machined so that it forms a well-fitting joint with the other pieces. If this machining is done badly, the chair will not fit together properly, though the individual pieces of wood may be fine in themselves. Similarly, in group accounts the individual accounts need to be aligned ('machined') before aggregation, so that a meaningful whole ('chair') is produced. If they are out of alignment, then the whole loses its meaning. Alignments necessary for conventional consolidation usually arise in two ways:
1. Where group companies trade with each other, the same transactions may not yet be reflected in *both* sets of records.
2. Adjustments are needed to reflect the change in scope from an individual company to a group basis.

Figure 5.1 illustrates types of alignment problems that may occur, assuming that a holding company takes a 100 per cent interest in a subsidiary on 31 December 1984. Thus, group retained earnings include all holding company retained earnings plus the subsidiary's since acquisition. The horizontal lines split the total into yearly components.

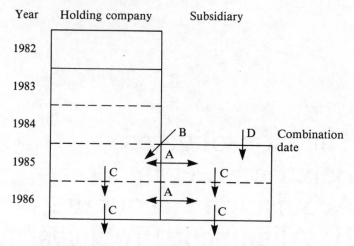

Key to types of alignment problems
A.   Intercompany transactions within a particular year not yet recorded by both companies.
B.   Subsidiary dividends from *pre*-acquisition retained earnings included in the holding company's *post*-acquisition retained earnings.
C.   Intercompany transactions where goods have not left the group. Since the goods have left the selling company, profits have been correctly realized by the individual company.
D.   Items owned by the subsidiary at acquisition transferred to the group whose historical cost to the group (i.e. at acquisition) is different from the historical cost to the subsidiary.

Figure 5.1   Types of alignment problems in group accounts: effects on group retained earnings

Category A adjustments on intercompany transactions result in alignment problems between companies *within* a single accounting period. Other categories all involve adjustments *between* periods. For example, when goods are sold between group companies in one period and then resold in the following period outside the group, profits are realized by the initiating company in the first period but by the group in the second, when goods leave the group. Thus, profits need to be reassigned from the first to the second period for group accounts purposes. The categories in Figure 5.1 will each be considered in turn.

Consolidated versus individual company alignment adjustments

Many alignment adjustments affecting consolidated accounts are not entered in individual company records (which correctly reflect the impact of the transactions on that company). These are often made on consolidated working papers at head office when the consolidation is done. Other adjustments (e.g. the incorrect recording of a transaction by an individual company) are made to the individual company records. Here the former are referred to as 'consolidation adjustments' and are separately labelled in cancellation tables. The latter are referred to as 'individual company adjustments' and will be treated accordingly.

It is important to understand the difference between the two classes of adjustments.

Type A adjustments: intercompany (intra-group) balances

When group companies trade, in principle debit (debtor) balances in one set of records should equal credit (creditor) balances in the other. On consolidation, these balances (totally internal to the group) should cancel. In practice, especially where the number of transactions is large, perfect agreement is rare and one of the major tasks in a large audit is agreement and/or reconciliation of intercompany balances before consolidation at head office. Much telexing and headscratching is often done before the balances are accepted. There are generally two reasons why balances do not agree:

1. Mistakes in recording by either company.
2. Timing differences caused by goods or cash in transit between companies at the end of the period, recorded by the originating company in the current period but not by the receiving company.

After reconciliation, mistakes are corrected by the individual companies. Timing differences are dealt with at head office by means of 'consolidation adjustments' so that both sets of balances will cancel. In this text, items in transit are usually treated as if they are at the *originating* company (i.e. as if the intra- (i.e. within) group transaction had not taken place prior to the year-end). This rule of thumb usually makes consolidation adjustments simpler than if the goods are treated as at the receiving company, though the latter assumption is valid logically. In principle, dividends declared by the subsidiary but not yet recorded by the holding company can be handled in a similar way.

Example 5.1   Type A adjustments

Acid plc and Alkali plc, two companies in the Corrosive Chemicals Group, trade regularly with each other. At 30 November 1986, Alkali is shown as a £20,000 debtor in Acid's records, whereas Acid is shown as a creditor of £4,000 in Alkali's records. The head office auditors, Delight, Hassle and Soles, contact the companies and find the following differences:

1. Stock despatched by Acid on 28 November but not received by Alkali until 2 December (cost £8,000) – £10,000.
2. Cash sent by Alkali on 29 November, not received by Acid until 1 December – £8,000.
3. Goods received by Alkali on 15 November still in stock, recorded by them at £5,000 instead of £3,000.

Consider now how this information would be treated for consolidation purposes. Note the differing characteristics of the three entries. The first two are *timing differences*. The transactions are treated correctly from the point of view of the individual companies, but are out of alignment for group purposes – the goods and cash are shown as being at neither company at the year-end (which is true, but they do belong to the group! Such timing differences are usually dealt with by consolidation adjustments at head office. The third is an *error* by Alkali and so will be dealt with by a correction at the individual company level.

Consider the following reconciliation and correction of these intercompany balances. The corrected *company* balances are the balances which will appear in each company's own individual accounts for the year. The aligned balance of £20,000 ensures consistent treatment of goods in transit to enable perfect cancellation in the *group* accounts.

Alkali's balance in Acid's records

Original balance	20,000
Corrected company balance	20,000
Goods in transit reversed	(10,000)†
Aligned consolidated balance	10,000

Acid's balance in Alkali's records

Original balance	(4,000)
Stock correction	2,000*
Corrected company balance	(2,000)
Cash in transit reversed	(8,000)†
Aligned consolidated balance	(10,000)

Notes
* A *mistake* by Alkali, corrected in *its own* records thus:
    Dr. Alkali interco. creditors 2,000   Cr. Alkali stocks 2,000
    Alkali's stocks are thus reduced by £2,000.
† *Consolidation adjustments* on working papers at head office:
    Goods
        Dr. Acid stocks   8,000   Cr. Acid intercompany debtors   10,000
        Dr. Acid P & L a/c   2,000

    Cash
        Dr. Alkali cash   8.000   Cr. Alkali intercompany creditors   8,000

The entries *reverse* the sale and cash payment as if they had not been made prior to the year-end. Where group companies have different (non-coterminous) year-ends, intercompany balances are usually brought into harmony by adjusting for transactions in the period between the year-ends. SSAP 14 recommends as far as possible that group companies should have coterminous year-ends.

Type B adjustments: dividends from pre-acquisition profits

The usual effects on group accounts of dividends from a wholly owned subsidiary are as follows:
1. Payment of the dividend usually has no effect on group accounts, since it is totally internal to the group.

2. If the dividend has been declared but not yet paid by the subsidiary and recorded as a debtor by the holding company, dividends payable by one and receivable by the other simply cancel out as intercompany balances.
3. If the dividend has been declared but not yet recorded by the holding company, the usual principles for dealing with timing differences within a single accounting period (type A adjustments) apply.

Dividends by a subsidiary out of pre-acquisition profits

Sometimes alignment differences occur across the pre-/post-acquisition boundary, for example when a subsidiary pays dividends to the holding company out of its profits earned prior to acquisition, e.g. if a subsidiary is purchased at its year-end, a dividend may have been *declared* in its accounts. The *payment* of the dividend to its shareholders (and hence to the parent) will occur sometime later (post-acquisition).

From the perspective of the individual accounts of the holding company, the current legal position, embodied in the Companies Act 1985, looks at such payments purely through the holding company's eyes, ignoring the underlying group situation, i.e. the holding company determines whether or not such a payment can be regarded as its income according to its usual fixed asset accounting principles, and no notice is taken of whether such dividends are pre- or post-acquisition. If the distribution from the subsidiary does not cause a permanent diminution in the amount of the investment, then it can be recognized as holding company income. If it causes such a diminution, then the investment should be written down by the amount of the diminution (probably easiest by crediting part of the dividend against the investment), and any remaining amount can be regarded as income. As discussed in Chapter 3, the distribution standard is thus easier when the merger relief provisions are applicable and the investment is stated at a nominal amount 'cost'.

When acquisition accounting is used in the group accounts, any amount of pre-acquisition dividends treated by the holding company as income in its individual accounts causes yet another case where its individual reserves are out of harmony with consolidated reserves (see page 61). Table 5.1 considers the effect on the consolidated accounts of the above individual accounts treatment.

Before the subsidiary's dividend declaration (shown in the top half of Table 5.1), its pre-acquisition retained earnings (and other equity components) would have been cancelled against the investment to determine goodwill. Its post-acquisition retained earnings would have been combined with the holding company's to form consolidated reserves. The strict dichotomy in treatment is represented by the broken line.

Suppose dividends from the subsidiary's pre-acquisition profits are declared and treated as income by the holding company (bottom half). Because it is totally internal to the group, the declaration or payment of a dividend by a wholly owned subsidiary should have no effect on the group accounts. However, to the extent that the dividend has been (legitimately) added to holding company reserves (i.e. treated as holding company income), pre-acquisition profits (equal to the dividend) are incorrectly (from a *consolidated* accounts perspective) included in consolidated reserves because the dividend has 'crossed the picket lines'. Further, group pre-acquisition reserves are too low and hence goodwill is overstated.

1. Prior to dividend declaration

Subsidiary retained earnings	Combined with			Gives in consolidated accounts
(pre-acquisition)	+	investment	=	goodwill
(post-acquisition)	+	(holding co. reserves)	=	(consolidated reserves)

2. After pre-acquisition dividend paid to holding co. and added to its reserves

Subsidiary retained earnings	Combined with			Gives in consolidated accounts
(pre-acquisition − dividend)	+	investment	=	goodwill + dividend
(post-acquisition)	+	(holding co. reserves + dividend)	=	(consolidated reserves + dividend)

Table 5.1   Effects on consolidated earnings of pre-acquisition dividends of subsidiary being treated as holding company income

Therefore, for *consolidation* purposes, to the extent that pre-acquisition dividends from pre-acquisition profits have been (legitimately) treated as holding company profits, a consolidation adjustment has to be made to align the group accounts as follows:

Dr. Consolidated reserves   Cr. Goodwill

Prior to the current legislative position, the individual accounts position on distributions from pre-acquisition profits required the holding company to look beyond its boundaries to a group perspective. All distributions from pre-acquisition profits were to be regarded as reductions in the investment, effectively as repayments of the consideration given for the subsidiary – since the holding company was not regarded as entitled to such income. This prior position was only really consistent with acquisition accounting, and so became untenable when the merger option was opened. However, for acquisition-type combinations, the current, more 'shortsighted' viewpoint (only looking as far as the company's boundaries) can in certain situations cause confusion of matters subsequent to acquisition with those prior, but a discussion of this area is beyond the scope of the book.

In the case of partly owned subsidiaries, the correcting entries are identical, as there is no distinction in treatment of pre- and post-acquisition profits of the minority.

Example 5.2   Type B adjustments

Consider the following balance sheets of Demarkation plc and Openplan Ltd on 31 March 1987 (in £000):

	Demarkation	Openplan
Assets less liabilities	400	175
Investment	200	
Share capital	(100)	(20)
Share premium	(150)	(30)
Retained earnings	(350)	(125)

Demarkation acquired a 100 per cent interest at 30 September 1986, Openplan's year-end before joining the group, when its retained earnings were £100,000. In the accounts of Openplan at that date were proposed dividends of £15,000 which were paid on 15 October 1986 and included in Demarkation's profit for the year ended 31 March 1987.

Consolidated accounts

If the dividend had never been declared, the retained earnings of both companies at 31 March 1987 would be (£350,000 − £15,000) = £335,000 and (£125,000 + £15,000) = £140,000 respectively. At acquisition (30 Sept.), Openplan's retained earnings would have been (£100,000 + £15,000) = £115,000. Consider Table 5.2 which shows the effects of Demarkation's treatment.

1. Prior to dividend declaration		
Subsidiary equity	Combined with	Gives in consolidated accounts
(pre-acquisition) (20 + 30 + 115)	+ investment 200	= goodwill 35
(post-acquisition) (140 − 115)	+ (holding co. reserves) (335)	= (consolidated reserves) (360)

2. After dividend declaration and inclusion		
Subsidiary equity	Combined with	Gives in consolidated accounts
(pre-acquisition) (20 + 30 + 100)	+ investment 200	= goodwill 50
(post-acquisition) (125 − 100)	+ (holding co. reserves) (350)	= (consolidated reserves) (375)

Table 5.2   Effects of including pre-acquisition dividend in holding company income: Demarkation–Openplan

Table 5.2 shows consolidated goodwill and consolidated retained earnings each overstated by £15,000 compared to the pre-dividend position.

Individual company versus consolidation adjustments

Demarkation can recognize income except to the extent that there has been a permanent diminution in the value of the investment. The treatment by Demarkation in its own accounts is correct if there had been no diminution in value below acquisition cost as a result of the receipt of the dividend. In this case, a *consolidation adjustment* would be made for the *group* accounts (only) as follows (reflecting the change in scope of the accounts):

Dr. Consolidated retained earnings 15,000   Cr. Goodwill 15,000

However, if the investment's value had, say, fallen as a result of the distribution to £185,000 (i.e. by the amount of the dividend) then Demarkation's treatment in its own accounts would have been incorrect. As a result of the dividend, the investment has diminished in amount below its acquisition amount, and £15,000 should have been written off the investment. The treatment of including the dividend as income, now effectively an *error*, should be corrected by an *individual company adjustment* as follows:

Dr. Demarkation retained earnings 15,000   Cr. Investment 15,000

If the diminution had been less than the full £15,000, then part of the dividend could legitimately be treated as holding company income and adjusted in the consolidated accounts by a consolidation adjustment, and the rest corrected in the individual accounts by an individual company adjustment to write down the investment.

Exercises

5.1   Explain how the following would be dealt with or corrected in consolidated accounts by either individual company or consolidation adjustments.

Haughty plc acquired a 100 per cent interest in Grovel Ltd on 30 June 1985.

(a)   In 1986, Grovel declared a dividend of £10,000 and in accounts at 30 April 1986 (the group year-end) showed dividends payable of £10,000. Haughty had made no entry in its own records to record the entry.

(b)   The same as (a) except that Haughty had wrongly recorded the amount due from Grovel as £8,000 dividends receivable.

(c)   In its accounts at 30 June 1985, Grovel declared dividends payable of £10,000. These were paid on 15 July 1985, and Haughty included its share in dividends income for the year ended 30 April 1986. The directors considered that after the dividend receipt, the investment in Grovel was still worth more than its acquisition cost.

(d)   As in (c) except that after the distribution, the investment's market value was £7,000 below its acquisition cost.

Be prepared to discuss the rationale for your position on each.

Type C adjustments: profits on intra-group transactions

Deferral of profits on operating transactions

This problem is caused by a change in scope of accounts to a group basis. Suppose one group company sells goods to another and the second resells outside the group, as shown in Figure 5.2.

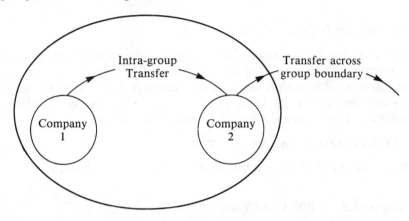

Figure 5.2   Transfers inside and outside the group

Profit on the intra-group transfer is 'realized' by company 1 immediately. However, group profit is realized only when goods leave the group. Consolidation adjustments are needed to remove profits on transfers which have not yet been resold across group boundaries – a 'deferring device'. Figure 5.3 illustrates the effects of these deferrals of profit, assuming that goods are resold outside the group in the year after they are sold within the group. Profits on 1982 internal sales are recognized by the group in 1983 when goods including such internal profits are resold across group boundaries. Thus, intra-group profits for 1982 are deferred to 1983 for group accounts purposes and so on. Consolidated retained earnings in the balance sheet comprises the total area in the diagram.

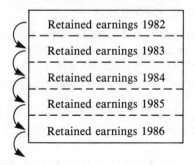

Figure 5.3   The effects of stock profits deferral on group reserves

Consolidated profit and loss

This flow statement is adjusted for intra-group stock profits in opening *and* closing intra-group stocks. Last year's deferrals (in opening stocks) are added to current year's group profits, and this year's deferrals (on closing stocks) are taken out of this year's profit to be deferred until next year's. Thus there are *two* adjustments.

Consolidated balance sheet

Only *one* adjustment is required for the balance sheet to defer profits on *closing* intra-group stocks to the next accounting period. Consolidated retained earnings is the aggregate of individual years' retained earnings. In this total, the deferral of one year cancels with its reinstatement in the next. The only deferral still outstanding is on closing stock, and is effected as follows:

> Dr. Consolidated reserves   Cr. Stocks

with the amount of profits on intra-group closing stocks still held.

Example 5.3   Type C adjustments

Ballcock Ltd and Looseat Ltd are both part of the Flushing Group. Ballcock sells washers to Looseat (at a mark up of 33⅓ per cent) which are incorporated into their high quality toilet seats. During 1985, total sales of washers by Ballcock to Looseat were £100,000. Stocks of such washers held by Looseat were £10,000 at 1 January, and £12,000 at 31 December.

The amount of 'profits' in Looseat's intra-group stocks is determined as follows. Cost to Looseat is Ballcock's selling price, which is 133⅓ per cent of original cost. The profit element is thus:

$$\text{Opening stock} \quad = \quad \frac{33\frac{1}{3}}{133\frac{1}{3}} \quad \times \quad 10,000 \quad = \quad 2,500$$

$$\text{Closing stock} \quad = \quad \frac{33\frac{1}{3}}{133\frac{1}{3}} \quad \times \quad 12,000 \quad = \quad 3,000$$

Thus, the consolidated profit and loss account will be credited with £2,500 and debited with £3,000 (a net decrease in profit of £500) to reflect the profit deferral on intra-group transfers. The consolidated balance sheet will show a decrease of £3,000 in consolidated reserves and a corresponding decrease of the same amount in stocks.

Minority interests

In the wholly owned case, the adjustment reduces stocks and equity. For partially owned subsidiaries, it can be argued that the 'equity' entry should be apportioned between majority and minority. Choices here are intimately related to views of the nature of a group and of the relative importance of the minority. It is fairly common in the UK to ignore the minority interest altogether and to eliminate the stock profits 100 per cent against the consolidated reserves (the majority being deemed to bear the whole effect of intra-group transfers). All that can be said in favour of this is that it is simple and conservative! A variety of rationales have been put forward for alternative treatment on intra-group transfers and these are examined briefly below.

Elimination procedures suggested by various authors have differed according to:

1. The direction of the intra-group transfer (upstream, downstream or sideways within the group).
2. The distribution of the amount eliminated between majority and minority, e.g. whether the whole (100 per cent) elimination should be entirely versus the majority, whether it should be divided proportionately (e.g. 75:25) between majority and minority, or whether *only* the majority fraction (e.g. 75 per cent) should be eliminated against stocks and *majority* share of retained earnings.
3. Whether the above proportions should depend on the ownership proportions of the buying or the selling company.

There are at least $3 \times 3 \times 2 = 18$ possible approaches to eliminating profits on intra-group transactions based on the above analysis (Eggington, 1965, provides a good review). Some of the most common are examined below.

Group-oriented views of profit elimination

Baxter and Spinney (1975) link the elimination of unrealized profits to various group concepts. In terms of criterion 3 above, they use the *selling* (originating) company's ownership proportions, as if the transaction had not taken place as far as the group is concerned. Transactions are regarded as incomplete and to be reversed if they are between group members. They then examine the effects of different group concepts within this overall 'group'-oriented context. The treatment of the minority under different group concepts (discussed in Chapter 4) is summarized in Figure 5.4.

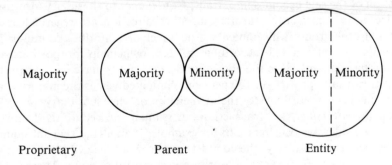

Figure 5.4   Treatment of minority under different group concepts

Proprietary

Since the subsidiary is accounted for fractionally, intra-group sales are to a fraction or from a fraction. The minority are treated as complete outsiders and only the *group's* portion of a transaction is eliminated as unrealized, versus consolidated reserves *and* stocks. If a partially owned subsidiary sells to another partially owned subsidiary, the proportion to be eliminated is obtained by multiplying ownership proportions, all sales by minority and to minority being 'realized' as outside the 'group'. For example, if an 80 per cent owned subsidiary sells to a 70 per cent subsidiary, then 80% × 70% = 56% of the profits is eliminated, as shown by the following grid:

		Sales from:	
		Majority (80%)	Minority (20%)
Sales to:	Majority (70%)	56%	14%
	Minority (30%)	24%	6%

Parent

Though the majority are considered to have an undivided interest in assets and liabilities of the subsidiary, the position of the minority is somewhat ambiguous. To accommodate this ambiguity, Baxter & Spinney (1975) subdivide the concept.

Pure parent This leans towards the proprietary end of the spectrum, treating the minority as outsiders. Like the proprietary approach only the majority portion is eliminated versus stocks and equity. Though a minority interest is disclosed between liabilities and shareholders' equity, no deferral against it is regarded as necessary. The minority interest in group accounts is the same amount as computed from the subsidiary's accounts. Supporters argue that minority shareholders in part of the group should not be affected by adjustments relating to an entity larger than one in which they have a share.

Parent company extension This variant leans towards the entity end of the spectrum. It views the minority as secondary owners *within* the group. Now the direction of the sale becomes important, from parent to subsidiary (downstream) or vice versa (upsteam). Transfers in either direction are regarded as *totally internal* to the group, whose members now include majority *and* minority.

Profits are eliminated according to the ownership proportions of the *originating* company since the goods are deemed not to have left the group – on downstream sales profits are 100 per cent eliminated versus the majority, and on upstream sales according to the ownership of the subsidiary (e.g. 75:25), notionally *reversing* the transaction. A similar procedure is followed on incomplete sideways transfers. So, for example, if an 80 per cent subsidiary sold to a 70 per cent subsidiary, the complete profit would be deducted from stocks, and apportioned 80:20 versus majority and minority reserves. There is now no multiplication since both majority and minority are deemed to be a part of the group entity.

Entity

This approach is exactly the same as the parent company extension with respect to operating transactions. It argues that the minority should be adjusted when the group as a whole is considered.

The effect of the different group concepts on 'stock profits' is summarized in Table 5.3 (in the case of transactions between holding company and 75 per cent owned subsidiary).

Consolidation concept	Direction of transaction	Apportionment Consolidated reserves	Minority
Proprietary	Upstream	75%	—
	Downstream	75%	—
Pure parent	Upstream	75%	—
	Downstream	75%	—
Parent company extension	Upstream	75%	25%
and entity	Downstream	100%	—
'Conventional' UK	Upstream	100%	—
	Downstream	100%	—

Table 5.3   Apportionment of unrealized profits on intra-group transactions

Example 5.4   Type C adjustments – minority interests

Suppose, in Example 5.3, Ballcock was a 75 per cent subsidiary and Looseat a 60 per cent subsidiary. Journal entries for eliminating intra-group closing stock profits (£3,000 in total) under the different approaches would be:

	Consolidation adjustment		
	Dr. Consol. Res.	Dr. Minority	Cr. Stocks
Sale Ballcock (75%) to Looseat:			
Proprietary (75 × 60)	(45%) 1,350		(45%) 1,350
Pure parent (75 × 60)	(45%) 1,350		(45%) 1,350
Parent extension	(75%) 2,250	(25%) 750	(100%) 3,000
Entity	(75%) 2,250	(25%) 750	(100%) 3,000
'Conventional' UK	(100%) 3,000		(100%) 3,000
Sale Looseat (60%) to Ballcock:			
Proprietary (60 × 75)	(45%) 1,350		(45%) 1,350
Pure parent (60 × 75)	(45%) 1,350		(45%) 1,350
Parent extension	(60%) 1,800	(40%) 1,200	(100%) 3,000
Entity	(60%) 1,800	(40%) 1,200	(100%) 3,000
'Conventional' UK	(100%) 3,000		(100%) 3,000

Component-oriented views on intra-group eliminations

Eggington (1965) criticizes approaches considering the group as a single 'entity' for missing an important dimension – that the group is composed of distinct and separate legal entities. He argues that the main reason for eliminating profits on uncompleted intra-group transfers is to prevent overstatement of profits not verifiable from *external* transactions; a transfer of legal rights has occurred and the company 'at risk' if the ultimate profit margin is not realized is the purchasing company, not the originating company. Under this viewpoint, ownership rights of the buying company should determine eliminations, since legally profit is recognized by the selling company, and cash may already have passed.

As Eggington (1965) points out, this approach is not without its problems. Suppose an 80 per cent owned subsidiary made a sale to the parent for £500 of goods costing £400, the goods remaining in stock. Under the 'component' view of the group, elimination of the £100 stock profits would be made according to ownership of the purchasing company (i.e. 100 per cent versus the majority). In the consolidated accounts, the majority shareholders would thus be shown as worse off by £20 than if the parent had never bought the goods, because of its £80 share of profits and £100 elimination!

Under this approach, the direction of the sale is important, but 'weights' are of the purchasing company. The rationales for the separate component and group viewpoints are quite different, according to how far one should look behind the corporate 'veil' in enforcing shareholders' rights. In some ways a group is not the same as its components, and in others it is not different! Eggington (1965) discusses other rationalizations for intra-group eliminations which are not examined here.

Current practice in the UK

The UK Survey of Published Accounts indicates that in general firms do not publish their policies on elimination of intra-group profits. Wilkins (1979) notes that in a survey of seventeen companies carried out in 1971–2, thirteen were found to eliminate 100 per cent versus the majority, and the remaining four to eliminate the majority's portion only. The former does not seem to be based on any consistent rationale.

SSAP 14, 'Group accounts', comments on '[the well understood] method of preparation of consolidated financial statements on an item by item basis, eliminating intra-group balances and transactions and unrealized intra-group profit', but gives no guidance to extent of total elimination or of apportionment between majority and minority interests. SSAP 1, 'Accounting for associated companies', also requires that where material, adjustments should be made for items such as unrealized profits in group–associate trading, but again gives no detailed guidance.

Eggington (1965) commented that in the USA, the most widely used approach was to eliminate 100 per cent of the 'stock profits' versus the majority and that ARB 51 (1961) recommends 100 per cent elimination. The standard does not preclude apportioning this total proportionately versus majority and minority. It is consistent with 'separate entities' or the 'group entity' criterion. Accounting Interpretation 1 of APB Opinion No. 18 (on the equity method) indicates that in the USA fractional elimination on upstream and downstream sales would be appropriate for joint ventures and investments under the equity approach (emphasizing the close link between the equity approach and the proprietary view of the group).

A reflection on elimination proposals

One might argue that the amounts involved are immaterial, so why eliminate such 'profits' at all? However, the potential for 'window dressing' without such eliminations would be enormous – to sell goods internally at an enormous mark-up and to hold them internally forever, recording an enormous profit. However, given the case for elimination, are the practical differences between alternatives (whatever their rationales) significant? No empirical work has been done in this area to evaluate sensitivity of reported profits of companies to different approaches, possibly because of paucity of available data on the extent of intra-group trading in general.

This problem might be a growing one as minority interests increase, with firms tending to acquire bare majorities. Certainly the differences on 51 per cent investments may be substantial. Case unproven owing to lack of evidence? Thus, the standardization of approach may be a significant aid to improving comparability or it may be immaterial! Wilkins (1979) argues that an alternative to exclusion of intra-group 'profits' might be full disclosure in the notes.

Exercises

5.2   The Integrated Group is organized in such a way that Rawmat plc, a 65 per cent owned subsidiary of Resell plc, manufactures components which it sells to Assembly plc, a 90 per cent fellow subsidiary, at a mark-up on cost of 25 per cent, as well as to non-group companies. Assembly incorporates these components in its own products and sells them to non-group companies. At the beginning of the current financial year Assembly has £10,000 of such components in stock, and at the end of the year £12,000.
(a)   Calculate the total stock profit deferral in the closing consolidated balance sheet for that year.
(b)   Explain the adjustment under the parent company extension concept of consolidation. How would your treatment differ if the transfers had been made from Assembly to Rawmat? Why?
(c)   Discuss treatments under other consolidation concepts.

Deferral of profits on intra-group capital transactions

As well as trading in operating items (e.g. stocks), group companies also trade in capital items which become fixed assets to the receiving company. Profits on the transfer of such fixed assets are deferred and realized not on external resale, but on a gradual basis as the assets are depreciated, in product or period costs.

It is abnormal to have the same item in stock at the beginning and end of a period. If this occurred, intra-group profits would need to be redeferred, resulting in a zero effect on this year's income, continuing the deferral until the item was sold. Fixed assets are similar except that the closing amount of the same fixed asset decreases each year as it is depreciated. The opening deferral which is reversed is on opening net book amount, and the closing deferral on the same asset is on closing book amount. Thus the reversal is bigger than the deferral, proportionate to the depreciation charge.

Example 5.5   Intra-group sales of fixed assets

Vanguard manufactures vans and in 1983 sold one to Grocer, its 100 per cent subsidiary, for £20,000 at a mark-up on cost of 25 per cent. Grocer estimated the van had a five-year life with no scrap value, straight line depreciation to be used.

The amount of Vanguard's profit incorporated in the cost to Grocer is:

$$25/125 \times £20,000 = £4,000$$

so the cost to the group of the van is £16,000.

'Profits' deferral is made by the following *consolidation adjustments:*

In 1983
Dr. Consolidated reserves 4,000   Cr. Fixed assets 4,000

From 1984 to 1988
Dr. Accum. depn. 800   Cr. Consolidated reserves (depn. expense) 800

The first entry (consolidated working papers) reverses profits recognized by Vanguard in its own records and ensures that the van appears at the cost to the *group.* The second entry (made each year for five years) reduces depreciation on the van from that on the cost to Vanguard (i.e. £4,000 per year) to cost to the group (i.e. 16,000 ÷ 5 = £3,200 per year). Effectively the £4,000 profit of Vanguard is recognized by the group at £800 per year as the van is depreciated. Some groups require subsidiaries to transfer fixed assets at *group* cost to avoid the need for making such (complex) entries.

Minority interests

Similar issues arise on the apportionment of such deferrals between minority and majority in partially owned subsidiaries. Again the apportionment depends on the consolidation concept used, and the reader is referred to the previous section. The comments made in the previous section on SSAPs 1 and 14 apply equally to the transfer of capital assets.

Exercise

5.3   Warped plc sold a weaving machine for £18,000 (whose cost of manufacture was £14,000) to its 80 per cent owned subsidiary, Weft plc, which Weft used to manufacture tablecloths. This machine has a life of ten years with no scrap value, and is to be depreciated on a straight line basis.

Required   Explain any adjustments necessitated in the consolidated financial statements by the above transaction.

Type D adjustments: revaluation of subsidiary assets on consolidation

SSAP 14 requires that in consolidated accounts under the acquisition approach, assets and liabilities of the subsidiary should be revalued at acquisition, again reflecting the change in scope of the accounts. These adjustments are very similar to type C except that they involve a change in value for the *same* company rather than in transactions between group companies. Such a revaluation may or may not be recognized by the subsidiary in its own financial records. The technical term for an actual company revaluation is 'push down' accounting, but often such revaluations are dealt with by consolidation adjustments at head office, particularly if the subsidiary is not wholly owned.

Asset revalued in subsidiary's own records

If a revaluation at acquisition is 'pushed down', the *individual company* entry would be:

> Dr. Fixed asset   Cr. Revaluation reserve

Such a revaluation reserve must be treated for cancellation as part of pre-acquisition equity (thus reducing the goodwill figure), and if there is a minority interest, be split between pre-acquisition equity and minority. Upsteam and downstream issues do not arise as the asset remains in the same company.

Asset not revalued in subsidiary's own records

If the revaluation is not recognized by the subsidiary, then the *consolidation* adjustment to effect the revaluation becomes:

> Dr. Consolidated fixed assets   Cr. Pre-acquisition equity (goodwill)
> (75%)
> Cr. Minority interests (25%)

The reader can check that this entry has the same effect at acquisition, on cancellation, as the above individual company entry. However, if the revaluation is recorded by consolidation adjustment, additional consolidation entries are required each year viz.:

> Dr. Consolidated reserves (depn.)   Cr. Consol. accumulated depreciation
> Dr. Minority interests

If the asset is revalued by the subsidiary, company cost equals *group* cost. So the company depreciation charge equals the group charge. The holding company–minority split will automatically occur in the cancellation table. However, if a consolidation adjustment is used, the company's *own* depreciation charge will be based on its original cost. Thus, a further adjustment is necessary each year to increase this to group cost, and to split this in the cancellation table between majority and minority.

Group concepts and revaluation of subsidiary assets at acquisition

This section can be omitted without loss of continuity. Figure 5.5 considers the effects of various group concepts on revaluation of subsidiary net assets at acquisition, using the example of Oppressor plc which acquires an 80 per cent interest in Victim Ltd. At acquisition, subsidiary net assets had a fair value of £200,000, and had originally cost Victim £100,000. Figure 5.5 shows the amount at which net assets of the subsidiary would be incorporated in the consolidated balance sheet and breaks this total down into its constituent elements of original cost to subsidiary (COST), and revaluation excess (REV). Consider each approach.

Proprietary/proportional
Majority (80%) Minority (20%)

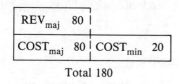

Total 160

Explanation

Only holding company's (80%) proportion (maj) of net assets is shown and revalued, i.e. at 80% × £200 = £160, made up of two components – original cost £80 and revaluation excess £80.

Pure parent
Majority (80%) Minority (20%)

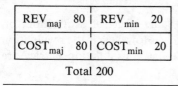

Total 180

100% of assets and liabilities (maj + min) reported. Since minority are outsiders, only the majority portion of fixed assets is revalued. Hence fixed assets are equal to 80% × £200 + 20% × 100 = 180. The minority share, £20, is the same as in subsidiary's own records. Each invididual asset, etc. is valued on a composite basis, 80% at revalued amount and 20% at original subsidiary cost.

Parent company extension
Majority (80%) Minority (20%)

REV_maj	80	REV_min	20
COST_maj	80	COST_min	20

Total 200

Conventional consolidation – 100% of assets and liabilities are completely revalued, viz. 80% × 200 + 20% × 200 = 200. The minority share of assets is stated at cost to the *group.*

Entity

Total 200

Identical to parent extension with regard to revaluation. In addition (not shown in this diagram) minority goodwill is revalued.

Figure 5.5   Components of asset valuation at acquisition under each approach (£000)

The *proprietary* consolidated balance sheet would incorporate 80 per cent of the subsidiary's net assets at cost to the *group* (£160,000). The *pure parent* consolidated balance sheet would incorporate 100 per cent of the net assets, but would only revalue the majority's portion, leaving these assets on a composite basis, 80 per cent at cost to the group and 20 per cent at cost to the subsidiary (£180,000). The minority interest section in the consolidated balance sheet would contain no revaluation reserves resulting from the acquisition. Under *parent company extension,* the consolidated assets would include 100 per cent of the net assets at *group* cost (£200,000), the minority interest now including revaluation reserves. The *entity* approach is identical to the parent extension with respect to revaluation at acquisition, but its minority interests section would include also a share in grossed-up goodwill at acquisition (see discussion of Figure 4.2).

Many of these problems disappear under current cost accounting since they arise out of deciding the appropriate date for determining historical costs. SSAP 14 requires revaluation where subsidiaries are 'purchased' but says nothing about the process of revaluation itself. Its wording does not seem to preclude composite revaluation or inclusion of minority goodwill.

A BRIEF EVALUATION OF THE DIFFERENT GROUP CONCEPTS

Different approaches to measurement and disclosure have been explored to show conventional consolidation as one part of a spectrum of alternatives. In practice group accounting is a composite of different approaches.

Should practice be more tightly specified by a particular 'theory' or group concept? An argument against this is that the concepts are poorly specified (e.g. the parent approach is 'defined' only in hybrid with proprietary or entity approaches). It could be argued that they are in fact merely labels for different technical calculations, useful to show a range of possibilities, but sometimes leading to peculiar hybrids, e.g. composite valuation, 80 per cent at group cost and 20 per cent at subsidiary cost.

The concepts may be useful in providing a framework for evaluating intra-group profit adjustments, an area notorious for '*ad hoc*'ery' though as Eggington (1965) points out, there are other approaches which emphasize separate legal entities within the group. Only a minor adjustment would be required to convert current practice to, say, the parent company extension approach on stock profits, at least allowing some uniformity in treatment. This approach is generally encouraged by US accounting texts.

The approaches highlight different disclosure possibilities for the minority. However, as will be discussed later, minority interests must be careful in using consolidated accounts to monitor their interests, and so there may not be too much pressure for increased disclosure from them. Further research is needed here.

The environment is more complex than is envisaged by these somewhat simplistic 'theories' of consolidation, and in practice a variety of different expansions are used by a single group in producing consolidated accounts. Further, changing practice should be examined in a wider context of user needs, and the conflicting demands of powerful vested interests are at very least a constraint and possibly a major determinant of practice. As stated in Chapter 3,

Watts and Zimmerman (1979) even hypothesize that accounting theories are excuses for vested interests, a theme to be re-examined later in the book. Whatever determines practice, it is important that accountants do not blindly accept current practice as the only possibility.

Example 5.6   Illustration of alignment problems

This example shows how various types of alignment problems are dealt with in conventional consolidation. The draft balance sheets of Ewing plc and Barnes plc at 31 March 1987 were as shown in Table 5.4.

		Ewing		Barnes
Land		10,000		13,000
Other fixed assets				
– cost	390,000		140,000	
– accumulated depreciation	(200,000)	190,000	(50,000)	90,000
Investment in Barnes plc		162,000		
Loan to Barnes plc		16,000		
Current assets:				
Stocks	190,000		42,000	
Dividends receivable	8,000		—	
Debtors	110,000		40,000	
Cash	70,000		25,000	
	378,000		107,000	
Creditors within one year:				
Creditors	(78,000)		(35,000)	
Dividends payable	(32,000)		(10,000)	
	(110,000)	268,000	(45,000)	62,000
Long-term loan by Ewing plc		—		(10,000)
		646,000		155,000
Capital and reserves:				
Ordinary shares		200,000		100,000
Share premium		154,000		20,000
Retained earnings		292,000		35,000
		646,000		155,000

Table 5.4   Ewing and Barnes balance sheets at 31 March 1987

Other information included:
1. Ewing purchased an 80 per cent interest in Barnes on 30 September 1986 by means of a share issue. At that date (which was Barnes's year-end) Barnes's retained earnings were £25,000.
2. In its financial report at 30 September 1986, Barnes had declared a final dividend of £5,000 which was paid on 27 October 1986. Ewing had included its share of this dividend in investment income for the year to 31 March 1987. The investment was correctly stated at acquisition.
3. Barnes had made a loan repayment to Ewing which had not been received by 31 March.
4. At acquisition, Barnes's land was revalued at £18,000, and the cost of its other fixed assets revalued upwards by 10 per cent. The useful lives and depreciation rates were not altered. At acquisition, the cost to Barnes of its other fixed assets was £140,000, and accumulated depreciation £40,000.
5. Since acquisition, Barnes had regularly sold items for resale to Ewing at a mark-up on cost of 20 per cent. At 31 March, Ewing's stocks of such items totalled £12,000. Ewing is shown as a debtor of £5,000 in Barnes's records and a corresponding amount is shown in Ewing's records.
6. Consolidated goodwill is amortized over ten years straight line.

Required
(a) Prepare a consolidated balance sheet for the Ewing–Barnes group at 31 March 1987 under the parent company extension approach.
(b) If Barnes were treated as an associate, show the disclosures required under SSAP 1.
(c) Show the breakdown of minority interests in the consolidated statement.

Part (a) – the consolidation

The extended cancellation table
Table 5.5 shows the acquisition cancellation table this time extended to incorporate alignment adjustments needed in the example. It is divided into two sections; the first being the earlier acquisition cancellation table dealing with consolidated equity; the other including balances to be aligned (adjusted) before aggregation. Only balances that do not add immediately to the corresponding consolidated balance appear in the table.

From top to bottom: Ewing's balances are recorded first as they are listed in its balance sheet, then Barnes's and finally consolidation adjustments are entered. It is helpful to leave a space between each horizontal section for any overlooked adjustments and also space for an extra column. Barnes's equity is split pre- and post-acquisition as before, and on a separate line Barnes's other balances are entered. Consider now how the 'other information' is used to determine alignment adjustments. Be careful, the adjustments cannot always be made in the order given. Here adjustment 2 (the pre-acquisition dividend) should be adjusted to revise pre-acquisition equity before determining goodwill (adjustment 1).

	Acquisition cancellation section						Interco. balances and other balances needing adjustment							
	Investment	Share cap.	Share prem.	Consol. res.	Goodwill pre-acq.	Minor. int.	Dividend	Loans	Land	Fixed assets	Stocks	Debtor	Cash	Creditors
Ewing														
Misc. balances	162	(200)	(154)	(292)	—	—	(32)	16	10	190	190	110	70	(78)
Pre-acq. div.	(4)			4			8							
Barnes														
Pre-acq. equity				(8)	(116)	(29)								
Post-acq. equity						(2)								
Other balances							(10)	(10)	13	90	42	40	25	(35)
Consolidation adjustments														
Cancellation	(158)				158			(6)						
Cash in transit													6	
Revaluations														
- Land					(4)	(1)			5					
- Other FA					(8)	(2)				10				
Extra depreciation				0.8		0.2				(1)				
Intra-group stock profits				1.6		0.4					(2)			
Interco. trading												(5)		5
Goodwill write-off				1.5	(1.5)									
Consolidated amounts	—	(200)	(154)	(292.1)	28.5	(33.4)	(32) (2)	—	28	289	230	145	101	(108)

Table 5.5 Ewing–Barnes group – extended cancellation table at 31 March 1987 (£000)

The treatment of alignment adjustments

2. The dividend out of pre-acquisition profits has been recorded as income by Ewing. The holding company's share is 80 per cent of 5,000 i.e. £4,000. Since the investment was correctly stated, Ewing should not treat the amount as income. The correction is thus an *individual company* adjustment, made in Ewing's own records, and so is shown under *Ewing's* balances.

1. Note this must be done after 2.

3. Cash in transit is reversed.

4. Under conventional consolidation, 100 per cent of the subsidiary's land and fixed assets are revalued at acquisition, the minority share thus including a revaluation reserve (20 per cent). Other fixed assets become 100,000 (net book value) $\times$ 1.1 = 110,000. Since no 'push down' has been advocated, revaluations have been recorded as consolidation adjustments. If individual company adjustments had been made, they would have been included in Barnes's section of the table. The majority share is treated as a part of pre-acquisition equity.

   In Barnes's own records, depreciation since acquisition on 'other fixed assets' was 50,000 − 40,000 = 10,000 on an original cost of 140,000. On the revalued amount, the depreciation would be 10,000 $\times$ 1.1 = 11,000, and so extra depreciation of 1,000 is split between majority (post-acquisition) and minority.

5. Under parent extension, intra-group stock profits are eliminated per ownership of the originating company, here the subsidiary. In practice, many companies would eliminate 100 per cent versus consolidated reserves. The intercompany *trading* balances are not included in the intercompany section of the table since they are not disclosed separately.

6. 30 $\times$ $\frac{1}{10}$ $\times$ $\frac{1}{2}$. Note the company has chosen the amortization approach (SSAP 22).

The balance of the intercompany dividends payable (2) belongs to the minority interest, and is shown at the foot of the dividends column to be shown as a current liability.

After much practice, only the left-hand section (as before) of the cancellation table need be used. Adjustments in the right-hand section can be made in memorandum form on the face of the balance sheets in an examination question. However, the extended table is recommended as an aid in understanding the *whole* process, and also in complex examples so that entries are not omitted. The consolidated balance sheet of the Ewing–Barnes group at 31 March 1987, shown in Table 5.6, is obtained from the table and by adding directly all balances not contained therein.

Part (b) – restatement as an associate – equity approach

Such a restatement might be required because of loss of effective control even though Barnes is still majority-owned (see page 88). The equity approach is to be used here, expanded into net assets and goodwill. The latter figure is as in the consolidated accounts. Net assets are a proportion of individual company net assets *now,* adjusted by consolidated adjustments (akin to the proportional

	£
Goodwill	28,500
Land	28,000
Other fixed assets	
– cost	544,000
– accumulated depreciation	(255,000)
	289,000
Current assets:	
Stock	230,000
Debtors	145,000
Cash	101,000
	476,000
Creditors within one year:	
Creditors	(108,000)
Dividends payable	
– holding company	(32,000)
– minority	(2,000)
	(142,000)
Net current assets	334,000
	679,500
Capital and reserves:	
Ordinary shares	200,000
Share premium	154,000
Retained earnings	292,100
	646,100
Minority interests	33,400
	679,500

Table 5.6   Ewing–Barnes group – consolidated balance sheet at 31 March 1987

consolidation approach) to obtain their 'group' accounts amount. The net assets figure is easy to obtain as it is equal to shareholders' equity (i.e. 120,000 + 35,000).

				£	£
Goodwill – per consolidation					28,500
Net assets (80%) per co. accounts	155,000 × 0.8		= 124,000		
Consolidation adjustments (80%) – proportional:					
Revaluation – land	0.8 ×	5,000	=	4,000	
– other fixed assets	0.8 ×	10,000	=	8,000	
Depreciation	0.8 ×	1,000	=	(800)	
Stocks	0.8 ×	2,000	=	(1,600)	
				9,600	
Net assets per group accounts					133,600
Equitized investment amount					162,100

SSAP 1 requires the goodwill figure of £28,500 and the group's share of net assets in associates, £133,600, to be disclosed as a note. The standard requires alignment adjustments to be made when they are material. It also requires disclosure of associate retained earnings since acquisition, and so the alternative expansion of the equitized investment (see page 78) is required, again adjusted in this more complex example for alignment data:

	£	£
Cost		158,000
Attributable profit:		
Post-acquisition retained earnings per individual accounts	8,000	
Consolidation adjustments:		
Depreciation	(800)	
Stock profits	(1,600)	
Goodwill write-off	(1,500)	
	(3,900)	
Post-acquisition retained earnings per consolidated accounts		4,100
		162,100

Attributable profit has been adjusted for alignment matters again on a proportional basis, consistent with proportional consolidation. SSAP 1 requires the disclosure of associated companies' reserves (£4,100) separate from other group reserves. Consolidated reserves would be here:

Holding company reserves   +   Associate reserves
adjusted for pre-acquisition
dividend
(292,000 − 4,000)   +   4,100   = £292,100

In this example consolidated reserves are the same under both parent company extension consolidation and latterly the equity method, i.e. £292,100. This is peculiar to the question, in which all consolidation adjustments were eliminated proportionately versus majority and minority, as sales were upstream. This is not always true (e.g. if sales had been downstream or if all intra-group stock profits were eliminated against the majority). Consolidated reserves under the equity approach are always equal to *proportional* consolidation. They may differ from other forms of consolidation owing to slightly different apportionments of alignment adjustments under each approach.

Part (c) – breakdown of minority interest
The minority interest of £33,400 is expanded in Table 5.7. Other splits are possible. The data for the following breakdown is obtained by reanalysing the minority column in the cancellation table (Table 5.5). The minority equity at 31 March 1987 before alignment is:

Minority share in current equity
= Pre-acquisition + post-acquisition = 29 + 2   = 31
= SC + SP + RE   = 20 + 4 + 7 = 31

		£	£
Share capital	100,000 × 0.2 =		20,000
Share premium	20,000 × 0.2 =		4,000
Retained earnings per individual accounts	35,000 × 0.2 = 7,000		
Consolidation adjustments:			
Depreciation	1,000 × 0.2 = (200)		
Stocks	2,000 × 0.2 = (400)		
Per group accounts			6,400
Revaluation reserves:			
Land	5,000 × 0.2 = 1,000		
Other fixed assets	10,000 × 0.2 = 2,000		
Per group accounts			3,000
			33,400

Table 5.7   Breakdown of minority: Ewing–Barnes

When calculating associated company or minority balances, start from company balances and note which alignment adjustments are necessary to convert to the corresponding group balance. The revaluation reserves are unrealized reserves per the Companies Act 1981. Note that minority interest excludes current dividends, which are included here in current liabilities. Texts seem divided on its treatment, with some (e.g. Shaw, 1973) including it in the single minority interests figure. It is interesting to reflect whether these different treatments imply different views as to the status of the minority (i.e. as more akin to equity or liabilities) or whether, even if the 'near equity' viewpoint is taken, a (current) liability to minority interests is deemed to arise when the subsidiary declares a dividend.

Exercise

5.4   Proud plc is the holding company of Humble Ltd. It acquired a 90 per cent interest on 1 January 1985 when the reserves of Humble were £50,000. Its directors decide that the investment should be accounted for under the acquisition method for group accounts purposes.

The balance sheets available for the year ended 31 December 1986 are shown in Table 5.8.

The following information is also available:
1.   Proud sold goods for £4,000 to Humble at a mark-up of 25 per cent on cost, but these were not received by Humble until after the group year-end. Also, when reconciling its bank statements, Proud has found a cash payment of £22,000 from Humble received on 29 December was wrongly recorded in its records as £20,000.

2. At acquisition, certain of Humble's fixed assets were revalued from £40,000 to £50,000. These assets are still held by Humble and are depreciated straight line in Humble's records at £4,000 per annum. No entry has been made to record their revaluation in Humble's records. No other assets were revalued.
3. You discover Proud's dividend income for the previous year included £4,000 from Humble in respect of the year ended 31 December 1985.
4. Humble has in stock at 31 December 1986, £16,000 of goods purchased from Proud (on the same basis as in 1 above). There are no outstanding debts relating to these items.
5. Goodwill is written off on the straight line basis over ten years.

	Proud (£000)		Humble (£000)	
Assets employed:				
Fixed assets		120		90
Investment in Humble		120		
Current assets:				
Stock	80		40	
Debtors	50		30	
Intra-group debtor	36			
Dividends receivable	9			
Cash	20		40	
	195		110	
Creditors due within one year:				
Creditors	(50)		(30)	
Dividends payable	(20)		(10)	
Intra-group creditor			(30)	
	(70)	125	(70)	40
		365		130
Financed by:				
Capital and reserves:				
Share capital	70		20	
Share premium	100		30	
Reserves	195		80	
		365		130

Table 5.8   Proud and Humble balance sheets at 31 December 1986

Required
(a) Prepare a consolidated balance sheet at 31 December 1986 for the Proud–Humble group.
(b) Suppose that Proud could no longer exercise control over Humble even though it held the majority of the ordinary share capital. Calculate the amount at which Humble would be disclosed as an associate, and present the additional disclosures prescribed by SSAP 1 for associates.
(c) Show in detail how the figure for minority interest is made up.

THE USEFULNESS OF THE CONSOLIDATED BALANCE SHEET

With the usual caveats about weaknesses of conventional accounting, it is undoubtedly true that for most groups the consolidated balance sheet gives a better picture of the size of the 'tools' at a group's disposal than the holding company balance sheet. This alone may justify its publication. However, it is important also to understand the limitations of such consolidated statements.

The averaging problem

Consolidation can be viewed as a process of averaging – the sum of a set of items is always a constant times their arithmetic average viz.

$$\bar{x} = \sum_{i=1}^{n} x_i /n \quad \text{and so} \quad \sum_{i=1}^{n} x_i = n \times \bar{x}$$

Under many circumstances averaging is misleading. For example, the consolidation of loss-making subsidiaries (without further disclosures) can hide variations in performance within the group. Another example is where businesses within the group are highly dissimilar, e.g. a heavy engineering firm owning an equal sized supermarket chain subsidiary. The former may have an extremely high current ratio because of long-term contracts in progress. The latter's current ratio may be less than unity because it collects cash from its customers much faster than it normally needs to settle its debts. The former may be heavily financed by long-term loans (i.e. be highly geared). The latter may be financed by retained earnings and short-term credit. If these two companies are consolidated, the 'average' balances and any ratios calculated therefrom are likely to be some meaningless amalgam which is difficult to interpret at all (conventional accounts do not report standard deviations!).

Though SSAP 14 has special provisions for excluding too dissimilar lines of business (with the consequence that many finance subsidiaries are not consolidated), the problem is one of degree. How dissimilar does a subsidiary have to be to require differential treatment? For example, how does one interpret ratios based on the consolidated statements of a conglomerate enterprise spanning highly diverse business sectors? SSAP 14 and the Companies Acts give no guidance on this issue. Segmental disclosures ease the problem somewhat, but as will be seen in Chapter 10, the requirements for such disclosures leave much to be desired in the UK. However, it still may be true (and this is very difficult to prove) that even under these circumstances a consolidated balance sheet *may be* more useful than a holding company balance sheet.

Some writers suggest that since financing subsidiaries are an inseparable part of large groups (often used as a means to solicit new customers for the rest of the group), non-consolidation may be misleading unless a great deal of prominence is given to the non-consolidated subsidiary. It becomes very difficult to compare two similar groups, one which finances its customers via its component companies, and the other via a financing subsidiary. The former will implicitly consolidate its financing 'wing'. Indeed Livnat and Sondhi (1986) suggest that the formation and non-consolidation of financing subsidiaries is an integrated decision, to reduce balance sheet volatility of the remaining consolidated balances and thus to reduce the possibility of default on debt. In an empirical investigation of forty-six US groups which formed financing subsidiaries in the period 1964–76 and did not consolidate them, they found that pre-formation balance sheets (with effective consolidation) were more volatile than post-formation ones (with financing subsidiaries excluded).

In the USA FAS No. 13 requires accounts of subsidiaries whose activity is principally leasing properties or facilities to the parent or other affiliated enterprises to be consolidated. However, this does not include all financing subsidiaries.

Sensitivity of tiered accounting treatment to marginal ownership changes

The crossing of the cost/equity tier at approximately 20 per cent ownership causes mainly a measurement change to include earnings retained in the affiliate, though there are disclosure consequences too (see Chapter 4). The crossing of the equity/consolidation tier at approximately 50 per cent ownership involves a major disclosure change/expansion.

So, for example, a 50 per cent holding will be accounted for as an equitized investment, with separate disclosure of attributable retained earnings and, as two figures in the notes, attributable net assets (as a *single* figure) and goodwill. A 51 per cent holding will necessitate an expansion of the components of this net assets figure and a collecting together, like with like, with corresponding components in other group companies. As the averaging section above (and Discussion Question 4.6) point out, for companies with quite different structures (e.g. a motorway contractor with an investment in a motoring discount shops chain), the differential effect between the inclusion of component balance sheet elements or the 'hiving' off into one lump (the equitized investment) can have a dramatic effect on balance sheet ratios. This major difference in accounting treatment between say 40 per cent plus and 50 per cent plus holdings is a potential hazard for analysts comparing similar groups where one invests in 'associates' and another with slightly larger proportionate holdings invests in 'subsidiaries'. It is present even apart from deliberate attempts to take advantage of the tiered disclosures by marginal changes in ownership (discussed, for example, in relationship to the cost/equity tier on page 85.

SSAP 1 requires more detailed information about the associate's tangible and intangible assets and liabilities and results if 'the interests [and results] in the associated companies are so material in the context of the financial statements that more detailed information about them would assist in giving a true and fair view' (paragraphs 23 and 30). However, because of the judgements involved here there is a potential grey area, and even if available, investors will have to scan the notes to the accounts carefully to find these additional disclosures. An interesting empirical question (not answered as yet to the author's knowledge) is how many groups in fact give these additional disclosures. It is also interesting that on the other side of the tier division, SSAP 14 requires the *equity* approach plus separate financial statements for subsidiaries *excluded* from consolidation because of too dissimilar activities, consistent with attempting to ameliorate the effects of a 'hard-edged' tier. On both sides of the tier it is quite difficult for outsiders and auditors to dispute managements' judgements which may align with their own interests. However, at least the ASC is aware of this problem area.

Rio Tinto Zinc Corporation is sufficiently concerned about this problem to provide a set of accounts under the proportional consolidation basis for all subsidiaries *and* associates alongside its conventional consolidated accounts (in which subsidiaries are (parent)-consolidated and associates treated under the equity approach). This is a novel treatment and perhaps further thought might be given to extending this supplementary disclosure to other groups.

Solvency evaluation and consolidated balance sheets

A 'group' is not a legal entity and so creditors (even of the holding company) would be mistaken if they look to group accounts to evaluate their security. They should look mainly to the individual accounts of subsidiaries, and creditors of the holding company mainly to its individual accounts. However, group accounts may be of limited help. The creditor may get a better feel of the strategic position of his company within the whole group, whether it is likely to be let slide or expanded, etc. However, their claims are only over the assets of the individual *legal* entity.

Walker (1978b) provides interesting counter-examples to illustrate that security of creditors often depends on the *order* in which companies in a group are liquidated – which depends on the whims of management, and often the amounts realized depend on intra-group debt guarantees. The accounts of the subsidiaries themselves may under these circumstances provide only minimally useful information. Thus, an appraisal of the overall financial position and strategy of the group may be extremely important to creditors of subsidiaries. The whole area is very complex.

The Companies Act 1985 requires in the accounts of the holding company details (in aggregate) of holding company loans to subsidiaries, and of loans by subsidiaries to the holding company. By themselves, these aggregate (i.e. 'average') figures can conceal a variety of different lending patterns, and for details of intercompany indebtedness the investor must try to piece together an incomplete jigsaw from the accounts of the subsidiaries. Subsidiary creditors have an even worse problem because only aggregate indebtedness to and, separately, from group companies is disclosed. SSAP 1 requires details of loans to and from associates to be disclosed separately in *consolidated* accounts and of short-term credit if material. The Act further requires a company to disclose guarantees entered into on behalf of other group companies, but to assess financial security in a marginally solvent group it is necessary to obtain a full picture of *interrelationships* in intra-group indebtedness, guarantees and likely order of liquidation.

Solvency evaluation has both a static and a dynamic aspect. It is possible to have healthy balance sheet ratios and still be in financial difficulties perhaps because creditors require payment before current assets are turned into cash. In Chapter 7, the consolidated funds statement is examined in this context.

The minority interest

Minority interests are set between creditors and holding company shareholders, having an interest in a *part* of the group. Presumably their primary source would be the consolidated accounts of the subsidiary in which they own shares, though their problems in evaluation would be analogous to those of a creditor. Probably this is why the entity approach, which sees them as co-equal owners of the group, has attracted little professional support. Rosenfield and Rubin (1986) provide evidence of confusion over the status of the minority, by quoting authors who respectively recommend minorities should be disclosed as liabilities, between liabilities and equity, and as a part of equity.

Differing conceptions of the group itself (e.g. as a single entity or as a collection of separate legal entities) and the position of the minority interests in it cause a lack of comparability in elimination adjustments to the minority. This, combined with a lack of disclosure, further minimizes the usefulness of consolidated accounts to the minority shareholder.

Discussion questions

5.5   Discuss why conventional consolidation may not always be the most appropriate accounting treatment for all subsidiaries, evaluating alternative forms of disclosure.

5.6   What changes in current practice would be necessary to change to an entity basis for consolidation? To what extent do you feel such changes would be appropriate?

5.7   Comment on whether you feel RTZ's approach of accounting for all subsidiaries *and* associates under proportional consolidation should *replace* conventional approaches used in group accounts. Give reasons.

SUMMARY

Alignment adjustments are mainly necessitated by the change in scope of the accounts from a company to a group basis. They are made either by companies themselves, 'individual company adjustments', or at head office when consolidation working papers are prepared, 'consolidation adjustments'.

For *intercompany (intra-group) balances,* errors are corrected by individual company adjustments and timing differences by consolidation adjustments.

Dividends from the subsidiary's pre-acquisition profits may be treated as income of the holding company, provided there is no diminution in the value of the investment below its carrying amount. However, in group accounts, transfers from pre-acquisition profits cannot increase group profits. Thus, any such profits recognized by the holding company need to be reversed by a consolidation adjustment, decreasing consolidated reserves and goodwill.

Profits on incomplete intra-group transfers are deferred by means of a consolidation adjustment to a later period. For partially owned subsidiaries, questions of apportionment of this amount between majority and minority are resolved differently according to whether the group is viewed as a *whole* (when the originating company's ownership proportions are used) or as a set of *separate legal entities* (in which case the receiving company's proportions are used). Within the 'group as a whole' perspective, there are a variety of characterizations – *proprietary, pure parent, parent company extension*, and *entity* – in order giving increasing importance to the minority. *Revaluations at acquisition* reflect alignments between periods for a single company. Again the different group concepts are reflected in different revaluation proposals.

Group concepts can be viewed merely as rationalizations for the different calculation bases, or as theories explaining consolidation. The concepts seem to be too poorly specified and oversimplified at present to perform the latter function.

In considering the usefulness of the consolidated balance sheet, difficulties often arise from 'averaging' dissimilar components. Users such as creditors and minorities having legal claims in a single company or part of the group need to be careful as they usually have no claim over 'successful' companies within the group. The position of the minority is ill-defined.

FURTHER READING

Alignment adjustments and group concepts

Baxter, G. C. and Spinney, J. C. (1975) A closer look at consolidated financial theory, *CA Magazine,* January 1975, pp. 31–5.

Eggington, D. (1965) Unrealized profit and consolidated accounts, *Accountancy,* May 1965, pp. 410–15.

Wilkins, R. M. (1979) *Group Accounts* (2nd edn), especially ch. 8, Institute of Chartered Accountants in England and Wales, London.

The usefulness of the consolidated balance sheet

Walker, R. G. (1978a) *Consolidated Statements: A History and Analysis,* especially chs. 15 and 16, Arno Press, New York.

Walker, R. G. (1978b) An evaluation of the information conveyed by consolidated statements, *Abacus,* Vol. 12, No. 2, pp. 77–115.

6 Consolidated Profit and Loss Accounts

The consolidated profit and loss account under both acquisition and merger accounting was considered briefly in Example 3.3. In the year of combination, revenues and expenses were included for the subsidiary only since acquisition under acquisition accounting, but for the whole year under merger accounting. This chapter examines in more detail the consolidated profit and loss account under the *acquisition* approach. Many issues in previous chapters (e.g. the spectrum of approaches to consolidation and the treatment of alignment problems) are reconsidered in condensed form. In this chapter *only*, revenues (credits) are positive and expenses (debits) negative. Such a departure makes profit and loss accounts here consistent with the usual convention that profits (credits) are shown as positive.

In the following section a simple example is presented, and subsequently elaborated and the facts modified, so that the sensitivity of the consolidated profit and loss account to different assumptions is shown. The basic data is shown in Example 6.1, and all subsequent examples (unless otherwise stated) start from these figures. In an expanded form the example will eventually be used in conjunction with Example 4.1 (the balance sheet) to show the interrelationship between consolidated balance sheets and profit and loss accounts. However, Example 6.1 is somewhat simpler (e.g. assuming a 100 per cent takeover).

A SIMPLE EXAMPLE

Example 6.1 Largesse–Smallnesse

Largesse has held a 100 per cent interest in Smallnesse for a number of years. Consider the profit and loss accounts for the year ended 31 March 1986.

Profit and loss accounts for the year ended 31 March 1986

	Largesse	Smallnesse
Sales	400,000	200,000
Cost of goods sold	(228,000)	(150,000)
Gross profit	172,000	50,000
Distribution costs	(70,000)	(14,000)
Administration expenses	(30,000)	(6,000)
Dividends receivable	8,000	—
Profit before tax	80,000	30,000
Corporation tax	(40,000)	(15,000)
Profit after tax	40,000	15,000
Dividends	(20,000)	(8,000)
Retained for year	20,000	7,000

The following further information is available:

1. Smallnesse sold £100,000 of goods to Largesse during the year but none of these goods were held at the end of the year.
2. Largesse acquired its interest for £100,000 at 31 March 1983, when the share capital, share premium and retained earnings of Smallnesse were £35,000, £15,000 and £30,000 respectively. At 31 March 1985 (the start of the year) retained earnings of Smallnesse had increased to £35,000. Goodwill on consolidation is to be written off over ten years.

When consolidating profit and loss accounts, there are two areas to consider:

(a) *Avoidance of double counting* by removing intra- (within) group flows. Here £100,000 of goods have been sold within the group and then resold externally in the same period. If the effects of this internal transfer are not removed, the goods will be counted twice.

(b) *Making alignment adjustments* to reflect the change in scope of the accounts to a group basis (e.g. by adjusting for consolidated goodwill, or intra-group stock 'profits').

Consider now the consolidation of the profit and loss accounts:

	Largesse	Smallnesse	Adjustments	Consolidated
Sales	400,000	200,000	(100,000)	500,000
COGS	(228,000)	(150,000)	100,000	(278,000)
Distribution costs	(70,000)	(14,000)		(84,000)
Admin. expenses	(30,000)	(6,000)		(36,000)
Goodwill			(2,000)	(2,000)
Dividends receivable	8,000		(8,000)	—
Corporation tax	(40,000)	(15,000)		(55,000)
Profit after tax	40,000	15,000	(10,000)	45,000
Dividends	(20,000)	(8,000)	8,000	(20,000)
Retained for year	20,000	7,000	(2,000)	25,000

Type (a) adjustments are the cancelling of intra-group sales, expenses and dividends. A type (b) adjustment is the amortization of goodwill (if SSAP 22's preferred treatment of immediate write-off had been adopted, the write-off would have been made directly against reserves, bypassing the profit and loss account). Adjustments in total do not add to zero since the double entry for type (b) adjustments is completed *outside the equity section*. Here, goodwill will be credited with £2,000, i.e. $\frac{1}{10} \times (100 - (35 + 15 + 30))$.

Exercise

6.1 Overbearing plc is the holding company of Inadequate Ltd. It acquired a 100 per cent interest on 1 July 1983 for £250,000 when the share capital, share premium and retained earnings of Inadequate were £50,000, £70,000, and £80,000 respectively. The directors decided to write off consolidated goodwill over a five-year period, and continued this treatment when SSAP 22 came into force. At 30 June 1985, Inadequate's retained earnings were £100,000. The individual profit and loss accounts of both companies were as follows.

Profit and loss accounts for the year ended 30 June 1986 (£000)

	Overbearing	Inadequate
Sales	900	500
Cost of sales	(300)	(250)
Gross profit	600	250
Distribution costs	(250)	(50)
Administration expenses	(150)	(70)
Dividends receivable	30	—
Corporation tax	(100)	(65)
Profit after tax	130	65
Dividends – interim	(30)	(10)
– final	(50)	(20)
Profit retained	50	35

Inadequate sold Overbearing £200,000 of goods during the year. No intra-group sales were in stock at the beginning or end of the year.

Required Prepare a consolidated profit and loss account for the Overbearing–Inadequate group for the year ended 30 June 1986, showing clearly the consolidation adjustments used.

CHANGES IN THE STATUS OF THE SUBSIDIARY

This section can be omitted without loss of continuity. Consider the effects of the following changes in assumptions on the profit and loss account. The three cases do *not* build on each other. Each refers back to Example 6.1 except for the changes specified. Assume sales, expenses, etc. accrue at an even rate. The dividend was declared in the accounts of Inadequate at 30 June 1986.

1. Acquisition of Smallnesse during the year.
2. Disposal of Smallnesse during the year.
3. Conversion of the subsidiary to an associate during the year.

Example 6.2   Acquisition of subsidiary during year

Assume the acquisition date was 30 September 1985 (half-way through the year). The equity (net assets) at acquisition is that at the start of the year adjusted for changes to the acquisition date, in £000:

$$(35 + 15 + 35) + \%_{12} \times £15 = £92.5$$

It is assumed that the subsidiary's dividend has not yet been recorded by Largesse. The transaction is *reversed* by consolidation adjustment, so profit *before* dividend is used.[1] Thus, goodwill at acquisition is 100,000 – 92,500 = £7,500, and will be written off for six months *since* acquisition, i.e. ½ × ¹⁄₁₀ × 7,500 = £375. Under the acquisition approach only earnings of Smallnesse *since acquisition* are included. There are two alternative presentations.

1. Only *post*-acquisition revenues and expenses of Smallnesse are added to those of Largesse. This is consistent with the spirit of acquisition accounting (i.e. as if Smallnesse had been purchased as a set of assets, liabilities and goodwill at 30 September).
2. Smallnesse's revenues and expenses for the whole year are added to those of Largesse, and pre-acquisition *profits* of Smallnesse are removed as a single figure deduction. Some argue that while the bottom line is consistent with acquisition accounting, the statement also gives full year figures for the group for forecasting purposes. The US standard ARB No. 51 (paragraph 11) expresses its preference for this approach, but the area is not discussed in UK standards, though the first approach seems to be more widely canvassed in UK accounting texts.

Note in the following that revenues and expenses of Smallnesse are halved before aggregation. Thus, pre-acquisition profits of the subsidiary are one half of its profits after tax for the year.

Consolidated profit and loss account: Largesse–Smallnesse group – year ending 31 March 1986

	Alternative 1	Alternative 2
Sales	450,000	500,000
COGS	(253,000)	(278,000)
Distribution costs	(77,000)	(84,000)
Admin. expenses	(33,000)	(36,000)
Dividends receivable	—	—
Goodwill	(375)	(375)
Corporation tax	(47,500)	(55,000)
Profit after tax	39,125	46,625
Less pre-acq. profits		(7,500)
Attributable profits for year	39,125	39,125
Dividends	(20,000)	(20,000)
Retained for year	19,125	19,125

Example 6.3   Disposal of subsidiary during year

The facts are as in Example 6.1 (i.e. Smallnesse was again acquired three years ago) but now assume that Smallnesse was disposed of on 30 September 1985 for £110,000.

Consolidation was characterized in Chapter 4 as *equitization and expansion*. When a subsidiary is disposed of, this expansion is reversed (*contracted*) and profit or loss calculated by comparing disposal proceeds with the *equitized amount* at disposal (treating the subsidiary analogously to an associate). In a number of areas in this chapter the link between the equity approach and consolidation is used, and so if this is hazy, the reader is advised to reread the relevant area in Chapter 4 – 'Full consolidation viewed as an expansion of the equity approach'.

SSAP 14 (paragraph 31) requires that where there is a material disposal, the subsidiary's results to the date of the disposal shall be included in the consolidated profit and loss account. Further, it requires that the profit or loss on sale shall be computed based on the holding company's share of the subsidiary's net assets at the date of disposal. So for the first six months, Smallnesse's component revenues and expenses will be added to those of Largesse. At disposal on 30 September 1985, all its balances will be *contracted* into a single amount, the equitized investment amount at that date (cost plus attributable retained earnings for the two and a half years it was owned), and matched with the proceeds to determine profit or loss. No later revenues, expenses and profits will be included as Smallnesse is no longer a part of the group.

Calculation of the equitized amount at 30 September 1985
The equitized investment will comprise cost plus attributable retained earnings for the period 31 March 1983 to 30 September 1985. Retained earnings of Smallnesse at 30 September 1985 $= 35,000 + \frac{1}{2} \times 15,000 = 42,500$. Now cost $= 100\,000$, and attributable retained earnings increment = Smallnesse retained earnings increment less consolidated adjustments (goodwill write-off) for the period

$$= (35,000 + \frac{6}{12} \times 15,000 - 30,000) - 2.5 \times 2,000$$
$$= \quad 7,500, \text{ so}$$

equitized investment $= 107,500$.

This figure equals the aggregate of all the assets, liabilities, goodwill (and in more complex examples minority interests) of Smallnesse at disposal, effectively a *contraction* of these balances. Consolidated goodwill write-off is at the same rate as in Example 6.1. Profit *before* dividend is used as Largesse sold its holding after 6 months, and so will not receive the final dividend.[2] The tax element on disposal profit is ignored here.

$$\text{Profit on disposal} = \text{Proceeds} - \text{Equitized investment}$$
$$= 110,000 - 107,500$$
$$= \quad 2,500$$

An intuitive way of thinking about this computation is that the investment is updated ('revalued') each year under *equitization* and the profit/loss is computed versus this 'revalued' amount. The *expansion* element of consolidation does not affect the *measurement* of income, but merely the *disclosure* of its components. The consolidated profit and loss account, which includes the first six months' revenues and expenses of Smallnesse is shown below. Each adjustment has a separate column. Note Largesse does not receive any dividend.

Consolidated P & L – Largesse–Smallnesse group (with disposal) for year ending 31 March 1986

	Largesse	Smallnesse 6 months	Intra-gp elim.	Disposal subsid.	Goodwill	Consol.
Sales	400,000	100,000	(50,000)			450,000
COGS	(228,000)	(75,000)	50,000			(253,000)
Other expenses	(100,000)	(10,000)				(110,000)
Goodwill					(1,000)	(1,000)
Corpn tax	(40,000)	(7,500)				(47,500)
Disposal profit				2,500		2,500
Dividends	(20,000)					(20,000)
Retd earnings	12,000	7,500	—	2,500	(1,000)	21,000

The totals of the adjustment columns complete the double entry. £2,500 will be debited (positive) to the investment realization account, and (£1,000) will be credited (negative) to consolidated goodwill (six months' write-off). Under SSAP 6 the disposal profit shown would be an extraordinary item. Corresponding to the alternative treatment on acquisitions, some suggest that the subsidiary's results for the first six months might merely be disclosed as profit after taxation, rather than as components, to assist comparisons with future years. ARB No. 51 in the USA expresses a preference for this treatment. SSAP 14 merely states that the subsidiary's *results* up to the date of disposal should be included, but it is not clear whether a single figure is an acceptable way to disclose such results.

The effects on the balance sheet cancellation table
Surprisingly, when a subsidiary is entirely disposed of, there are *no* effects on the closing consolidated balance sheet cancellation table if it is calculated from scratch. Only subsidiaries at the *year-end* are consolidated. Thus, Smallnesse will be completely omitted. Unexpectedly, this will give the correct total consolidated retained earnings figure. The *total* effects of the subsidiary on consolidated retained earnings since acquisition come from two sources, retained earnings contributed to the group over the years, and the effects of the disposal itself. These are shown below, the disposal being broken down line by line into its components:

Consolidated retained earnings contribution
= Change in retained earnings (RE) (of subsidiary)
− Consolidated goodwill write-off

Consolidated gain on disposal
= Proceeds − Equitized investment
= Proceeds − (Cost + attributable RE)
= Proceeds − (Cost + (Change in RE − Consol. g/w w/o))

Adding these, we get

Consolidated RE contribution
+ Consolidated gain on disposal
= Proceeds − Cost

Thus the consolidated total contribution of the subsidiary equals the gain on disposal calculated on its original historical cost. But this amount will automatically be calculated in the holding company's own records when the subsidiary is not consolidated. SSAP 14 is concerned that the contribution to retained earnings and the gain/loss on disposal is correctly determined in the *consolidated* profit and loss account, hence the calculations above. However, the consolidated balance sheet is concerned with totals, and consolidated profit and loss calculations are merely subdivisions within the same overall total. Where the balance sheet cancellation table is updated from the previous year, this simple result does not hold. This is discussed in Chapter 8.

Example 6.4   Conversion from subsidiary to associate

Suppose the facts are as in Example 6.3, except on 30 September Largesse sells only 60 per cent of its holding in Smallnesse. Assume the proceeds are now 60 per cent of £110,000, i.e. £66,000. The equitized amount at 30 September of the disposed portion would be 60% × £107,500 = £64,500, and the profit on disposal £66,000 − £64,500 = £1,500 (i.e. 60% × £2,500).

The equity method has been described earlier as 'one line' consolidation, and there is an analogous profit and loss treatment. For subsidiaries, revenues and expenses are added component by component to the holding company's. For associates (SSAP 1) there is no such *expansion*. SSAP 1 requires the following to be disclosed for associated companies:
(a)   profits attributable to the associate before tax;
(b)   attributable tax charge of the associate;
(c)   attributable extraordinary items of the associate;
(d)   as a note, attributable retained earnings of the associate.

Effectively these disclosures *contract* revenues and expenses of the associate to a single figure of profit before tax (PBT) analogous to the balance sheet treatment. Consider now the calculation of these components.

Attributable retained earnings 30 September 1985 to 31 March 1986
= 40% × Smallnesse PBT (last 6 months) − 40% × Consol adj (g/w) (last 6 months)
= 40% × $\frac{6}{12}$ × 30,000 − 40% × $\frac{6}{12}$ × 2,000
= 5,600

Attributable tax charge = 40% × $\frac{6}{12}$ × 15,000 = 3,000
Attributable RE = Attrib. PBT − Attrib. tax − 40% × dividends
            = 5,600 − 3,000 − 3,200 = (600)

Consider the cancellation table based on the above calculations

Consolidated P & L - Largesse-Smallnesse group (conversion to associate)

	L	S 6 months	Intra-gp elims.	Disposal subsid.	Assoc. co.	G/will	Consol.
Sales	400,000	100,000	(50,000)				450,000
COGS	(228,000)	(75,000)	50,000				(253,000)
Distr. cost	(70,000)	(7,000)					(77,000)
Admin. exp.	(30,000)	(3,000)					(33,000)
Goodwill						(1,000)	(1,000)
Divs. rec.*	3,200				(3,200)		—
Profit assoc.					5,600		5,600
Corpn tax	(40,000)	(7,500)					(47,500)
C tax assoc.					(3,000)		(3,000)
Profit disp.†				1,500			1,500
Dividends	(20,000)						(20,000)
Retained	15,200	7,500	—	1,500	(600)	(1,000)	22,600

* Dividend is received for the whole year on the 40% holding, i.e. 40% × £8,000.
† Disclosed as an extraordinary item under SSAP 6.

The profit on disposal is scaled down to 60 per cent. Otherwise the only change from Example 6.3 is the inclusion of the associate for the last six months. As discussed in Chapter 4 – under 'Accounting for substantially owned investments – the equity method' – it is associated company *profits* which affect the profit and loss account, not dividends. Hence the dividends (£3,200) are removed and replaced by profits (£5,600 − £3,000).

Consider now the adjustment columns. The sum of £1,500 will go (as before) to the debit of the investment realization account. Consolidated goodwill will be credited by six months' write-off (£1,000) whilst Smallnesse was still a subsidiary. The net credit (decrease) to the investment in associate from 30 September to 31 March will be (£600). The equitized investment will be increased by the profits earned, £2,600, and decreased by dividends received, £3,200. Because the profit before tax of the associate is contracted to 'one line', the write-off of attributable goodwill on Smallnesse for the *second* six months is included in that one figure and not in the group goodwill write-off.

Effects of the conversion on the consolidated balance sheet cancellation table

Using similar reasoning to the complete disposal case, it can be shown that if the remaining 40 per cent is treated as if it had been an associated company from the original acquisition date of the subsidiary in 1982, then the consolidated balance sheet cancellation table, if calculated from scratch, will be correct. The 60 per cent disposed of will again not be consolidated, and the gain on disposal against original historical cost, i.e £66,000 − 60% × 100,000 = £6,000, will be shown in the holding company's own records.

The equitized investment at 31 March 1986 for the remaining 40 per cent will be:

$$\text{Equitized investment} = \text{Cost} + \text{Attributable RE since 31 March } 1983$$
$$= \text{Cost} + (\text{Change in RE} - \text{goodwill w/o})$$
$$= 40\% \times £100 + 40\% \times (35 + 7 - 30) - 40\%$$
$$\times (2.5 \times 2.0)$$
$$= 42,800$$

Everything is calculated on the remaining 40 per cent and the 'associate' is treated as acquired at the subsidiary acquisition date, two and a half years ago.

Exercises

In the following, prepare consolidated profit and loss worksheets for the Overbearing–Inadequate group for the year ended 30 June 1986.

6.2   In Exercise 6.1, assume that Inadequate was acquired on 31 March 1986, for £286,250. All revenues and expenses can be apportioned on a time basis.

6.3   Assume Inadequate Ltd was disposed of on 31 March 1986 for £300,000.

(a)   Calculate the equitized investment in Inadequate Ltd at disposal.

(b)   Prepare a consolidated profit and loss account for the group at 30 June 1986.

6.4   Assume that on 31 March 1986, 70 per cent of the holding of Inadequate was disposed of for £210,000.

TREATMENT OF MINORITY INTERESTS – DIFFERENT GROUP CONCEPTS

Analogous to balance sheet treatments (see pages 78–81), this section illustrates the spectrum of possible treatments (expansions) for minority interests in the consolidated profit and loss account, setting into context the alternatives used in practice. Example 6.1 (repeated here for reference), is now modified to include minority interests.

Example 6.5   Minority interests

The facts are unchanged except that Largesse now holds an 80 per cent interest in Smallnesse throughout the year (i.e. a minority interest of 20 per cent) and the investment is scaled down to 80 per cent of its former amount (80% × £100,000 = £80,000). So that the dividends receivable by Largesse can remain at £8,000, dividends payable by Smallnesse must be increased to £8,000 × $\frac{10}{80}$ = £10,000. Consequently its retained earnings become £5,000.

Profit and loss accounts for the year ended 31 March 1986

	Largesse	Smallnesse
Sales	400,000	200,000
Cost of goods sold	(228,000)	(150,000)
Gross profit	172,000	50,000
Distribution costs	(70,000)	(14,000)
Administration expenses	(30,000)	(6,000)
Dividends receivable	8,000	—
Profit before tax	80,000	30,000
Corporation tax	(40,000)	(15,000)
Profit after tax	40,000	15,000
Dividends	(20,000)	(10,000)
Retained for year	20,000	5,000

The following further information is available:
1. Smallnesse sold £100,000 of goods to Largesse during the year but none of these goods were held at the end of the year.
2. Largesse acquired its interest for £80,000 at 31 March 1982, when the share capital, share premium and retained earnings of Smallnesse were £35,000, £15,000 and £30,000 respectively. At 31 March 1985 (the start of the year) retained earnings of Smallnesse had increased to £35,000. Goodwill on consolidation is to be written off over ten years.

Goodwill is recalculated (£000) as £80 − 80% × (35 + 15 + 30) = £16, 80 per cent of its former amount, and written off at £1,600 per year. Under the equity approach profit after tax for the year of Smallnesse would be:

Equitized profit for the year
= (80% × Profit after tax) − Consol. adj. g/w
= (80% × 15,000) − 1,600 = £10,400

Group profit after tax is obtained by aggregating this with the holding company (£40,000) to get £50,400. The £10,400 is expanded in Table 6.1 corresponding to various consolidation concepts. Intra-group sales, etc. are eliminated against sales, etc. of the subsidiary to keep the presentation simple. Thus, the *increment* to get consolidated sales is (subsidiary 200,000 − intra-group sales 100,000) = £100,000. Going from left to right in Table 6.1, the single figure is expanded progressively.

SSAP 1 requires profit before taxation *and* taxation to be shown separately for associates. The *proprietary* approach, closely linked to the equity approach, expands equitized profit into its components (each 80%). Conventional (*parent*) consolidation shows 100 per cent of revenue and expense components (except goodwill which is based on the holding company share (80 per cent) only). In practice minority interests are shown as a *single figure* deduction from profit *after* tax. Goodwill is not included in determining the minority share.

Minority = 20% × (Sales − COGS − Distn and Admin. − Tax)
= 20% × (100,000 − 50,000 − 20,000 − 15,000) = £3,000

Under the *entity* approach, minority goodwill is included in the balance sheet, and so is written off in the profit and loss account. Its amount is the difference between the parent goodwill write-off (£1,600) and entity goodwill write-off ($\frac{100}{80}$ × £1,600 = £2,000) i.e. £400. Thus, the entity minority is reduced in total to £3,000 − £400 = £2,600. Further, under the entity approach, minority disclosure is the same as for the majority, i.e. expanded to show share of minority dividend (i.e. 20% × 10,000) and the minority retained earnings (£600). No such distinction is made under conventional consolidation where it is lumped into one figure.

Profit *before* tax differs under each approach. Under the proportional approach, it is equal to equity profit (80 per cent). Under the entity approach it is grossed up to equal 100/80 × equity profit. Under conventional consolidation all items are grossed up *except* goodwill (80 per cent). The consolidated profit and loss account under each approach, obtained by aggregating expansions with the holding company figures is shown in Table 6.2.

Equity	SSAP 1	Proportional		Conventional		Entity	
		Sales	80,000	Sales	100,000	Sales	100,000
		COGS	(40,000)	COGS	(50,000)	COGS	(50,000)
		Distribn.	(11,200)	Distribn.	(14,000)	Distribn.	(14,000)
		Admin.	(4,800)	Admin.	(6,000)	Admin.	(6,000)
		Goodwill	(1,600)	Goodwill	(1,600)	Goodwill	(2,000)
		Prop. PBT	22,400	Parent PBT	28,400	Entity PBT	28,000
80% PBT 22,400							
10,400							
80% tax (12,000)	80% tax (12,000)	80% tax	(12,000)	Tax	(15,000)	Tax	(15,000)
				Minority	(3,000)		
						Minority dividend	(2,000)
						Minority retained	(600)

Table 6.1 Alternative expansions of equitized profit

	SSAP1	Proportional	Conventional	Entity
Sales	400,000	480,000	500,000	500,000
COGS	(228,000)	(268,000)	(278,000)	(278,000)
Distribn. expenses	(70,000)	(81,200)	(84,000)	(84,000)
Admin. expenses	(30,000)	(34,800)	(36,000)	(36,000)
Goodwill		(1,600)	(1,600)	(2,000)
Associate PBT	22,400			
Profit before tax	94,400	94,400	100,400	100,000
Corporation tax	(40,000)	(52,000)	(55,000)	(55,000)
Corpn tax assoc.	(12,000)			
Profit after tax	42,400	42,400	45,400	45,000
Less minority			(3,000)	
Attrib. profit	42,400	42,400	42,400	45,000
Dividends – L	(20,000)	(20,000)	(20,000)	(20,000)
Dividends minority				(2,000)
Retained earnings	22,400	22,400	22,400	23,000*

* £22,400 (majority share) + £600 (minority share).

Table 6.2   Consolidated P & L under different expansions

Under the entity approach the minority share of retained earnings is aggregated with the majority share to give *entity* retained earnings. Under conventional consolidation it is included in the *single* figure for minority interests in the balance sheet.

Consolidated profit and loss accounts under proportional and entity consolidation are homogeneous, dealing with the subsidiary on an 80 per cent and 100 per cent basis respectively. *Conventional consolidation* is a *two-tier hybrid*. Revenues and expenses are reported on a 100 per cent basis. Half-way down the minority is removed as a single lump, and then the rest is on an 80 per cent basis, focusing on profits attributable to parent company shareholders.

Again consolidation can be viewed conceptually as *equitization and expansion*. However, the *means* of obtaining the desired result is via a cancellation worksheet, to be discussed later.

Example 6.6   Disposal of majority owned subsidiary

(This example can be omitted without loss of continuity.) To complete the discussion on disposal of subsidiaries, assume the 80 per cent owned subsidiary is disposed of half-way through the year for £88,000 (i.e. 80 per cent of disposal proceeds for the 100 per cent owned subsidiary in Example 6.3). Again, its results should be included to the date of disposal (SSAP 14), and profit on disposal be calculated against the equitized amount at disposal. This is evaluated by *contracting* the subsidiary's balances (assets, liabilities, goodwill *and* minority) into a single amount. By the fundamental identity in Chapter 4, this equals cost plus attributable retained earnings:

Equitized investment

= Cost + Attributable RE 31 March 1983 to 30 September 1985

= Cost + (80% × Smallnesse RE – Consol. adj. (g/w))

= 80,000 + 80% × (37,500 – 30,000) – 2.5 × 1,600 = 82,000

Profit on disposal = 88,000 – 82,000 = 6,000

The profit and loss worksheet in this case is shown below. Again there is no effect on the balance sheet cancellation table. (For comparison, all calculations here are 80 per cent of the earlier disposal of the 100 per cent subsidiary in Example 6.3.)

Consolidated P & L – complete disposal of 80 per cent subsidiary – year ending 31 March 1986

	Largesse	Smallnesse 6 months	Intra-gp elim.	Disp. of subsid.	G/will 6 months	Minor.	Consol.
Sales	400,000	100,000	(50,000)				450,000
COGS	(228,000)	(75,000)	50,000				(253,000)
Other exp.	(100,000)	(10,000)					(110,000)
Goodwill					(800)		(800)
Corpn tax	(40,000)	(7,500)					(47,500)
Minority						(1,500)	(1,500)
Disp. profit*				6,000			6,000
Dividends	(20,000)						(20,000)
Ret. earnings	12,000	7,500	–	6,000	(800)	(1,500)	23,200

* SSAP 6, discussed later in this chapter, requires such disposals to be disclosed as extraordinary items; and a breakdown of the total.

Exercises

6.5   Assume the facts as in Exercise 6.1, except that Overbearing acquires a 60 per cent stake in Inadequate for £150,000 (i.e. 60% × £250,000) and that the interim and final dividends payable by the subsidiary are respectively £20,000 and £30,000. So Inadequate's retained earnings become £15,000.

(a)   Calculate the equitized share in the group profit after tax for the year applicable to Inadequate.

(b)   Produce a table showing expansions of this equitized figure according to various concepts of consolidation.

(c)   Produce consolidated profit and loss accounts under the various concepts of consolidation.

(d)   Contrast the treatment of minorities under the different approaches.

6.6   Assuming a 60 per cent original takeover as in Exercise 6.5, the investment in Inadequate was completely disposed of on 31 March 1986 for £180,000 (i.e. 60% × 300,000).

(a)   Calculate the amount of the equitized investment on disposal.

(b)   Prepare a profit and loss worksheet for the group at 30 June 1986.

ALIGNMENT ADJUSTMENTS
UNDER CONVENTIONAL CONSOLIDATION

For the purposes of later sections, the following information is added to Example 6.5 (minority interests).

1. Smallnesse sold to Largesse £100,000 of goods during the year. The opening stock of such goods held by Largesse was £10,000, and the closing stock was £15,000. The mark-up on cost of such goods was 25 per cent. These intra-group stocks are included in total opening and closing stocks held by both companies as follows:

	Largesse	Smallnesse
Opening stock	40,000	25,000
Closing stock	50,000	30,000

(b) At acquisition, fixed assets of Smallnesse used for distribution were revalued upwards by £10,000 for consolidation purposes only. The fixed assets concerned were depreciated straight line over a four-year period.

Case 1: intra-group transfers

Stock profits in opening and closing stocks as a result of incomplete intra-group transfers are calculated as follows. Since stock figures represent 125 per cent of cost, stock profits unrealized by the group are:

Opening stock £10,000 × 25/125 = £2,000
Closing stock £15,000 × 25/125 = £3,000

The former is a *deferral* from last year to this year. The latter is a deferral from this accounting period to the next (see pages 109–10).

Consider sales and cost of sales of both companies. From the example data and the calculations above, consider the following analysis:

	Largesse	Smallnesse	Transfers elimination	Profits	Consolidated
Sales	400,000	200,000	(100,000)		500,000
Cost of sales:					
Opening stock	(40,000)	(25,000)		2,000	(63,000)
Purchases	(238,000)*	(155,000)*	100,000		(293,000)*
Closing stock	50,000	30,000		(3,000)	77,000
	(228,000)	(150,000)	100,000	(1,000)	(279,000)
Gross profit	172,000	50,000	—	(1,000)	221,000

Purchases are obtained by differencing (*). Intra-group sales of one company are purchases of the other and are eliminated to prevent double counting. Opening stock would have been adjusted to cost to the *group* in the *previous* period by a consolidation adjustment. This reduced cost now flows through into the consolidated profit and loss account. Thus, consolidated cost of sales is lower than the sum of the two companies' cost of sales by the amount of the adjustment. Closing stock is also adjusted to consolidated cost to the group, increasing consolidated cost of sales. In terms of Figure 5.3, consolidated profit is *increased* by the deferral from *last* year, and *decreased* by the deferral from *this* year. The net change in the consolidated adjustment to stocks is an *increase* in the credit (i.e. reduction) by £1,000, to £3,000, this increase being the subtotal of the 'profits elimination' column.

Case 2: fixed asset revaluation and extra depreciation

Equity at acquisition of the subsidiary is increased by £10,000, the majority share of which is 80% × £10,000 = £8,000, and hence goodwill is decreased from £16,000 to £8,000. Hence the annual amortization of goodwill will now be £8,000/10 = £800. A consolidation adjustment increases the depreciation charge by £2,500 (i.e. £10,000/4), forming a part of distribution expenses.

The consolidated profit and loss account worksheet

Table 6.3 comprises the worksheet *including* alignment adjustments. It is very important and forms the basis for consolidating profit and loss accounts in this book.

Adjustment columns

There is a column for each adjustment and as before, the subtotal of each column shows the destination and sign (debit or credit) of the entry outside equity. At the start of the year the provision for unrealized profits on intra-group stocks was £2,000. The total of the 'profit elim.' column shows that this is to be credited (negative) with a further £1,000, to bring to £3,000 the deduction from stocks. The net change in minority interests in the balance sheet is an increase (credit, negative) of £300, a share of profits of £2,300 less dividends received of £2,000. Consolidated goodwill is to be credited with £800. Note that accumulated depreciation is to be increased by £2,500 to its consolidated amount. All these are *consolidation adjustments* made in the consolidated working papers. Thus, the aggregate of the individual company profit and loss accounts is replaced by a consolidated total, and a number of adjustments to other balance sheet accounts.

In order to allow non-publication of a holding company profit and loss account, the amount of the profit dealt with in the accounts of the holding company, here £40,000, must be disclosed as a note.

Minority interests

The minority share of profit *after* tax is £2,300, and not £3,000 as previously, because of alignment adjustments for stock profits (£200) and extra depreciation (£500). Intra-group stock transfers are *upstream* and are eliminated according to the parent company extension approach (i.e. *originating* company's ownership,

	Largesse	Smallnesse	Intra-grp transfers	Profit elim.	Intra-grp dividends	Minority interests	Goodwill	Extra depn	Consol.
Sales	400,000	200,000	(100,000)						500,000
Cost of sales:									
Opening stock	(40,000)	(25,000)		2,000					
Purchases	(238,000)	(155,000)	100,000						(279,000)
Closing stock	50,000	30,000		(3,000)					
Distribution costs	(70,000)	(14,000)						(2,500)	(86,500)
Admin. expenses	(30,000)	(6,000)							(36,000)
Goodwill							(800)		(800)
Dividends receivable	8,000				(8,000)				–
Corporation tax	(40,000)	(15,000)							(55,000)
Minority interests						(2,300)			(2,300)
Dividends	(20,000)	(10,000)			8,000	2,000			(20,000)
Retained earnings	20,000	5,000		(1,000)	–	(300)	(800)	(2,500)	20,400

Table 6.3　Consolidated profit and loss account – Largesse–Smallnesse group (includes minority and stock adjustment) – year ended 31 March 1986

here 80 per cent). Therefore, holding company shareholders should bear 80 per cent of the *increase* in the provision, and minority 20 per cent. To prevent majority shareholders bearing the full £1,000, the minority share in profit is *reduced* (i.e. deferred) by £200, i.e. 20 per cent, leaving the majority to bear £800. Similarly, 20 per cent of extra depreciation (£2,500) charged in the top part of the statement (i.e. £500) is recharged to the minority, leaving the net charge to the majority of £2,000. Thus,

$$\text{Minority share} = 20\% \times (\text{Net profit } after \text{ tax} - \text{Stock adj.} - \text{Extra depn})$$
$$= 20\% \times (15,000 - 1,000 - 2,500) = £2,300$$

Exercise

6.7   The facts are as in Exercise 6.8, except for the following:
(a)   Ignore the balance sheet data.
(b)   Only consider profit and loss data as far as profit retained for the year (i.e. ignore retained profit b/f and c/f).
Required   Prepare a consolidated profit and loss account worksheet at 30 June 1986, including the effects of the above adjustments.

THE LINK WITH THE CONSOLIDATED BALANCE SHEET

A major objective of this book is to show how the various consolidated financial statements are interrelated, and so this section is extremely important. In a profit and loss account it is usual to show not only current year's transactions, but also retained earnings brought forward and carried forward. These figures link with retained earnings figures in the opening and closing balance sheets respectively; this section shows how to incorporate these linking figures into the cancellation table. At this point the profit and loss example in this chapter is linked with the Largesse–Smallnesse balance sheet in Example 4.1 (page 73), which is modified very slightly to include the consolidation adjustments introduced in this chapter (i.e. on stock profits, depreciation and amortization of goodwill).

The consolidated balance sheet

Table 6.4 takes the original balance sheet cancellation table in Table 4.1 and modifies it to include the alignment adjustments. Since stocks and fixed assets are to be adjusted, they are given additional columns. Goodwill is adjusted from £16,000 to £8,000 because of the fixed asset revaluation at acquisition. The goodwill write-off since acquisition is 3 × £800 = £2,400, and extra depreciation is 3 × £2,500 = £7,500. Only the *closing* deferral of stock profits affects the consolidated balance sheet.

	Inv.	Share capital	Share premium	Retained earnings	Goodwill	Minority	Stock	Other assets
Largesse	80	(130)	(70)	(120)	—	—	50	250
Smallnesse								
– at acquisition					(64)	(16)		
– post-acquisition				(8)		(2)		
Elimination	(80)				80			
Subtotal (as Table 4.1)	—	(130)	(70)	(128)	16	(18)	50	250
Additional information:								
Smallnesse								
– other balances							30	60
Consolidation adj.:								
– fixed asset rev.					(8)	(2)		10
– extra depn (3 yrs)				6		1.5		(7.5)
– goodwill w/o (3 yrs)				2.4	(2.4)			
– stock profits				2.4		0.6	(3)	
Consolidated	—	(130)	(70)	(117.2)	5.6	(17.9)	77	312.5

Table 6.4   Balance sheet cancellation table: acquisition approach

Deducing consolidated reserves brought forward and carried forward

Consider the amounts for each company. Smallnesse's changes in retained earnings prior to acquisition are segregated, since such earnings need to be eliminated. In the following analysis, the closing reserves of both companies and the reserves at acquisition of Smallnesse are obtained from the balance sheet data in Example 4.1, and the change in retained earnings for the year for both companies from the profit and loss account data in this chapter. The missing data is obtained by differencing.

	Largesse	Smallnesse
Reserves at acquisition – 31 March 1983		30,000
Change in retained earnings from acquisition to 31 March 1985 (differencing)		5,000
Opening reserves – 31 March 1985 (differencing)	100,000	35,000
Change in retained earnings for year	20,000	5,000
Closing reserves – 31 March 1986	120,000	40,000

For the subsidiary, the following relationship holds:

Closing RE = RE at acq. + Change from acq. to start of year + Change for year
40,000 = 30,000 + 5,000 + 5,000

To determine its contribution to *consolidated* retained earnings, pre-acquisition earnings of £30,000 are eliminated. The following equation shows its contribution (80 per cent) *after* removing the pre-acquisition portion:

Contrib to consol. RE = Change from *acq.* + Change for year
                         to *start* of yr

(closing)   (opening)   (P & L)
80% × 10,000   = 80% × 5,000   + 80% × 5,000

And hence consolidated retained earnings (CRE) would be:

Opening CRE = Holding co. + Subsid. contrib. to start of year
           = 100,000   + 80% × 5,000 = 104,000

Closing CRE = Opening   + HC retained + Subsid. retained for year
           = 104,000   + 20,000   + 80% × 5,000
           = 128,000

Analysis of Smallnesse retained earnings

A systematic way of obtaining the above results is via a diagrammatic analysis as in Table 6.5. The retained earnings of the subsidiary are split (as described above) into three time periods; pre-acquisition, the time from acquisition to the start of the current year, and the current year. For each of these subperiods, the change in retained earnings is apportioned between the majority share and the minority share.

Date	Majority share (80%)	Minority share (20%)	Time period
31 March 1983 (30)	80% × 30 = 24	20% × 30 = 6	Pre-acquisition
31 March 1985 (35)	80% × 5 = 4	20% × 5 = 1	Prior year
31 March 1986 (40)	80% × 5 = 4	20% × 5 = 1	Current year

Table 6.5   Analysis of Smallnesse's retained earnings

Since the minority interest is ongoing, there is no need to split pre-acquisition and prior year, and the 6 + 1 = 7 can be combined. The holding company's portion (80 per cent) of pre-acquisition retained earnings of Smallnesse, £24,000, is eliminated in determining consolidated goodwill.

Deducing reserves brought forward and carried forward – with alignment adjustments

The diagrammatic analysis in Table 6.5 can be expanded to include alignment adjustments. Using the same format, alignment adjustments are split between majority and minority and are placed respectively on the left and right hand sides of the diagram according to the period to which they relate. Table 6.6 encapsulates the contribution of subsidiary retained earnings to both consolidated balance sheets and profit and loss accounts.

Date	Majority share (80%) Alignment adj. G/will Stock Depn					Minority share (20%) Alignment adj. Stock Depn		Time period
31 March 1983 (30)				24	7			Pre-acquisition
31 March 1985 (35)	(1.6)	(1.6)	(4.0)	4		(0.4)	(1.0)	Prior year
31 March 1986 (40)	1.6 (0.8)	(2.4)	(2.0)	4	1	0.4 (0.6)	(0.5)	Current year

Table 6.6   Analysis of alignment adjustments

Alignment adjustments

Two years' goodwill was written off prior to 31 March 1985, and one year more in the year to 31 March 1986. Since minority share of goodwill is not recognized under conventional consolidation, its write-off is made only against the majority. For the stock adjustments, in *upstream* sales as in this example, 'profit' eliminations are made according to the ownership proportions of the *originating* company. Hence the adjustments (£2,000 at 31 March 1985, and £3,000 at 31

March 1986) are split 80:20. Extra depreciation is split 80%:20%.

The subsidiary's contribution to the current year's consolidated retained earnings is obtained by adding together the majority share of profit ($+4$) plus all the alignment adjustments in the bottom left-hand corner of Table 6.6 (viz. $+1.6$ $-0.8 - 2.4 - 2.0$) making 0.4 (i.e. £400). Note how the *current year* change in retained earnings (i.e. the bottom line of the consolidated profit and loss account) is affected by the reversal of the previous year's stock adjustment, 1.6, and the setting up of this year's, (2.4). When this is added to previous years' retained earnings to get the *balance sheet* total, the 1.6 of the current year and the (1.6) of prior years cancel to zero and *only* the *closing* adjustment (2.4) is left.

Calculating opening and closing reserve figures for the cancellation table

From Table 6.6 we can deduce the following relationships (£000):

Subsidiary contribution to consolidated opening reserves (middle left)

$$= (1.6) + (1.6) + (4.0) + 4 = (3.2)$$
   G/Will Stock Depn

Subsidiary contribution to consolidated retained earnings for current year (P & L)

$$= (0.8) + 1.6 + (2.4) + (2.0) + 4 = 0.4$$

   G/Will   Stock   Depn

Thus, subsidiary contribution to consolidated closing reserves

$$= (3.2) + 0.4 = (2.8)$$

Hence:

Consolidated opening reserves	= Holding company + Subsidiary
	= 100,000 − 3,200 = 96,800
Consolidated ret. earnings (P & L)	= 20,000 + 400 = 20,400
Consolidated closing reserves	= 120,000 − 2,800 = 117,200

The following relationships can be deduced for minority interests (£000):

Minority opening retained earnings
$$= (0.4) + (1.0) + 7 = 5.6 \text{ (top right)}$$
   stock   depn

Minority current year *retained*
$$= 0.4 + (0.6) + (0.5) + 1 = 0.3 \text{ (bottom right)}$$
      stock

Minority closing retained earnings
$$= 5.6 + 0.3 = 5.9 \text{ (total right)}$$

Details	Individual statements		Intra-group transactions			Goodwill	Minority	Pre-acq. profits	Extra depn	Consol.
	Largesse	Smallnesse	Sales	Stock pr.	Dividends					
Reserves b/f	100,000	35,000		(2,000)		(1,600)	(5,600)	(24,000)	(5,000)	96,800
Sales:	400,000	200,000	(100,000)							500,000
Cost of sales:										
Opening stock	(40,000)	(25,000)		2,000						
Purchases	(238,000)	(155,000)	100,000							(279,000)
Closing stock	50,000	30,000		(3,000)						
Distribution costs	(70,000)	(14,000)							(2,500)	(86,500)
Admin. expenses	(30,000)	(6,000)								(36,000)
Goodwill						(800)				(800)
Divs. receivable	8,000				(8,000)					
Corporation tax	(40,000)	(15,000)								(55,000)
Minority interests (in after-tax profits)							(2,300)			(2,300)
Dividends:										
– interim	(10,000)				8,000		2,000			(10,000)
– final	(10,000)									(10,000)
Profit for year retained (subtotal)	20,000	5,000		(1,000)		(800)	(300)		(2,500)	20,400
Reserves c/f	120,000	40,000		(3,000)		(2,400)	(5,900)	(24,000)	(7,500)	117,200

Table 6.7 Consolidated profit and loss account – Largesse–Smallnesse group (includes opening/closing reserves) – year ended 31 March 1986

The complete profit and loss cancellation worksheet

Consider now how these relationships are incorporated into the final worksheet presented in this chapter, Table 6.7, which is similar to earlier worksheets except that it now includes a top line for consolidated reserves brought forward, and a bottom line for such reserves carried forward.

Reconciling reserves brought forward with the diagrammatic analysis in Table 6.6

The top line, opening retained earnings, is a grossed-up version of the diagrammatic analysis of consolidated retained earnings in Table 6.6, in which the starting point comprises the *whole* of the subsidiary's retained earnings, from which pre-acquisition and minority retained earnings are removed to determine the consolidated figure. Under the diagrammatic approach, the subsidiary's contribution starts as a *net* figure. The top line (gross) approach and the diagrammatic (net) approach can be reconciled easily by breaking down the minority figure (£5,600) and reallocating its components as follows.

The top line (in £000) is:

L	*S*	*Stock pr.*	*Goodwill*		*Minority*	*Pre-acq.*	*Depn*	*Consol.*
100	+ 35	− 2	− 1.6	−	5.6	− 24	− 5	= 96.8

$$- (7 - 0.4 - 1)$$

Stock Depn

Reallocating and netting off the minority components and pre-acquisition profits, we get:

L	*S*	*Stock pr.*	*Goodwill*	*Depn*	*Consol.*
100 + (35 − 24 − 7)	− (2 − 0.4)	− 1.6	− (5 − 1)	= 96.8

Which is then the net version used in the diagrammatic analysis, viz.:

L	*S*	*Stock pr.*	*Goodwill*	*Depn*	*Consol.*
100	+ 4	− 1.6	− 1.6	− 4	= 96.8

Thus the diagrammatic analysis can be used as a check on the (grossed-up) top line for opening reserves, and to provide many other of its elements (e.g. pre-acq. profits, 24, and minority, 5.6). Note however that in the cancellation table top line, the stock profit and extra depreciation figures are *100 per cent* figures, not *majority* figures as in the diagrammatic analysis. Similar relationships can be deduced for the profit for the year subtotal and for the closing reserves (bottom line).

Totals of adjustment columns – completing the double entry

Previously subtotals of adjustment columns gave the *increment or decrement* to consolidated provisions, etc. Here the bottom line gives *total* consolidated provisions/balances in the consolidated balance sheet.

£(3,000) is the *total* credit to consolidated stocks
£(2,400) is the *total* written off (credit) consolidated goodwill
£(5,900) is the *total* retained earnings in minority interests
£(24,000) is the *total* retained earnings eliminated to obtain goodwill

The balance sheet minority interest figure also includes its share capital, share premium *and* retained earnings, and pre-acquisition equity is merely one element in computing goodwill. From the original data (page 72):

Minority interest at 31 March 1986
= 20% × s. cap. + 20% × s. prem. + 20% × rev. res. + 20% × RE
= 20% × 35 + 20% × 15 + 20% × 10 + 5.9 = 17.9

Goodwill
= Inv. − 80% × s. cap. − 80% × s. prem. − 80% × rev. res. − 80% RE at acq.
= 80 − 80% × 35 − 80% × 15 − 80% × 10 − *24* (above) = 8

less accumulated write-off (£2,400), gives £5,600. The figures for minority and goodwill thus both tie up with the balance sheet table in Table 6.4.

Using the diagrammatic analysis to check minority interests in current year profits

Directly from the subsidiary's profit and loss account we can deduce that the minority interest in profit *after* tax (including alignment adjustments is 20% × (15,000 (profit after tax) − 1,000 (stock profit increase) − 2,500 (extra depreciation)) = £2,300. The diagrammatic analysis can be used to check this direct computation. In it the minority interest in *retained earnings* for the year was deduced as £300. These two figures can be linked by adding back minority dividends viz.:

Minority interest in *retained earnings* for the year =   300 (diagram)
+
Minority dividends   = 2,000
=
Minority interest in *profits* for the year   = 2,300 (P & L)

Such a check is extremely useful in more complex examples, where a separate diagrammatic analysis can be produced for each subsidiary.

Alignment adjustments

In the diagrammatic analysis in many instances, consolidated reserves only include the majority share of alignment adjustments (e.g. on incomplete upstream intra-group transfers). However, in the revenue and expense section of the cancellation worksheet, alignment adjustments are disclosed at their gross (100 per cent) amount, and the minority share (where appropriate) is deducted in the single figure, minority share in profits *after* tax. Thus, the consolidated retained earnings for the year subtotal incorporates net amounts for the adjustments and hence ties up with the diagrammatic analysis.

Abbreviating the consolidation process

When the reader is familiar with the above relationships and is proficient in their *practice*, one can afford to dispense with the diagrammatic analysis of reserves, and to do calculations directly on the cancellation table. Also, as a further short-cut, the analysis columns can be abridged into two, a debit and a credit column as shown in Table 6.8, the approach taken by many accounting texts. Fine for examination purposes *after* one understands the relationships discussed earlier – it is not very helpful in aiding an initial understanding of these relationships. It is prone to error, and in complex examples in practice, a fuller layout is often used. The reader is advised to become familiar with the full approach before abridging it.

	Largesse	Smallnesse	Adjustments Debit	Credit	Consolidated
Ret. earnings b/f	100,000	35,000		(2,000)	96,800
				(1,600)	
				(5,600)	
				(5,000)	
				(24,000)	
Sales	400,000	200,000		(100,000)	500,000
Cost of sales:					
Opening stock	(40,000)	(25,000)	2,000		
Purchases	(238,000)	(155,000)	100,000		(279,000)
Closing stock	50,000	30,000		(3,000)	
Distribution costs	(70,000)	(14,000)		(2,500)	(86,500)
Admin. expenses	(30,000)	(6,000)			(36,000)
Goodwill				(800)	(800)
Divs. receivable	8,000			(8,000)	—
Corporation tax	(40,000)	(15,000)			(55,000)
Minority interests				(2,300)	(2,300)
Dividends – interim	(10,000)	(10,000)	10,000		(10,000)
– final	(10,000)				(10,000)
Ret. profit for year	20,000	5,000	112,000	(116,600)	20,400
Ret. earnings c/f	120,000	40,000	112,000	(154,800)	117,200

Table 6.8   Consolidated P & L account in abbreviated format – year ended 31 March 1986

Exercise

6.8   The Overbearing–Inadequate example is repeated with additional data to show the link between statements. Overbearing plc is the holding company of Inadequate Ltd. It acquired a 60 per cent interest on 1 July 1983 for £150,000, when the share capital, share premium and retained earnings of Inadequate were respectively £50,000, £70,000 and £80,000. The draft financial statements are as follows:

Profit and loss accounts for the year ended 30 June 1986 (£000)

	Overbearing	Inadequate
Sales	900	500
Cost of sales	(300)	(250)
Distribution costs	(250)	(50)
Administration expenses	(150)	(70)
Dividends receivable	30	—
Corporation tax	(100)	(65)
Dividends – interim	(30)	(20)
– final	(50)	(30)
Profit retained for year	50	15
Retained profit b/f	200	140
Retained profit c/f	250	155

Balance sheets at 30 June 1986 (£000)

	Overbearing	Inadequate
Fixed assets	300	200
Investment in Inadequate	250	—
Stocks	220	180
Other assets	120	170
Liabilities	(320)	(275)
Share capital	(100)	(50)
Share premium	(220)	(70)
Retained earnings	(250)	(155)

Other information

1. The directors of Overbearing decided to write off consolidated goodwill over a five-year period. When SSAP 22 came into force, they decided to continue this policy.
2. Overbearing sold to Inadequate £200,000 of goods during the year. Opening stocks of such goods held by Inadequate amounted to £12,000, and closing stocks £14,000. The mark-up on cost of such goods was 33⅓ per cent.
3. At acquisition, certain buildings used by central administration were revalued from £60,000 to £80,000. The remaining life of those buildings at that time was estimated at twenty years (straight line).

Required

(a) Prepare a balance sheet cancellation table at 30 June 1986.
(b) (i) Analyse diagrammatically Inadequate's retained earnings at that date.
    (ii) Incorporate alignment adjustments into the diagram.
    (iii) Calculate consolidated reserves and minority interests at 30 June 1986.
(c) Prepare a profit and loss worksheet for the year ended 30 June 1986, linking the reserves c/f with the balance sheet cancellation in (a). (The solution to Exercise 6.7 can be adapted by adding a top (retained earnings b/f) line and a bottom line (c/f).)
(d) Discuss the relationships between figures in the profit and loss worksheet and the balance sheet cancellation table.

DISCLOSURES IN THE CONSOLIDATED PROFIT AND LOSS ACCOUNT

This section reviews disclosure requirements for published consolidated profit and loss accounts. Some knowledge is assumed of the relevant pronouncements in the context of individual company statements.

Companies Act 1985 – profit and loss account formats

The Companies Act 1985, in Schedule 4 Part 1, requires the choice of one from four possible formats for the profit and loss account. Formats 1 and 2 are in vertical format, whereas 3 and 4 which segregate income from charges are rarely used in the UK. The choice between 1 and 2 is significant, in that 1 analyses expenses by *function* (e.g. cost of sales, distribution costs, administrative expenses), whereas 2 analyses expenses by *type* (e.g. cost of raw materials used, depreciation, staff costs, etc.). In this chapter, the examples comply with Format 1.

If Format 1 is used, items like depreciation, goodwill, etc. are apportioned over the relevant functional headings (e.g. manufacturing depreciation will be classified as cost of goods sold, etc.). The Act does not make clear how goodwill write-off is to be classified. Most companies using Format 1 (see, for example, the survey by Hardcastle and Renshall, 1985) do not disclose where goodwill is included when gradual amortization is chosen. If this option is chosen, SSAP 22 requires an analysis of movements on the goodwill account, including the amount amortized in the year, but not the disclosure of the heading under which this amount is included. Using the Act's flexibility to allow increased disclosure, goodwill amortized is given a separate heading in the examples here, since it is difficult to classify under another functional heading.

In this chapter it is assumed that fixed assets revalued are related to distribution. If they relate to manufacturing, part of extra depreciation relates to cost of sales, and part to closing stocks if absorption costing is used. The charge for cost of goods sold should therefore strictly include any extra depreciation in opening stocks, plus the extra depreciation charge for the year, less extra depreciation in closing stocks. In practice, the accounting policies of companies in this area are rarely disclosed. Possibly companies make such an adjustment, or decide it is immaterial in a subsidiary where intra-group stock levels remain approximately constant. However, it may not be immaterial if a new subsidiary is acquired during the year, the revaluation adjustment is large, stock levels change substantially, or the absorption basis or rates change substantially. This problem arises under all formats.

The order of presentation in group accounts

Paragraph 35 of SSAP 14 requires that minority interests 'should be shown separately . . . after arriving at group profit or loss after tax [i.e. should be measured after tax but before extraordinary items]. Minority interests in extraordinary items should be deducted from the related amounts in the consolidated profit and loss account.'

SSAP 1 requires for associated companies the separate disclosure of the holding company's share of:
(a) profit before tax;
(b) taxation;
(c) extraordinary items;
(d) net profit retained by associated companies.
If additional information is to be given (e.g. turnover, depreciation, etc.) it should be done by means of a note, not in the statements themselves.

Extraordinary items: SSAP 6

SSAP 6 (revised 1986), entitled 'Extraordinary items and prior year adjustments', considers disclosure issues concerning items which affect the profit and loss account. One of the purposes of SSAP 6 is to standardize presentation and ensure most current year items do not bypass the profit and loss account (i.e. an 'all-inclusive' income concept). It tries to ensure proper disclosure of matters significant for an appreciation of a company (or group's) performance. It distinguishes:

1. *Exceptional* items – material items which derive from the ordinary activities of the entity and which, because of their size and incidence, need separate disclosure to give a true and fair view. These are disclosed as a part of profit *before* taxation and extraordinary items.

2. *Extraordinary* items – 'material items which derive from events or transactions that fall outside the ordinary activities of the company and which are therefore not expected to recur frequently or regularly' – disclosed net of tax under a separate heading *after* profit after taxation.

3. *Prior year adjustments*, which are defined in a legalistic way, only include 'material adjustments ... arising from changes in accounting policies or from the correction of fundamental errors. They do not include normal recurring corrections or adjustments of accounting estimates made in prior years.' These are shown as a restatement of retained earnings brought forward and do not have to appear on the face of the profit and loss account. Comparatives need to be restated too.

4. *Reserve movements* – under SSAP 6 only specifically defined items can bypass the profit and loss account and be taken direct to reserves. These tightly defined items include the immediate write-off of goodwill (SSAP 22) and foreign currency translation gains or losses under the closing rate approach (SSAP 20) (discussed in Chapter 9). The revised standard (unlike its original version or revised exposure draft ED 36) explicitly ignores revaluations of fixed assets. However, under Schedule 4 to the Companies Act 1985, 'Alternative accounting rules', such revaluation surpluses should be taken to a revaluation reserve, bypassing the profit and loss account.

Only extraordinary items are discussed further here. These form part of the *second tier* of the consolidated profit and loss account and so their *aggregate* shows only the *majority portion* of such items (80 per cent). SSAP 6 requires components making up this amount (including the amount attributable to minority interests) to be disclosed either on the face of the profit and loss account or as a note, and the amount of taxation relating to extraordinary items. SSAP 1 does *not* seem to require the separate disclosure of the tax element of *associates'* extraordinary items.

Where a group chooses the gradual amortization policy for goodwill under SSAP 22, the gradual amortization itself is not regarded as extraordinary. Where this policy is followed and it is necessary for, say, the holding company to make a provision for the permanent diminution in value of the investment, whether the consequent write-down of consolidated goodwill is extraordinary or exceptional depends on whether the event giving rise to the write-down is itself extraordinary or not (paragraph 4(d)). If the immediate write-down policy for goodwill is chosen under SSAP 22, the amount goes to reserves, bypassing the profit and loss account.

SSAP 6 gives the discontinuation of a business segment through termination or disposal as an example of a possible extraordinary item (paragraphs 4(a) and 11). Costs relating to reorganization of or redundancies arising from *continuing* business segments are, if material, exceptional not extraordinary. The definition of a 'business segment' does not concern us here except to note that a subsidiary qualifies as a business segment. Another example of a possible extraordinary item is the 'sale of an investment not acquired with the intention of resale, such as investments in subsidiary and associated companies' (paragraph 4(b)).

Thus, the profit or loss on the termination (e.g. by liquidation) or disposal of a subsidiary could be treated as an extraordinary item, if surrounding circumstances warrant it. In accordance with SSAP 14, results to the date of disposal/termination should be included in the consolidated profit and loss account. In paragraph 12, SSAP 6 states that 'Such provisions [for termination] are not prevented from being treated as extraordinary items merely because they occur and are recognized over a number of accounting periods where this is either the ongoing result of a single decision or because of a number of separate decisions.'

Example 6.7   Published consolidated profit and loss account layout

Suppose the following is added to the previous examples: Smallnesse's profit and loss account included the following extraordinary item, giving a consolidated profit and loss account as shown in Table 6.9.

Loss from expropriation of assets in Niganda	9,000
Taxation relating thereto	(5,000)
	4,000

Turnover:		£
Sales for year		500,000
Less: Cost of sales		(279,000)
Gross profit		221,000
Distribution costs		(86,500)
Administration expenses		(36,000)
Goodwill amortization		(800)
Profit on ordinary activities before taxation		97,700
Taxation on profit on ordinary activities		(55,000)
Profit on ordinary activities after taxation		42,700
Minority interests		(2,300)
Attributable profits on ordinary activities after taxation		40,400
Extraordinary items:		
Extraordinary charges: expropriation of assets	(9,000)	
Taxation on extraordinary loss	5,000	
Minority interests in extraordinary loss	800	(3,200)
Profit for the financial year		37,200
Dividends		
– interim		(10,000)
– final		(10,000)
Retained profit for the financial year		17,200

Note: A statement of movement in reserves is disclosed on page xx.

Table 6.9 Largesse–Smallnesse group – consolidated profit and loss account – year ended 31 March 1986

Note that the *total* amount for extraordinary items is net of minority interests. The total minority share in *profits* for the year is now:

Ordinary activities (2,300) – Extraordinary activities 800 = £(1,500)

A statement of movement on reserves (including movement on retained earnings) is required and an indication on the face of the profit and loss account as to where it is included (paragraph 35).

SUMMARY

Two areas are important; the *elimination* of intra-group *flows* (e.g. sales, purchases, dividends), and making *alignment adjustments* to reflect the change in scope of the accounts to a group basis.

When subsidiaries are *acquired* during the year, either the revenues and expenses can be included from the date of acquisition, or included for the whole year and a single amount for pre-acquisition profits removed. When subsidiaries are *disposed of*, all their balances are *contracted* into a single *equitized* amount at the date of disposal, and the profit or loss on disposal matches this amount with the proceeds. When subsidiaries are *converted to associates*, a similar procedure is followed as on disposals. From the date of conversion, the associate profit before tax, tax and retained earnings are separately disclosed (a variant of one line consolidation).

As in the balance sheet there is a *spectrum* of approaches for the treatment of minority in the consolidated profit and loss account. Conventional consolidation (the parent approach) results in a *two-tier* profit and loss account. Above minority, 100 per cent of revenues and expenses are shown (except for goodwill). The minority share in profits *after* tax is removed and below this, the statement deals with the majority share only.

Alignment adjustments follow the same logic as in Chapter 5. Note that stock adjustments for the previous period are reversed and for this period deferred. The minority calculation is affected by certain alignment adjustments (e.g. where they are split pro rata in upstream sales). The link between balance sheet and profit and loss account was demonstrated by using a *diagrammatic* analysis of the subsidiary's retained earnings and alignment adjustments.

Finally, Companies Act layouts and the treatment of extraordinary items in group accounts were discussed. Minority interests in profits *after* tax are deducted *before* the extraordinary items section. Thus, *in aggregate*, extraordinary items are shown net of the minority (though SSAP 6 requires disclosure of the components making up this total including taxation and the minority share). The termination or disposal of a 'business segment' (which includes a subsidiary) is cited as a *possible* extraordinary item.

NOTES

1. If the dividend for the first 6 months (£4,000) *had* been recorded by Largesse it would be pre-acquisition, reducing the investment. Subsidiary profit *after* dividend would be used in computing goodwill, giving the same result as if the transaction were reversed, i.e.

   $(100-4) - ((35 + 15 + 35) - \frac{6}{12} \times 7) = £7.5.$

2. Shares are bought or sold *cum div* (with rights to receive forthcoming dividends) or *ex div* (without such rights). If subsidiary shares are purchased *cum div*, the investment is reduced by the forthcoming dividend; if *ex div*, no such adjustment is needed. If they are sold *cum div*, dividends go to the new holder, so subsidiary profits *before* dividends contribute to equitized cost; if *ex div*, profits *after* dividends can be used.

FURTHER READING

The further reading for this chapter is technical. However, many of the arguments and readings of the previous two chapters apply.

Accounting Standards Committee (1971) *SSAP 1 – Accounting for associated companies* (revised 1982), paragraphs 19–23, ASC, London.

Accounting Standards Committee (1974) *SSAP 6 – Extraordinary items and prior year adjustments* (revised 1986), ASC, London.

Accounting Standards Committee (1978) *SSAP 14 – Group Accounts*, paragraphs 30–1, ASC, London.

7 Consolidated Statements of Sources and Applications of Funds

The statement of sources and applications of funds is probably the least understood of the major financial statements. Produced as a by-product from the other consolidated statements, it is frequently defined in terms of the methods used to prepare it, rather than conceptually. Often it is (mistakenly) viewed as being the statement which links the other statements or reaches *all* the parts other statements do not reach! Heath (1977) argues that, as a result of trying to pack too much into published funds statements, the term 'funds' becomes so broad as to become meaningless and the statement, in trying to include too much, ceases to communicate information effectively. This assertion is examined later.

The first section of this chapter explores the nature of funds statements using a *matrix* approach. This approach is then used in the second section to prepare consolidated funds statements, focusing on specific aspects relating to group accounts, and in the next chapter to explain the translation of foreign currency financial statements. The third section examines the usefulness of such statements.

INTERRELATIONSHIPS BETWEEN FINANCIAL STATEMENTS: THE FUNDS FLOW MATRIX

The funds flow matrix is introduced as a useful method for producing funds statements, and also to clarify the interrelationships between the balance sheet, profit and loss account, and statement of sources and application of funds. Consider the following example.

Example 7.1   Marx and Sparks – the funds flow matrix

Marx and Sparks plc owns a revolutionary chain of clothes shops. Its draft opening balance sheet at 31 December 1985 is shown in Table 7.1.

	£	£
Fixed assets – cost		50,000
– accumulated depreciation		(30,000)
		20,000
Current assets:		
Stocks	30,000	
Debtors	43,000	
Cash	10,000	
	83,000	
Creditors within one year:		
Merchandise creditors	(35,000)	
Dividends	(5,000)	
	(40,000)	
Net current assets		43,000
Creditors more than one year: Loans		(13,000)
		50,000
Capital and reserves:		
Share capital and premium		10,000
Reserves		40,000
		50,000

Table 7.1   Marx and Sparks plc – balance sheet at 31 December 1985

Over the year, the following transactions took place:
1. Sales on credit £543,000. Receipts from debtors £521,000.
2. Merchandise purchases £475,000. Payments to creditors £470,000.
3. Fixed asset purchase £20,000, of which £10,000 was paid in cash, and the balance by a share issue to the supplier of the asset.
4. Further share issue £5,000 and loan issue £4,000, both for cash.
5. £9,000 of the loans were redeemed for £7,000 in cash.
6. Fixed asset (cost £10,000, accumulated depreciation £7,000) sold for £2,000 cash.
7. Miscellaneous expenses £19,000 paid in cash.
8. Closing stock was valued at £28,000.
9. Depreciation for the year was £5,000.
10. Dividends proposed for 1986 were £6,000.

Normally, the above transactions would be dealt with via 'T' accounts. Here the same process has been summarized in Table 7.2 using the funds flow matrix.

Details	Cash	Debtors	Stock	Fixed assets	Accum. depn	Creditors	Divs. payable	Loan	Share cap./prem.	Retained earnings
Opening balance sheet	10	43	30	50	(30)	(35)	(5)	(13)	(10)	(40)
Bookkeeping entries:										
Sales		543								(543)
Receipts	521	(521)								
Purchases			475			(475)				
Payments	(470)					470				
New fixed asset	(10)			20					(10)	
Share issue	5								(5)	
Loan issue	4							(4)		
Loans redeemed	(7)							9		(2)
Sale of fixed asset	2			(10)	7					1
Miscellaneous expenses	(19)									19
Dividends proposed							(6)			6
Depreciation					(5)					5
Deduced by difference:										
Dividends paid	(5)						5			
COGS			(477)							477
Closing balance sheet	31	65	28	60	(28)	(40)	(6)	(8)	(25)	(77)

Table 7.2   Marx and Sparks plc – transactions matrix (£000)

The basic layout of the matrix in Table 7.2 is as follows:

Opening balance sheet balances
Transactions
Amounts found by differencing
Closing balance sheet balances

Each column represents a balance sheet account. Consider dividends payable.

'T' Account

Dividends payable

Divs. paid	5,000	Balance b/f	5,000
		Divs. payable	6,000
Balance c/f	6,000		
	11,000		11,000
		Balance b/f	6,000

Column

Details	Divs. payable
Opening balance	(5,000)
Divs. payable	(6,000)
Divs. paid	(5,000)
Closing balance	(6,000)

The column mirrors a 'T' account but in vertical format. Debits are represented as positive (+) and credits as negative (−). Debits equal credits (each entry adds to zero across the matrix). The top and bottom lines of the matrix show opening and closing balance sheets and the right-hand column the profit and loss account. The profit and loss account is a *flow* statement, showing why retained earnings have changed over the period.

A funds statement is also a flow statement. A funds flow statement can be defined as a statement which shows *why* a particular set of accounts has changed over a period, e.g. a working capital flow statement shows why current assets less current liabilities in aggregate have changed. The change can be deduced by differencing opening and closing working capital *balances*, but the *flow* statement shows *why*. In practice in the UK, published funds statements are often (but not necessarily) based on working capital.

Consider now a funds statement based on working capital. For reasons discussed later, working capital is defined here as current assets less current liabilities *excluding dividends payable*. What flows affect the working capital 'fund'? To determine this we add together the four columns (accounts) – stock, debtors, cash and creditors – to see which flows (i.e. double entries) affect the *aggregate* of these columns (accounts). The matrix can be condensed to show this by aggregating the accounts (columns) comprising working capital into a single column. In the condensed matrix in Table 7.3, the first column does this.

What sort of flows affect working capital? Not 'purchases' since it is *totally internal* to the four working capital accounts. The debit (+) to stock and credit (−) to creditors cancel out when the four columns are added. 'Cost of goods sold' is a flow since the double entry is *partially internal* (stock) and *partially external* (retained earnings) to the four columns. 'Dividends paid' is also a flow for the same reasons – cash (internal) and dividends payable (external). 'Dividends payable' is *not* a flow because the double entry is *totally external* to the four columns (i.e. dividends payable and retained earnings).

Details	Working capital	Fixed assets	Accum. depn	Dividends payable	Long-term loan	Share cap./prem.	Retained earnings
Opening balances	48	50	(30)	(5)	(13)	(10)	(40)
Transactions:							
Sales	543						(543)
Fixed asset purchase	(10)	20				(10)	
Share issue	5					(5)	
Loan issue	4				(4)		
Loan redemption	(7)				9		(2)
Fixed asset sale	2	(10)	7				1
Misc. expenses	(19)						19
Depreciation			(5)				5
Divs. payable				(6)			6
By differencing:							
COGS	(477)						477
Dividends paid	(5)			5			
Closing balances	84	60	(28)	(6)	(8)	(25)	(77)

Table 7.3   Marx and Sparks plc: working capital condensed funds flow matrix (£000)

A working capital flow statement is a listing of the working capital column. Similarly, it is possible to produce flow statements for other concepts of funds (see for example Miller, 1981). A cash flow statement is a listing of the cash column. A net asset flow statement is an aggregation of *all* the columns except retained earnings, i.e. the profit and loss account. In Chapter 7 it will be shown that the process of foreign currency translation is based on these basic ideas. Cash, working capital and net asset (profit and loss) flow statements are shown in Table 7.4.

Cash		Working capital		Net assets (P & L)	
Receipts from debtors	521	Sales	543	Sales	543
Payments to creditors	(470)	COGS	(477)	COGS	(477)
Misc. expenses	(19)	Misc. expenses	(19)	Misc. expenses	(19)
Funds from operations	32	Funds from operations	47		
Investing		Investing		Investing	
– fixed assets:		– fixed assets:		– fixed assets:	
Cash purchase	(10)	Cash purchase*	(10)	Depreciation[†]	(5)
Sale proceeds	2	Sale proceeds*	2	Loss on sale[†]	(1)
	(8)		(8)		
Financing:		Financing:		Financing:	
Share issue	5	Share issue*	5		
Loan issue	4	Loan issue*	4		
Loan redemption	(7)	Loan redemption*	(7)	Gain on loan redemption[†]	2
Dividends paid	(5)	Dividends paid*	(5)	Dividends payable[†]	(6)
	(3)		(3)		
				Change in net assets/retained	
Change in cash	21	Change in working capital	36	earnings	37

Table 7.4   Funds flow statements for the year ended 31 December 1986 (£000)

Suppose we compare the working capital and net asset flow statements in Table 7.4. Double entries affecting a working capital account and retained earnings are common to both funds and are seen in the top half of both statements. Flows between a working capital account and long-term assets and liabilities (denoted*) are not in the net assets flow statement since they are *totally internal* to net assets. Flows between long-term assets and retained earnings (denoted[†]) are not in the working capital flow statement since they are totally external to working capital.

The wider the fund definition, the more developed the accrual concept and the more smoothed the flows. In a cash flow statement the flow relating to stocks (inventory) is payments to creditors. For net monetary assets, it is purchases (i.e. payments matched to a period). For working capital and net assets it is COGS (purchases matched to output). Similar effects can be seen for fixed assets. Narrower definitions have more of a solvency perspective and broader ones more a profitability perspective.

The most common type of funds statement in the UK is based around working capital. At present in the USA, 'cash' and working capital statements are acceptable, with a trend towards cash. A recent FASB exposure draft, 'Statement of cash flows', issued in July 1986, proposes all US funds statements should be cash-based with a layout similar to the cash column in Table 7.4

Exercise

7.1   Consider cash, net liquid assets (debtors, cash, creditors), net monetary assets, working capital and net assets as fund definitions. Explain why the following items are or are not flows of each fund:
(a)   receipts from debtors;
(b)   long-term loan repayments;
(c)   depreciation;
(d)   profits on sale of fixed assets;
(e)   proceeds from sales of fixed assets;
(f)   share issues;
(g)   purchases of merchandise.

Published funds statements and SSAP 10

Two further concepts are necessary to understand funds statements per SSAP 10, 'Statements of sources and applications of funds', namely the derived format and the inclusion of expanded flows.

The derived format

The 1984/5 Survey of Published Accounts showed that all listed companies surveyed produced their funds statement in a derived format which reconciles 'funds from operations' to the profit figure in the profit and loss account. Consider the following from Table 7.4.

Working capital – funds from operations		Profit	
Sales	543	Sales	543
COGS	(477)	COGS	(477)
Misc. expenses	(19)	Misc. expenses	(19)
		Depreciation	(5)
		Loss on fixed asset	(1)
		Profit on loan	2
	47		43

The difference between funds from operations and profit is the subtraction of depreciation and loss on fixed asset, and the addition of profit on redemption of the loan. If we wish to reconcile profit to 'funds from operations', then we adjust these to get:

Derived format		Actual format	
Profit	43	Sales	543
Items not involving a movement of funds:		COGS	(477)
Depreciation	5		
Loss on fixed asset disposal	1	Misc. expenses	(19)
Profit on loan redemption	(2)		
Total generated from operations	47	Total generated from operations	47

The left-hand side is called the 'derived format' for funds from operations and the right-hand side the 'actual flow format'. The derived format reconciles easily with the profit and loss account and, some argue, also highlights certain allocations included in profits. However, it loses much of its intuitive meaning. Depreciation and loss on sale of fixed assets are often wrongly considered flows of working capital. They are merely items reconciling something having no meaning in terms of working capital flows (i.e. profit) into something which has a meaning (i.e. the subtotal of short-term operating flows of working capital) – the actual flows being shown on the right-hand side. The rest of a derived funds statement is *exactly the same* as its actual flow counterpart.

Derived funds statements were popular prior to the Companies Act 1981 (previous Acts requiring no breakdown of profit before tax) in that actual flow statements would have required further breakdowns. It will be interesting to see whether the more comprehensive profit and loss disclosure provisions in the Companies Act 1985 will result in a more comprehensible statement of sources and applications of funds in this respect. SSAP 10 allows either derived or actual format, provided a reconciliation to profit is given as a footnote.

Expanded funds statements – the 'all financial resources' statement

A problem with flow statements defined as the movement on a set of accounts is that they exclude certain important transactions. Suppose a fixed asset which cost £20,000 is financed £10,000 in cash and by issuing £10,000 in shares to the former owners in lieu of cash. Here the flow of *working capital* is only £10,000 (cash) since the share-financed portion is *totally external* to working capital. Proponents of what is termed the 'all financial resources' view of funds statements argue that all investing and financing flows should be included whether or not they affect working capital. One way of reconciling the two approaches is to 'expand' the pure working capital statement by treating external flows *as if* they went into working capital to purchase the fixed asset. This 'expansion' then conforms in a technical sense to the 'all financial resources' rationale (i.e. a statement showing all investing and financing flows).

The changes to the *pure* working capital funds statement to achieve publishable format are shown below. On the left is the pure working capital statement shown earlier, converted in the middle to the derived format which is then expanded by including the share-financed purchase (£10,000) of the fixed asset.

Statement of sources and application of funds – year ended 31 December 1986

Pure actual		Pure derived		Expansion	Published
Sales	543	Profit	43		43
COGS	(477)	Depreciation	5		5
Misc. expenses	(19)	Loss on FA	1		1
		Profit on loan	(2)		(2)
Operations	47		47		47
FA purchase	(10)	FA purchase	(10)	(10)	(20)
FA sale proceeds	2	FA proceeds	2		2
Share issue	5	Share issue	5	10	15
Loan issue	4	Loan issue	4		4
Loan redemption	(7)	Loan redemption	(7)		(7)
Dividends paid	(5)	Dividends paid	(5)		(5)
Change in working capital*	36	Change in working capital*	36	—	36

*84 – 48, per working capital column in Table 7.3.

What are published funds statements? A closer look

The intuitive rationale presented thus far for many published funds statements is that they are expanded, derived working capital flow statements. However, this is not the only rationale. In order to consider other rationales, consider again the original matrix diagram in Table 7.2. The top line shows the opening balance sheet and the bottom line the closing one. The realm of flow statements is the section between these. The current US title for funds statements, 'Statements of changes in financial position', reflects this general observation. The full matrix captures all flow changes. The debate about funds statements is about which flows should be reported from this whole set of flows – in effect, defining a sample selection rule. Some sampling rules which have been proposed include the following:

1. Report flows which affect a particular account or sets of accounts – see for example Taylor (1979a). If followed dogmatically, such an approach can omit certain 'significant' flows external to this set.
2. Report certain 'significant' flows regardless of which accounts they affect (e.g. report all long-term investment and financing flows regardless of which accounts they affect – the 'all financial resources' rationale). Other authors suggest the reporting of all flows resulting from external transactions of the entity (omitting book entries, e.g. depreciation) – see for example McKinnon, Martin and Partington (1983). The problem with such approaches is that they tend to be vague operationally as to which flows to include and exclude (see for example Robb, 1985).
3. Gross up balance sheet differences in some (undefined) way so that the statement can be easily reconciled with published balance sheet and profit and loss account data. Heath (1977) criticized such approaches as confusing the textbook method used to produce funds statements with the concepts underlying the statements.

SSAP 10 does not clarify which rationale is to be used, and in practice the published funds statement is a hybrid which can be rationalized from each of the above perspectives. The expanded working capital rationale has been used in this book since it is in the author's view the easiest to understand intuitively, is consistent with most published funds statements, and allows a systematic approach to the preparation of funds statements. It is interesting to note a movement in the rationale for funds statements in the USA. The new FASB exposure draft, 'Statement of cash flows' (July 1986), requires movements in *cash* (and cash equivalents) in actual or derived format and explicity supports the 'expansion' concept by allowing expansions either to be included in the statement or be presented as *a supplementary note* to a 'pure' cash statement. How this draft will be amended in its conversion into a standard will be interesting to see as it is a significant departure from existing practice in the USA.

Exercise

7.2   Consider the draft financial statements of Rundown plc which are shown in Table 7.5.

Balance sheets at 31 March (£000)	1985		1986	
Fixed assets – cost	250		400	
– accumulated depn	(130)		(145)	
		120		255
Current assets:				
Stock	100		140	
Debtors	70		85	
Cash	30		—	
	200		225	
Creditors within one year:				
Creditors for goods	(30)		(55)	
Dividends payable	(20)		(30)	
	(50)		(85)	
Net current assets		150		140
Long term loans		(70)		(75)
		200		320
Capital and reserves:				
Share capital and premium		100		170
Retained earnings		100		150
		200		320

Profit and loss account for the year ended 31 March 1986	
Sales	1,000
Cost of sales	(505)
	495
Depreciation	(15)
Other expenses	(400)
Net profit	80
Dividends payable	(30)
Retained earnings	50

Table 7.5   Financial statements of Rundown plc

Note
1.   All purchases and sales of goods were on credit.
2.   £60,000 of the fixed asset purchases for the year were financed by giving the suppliers an equity stake in the company. There were no disposals of fixed assets during the year.
3.   All other transactions were for cash.

Required
(a)   Prepare a funds flow matrix for the above example. (Hint: the information given allows you to start with the top line of the matrix, the bottom line and the right-hand column. Deduce the rest.)
(b)   From the matrix prepare a pure working capital funds flow statement, and compare this with the profit and loss account given.
(c)   Show the adjustments necessary to obtain a derived expanded funds statement, and discuss their rationale.

CONSOLIDATING STATEMENTS OF SOURCES AND APPLICATIONS OF FUNDS

Consolidated statements of sources and applications of funds can be prepared in two ways:
(a)   *Direct aggregation* – as with other consolidated statements, by adding the individual company statements (here, funds statements), making adjustments to reflect the change in scope of the accounts.
(b)   *Indirect derivation* – just as individual funds statements can be prepared from balance sheets and profit and loss account, so the consolidated funds statement can be prepared from consolidated balance sheets and consolidated profit and loss account.

In large groups, approach (b) is computationally more efficient in practice because only three statements are involved, and no additional consolidation adjustments need to be calculated. The consolidated funds flow matrix prepared under (b) is also a useful summary of links between consolidated statements. Only (b) is discussed here. However, use of this approach could lead to the mistaken view that the funds statement is merely a supplementary statement, derived from other (primary) statements, not a full statement in its own right – confusing *method* of preparation (approach (b)) with the *concept* of the statement (approach (a)).

Conceptually, the whole consolidation process can be viewed in terms of aggregating funds flow matrices in their entirety. Earlier chapters on individual statements can be viewed as aspects of this process – balance sheet consolidation involving aggregation of top and bottom lines, profit and loss accounts of right-hand columns, and funds statements of left-hand columns. Consider now how a funds flow matrix is prepared (the steps being similar to those in Exercise 7.2).

Example 7.2   A consolidated statement

The accountant of the Fundsflow Group produces the draft accounts shown in Table 7.6, asking you to prepare a consolidated funds statement.

The steps to be taken in producing a consolidated funds statement to comply with SSAP 10, which will be considered in turn, are as follows:

1. *Construction* of the funds flow matrix (first in actual flow format for ease of understanding, and then demonstrating and contrasting the procedures for the derived format).
2. *Expanding* certain investing and financing flows (using standard procedures).
3. Providing *additional disclosures* required by SSAP 10.

The standard does not specify a particular concept of fund for published funds statements, but in its appendix (for guidance only) it shows a statement based on *working capital*, and this is taken as the basis for the statement prepared below, though other funds concepts, e.g. net liquid assets, are also permitted. SSAP 10 requires dividends *paid* to be disclosed, and in its example shows taxation *paid*, which implies that dividends and taxation are to be *excluded* from 'working capital' (otherwise the entry would be dividends and taxation *payable*). Thus, here dividends and tax have columns separate from working capital. Consider the preparation of a working capital statement in *actual flow* format.

Constructing the matrix in actual flow format: the steps

1. Fill in matrix headings from balance sheet captions (noting that for funds statement purposes some can be combined, e.g. fixed assets and accumulated depreciation, and share capital and premium).
2. Fill in top and bottom lines with opening and closing balance sheet.
3. Top section – enter each item in the profit and loss account in the right-hand column, and reconstruct its double entry.
4. Middle section – reconstruct double entries from the accounts notes.
5. Bottom section – subtotal each column and calculate the difference between the subtotals and the bottom line (closing balance sheet). Complete double entries by deducing the nature of missing items. Step 4 comes before step 5 since it enables a grossing of some differences.

Steps 1, 2 and 3 – the matrix as far as 'subtotal'/retained earnings
Working capital opening and closing balances are calculated below. SSAP 10 requires disclosure of the *component* changes in working capital. The total flow is £240.5 − £231.5 = £9.0. Dividends and tax are *not* included.

	1986	1985
Stocks	239.0	243.0
Trade debtors	134.5	116.0
Cash	21.5	12.0
Creditors (<1 year)	(154.5)	(139.5)
	240.5	231.5

Consolidated balance sheets at 31 December (£m)

	Note	1986		1985	
Fixed assets:					
Tangible assets	1	165.5		164.0	
Investment in related companies	4	38.0		35.0	
			203.5		199.0
Current assets:					
Stocks		239.0		243.0	
Trade debtors		134.5		116.0	
Cash		21.5		12.0	
		395.0		371.0	
Current liabilities:					
Creditors (<1 year)		(154.5)		(139.5)	
Dividends payable		(8.0)		(10.0)	
Current taxation		(40.5)		(40.5)	
		(203.0)		(190.0)	
Net current assets			192.0		181.0
Creditors (>1 year) – debentures			(77.0)		(98.0)
Provisions – deferred taxation			(6.0)		(4.0)
Minority interests			(29.0)		(25.0)
			283.5		253.0
Capital and reserves:					
Called up share capital (£1 ord.)	3		49.0		40.0
Share premium	3		65.0		56.0
Profit and loss			169.5		157.0
			283.5		253.0

Consolidated profit and loss account – year ended 31 December 1986 (£m)

Turnover: sales		779.5
Cost of sales		(496.0)
Gross profit		283.5
Depreciation		(17.0)
Other expenses		(202.0)
Loss on fixed asset disposal		(3.5)
Profit on debenture redemption		3.0
Income from associated companies		10.0
Profit before taxation		74.0
Taxation – associate	(5.0)	
– deferred	(2.0)	
– other	(32.0)	
		(39.0)
Profit after taxation		35.0
Minority interests		(7.5)
Profit for the financial year		27.5
Dividends		(13.0)
Retained profits for the year		14.5

Notes to the accounts

1. Fixed assets – net book values

Opening balance	164.0
Additions	32.0
Disposals	(20.5)
Depreciation	(17.0)
Acq. of subsidiary	7.0
Closing balance	165.5

2. Acquisition of subsidiary

An 80 per cent interest in Subservient was acquired at 30 June for £10 million. At that time its balances were:

Fixed assets	7	Creditors	3
Stocks	4	Taxation	2
Debtors	3	Share capital	2
Cash	1	Share premium	3
		Retained earnings	5
	15		15

Consolidated goodwill on all acquisitions is written off to retained earnings in the year of acquisition.

3. Share issues

	Nominal	Premium	Total
Acquiring Subservient (part cash)	4	4	8
To redeem debentures (part cash)	2	3	5
To acquire fixed assets (part cash)	3	2	5
	9	9	18

4. Associated companies

	1986	1985
Cost	20	20
Attributable retained earnings	18	15
Per balance sheet	38	35

The total amounts here represent net assets only, since goodwill is written off immediately on acquisition.

Table 7.6   Draft accounts of Fundsflow Group

In Table 7.7, fixed assets/accumulated depreciation and share capital/premium should be combined for efficiency. *Profits or losses on disposals of assets and liabilities are reconstructed directly to the asset or liability account itself* (see step 5). 'Funds from operations' is in this example, the subtotal of profit and loss account items from *ordinary* activities, which affect working capital.

Step 4 – reconstruction from the notes
The following table shows the acquisition of Subservient – the conversion from the balances in Table 7.6, note 2, to the line in matrix.

	Original balances	Reclassify equity	Investment recording	Elim.	Consol.
Working capital	5		(2)		3
Fixed assets	7				7
Investment			10	(10)	—
Taxation	(2)				(2)
Share cap. and prem.	(5)	5	(8)		(8)
Retained earnings	(5)	5			—
Minority interests		(2)			(2)
Goodwill		(8)		10	2

The equity at acquisition, $2 + 3 + 5 = 10$, is split 80:20 between goodwill and minority. The investment is recorded, and then eliminated to get consolidated balances in the final column. This records the consolidated assets acquired *net* of consideration given, viz.:

$$(5 + 7 + 2 - 2 - 2) - (2 + 8) = 0$$
WC   FA   G/W   Tax   Mino.   WC (cash)   Shares

Net assets acquired   Consideration given

Goodwill is immediately written off versus retained earnings in the matrix. A similar procedure can be used to deal with disposals of subsidiaries. The fixed asset disposal and debenture redemption involve differencing so are dealt with in step 5.

Step 5 – differencing
In step 3, profits or losses on disposals of assets and liabilities were entered directly to the columns representing those assets and liabilities. Consider why. Suppose opening fixed assets were £10. Some of these with a book value of £2 were sold for £5. The closing book amount is thus £8, and the profit on disposal £3. Consider how these transactions would be dealt with in the matrix.

	Working capital	Fixed assets	Retained earnings
Opening balance sheet	xx	10	xx
Step 3: reconstruct P & L			
Profit on fixed asset		3	(3)
Subtotal	xx	13	xx
Step 5: differencing			
Proceeds on disposal	5	(5)	
Closing balance sheet	xx	8	xx

Details	W cap	Fixed assets	Assoc. co.	Divs. p'ble	Current tax p'ble	Debents.	Deferred tax	Minority	S cap & s prem	Retained earnings
Opening balance sheet	231.5	164.0	35.0	(10.0)	(40.5)	(98.0)	(4.0)	(25.0)	(96.0)	(157.0)
Reconstruct profit & loss:										
Sales	779.5									(779.5)
Cost of sales	(496.0)									496.0
Depreciation		(17.0)								17.0
Loss on fixed asset disposal		(3.5)								3.5
Other expenses	(202.0)									202.0
Income from associate			10.0							(10.0)
Profit on debenture redempt.						3.0				(3.0)
Taxation – associate			(5.0)							5.0
– other					(32.0)		(2.0)			34.0
Funds from operations	81.5									
Minority interest								(7.5)		7.5
Dividends				(13.0)						13.0
Retained earnings										(14.5)
Subtotal	313.0	143.5	40.0	(23.0)	(72.5)	(95.0)	(6.0)	(32.5)	(96.0)	(171.5)
Reconstruction from notes:										
FA – additions*	(27.0)	32.0								
– disposal proceeds	17.0	(17.0)								
Acquisition of subsidiary:										
– assets acquired*	5.0	7.0			(2.0)			(2.0)	(5.0)	
– consideration given*	(2.0)								(8.0) (g/w w/o)	2.0 (g/w w/o)
Debenture redemption*	(13.0)					18.0			(5.0)	
Differencing:										
Dividends from assoc. co.	2.0		(2.0)							
Dividends paid	(15.0)			15.0						
Taxation paid	(34.0)				34.0					
Dividends to minorities	(5.5)							5.5		
Closing balance sheet	240.5	165.5	38.0	(8.0)	(40.5)	(77.0)	(6.0)	(29.0)	(114.0)	(169.5)

Table 7.7 Fundsflow Group – full funds flow matrix (actual format)

Normally the balance removed on disposals in a fixed asset account is the *net book amount*. However, since in step 3 the profit or loss on disposal was taken to the fixed asset account, the balance removed then becomes *proceeds* on disposal (i.e. proceeds = profit + book amount). This then gives us the flow of working capital required. All the other differences here represent *payments* to or from the relevant parties.

The matrix in derived format

In the author's view, the actual flow format is more informative than the derived one, SSAP 10 allowing this provided a reconciliation to profit for the period given. However, most companies still produce derived funds statements (in which profit is reconciled to funds from operations as shown earlier in this chapter). The *only* difference between actual and derived statements is in the alternative layout for 'funds from operations', i.e. the *top* part of the matrix. An alternative procedure for this top part in derived format is now discussed. Before recomputing the matrix consider, for the example, funds from operations in actual and derived format.

Funds from operations

Actual format		Derived format	
Sales	779.5	Profit before tax	74.0
COGS	(496.0)	Adjustments not involving funds movement:	
Other expenses	(202.0)	Depreciation	17.0
		Loss on fixed assets	3.5
		Profit on debenture	(3.0)
		Income from assoc. co.	(10.0)
	81.5		81.5

Since funds from operations only includes a subset of the items comprising profit before tax (for example, not including depreciation and loss on fixed asset – see left-hand side of above), to reconcile profit to funds from operations the items not in common need to be reversed[1] and adjusted against profit before tax as shown on the right.

It is comparatively easy to reformat the top part of the matrix to get the derived format *directly*. This is shown in Table 7.8.

The procedure to be used in the top part of the matrix to obtain directly the derived format is as follows. After entering the opening balance sheet:

(a) *Decomposition of retained earnings* – start with the line 'profit before tax'. Profit before tax is entered in the working capital column (positive) and in the retained earnings column (negative).

(b) *Adjustments not involving a movement of funds* – transfer out of the working capital column all the elements of profit before tax which do not affect working capital. These are transferred into the accounts which would have been affected in an actual flow statement.

(c) *Items below profit before tax* – these are treated identically to the actual flow statement, as are all other items in the matrix.

Step (a) is a first approximation, treating all items comprising profit before tax as if they were working capital flows. Step (b) removes 'incorrectly' treated items,

Details	W cap	Fixed assets	Assoc. co.	Divs. p'ble	Current taxation	Debents.	Deferred tax	Minority	S cap & s prem	Retained earnings
Opening balance sheet	231.5	164.0	35.0	(10.0)	(40.5)	(98.0)	(4.0)	(25.0)	(96.0)	(157.0)
Decomposition of retained earnings:										
Profit before tax	74.0									(74.0)
Taxation – associate			(5.0)							5.0
– deferred							(2.0)			2.0
– other					(32.0)					32.0
Minority interests								(7.5)		7.5
Dividends				(13.0)						13.0
						Retained earnings				(14.5)
Adjustments not involving a movement of funds:										
Depreciation	17.0	(17.0)								
Loss on fixed asset disposal	3.5	(3.5)								
Profit on debentures	(3.0)					3.0				
Profit on associate	(10.0)		10.0							
Funds from operations	81.5									
Subtotal	313.0	143.5	40.0	(23.0)	(72.5)	(95.0)	(6.0)	(32.5)	(96.0)	(171.5)

Table 7.8   Fundsflow Group – reconstruction of P & L in funds flow matrix (derived format)

transferring them to 'correct' columns. Steps (a) and (b) together give the same subtotals as the actual flow matrix. The remainder of the matrix is identical to the actual approach. Differencing will locate omissions in stage (b). To check step (a), the 'subtotal' in the retained earnings column should equal retained earnings for the year.

Expanding the working capital funds statement
Most funds statements in practice are *expanded* working capital statements with funds from operations in derived format. None of the expansions affects funds from operations. A 'pure' working capital flow statement is obtained by listing the flows in the first column of the matrix. However, as explained earlier in this chapter, to satisfy SSAP 10 certain investing and financing flows are expanded *as if* all their components affected working capital. Intuitively, investing and financing flows involve such events as acquisition and disposal of fixed assets, subsidiaries, and debentures.

Acquisition of fixed assets – the working capital outflow of £27 million excludes share-financed purchases of £5 million. Hence it is expanded into two figures:

	£m
Source: Share issue	5
Application: FA purchase	(32)
Net application of working capital	(27)

Acquisition of subsidiary – a net inflow of working capital of £3 million (Subservient's working capital acquired (£5 million) less working capital expended (£2 million)), can be expanded as follows:

'Sources'	
Share issue	8
Current taxation	2
Minority	2
	12
'Applications'	
Fixed assets	(7)
Goodwill	(2)
	(9)
Net source of working capital	3

The meaning of such an expansion is explored later. Table 7.9 shows the pure working capital flow statement in derived format (from the first column of the matrix) and the expansions necessary to produce an SSAP 10 funds statement (the final column). The statement is effectively divided into three parts: funds from operations, other sources, and applications.

Expanding the funds statement – a procedural basis
Consider the following algorithm for deducing expansions.
(a)   Look along each transaction line in the matrix to see if there is more than one entry outside the working capital column. If so the transaction is a candidate for expansion.

	'Pure' WC	FA acq.	Expansions Deb. red.	Subsid. acq.	Expanded WC
SOURCES					
Profit before tax	74.0				74.0
Adjustments:					
Depreciation	17.0				17.0
Loss on FA	3.5				3.5
Profit on debentures	(3.0)				(3.0)
Income from associate	(10.0)				(10.0)
Funds from operations	81.5				81.5
Other sources:					
FA disposals	17.0				17.0
Subservient acq.	3.0			(3.0)	—
Divs. from associate	2.0				2.0
Share issues		5.0	5.0	8.0	18.0
Current tax				2.0	2.0
Minority				2.0	2.0
Other sources	22.0	5.0	5.0	9.0	41.0
Total sources	103.5	5.0	5.0	9.0	122.5
APPLICATIONS:					
FA acquisitions	(27.0)	27.0 (32.0)		(7.0)	(39.0)
Debenture redeemed	(13.0)		13.0 (18.0)		(18.0)
Dividends paid	(15.0)				(15.0)
Taxation paid	(34.0)				(34.0)
Divs. to minorities	(5.5)				(5.5)
Goodwill				(2.0)	(2.0)
Total applications	(94.5)	(5.0)	(5.0)	(9.0)	(113.5)
NET CHANGE IN WC	9.0	—	—	—	9.0

Table 7.9   Fundsflow Group – expanded flow statement – year ended 31 December 1986

(b) Replace the single working capital flow (which may be zero) with all the other separate flows in the line, *with their signs reversed*.

The relevant flows in (a) for the Fundsflow Group example are marked* in Table 7.7. In step (b) the rest of the line is the *other side* of the double entry for the working capital figure. Reversing the sign reconstructs the working capital side of the double entry in *component* form.

Exercises

7.3   Consider the consolidated financial statements for the Gruppe Group for the year ended 31 March 1986 as shown in Table 7.10.

Consolidated balance sheets at 31 March (£000)

	1986		1985	
Assets employed:				
Fixed assets:				
Goodwill	18		12	
Other	55		31	
Investment in related companies	5		10	
		78		53
Current assets:				
Stocks	29		22	
Trade debtors	28		18	
Cash	10		5	
	67		45	
Current liabilities:				
Creditors	34		30	
Dividends payable	6		5	
Taxation payable	10		8	
	50		43	
		17		2
		95		55
Financed by:				
Capital and reserves:				
Share capital	19		11	
Share premium	25		9	
Reserves	33		23	
		77		43
Minority interests		18		12
		95		55

Consolidated profit and loss account – year ended 31 March 1986 (£000)

Turnover	106
COGS	(49)
Gross profit	57
Depreciation	(4)
Goodwill	(2)
Profit on sale of fixed assets	3
Other expenses	(23)
Share of profits of associated companies	4
Profit before taxation	35
Taxation	(11)
Profit after taxation	24
Minority interests	(4)
Attributable profit before extraordinary items	20
Extraordinary items (Note 1)	(4)
Attributable profit for the financial year	16
Dividends	(6)
Profits retained	10

Notes to the accounts

1. Loss on sale of associate, whose net book amount at the date of sale was £6,000.
2. Fixed asset purchases amounted to £25,000 of which £10,000 was financed by share issue direct to the supplier.
3. A 75 per cent interest in Appendage Ltd was acquired on 31 January for £14,000 in shares and £6,000 in cash. At that date, Appendages's balances were:

Fixed assets	8	Creditors	5
Stock	7	Share capital	4
Debtors	4	Share premium	6
Cash	2	Retained earnings	6

Table 7.10 Consolidated financial statements for Gruppe Group

Required   Prepare a funds flow matrix.

7.4 For the example in Exercise 7.3, produce the top section of the matrix in derived format, and compare funds from operations with actual format.

7.5 From the matrix in Exercise 7.3 or 7.4, prepare an expanded working capital statement, showing clearly the nature of the individual expansions.

Incorporating additional information required by SSAP 10

In addition to the expanded funds statement described earlier, SSAP 10 requires a breakdown of the components of working capital (separately disclosing net liquid funds), and a note disclosing components relating to the acquisiton and disposal of subsidiaries. These are discussed in detail in the next section.

SSAP 10, 'STATEMENTS OF SOURCE AND APPLICATION OF FUNDS' – AN ANALYSIS

SSAP 10, issued in July 1975, had immediate impact by requiring publication of funds statements. This section confines itself to a technical analysis of the standard's contents. A more conceptual analysis will be made later.

Objectives and disclosures

The standard, in common with its US counterpart, hedges as to the objectives of a funds statement, paragraph 2 stating that 'The objective of such a statement is to show the manner in which the operations of a company have been financed and in which its financial resources have been used.' However, in paragraph 4 it also states

> the funds statement will provide a link between the balance sheet at the beginning of the period, the profit and loss account for the period and the balance sheet at the end of the period. A minimum of netting off should take place . . . The figures from which the funds statement is constructed should generally be identifiable in [the other financial statements].

Paragraph 3 says 'It should show clearly the funds generated or absorbed by the operations of the business.' These statements embrace most of the characterizations of funds statements, and are fairly non-specific.

The corresponding US standard, APB Opinion No. 19 issued in 1971, emphasizes a statement disclosing all financing and investing activities regardless of form, based on a broad concept embracing all changes in financial position and calls the resulting statement 'Statement of changes in financial position'. However, it states that funds from operations can be, for example, on a cash or working capital basis. Again ambiguity, a statement rationalizable from a variety of angles. The new (1986) FASB Exposure Draft, 'Statement of cash flows', is more specific and comments that a (cash-based) funds statement should help investors, creditors and others to predict future cash flows, assess ability to meet and utilize financial obligations, contrast cash flow with profit, and throw light on investing and financing transactions.

SSAP 10 makes no attempt to define a fund or which concept of fund should be used, merely requiring (paragraphs 11 and 12) the disclosure of specific items:

> The statement should show the profit and loss for the period together with the adjustments required for items which did not use (or provide) funds in the period. The following other sources and applications of funds should, where material, also be shown:
> (a) dividends *paid*;
> (b) acquisitions and disposals of fixed and other non-current assets;
> (c) funds raised by increasing, or expended in repaying or redeeming, medium or long-term loans or the issued capital of the company;
> (d) increase or decrease in working capital subdivided into its components, and movements in net liquid funds.
> Where the accounts are those of a group, the statement of source and application of funds should be so framed as to reflect the operations of the group.

SSAP 10's specimen statements suggest a working capital based statement. The standard's insistence on dividends *paid* requires that dividends should be excluded from working capital. In the appendix, taxation *paid* is shown in the examples suggesting taxation should also be excluded. Requirements (b) and (c) which require *all* investing and financing flows to be shown suggest an 'all financial resources' (expanded) statement. The preamble quoted above suggests a derived statement, but could be satisified by an actual flow statement with a note reconciling funds from operations to reported profit.

Disclosure of changes in working capital components

The following (based on Example 7.2) satisfies requirement (d):

Increase in working capital	£m
Stock decrease	(4.0)
Trade debtors increase	18.5
Creditors increase	(15.0)
Movement in net liquid funds: cash increase	9.5
	9.0

The standard requires the separate subtotalling of items comprising 'net liquid funds', defined as 'cash at bank and in hand and cost equivalents (e.g. investments held as current assets) less bank overdrafts and other borrowings repayable within one year of the accounting date' (paragraph 8).

Funds from operations

SSAP 10 requires the funds statement to show profit and loss for the period, but surprisingly does not *require* the disclosure of funds from operations (unlike the US standard). Its explanatory note (paragraph 3) states clearly that '[a funds statement] should show clearly the funds generated or absorbed by the operations of the business', but this is not in the requirements section and therefore is only a recommendation. Further, nowhere does SSAP 10 define 'funds from operations'.

It is not surprising therefore that the 1984/5 Survey of Published Accounts (Skerratt and Tonkin, 1985) shows a remarkable diversity in disclosure and treatment of items comprising funds from operations – for example, the term 'profit' at the head of the funds statement is defined in at least six different ways (e.g. before or after tax, before or after minorities, ditto for associates, ditto for extraordinary items, etc.). Also the flows included in funds from operations vary considerably as shown by Table 7.11 summarizing the survey results. In the USA APB Opinion No. 19 requires funds from operations to be shown exclusive of extraordinary items, and then extraordinary items to be separately disclosed but there is no such requirement in the UK.

Nature of flow	Included (%)	Excluded (%)
Taxation	17	83
Extraordinary items	56	44
Minority dividends	17	83
Associated company dividends or profits	85	15

(Based on the 300 companies in the 1984/5 Survey of Published Accounts)

Table 7.11   Definition of funds from operations

In the derived format, because the starting point, 'profit', is defined so diversely, it takes detective work to establish which of the above items have been included in or deducted from funds from operations. Consider for example the treatment of taxation. If the starting point of the derived statement is profit *after* tax, the starting point is *net* of taxation and so consequently funds from operations is determined *after* deducting taxation. Where the starting point is profit *before* tax, usually tax *paid* is shown as a flow later in the statement. Hence, now funds from operations is *gross* of taxation.

But further, in the case of taxation only, the two treatments correspond to different working capital definitions and measurements of the taxation flow. In the after-tax treatment, the starting point is after deducting tax *payable*, which is the implicit flow relating to taxation. For this to be the working capital flow, working capital must *include* taxation payable. The before-tax treatment shows tax *paid* as the taxation flow. Hence, under this treatment, taxation payable is *excluded* from working capital (as exemplified by the example for guidance only in SSAP 10's appendix). Thus, in this simple change in starting point is an alternative measurement of funds from operations *and* of working capital.

Minority interests

The standard's silence on minorities results in diverse treatments. Again starting with profit before (as in the Fundsflow example – Example 7.2) or after minorities (as in SSAP 10's example) affects the definition of funds from operations. Consider Table 7.12 based on the Fundsflow data. Only the particular components relating to minorities are shown, and the subtotals therefore include other figures in addition.

Fundsflow format (Example 7.2)		SSAP 10 example format	
Profit before tax & minority Adjustments (including):	74.0	Profit before tax after minority Adjustments (including):	66.5
Misc. other items	7.5*	Minority interest in retained earnings	2.0
		Misc. other items	7.5*
Funds from operations	81.5	Funds from operations	76.0
Applications (including):			
Minority dividends	(5.5)		

* Misc. other items = depn 17.0 + loss FA 3.5 − profit deb. 3.0 − assoc. 10.0.

Table 7.12   Flows relating to minority interests

The following figures from the Fundsflow example are used to explain the difference between the approaches.

Profit before tax and minority interests	74.0
Less minority interests in profit after tax	(7.5)*
Profit before tax after minority interests in profit	66.5
Minority interest in retained earnings	2.0*
Profit before tax but after minority dividends	68.5

* Note minority profit 7.5 − minority retained earnings 2.0
= minority dividend 5.5.

In the Fundsflow example in Table 7.12, its starting point is profits *before* minorities, 74.0. Minority dividends, 5.5, is shown as an application *later* in the statement. The net overall effect on the funds statement is 76.0, but the positioning of the flows means that funds from operations is *gross* of minority dividends. The example for guidance in SSAP 10's appendix starts with profit *after* minorities, 66.5, and adds back minority retained earnings, 2.0, in the 'adjustments not involving a movement of funds' section. From the breakdown above it can be seen that such a treatment again results in an overall effect of 76.0, but now funds from operations is stated *net* of minority dividends. As shown in Table 7.11, 83 per cent of companies exclude minority dividends and 17 per cent include it. SSAP 10 permits either treatment.

Associated companies

There is an identical split for associates – to start with profits *before* associates and to show associate dividends as a source later in the statement (i.e. to measure funds from operations *net* of associate dividends), or to start with profit *after* associates and adjust for associate retained earnings (measuring funds from operations *gross* of such dividends). However, a few companies adopt a third treatment, starting with profits *after* associates, but making the adjustment for retained earnings not as an 'adjustment not involving the movement of funds' (i.e. within funds from operations), but later in the funds statement in the 'applications' section, often labelling it 'investment in associate', as shown in Table 7.13.

Excluded		Included		Included and expanded	
Profit before assoc.	64.0*	Profit after assoc.	74.0	Profit after assoc.	74.0
Adjustments (incl.):		Adjustments (incl.):		Adjustments (incl.):	
Misc. items	17.5**	Assoc retained	(5.0)	Misc. items	17.5**
		Misc. items	17.5**		
Funds from ops.	81.5	Funds from ops.	86.5	Funds from ops.	91.5
Sources:				Applications:	
Assoc. dividends	5.0			Inv. in associate	(5.0)

* Equals profit after associate, 74.0, less associate profit, 10.0.
** Equals depreciation, 17.0, plus fixed asset loss, 3.5, loss debenture profit, 3.0.

Table 7.13   Flows related to associated companies

Though the overall impact on the funds statement seems the same, the effect of the third treatment on the statement is conceptually different in that it effectively *expands* the associate's contribution from dividends to attributable profit and reinvestment – as if the earnings retained in the associate had flowed into working capital (via funds from operations) and were reinvested in the associate as an application.

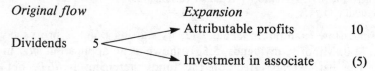

Original flow   *Expansion*
                       Attributable profits   10
Dividends   5
                       Investment in associate   (5)

This treatment stretches to the limit the criterion for expanding flows in that here no external transaction has taken place, merely the accrual of profits under the equity approach. It is highly questionable whether such flows should be regarded as investing and financing flows.

Suggestion   A format for funds from operations analogous to the profit and loss account, which would obviate some of the difficulties discussed is

Group funds from operations		xx
Less: Minority dividends		(xx)
Attributable funds from operations		xx
Less: Extraordinary items per P & L	(xx)	
Adjustments for extraordinary items not affecting working capital	xx	
		(xx)
Attributable funds from operations after extraordinary items		xx

APB Opinion No. 19 at least covers extraordinary items. Even the international standard IAS No. 7 requires the separate disclosure of 'unusual' flows, but not SSAP 10!

The acquisition and disposal of subsidiaries

SSAP 10 in its explanatory foreword recommends (paragraph 5):

[Funds statements] should reflect any purchases or disposals of subsidiary companies either
(a) as separate items, or
(b) by reflecting the effects on the separate assets and liabilities dealt with in the statement, so that the acquisition of a subsidiary company would be dealt with as an application of funds in acquiring the fixed assets (including goodwill) of that subsidiary and as a change in working capital.

In either case, in the interests of clarity, it will generally also be necessary to summarize the effects of the acquisition or disposal by way of a footnote indicating, in the case of an acquisition, how much of the purchase price has been discharged in cash and how much by the issue of shares.

A footnote satisfying SSAP 10 can be obtained directly from the calculations on page 178 by disaggregating the working capital element, viz.:

Summary of the effects of the acquisition of Subservient Ltd

Net assets acquired		*Discharged by*	
Goodwill	2		
Fixed assets	7	Shares issued	8
Stocks	4	Cash paid	2
Debtors	3		
Cash	1		
Creditors	(3)		
Taxation	(2)		
Minority interest	(2)		

The 1984/5 Survey of Published Accounts (Skerratt and Tonkin, 1985) indicated that of 249 companies which acquired or disposed of subsidiaries, only 47 per cent summarized the effects of such transactions in such a footnote. Of these 249 companies, 64 per cent followed approach (a), and 36 per cent (b).

Consider now approach (b).

Component format (b) – effects on separate assets and liabilities

Used in the Fundsflow example earlier, this approach expands the working capital flow relating to the acquisition or disposal, *as if* the rest of the transaction had not bypassed working capital. SSAP 10 recommends a footnote showing separately the effects of the acquisition of the subsidiary. A columnar presentation is used here to illustrate the component format and can also be used in published funds statements as a clearer alternative than footnote disclosure. It has three columns, the first *excluding* the acquisition, the second showing its effects (expansion), and the third *including* it by aggregating the first two columns, as in Table 7.14. Note the working capital flow (a net source) to be expanded is the *net* of subsidiary working capital acquired (£5 million) less *working capital* consideration given (£2 million).

Fundsflow Group – statement of sources and applications of funds – year ended 31 December 1986

	Excluding expansion	Acquisition effects	Including expansion
SOURCES:			
Profit before tax	74.0		74.0
Adjustments for items not involving a funds movement			
Depreciation	17.0		17.0
Loss on fixed asset	3.5		3.5
Profit on debenture	(3.0)		(3.0)
Income from associate	(10.0)		(10.0)
Funds from operations	81.5		81.5
Funds from other sources:			
Fixed asset disposal proceeds	17.0		17.0
Share issues	10.0	8.0	18.0
Net working capital on acquisition	3.0	(3.0)	–
Dividends from associate	2.0		2.0
Current tax on acquisition		2.0	2.0
Minority interests on acquisition		2.0	2.0
	113.5	9.0	122.5
APPLICATIONS:			
Fixed asset acquisitions	(32.0)	(7.0)	(39.0)
Debenture redemption	(18.0)		(18.0)
Goodwill on acquisition		(2.0)	(2.0)
Dividends paid – group	(15.0)		(15.0)
– minority	(5.5)		(5.5)
Taxation paid	(34.0)		(34.0)
	(104.5)	(9.0)	(113.5)
Increase in working capital	9.0	–	9.0
Comprising:			
Decrease in stocks			(4.0)
Increase in trade debtors			18.5
Increase in creditors (excluding dividends and tax payable)			(15.0)
Movement in net liquid funds: increase in cash			9.5
Increase in working capital			9.0

Table 7.14   Acquisition of subsidiary – component format

The first column here is the sum of the first three columns in Table 7.9 (which shows every expansion individually) including all expansions *except* the acquisition of subsidiary, shown in the first column as a single figure. The second column here is identical to the fourth column in Table 7.9 in expanding this into components.

Single figure format (a)

This approach treats the subsidiary acquisition as if it were the acquisition of a *trade investment*. Hence the individual balances of the subsidiary are not included in the funds statement. Table 7.15 compares the matrix lines for the acquisition of subsidiary under the separate component treatment (as in Table 7.7) and under the assumption that the subsidiary was acquired as a trade investment.

Details	WC	Fixed assets	Invest-ment	Tax	Minor-ity	S cap and s prem	Retained earnings
Component format:							
Assets acquired	5.0	7.0		(2.0)	(2.0)		(2.0)g/w
Consideration	(2.0)					(8.0)	
Single item format:							
Investment acquired			(10.0)				
Consideration	(2.0)					(8.0)	

Table 7.15   Comparison of matrix lines for acquisition of subsidiary under separate component and single item formats

The basic difference is that under the component (consolidated) format, the investment at acquisition of 10.0 is broken down into component assets, liabilities and goodwill, whereas under the single item approach they are not. Analogous to a fixed asset purchase for cash and shares (discussed earlier), under the single item approach the cash consideration (£2.0) is expanded as if the share-financed portion (£8.0) of the subsidiary purchase flowed into working capital to purchase the investment. In contrast, under the component approach it is the net balance of (£5 million − £2 million) which is expanded into components. Table 7.16 illustrates the single item approach.

The first column is identical to Table 7.14 (approach (b)), except that it now shows the working capital flow relating to the acquisition of the subsidiary as an application of £2 rather than as a *net* source of £3 million (£5 million − £2 million) as discussed above. The second column shows the expansion of this £2 million. However, the change in working capital under the single item approach does *not* equal the change in consolidated working capital balance sheet amounts, since the funds statement treats the acquisition as a *non-consolidated* trade investment, whereas the change between consolidated balance sheets (viz. the separate component approach) incorporates component balances of the subsidiary on a consolidated basis. Thus the funds statement does not articulate with the other statements without further reconciliation.

Non-columnar presentations

The columnar presentation is, in the author's view, the most helpful way of presenting the effects of the acquisition and disposal of subsidiaries. It has been used here particularly because it aids the comparison between the two approaches. In practice the most frequent approach is to use a footnote as mentioned earlier. When this is done only the final column of the funds statements of approach (a) or (b) is disclosed, together with the footnote.

Fundsflow Group – statement of sources and applications of funds – year ended 31 December 1986

	Excluding acquisition	Acquisition effects	Including acquisition
SOURCES:			
Profit before tax	74.0		74.0
Adjustments for items not involving a funds movement			
Depreciation	17.0		17.0
Loss on fixed asset	3.5		3.5
Profit on debenture	(3.0)		(3.0)
Income from associate	(10.0)		(10.0)
Funds from operations	81.5		81.5
Funds from other sources:			
Fixed asset disposal proceeds	17.0		17.0
Share issues	10.0	8.0	18.0
Dividends from associate	2.0		2.0
	110.5	8.0	118.5
APPLICATIONS:			
Fixed asset acquisitions	(32.0)		(32.0)
Investment in subsidiary	(2.0)	2.0	
		(10.0)	(10.0)
Debenture redemption	(18.0)		(18.0)
Dividends paid – group	(15.0)		(15.0)
– minority	(5.5)		(5.5)
Taxation paid	(34.0)		(34.0)
	(106.5)	(8.0)	(114.5)
Increase in working capital	4.0	—	4.0
Comprising:			
Decrease in stocks[*]			(8.0)
Increase in trade debtors[*]			15.5
Increase in creditors[*]			(12.0)
Movement in net liquid funds: cash[*]			8.5
Increase in working capital			4.0

[*] As Table 7.14 except working capital components of subsidiary acquired are removed. (A footnote is required to show the component effects of the acquisition.)

Table 7.16   Acquisition of subsidiary – single item format

A comparison of the approaches

The separate component approach provides ease of reconciliation with other financial statements, but with loss of an easy intuitive understanding. The expansion raises difficult questions, e.g. 'How can the minority interests or current taxation of the subsidiary be regarded as (imputed) sources of funds?', or 'How can goodwill be regarded as an application?' All expansions of flows can be viewed as hypothetical flows of working capital, but some stretch the imagination! Even from an 'all financial resources' perspective, the transaction took place as a single whole and not as components. However, the expansion is consistent with a view of the funds statement as reconciling balance sheet changes, showing how new balances were introduced into the consolidation process.

The single item format is easier to understand intuitively and is consistent with the 'all financial resources' viewpoint, showing the actual transaction that took place. However, after acquisition, the acquired subsidiary will be dealt with on a component by component (consolidated) basis. It seems anomalous to treat the acquisition as a trade investment, but subsequent results as a *consolidated* subsidiary. There are no easy answers to these inconsistencies.

Whichever approach is used, given the funds statement and the footnote, analysts can (in principle) reconcile one approach with the other. Is the choice of approach therefore significant? Efficient markets research discussed earlier suggests that investors in aggregate are probably not fooled by differing presentations of accounting data, provided they are given enough information to convert from one format to another. However, empirical studies have not examined this particular area, and it may be dangerous to extend general results to this area, which is not well understood by users.

Exercises

7.6 Using the data in Exercise 7.3 (and its matrix), produce a statement of sources and applications of funds satisfying SSAP 10.

7.7 Using the same data, calculate the alternative presentations for minorities, associates and the acquisition of the subsidiary, discussed in the preceding sections of the book. Discuss the rationales for these alternatives.

THE USEFULNESS OF CONSOLIDATED STATEMENTS OF SOURCES AND APPLICATIONS OF FUNDS

Most funds statements produced are consolidated statements. Similar problems arise as for other financial statements, for example the averaging of dissimilar activities and the difficulties arising from the fact that stakeholders have claims on individual companies and not the group. However, many difficulties in interpreting and using consolidated funds statements arise from confusions and disagreements over the nature and purpose of the statement itself.

Miller (1981), for example, writes:

> [SSAP 10] runs together more funds concepts than any other standard. Although SSAP 10 is far from being explicit on all points, the text and examples seem to embrace an all

financial resources concept of funds, income tax and dividends included on a cash basis, and funds from operations and most other items presented on a working capital basis. Further, the movement in 'funds' is reconciled to both working capital (excluding income taxes and proposed dividends) and 'net liquid funds' . . . The [non-Australian] standard setting bodies have been remarkably coy about the funds concepts underlying their standards.

Some of these difficulites are now examined.

The derived format

Heath (1977) in an excellent review of funds statements, suggests that the derived format arose historically because accounts did not include funds statements. As a result 'balance sheet change' statements arose as a tool for externally analysing financial statements. The derived format simply resulted from a lack of disclosure. Because of this origin, funds statements have been viewed as secondary statements, summarizing the information in the other financial statements. However, Heath points out that it is easy to set up the bookkeeping system to produce funds statements directly (especially with computer-based systems). Firms still have a vested interest in preserving the derived format to minimize disclosure.

Confusions arise over whether depreciation is a source of funds (discussed earlier), and Heath (1977) cites mistaken views of a funds statement as showing where a company's profits 'went'. Clearly profits are not a physical thing like cash, but the *change* in net assets – not an asset itself. Again mere reconciling items have been mistakenly ascribed 'meaning'. Mason (1983, p. 98) comments that a survey by Lee and Tweedie (1977) on the comprehension and use of company financial reports by private and institutional shareholders indicated that private shareholders 'only had the haziest notion of the differences between profits and cash'.

To what extent do current derived statements add *additional* information to other statements – or are they just a rearrangement? SSAP 10, for example, states (paragraph 4) 'the information which it contains is a selection, reclassification and summarization of information contained in [the other] statements'. Heath (1977) quotes numerous examples of this view, including where an author considers it is the function of the funds statement to make the others more readable! If so, efficient markets research suggests they may not be very valuable to sophisticated users!

Providing complementary information

Heath (1977) comments that some of the above misconceptions have arisen because the profit and loss account has been viewed as *the* connecting link between balance sheets, *the* operating statement. Arising from this misconception is the slightly more sophisticated viewpoint that the funds statement shows investing and financing flows, whereas the profit and loss account is the operating statement. He points out that the profit and loss account reports only the effects of 'selected operating activities, selected financing activities [e.g. repayment of debt at less than book value], selected investing activities [sale of fixed assets at more or less than book value]' (Heath, 1977, p. 97). The 'third' statement will thus report *complementary* facets of investing, financing *and* operating flows.

The very title of the current US statement, the 'Statement of changes in financial position', indicates a lack of guidance in this area. Heath (1977) orients his discussion towards the evaluation of *solvency* which he defines as the ability of a company to pay its debts when due, rather than *profitability* which refers to a company's ability to increase its wealth. The funds statement provides part of the information needed to evaluate solvency, which he sees as distinct from and complementary to profitability evaluation, requiring different types of information.

His main criticism of published funds statements is that they are confused because they have ill-defined objectives and try to do too much within a single statement, ending up with an unhelpful compromise. He suggests in effect multiple funds statements, showing the movements in specific sets of assets and liabilities. In terms of the original matrix, he suggests disclosing multiple columns of the matrix – cash, fixed assets, long-term financing and equity – rather than expanding a single column, working capital. This he feels would capture the flows in a more helpful and interactive way. This proposal would link with other corporate disclosures in order to aid solvency evaluation, but these are beyond the scope of the present chapter. However, Heath's (1977) view of objectives is not universally agreed (see, for example, pages 172–3), but it is discussed here because of its penetrating critique of current statements.

Clarifying the objectives of the funds statement would help resolve the extent to which it would be useful to identify a specific type of fund (e.g. cash, net liquid assets or working capital) for particular types of entities, and also in deciding on a single treatment for the acquisition and disposal of subsidiaries. The recent FASB Exposure Draft, 'Statement of cash flows', goes some way towards narrowing treatments. The Draft defines the focus of such statements as cash plus cash equivalents (not allowing a reconciliation to working capital). It also requires cash flows to be analysed between operating, investing and financing flows rather than general sources and applications (uses) headings, giving detailed guidance on classification (see the first column of Table 7.4 for an example of this format). Unlike Heath's (1977) proposals it goes for an expanded statement. Further, it allows flexibility in choosing actual or derived format, and in whether to include expansions as a part of the statement or as a separate note. So Heath's criticisms of the derived format and that the statement includes too much may still apply if certain options are taken.

The lack of comparability

Arising from the lack of clarity evidenced in SSAP 10 is the incredible diversity in presentation and measurement illustrated earlier in the chapter. This lack of comparability makes the consolidated statement of sources and applications of funds the most confusing and difficult statement to analyse. Any self-respecting analyst would be advised to bypass the statement except as a last resort and produce his own analytical statements on a comparable basis. Mason (1983, p. 98) quotes Lee and Tweedie (1977) commenting that 'no less than 64 per cent of professional investment managers have no understanding of funds statements, although 67 per cent claimed to read them thoroughly'. He further points out that the derived format in practice is not even reconcilable to other figures in the accounts, so it seems that at present no objectives are being satisfactorily attained in a mire of uneasy compromise.

Discussion questions

7.8   Discuss the potential uses of the consolidated funds statement to analysts. What information might be obtainable from such a statement, not obtainable from the other consolidated statements. How far does the funds statement under SSAP 10 satisfy those potential uses?

7.9   Explain intuitively the rationales for the two approaches for accounting for the acquisition and disposals of subsidiaries in SSAP 10. Should both be allowed as alternatives?

SUMMARY

The *funds flow matrix* shows interrelationships between financial statements, and illustrates flow statements. One way of characterizing funds statements is as the movement on a set of accounts (a fund). Transactions are flows of a 'fund' if *one side* of the double entry is *within* the set of accounts comprising the fund. Transactions for which neither or both double entries are within are not flows of that 'fund'.

An *actual* flow statement is one where the transactions affecting funds from operations are disclosed. In a *derived* flow statement, profit is *reconciled* to funds from operations. An *expanded* flow statement includes transactions external to working capital as if they flowed into and out of working capital (an unexpanded statement is called here a 'pure' flow statement). Some characterize funds statements as 'all financial resources' statements including all investing and financing flows, statements resulting from a *grossing-up* of balance sheet differences, or statements of external transactions. The matrix can be used under all these approaches.

SSAP 10 does not define a 'fund' but requires certain disclosures. It requires *dividends paid* to be disclosed and suggests taxation paid. It also *suggests* the disclosure of 'funds from operations' (which is also not defined), and a footnote to show the effects of acquisitions and disposals of subsidiaries, which can be disclosed as a single item or as components. It *allows* an actual format only if funds from operations are reconciled with profits, and *requires* a breakdown of changes in working capital and net liquid funds. The diversity in practice in relation to group accounting matters (e.g. minorities, associates, and the acquisition and disposal of subsidiaries) was examined.

An examination of usefulness revealed a lack of clarity over objectives, and a consequent confusion over meaning. Such confusion resulted in a vast diversity of treatments, causing non-comparability.

NOTES

1. Under absorption costing, the depreciation charge to be added back should be that in the profit and loss account and not the amount written off fixed assets, since the latter is absorbed into production and may not appear in profit and loss until future periods.

FURTHER READING

Conceptual

Heath, L. C. (1977) *Financial Reporting and the Evaluation of Solvency*, Accounting Research Monograph No. 3, American Institute of Certified Public Accountants, New York.

Hendricksen, E. S. (1982) *Accounting Theory* (4th edn), ch. 10, Irwin, Homewood, Illinois.

Miller, M. C. (1981) The funds statement debate: a reconsideration of objectives and concepts, *The Chartered Accountant in Australia*, August 1981, pp. 55–8. (See also comment by Clift in the same journal, September 1982, pp. 30–2.)

In practice

Accounting Standards Committee (1975) *SSAP 10 – Statements of Source and Application of Funds*, ASC, London.

Knox, R. W. (1977) *Statements of Source and Application of Funds: A Practical Guide to SSAP 10*, Institute of Chartered Accountants in England and Wales, London.

Skerratt, L. and Tonkin, D. (eds.) (1984) *Financial Reporting 1984/5: A Survey of UK Published Accounts*, pp. 217–42, Institute of Chartered Accountants in England and Wales, London.

PART III

OTHER ISSUES
IN GROUP ACCOUNTING

8 Consolidated Accounts in Practice

Previous chapters examined each major financial statement in the context of a holding company and single subsidiary or associate, allowing an analysis of the techniques, concepts and issues underlying consolidation without distracting complex calculations. The first part of this chapter explores certain technical complexities. Each topic is self-contained so that the reader can sample some areas and omit others without loss of continuity. Its aim is to give a taste of the issues involved, and hence does not attempt to be exhaustive. The second part examines the widespread use of computer packages in large consolidations. ICI plc, for example, has over four hundred subsidiaries, operating in more than fifty currencies.

The technical areas covered are:
1. Acquiring or disposing of a subsidiary or associate in a series of transactions (*piecemeal* acquisitions and disposals).
2. Groups with complex holding structures, *vertical* groups, *mixed* groups and *cross-holdings*. Each can be covered without its successors.
3. Acquiring preference shares and debentures as well as ordinary shares.

Subsequent write-off of consolidated goodwill is ignored here so as not to obscure principles of cancellation in more complex examples.

COMPLEX GROUP STRUCTURES: TECHNICAL ISSUES

Acquiring or disposing of holdings in a series of transactions

Piecemeal acquisitions

Frequently, holding companies do not acquire holdings as a single transaction but over a period, e.g. a 15 per cent holding at one date, and later a further 45 per cent holding. An interesting issue is whether control is acquired at a single date or piecemeal throughout the series of transactions.

Example 8.1   The Hangover–Shady acquisition

Consider the following balance sheets at 31 December 1986:

	Hangover (£000)	Shady (£000)
Assets	5,000	2,000
Investment in Shady	600	
Liabilities	(2,600)	(1,000)
Share capital	(700)	(200)
Share premium	(800)	(200)
Retained earnings	(1,500)	(600)

Hangover had acquired its 60 per cent stake in Shady in two separate transactions:

Transaction date	% acquired	Consideration	Shady reserves
31 March 1985	15	150,000	300,000
30 September 1985	45	450,000	400,000
Total	60	600,000	

One possibility is to compute pre-acquisition reserves at the date control was finally acquired. Another is on a 'step by step' basis according to proportionate holdings at each purchase. The second, layered approach increases consolidated reserves and goodwill, since pre-acquisition profits are less and post-acquisition greater. Early recommendations by a research committee of the Institute of Chartered Accountants in 1949 (see Wilkins, 1979, p. 89), now withdrawn, regarded intent at the time of purchase as significant. If the intention was eventually to acquire control, then the 'step by step' approach was permissible, otherwise the single date approach was recommended. Subsequently there has been a movement to the step by step approach in all situations except where it is inconvenient, e.g. for a series of small purchases (for example ARB 51, paragraph 9, in the USA). SSAP 14 is silent on the matter.

In a survey in the early 1970s, Wilkins (1979, p. 91) found five cases of piecemeal acquisition, all of which used the 'step by step' approach. Shaw (1973, pp. 121–2) comments that it seems incorrect to deprive a holding company of dividend income to which it would have been entitled (after the first purchase) by later capitalizing the reserves of its subsidiary prior to total control. The consolidated equity components under both approaches (£000) are now contrasted.

Computation at the date of final control

Goodwill

= Total consideration − 60% of Shady's equity at control (September)

= (150 + 450)   − 60% × (200 + 200 + 400) = 120

Consolidated reserves

= Hangover's reserves + Shady's post-acquisition reserves

= 1,500   + 60% × (600 − 400) = 1,620

Computation step by step

Goodwill

= Goodwill at first purchase + Goodwill at second purchase
= $(150 - 15\% \times (200 + 200 + 300)) + (450 - 45\% \times (200 + 200 + 400)$
= $45 + 90 = 135$

Consolidated reserves

= Hangover's + post-acq. first parcel + post-acq. second parcel
= $1,500 + 15\% \times (600 - 300) + 45\% \times (600 - 400)$
= $1,635$

Under the step by step approach, Hangover's share of Shady's reserves between first purchase and control (calculated as $15\% \times (400 - 300) = 15$) is post-acquisition, increasing both consolidated reserves and goodwill (the latter because of a corresponding reduction in pre-acquisition equity). Minority interests of 400,000 ($40\% \times (200 + 200 + 600)$) are unaffected by the choice of approach, as the dichotomy in pre- and post-acquisition treatment does not apply to their ongoing holding. Figure 8.1 analyses Shady's equity under the step by step approach.

Time period	Slices of Shady equity		Analysis of equity slices		
			15%	45%	40%
			purchase	purchase	minority
Equity to 31/12/84	(200 + 200 + 300) =	700	105	315	280
Retained earnings 12/84–6/85	(400 – 300) =	100	15	45	40
Retained earnings 6/85–12/86	(600 – 400) =	200	30	90	80
Total equity at 31/12/86	(200 + 200 + 600) =	1,000	150	450	400

Figure 8.1   Piecemeal acquisition – analysis of subsidiary equity

In Figure 8.1, the left-hand column analyses Shady's equity chronologically. The key dates are those of first purchase (31 March 1985) when Shady's equity was 700,000, second purchase (30 September 1985) when it increased by 100,000 to 800,000, and the closing financial statement date when it increased by a further 200,000 to 1,000,000. These increments are analysed horizontally in the ratios 15 per cent (first purchase), 45 per cent (second purchase) and 40 per cent (remaining minority).

Pre-acquisition equity is shaded. It can be analysed according to purchase (in £000): 105 ($15\% \times 700$) first purchase, and $315 + 45 = 360$ (i.e. $45\% \times (700 + 100)$) second purchase as above; or chronologically (to construct a cancellation table) as 420 (105 + 315 or 60% × 700) to 31 March 1985, and 45 (45% × 100) from 31 March to 30 September 1985. Shady's *post*-acquisition reserves can also be analysed according to purchase – 15 + 30 = 45 first, and 90 second, as above – or chronologically, 15 from 31 March to 30 September 1985 and 30 + 90 = 120 from 30 September 1985 to 31 December 1986. Adding Hangover's 1,500 retained earnings to these two increments gives £1,635 consolidated reserves as before. Consider the cancellation table (Table 8.1) which uses the chronological breakdowns of Figure 8.1.

The consolidated profit and loss account in the year of acquisition
In the year to 31 December 1985 when control was achieved, the consolidated profit and loss account would probably treat Shady as an associate from 31 March to 30 September (when a 15 per cent stake was held), and include all its revenues and expenses less a 40 per cent minority for the last three months (60 per cent stake held). The latter treatment would be used in future years. To reconcile opening and closing minority interests, it is necessary to expand associate (15 per cent) profit into profit less 85 per cent minority.

The interaction between piecemeal acquisition and the tiers of disclosure

As discussed earlier, accounting for investments in the UK is a three tiered affair: broadly cost (less than 20 per cent), equity method (20–50 per cent) and full consolidation (over 50 per cent). The accounting treatment is affected when the increases in proportionate holdings cross barriers between tiers as illustrated in Table 8.2.

Consider the case where an incremental purchase converts a trade investment to an associate. For illustration, the figures above are used (though strictly the treatment would not comply with SSAP 1). Attributable retained earnings of the associate would comprise 15 per cent from the date of the first purchase, and 45 per cent from the second. Thus the investment would be (in £000):

Investment
= Cost + Attrib retained earnings + Attrib retained earnings
            from first purchase   from second purchase
= 600   + 15% × (600 − 300)   + 45% × (600 − 400) = 735

The alternative expansion is net assets *now* plus goodwill at acquisition (the latter already calculated above), i.e.

Investment
= Net +   Goodwill from   + Goodwill from
   assets   first purchase   second purchase
= 60% × (2,000 − 1,000) + 45   + 90   = 735

	Proportions pre/post/mino.	Investment	Share capital	Share premium	Goodwill	Consolidated ret. earnings	Minority interest
Hangover		600	(700)	(800)		(1,500)	
Shady:							
Prior to 12/84	60%/ 0%/40%				(420)		(280)
12/84–6/85	45%/15%/40%				(45)	(15)	(40)
6/85–12/86	0%/60%/40%					(120)	(80)
Cancellation		(600)			600		
Consolidated		—	(700)	(800)	135	(1,635)	(400)

Table 8.1 Cancellation table for piecemeal acquisition

Extra purchase causes change		Discussion
From	To	
Cost	Consolidation	Situation as already discussed in the text.
Cost	Equity	Similar to above. Attributable profit on acquisition is on a 'step by step' basis.
Equity	Consolidation	Already consolidated reserves will include holding company profit relating to first purchase. Compute goodwill and post-acquisition profits on a 'step by step' basis.
Consol.	Consolidation	For example, from 55 per cent to 75 per cent subsidiary. Use straightforward 'step by step' approach.

Table 8.2   Effects of changes in tier on accounting for piecemeal acquisitions

Revaluations and piecemeal acquisitions

Holgate (1986b) discusses whether assets and liabilities should be revalued at each (sometimes insignificant) incremental purchase, an aspect not discussed in accounting standards. There is a requirement to revalue when the company becomes a subsidiary (SSAP 14), but subsequently he cites three alternatives:

(a) to revalue at each incremental purchase;
(b) to ignore revaluations and use valuations established when the company became a subsidiary;
(c) to revalue only the incremental slice of assets acquired (causing a composite basis akin to pure parent consolidation (see pages 118–19 except now caused by different purchases not different owners).

He prefers (a), commenting that (c) is difficult to rationalize. Alternative (b) is simple, but goodwill on incremental purchases is then not calculated against fair value at the purchase date. Presumably (b) would be used on small purchases on materiality and cost-saving grounds.

Institutional requirements

The City Code on Takeovers and Mergers requires that in piecemeal acquisitions, once a company owns 30 per cent of the voting rights of another company, it must make an offer for the remaining shares. The offer should be at a price not less than the highest price paid in the last twelve months and must include a cash alternative. This code is not backed by law, but according to Cooke (1986) is effective. See Cooke for further information.

Piecemeal disposals

Similarly, crossing the tiers affects the treatment of disposals. In Chapter 6, the complete disposal of wholly and majority owned subsidiaries was considered, and also a simple case of piecemeal disposal, a wholly owned subsidiary being converted to an associate.

General rules for disposals, discussed in Chapter 6, were:
1. Subsidiary asset and liability balances disposed of are effectively *contracted* into their equitized equivalent, and compared with disposal proceeds to determine *consolidated* gain or loss.
2. In the consolidated profit and loss account, the treatment prior to disposal reflects the tier which the affiliate belonged to for that period (subsidiary or associate). The treatment for the remainder of the year reflects the tier to which the *remaining* portion belongs.
3. In the holding company profit and loss account, the gain or loss is calculated against original cost.
4. If a closing balance sheet cancellation table is calculated from scratch based on *end of period* holdings, then it is not necessary to make special entries to reflect the disposal.

The reader is referred to Chapter 6 for further discussion. These principles apply to the spectrum of:
(a) reduction of control within the consolidation tier (e.g. sale of 20 per cent of a 75 per cent subsidiary);
(b) change of status from subsidiary to associate (e.g. sale of 20 per cent of a 55 per cent owned subsidiary);
(c) reduction in influence within the equity accounting tier (e.g. 20 per cent sale of 45 per cent owned associate);
(d) change of status from subsidiary or associate to cost (sale of 45 per cent of a 55 per cent owned subsidiary).

Calculations are more complex when opening and closing reserves are included in the consolidated profit and loss account, or when the balance sheet cancellation table *updates* the previous year's table to the current year position since, for example, opening and closing minority interests might need to be reconciled after a piecemeal disposal. A simple example of the updating form of the balance sheet cancellation table (widely used in practice) is discussed later in this chapter, but many of these reconciliation issues are beyond the scope of this book.

Example 8.2 Reduction of control

Consider the disposal of 20 per cent of a 75 per cent owned subsidiary half-way through the accounting period – in the consolidated profit and loss account, 75 per cent of the subsidiary's attributable profits will be included for the first half of the period. At disposal, total consolidated reserves will include 75 per cent of the subsidiary's retained earnings since acquisition. The subsidiary's component net assets plus goodwill at disposal equal in total the amount of a 75 per cent equitized investment at that date (see page 78 *et seq.*)

On disposal, 20 per cent of the equitized investment amount will be removed against proceeds to determine the *consolidated* profit or loss on sale. The 55 per cent remainder will continue to accrue earnings for the rest of the year as a subsidiary. Thus, in the second half of the period, 55 per cent of the subsidiary's attributable profits will be included in consolidated profit or loss. Both prior to and after the partial disposal, the investment is majority owned and hence consolidated. Under conventional consolidation, the 75 per cent and 55 per cent contributions will be recorded by including 100 per cent of revenues and expenses, removing minority interest in profit after tax, for each subperiod (i.e. 25 per cent and 45 per cent respectively). Calculations relating to a piecemeal disposal are dealt with in Example 6.4.

Exercise

8.1   Gradualist plc has acquired its 75 per cent stake in Prey Ltd in two stages; 25 per cent on 30 November 1982 for £3,000,000 when the reserves of Prey were £4,000,000, and a further 50 per cent on 30 November 1985 for £9,000,000, when Prey's reserves were £8,000,000. Ignore for the purposes of this example, the write-off of goodwill.

The balance sheets of both companies at 30 November 1986 were:

	Gradualist (£000)	Prey (£000)
Assets	183,000	20,000
Investment (75 per cent)	12,000	
Liabilities	(80,000)	(5,000)
Share capital	(15,000)	(2,000)
Share premium	(30,000)	(4,000)
Retained earnings	(70,000)	(9,000)

Required
(a)   Analyse the equity of Prey diagrammatically along the lines of Figure 8.1.
(b)   Prepare a consolidated balance sheet for the group at 30 November 1986, using the cancellation table as in Table 8.1.
(c)   Show how the incremental purchase would have been treated in the consolidated balance sheet at 30 November 1986 if Prey were treated as an associate.

Complex group shareholding structures

This section considers where groups have subsidiaries which themselves own subsidiaries (vertical groups), where in addition to this the holding company has direct holdings in sub-subsidiaries (*mixed* groups), and where subsidiaries have bilateral shareholdings in each other (*cross-holdings*).

Vertical groups – the case of sub-subsidiaries

In Example 8.3 a group has the following structure:

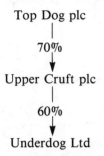

Top Dog plc

|

70%

▼

Upper Cruft plc

|

60%

▼

Underdog Ltd

Top Dog holds a 70 per cent stake in Upper Cruft, which itself holds a 60 per cent stake in Underdog. Thus, Top Dog holds a 42 per cent (i.e. 70% × 60%) indirect stake in Underdog. The group minority is made up of two components; 30 per cent (i.e. 100% – 70%) in Upper Cruft, and 58 per cent (i.e. 100% – 42%) in Underdog. The makeup of the 30 per cent is obvious, but consider now how the 58 per cent is made up using Figure 8.2.

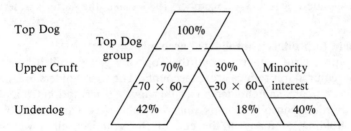

Figure 8.2   Disposition of shareholdings in vertical group – Example 8.3

The main group comprises Top Dog, a 70 per cent holding in Upper Cruft, and a 42 per cent indirect holding in Underdog, represented by the left-hand diagonal area. The minority interest is made up of three components: a 30 per cent minority in Upper Cruft; its 30% × 60% = 18% indirect stake in Underdog, forming a subgroup, and, separately, a direct minority holding of 40 per cent in Underdog itself (i.e. 100 – 42 – 18), the last two comprising the 58 per cent minority in Underdog. Under the Companies Act (see Chapter 2), Underdog is a subsidiary as the subsidiary of a subsidiary, even though the group's interest is only 42 per cent. In such vertical groups 'minority interests' in the consolidated balance sheet (here 58 per cent, in effect the majority holding in Underdog) could be extremely large if sub-subsidiaries are large in relation to the senior companies, e.g. in a reverse takeover situation. Consider where one company holds 51 per cent of another, which holds 51 per cent of another, which holds 51 per cent of a fourth. The fourth is a subsidiary with a 51% × 51% × 51% = 13 per cent indirect holding, and a 'minority' of 87 per cent. Maybe the case for proportional consolidation is not so outlandish!

Example 8.3   The Top Dog group

The balance sheets of the three companies at 31 December 1986 were:

	Top Dog (£000)	Upper Cruft (£000)	Underdog (£000)
Assets	9,500	7,300	2,000
Investment in Upper Cruft	2,500		
Investment in Underdog		700	
Liabilities	(7,000)	(5,000)	(1,000)
Share capital	(1,000)	(700)	(150)
Share premium	(1,500)	(800)	(250)
Retained earnings	(2,500)	(1,500)	(600)

Top Dog acquired a 70 per cent interest in Upper Cruft on 31 December 1984 when the latter's reserves were £1,000,000. Upper Cruft acquired a 60 per cent interest in Underdog on 31 December 1985 when the latter's reserves were £400,000.

Requirement to produce consolidated accounts
Both the Upper Cruft subgroup *and* the Top Dog group (called here the main group) are required to produce group accounts. The shareholders in Upper Cruft are holding company shareholders in a subgroup. An exemption from producing such a subgroup consolidation is only available (see Chapter 2) where the subgroup holding company at the end of the year is itself a wholly owned subsidiary. This seems reasonable since in that case only main group shareholders are involved.

Approaches to producing group accounts for the ultimate group
There are two approaches to consolidating the Top Dog group:
1. *Sequential approach* – the group accounts for the Underdog subgroup are prepared in the manner described in previous chapters, and are themselves consolidated with the accounts of the holding company.
2. *Simultaneous approach* – the group accounts for the whole group are produced directly by using ownership proportions attributable to the ultimate holding company (in this example 42 per cent).
   In practice, it is necessary for subgroup consolidations to be prepared to satisfy legal requirements. Also in large groups, head office is supplied with subconsolidated information to manage the quantity of data processed centrally.

Sequential approach
Table 8.3 shows the cancellation table for the Upper Cruft–Underdog subgroup.
   These consolidated balances are themselves consolidated with Top Dog's in Table 8.4, producing consolidated accounts for the main group.

	Investment	Share capital	Share premium	Goodwill	Consolidated reserves	Minority interests
Upper Cruft	700	(700)	(800)		(1,500)	
Underdog (60:40):						
Pre-acquisition (150 + 250 + 400)				(480)		(320)
Post-acquisition (600 − 400)					(120)	(80)
Cancellation	(700)			700		
Consolidated balances	—	(700)	(800)	220	(1,620)	(400)

Table 8.3 Sequential approach: cancellation table for subgroup

	Investment	Share capital	Share premium	Goodwill	Consolidated reserves	Minority interests
Top Dog	2,500	(1,000)	(1,500)		(2,500)	
From subconsolidation table (70:30):						
(a) Upper Cruft related components:						
Pre-acquisition (700 + 800 + 1,000))				(1,750)		(750)
Post-acquisition (1,500 − 1,000)					(350)	(150)
(b) Underdog related components:						
Post-acquisition by main group (1,620 − 1,500 = 120)					(84)	(36)
Goodwill				220		
Minority interest (40%)						(400)
Cancellation	(2,500)			2,500		
Consolidated balances	—	(1,000)	(1,500)	970	(2,934)	(1,336)

Table 8.4 Sequential approach: cancellation table for main group

Consider the following procedural matters relating to Table 8.4:
1. Consolidated balances in Table 8.3 have been broken down between Upper Cruft and Underdog for explanatory purposes.
2. Pre-acquisition balances all relate to Upper Cruft as Underdog's were removed in computing goodwill in the prior subgroup consolidation.
3. Subgroup consolidated reserves (in £000) of £1,620 are broken down into three components: £1,000 pre-acquisition retained earnings of Upper Cruft (combined with its share capital and premium to get its pre-acquisition equity); £500 post-acquisition profits of Upper Cruft; and £120, the subgroup's share of post-acquisition profits of Underdog.
4. In Table 8.4, subgroup goodwill and minority interests (the latter being the 40 per cent outside interest in Underdog) are taken direct to goodwill and minority columns.

The treatment of goodwill

Under the cancellation approach adopted above (in £000), goodwill of £970 is that of the main group *and* the subgroup, comprising £750 relating to Upper Cruft $(2,500 - 70\% \times (700 + 800 + 1,000))$, and £220 relating to Underdog $(700 - 60\% \times (150 + 250 + 400))$. It therefore includes all the subgroup's goodwill (£220) in the sub-subsidiary, even though the main group only owns 70 per cent. Should the main group accounts include goodwill arising in the whole group, or just goodwill attributable to main group shareholders? Many writers (e.g. Shaw, 1973, pp. 69–70) recommend the latter, that only $70\% \times £200 = £154$ relating to the sub-subsidiary should be included. Thus, both consolidated goodwill and minority interests in Table 8.4 should be reduced by $(220 - 154) = 66$, revising the figures from £970 and £1,336 to £904 and £1,270.

The effects of removing minority goodwill

This subsection can be omitted without loss of continuity. To see clearly the implications of the above alternatives for goodwill on minority interests (MI), it is necessary to analyse the minority figure of £1,336. Consider the following breakdown using the numbers from Table 8.4.

$$MI = (400) + (750 + 150) + (36) = (1,336)$$

The first term represents the 40 per cent outside minority's share in Underdog's equity, the second (900) the 30 per cent outside minority's share in Upper Cruft's equity, and the third, $30\% \times 60\%$ of *post*-acquisition retained earnings of Underdog. What a motley array of items! To understand the effects of the adjustment proposed above, it is necessary to rearrange these terms using familar balance sheet relationships and the fundamental consolidation equation.

Using balance sheet relationships, for Underdog, equity = assets − liabilities (denoted below as NA_{UD} 'net assets of Underdog'). Because Upper Cruft has an investment in Underdog, its equity = assets − liabilities + *investment* in Underdog (denoted below as $NA_{UC} + INV_{UD}$). Finally, if we denote the post-acquisition retained earnings of Underdog as ΔRE_{UD}, the above equation can be expressed:

$$\text{MI} = 40\% \times NA_{UD} + 30\% \times (NA_{UC} + INV_{UD}) + 30\% \times 60\% \times \Delta RE_{UD}$$
$$= 40\% \times (2{,}000 - 1{,}000) + 30\% \times (7{,}300 - 5{,}000 + 700) + 30\% \times 60\% \times (600 - 400)$$

Rearranging terms, we get

$$\text{MI} = 40\% \times NA_{UD} + 30\% \times NA_{UC} + 30\% \times (INV_{UD} + 60\% \times \Delta RE_{UD}) \qquad 8.1$$

Using the fundamental consolidation identity, the last term is merely an expression for 30 per cent of the equitized investment. The fundamental consolidation equation (using equation 4.2 on page 78) is:

$$INV_{UD} + 60\% \times \Delta RE_{UD} = 60\% \times (NA_{UD} + G/W_{UD}) \qquad 8.2$$

Substituting for the last term of the equation above, we get

$$\text{MI} = 40\% \times NA_{UD} + 30\% \times NA_{UC} + 30\% \times 60\% \times (NA_{UD} + G/W_{UD})$$
$$= 58\% \times NA_{UD} + 30\% \times NA_{UC} + 18\% \times G/W_{UD}$$

Thus the main group minority interest has a direct and indirect share (58 per cent) in the net assets of Underdog, a direct share (30 per cent) in the net assets of Upper Cruft and, in its capacity as *subgroup* holding company shareholder, it owns 30 per cent of the subgroup's goodwill.

The situation where the minority owns goodwill is seemingly at odds with the parent company approach to consolidation. However, here minority goodwill arises from a *transaction* and is not a result of grossing up holding company goodwill (on a hypothetical basis) as in Chapter 4. In vertical groups, there are (at least) *three* tiers of shareholders; in the ultimate group, in the subgroup(s) and in ultimate sub-subsidiaries. Effectively we are asking here whether group accounts should treat all classes of minorities the same or allow differential treatments for more 'influential' subholdings.

Anecdotal evidence (plus a review of professional texts) suggests that the most used alternative is to state consolidated goodwill at the amount attributable to main group shareholders, and thus to remove the minority's share of subgroup goodwill. This implies *all* minority interests are stated at share of *net assets* in the subsidiaries they own (i.e. the third term above would be removed). However, it does not coincide with their proportionate share in the group accounts of the subgroup which they partially own. If the subgroup adopted the policy of immediate write-down of goodwill, no problems arise. However, if it did not, the treatment 'enforces' immediate write-down on the minority where it is not practised by the majority. Neither SSAP 14 nor SSAP 22 deals with this issue.

Simultaneous approach
Under this approach, the subgroup consolidation is ignored and the main group consolidation is done from scratch using multiplicative ownership proportions (e.g. $70\% \times 60\% = 42\%$). The approach is useful for examination purposes, being simple for small groups, though it may cause data management problems in

large groups (see later). Table 8.5 shows the simultaneous cancellation table for the main Top Dog group.

The only new technical procedure is that the subgroup investment in the sub-subsidiary (Underdog) is apportioned between the investment column and minority according to the holding company's stake in Upper Cruft (70:30). As can be seen by comparing the final figures with those above, the simultaneous approach implicitly *excludes* minority goodwill from the main group statements. The figure for minority interests can thus simply be checked as 70 per cent of Upper Cruft's net assets (70% × (7,300 − 5,000)) plus 58 per cent of Underdog's (58% × (2,000 − 1,000)). Consolidated reserves (£2,934) comprise holding company reserves (£2,500) plus (£350), 70 per cent of Upper Cruft's reserves since acquisition (i.e. 70% × (1,500 − 1,000)), plus (£84), 42 per cent of Underdog's reserves since its acquisition (i.e. 42% × (600 − 400)).

Sub-subsidiary acquired before the subsidiary joined the group

In Example 8.3, the sub-subsidiary was acquired *after* the subsidiary joined the group, hence the date for determining its post-acquisition profits for the main group is identical to the date on which it entered the subgroup. Suppose the subgroup purchases its holding in the sub-subsidiary *before* the holding company acquires the subgroup. Now some *post*-acquisition profits of the *subgroup* become *pre*-acquisition profits of the *main group*.

Example 8.4　Sub-subsidiary acquired first

Suppose Upper Cruft had acquired its interest in Underdog on 31 December 1982 when the retained earnings of Underdog were £200,000. Assume that on 31 December 1984 when Top Dog acquired its interest in Upper Cruft, retained earnings in Underdog were £400,000.

A short-cut approach usually recommended in this case is to treat the date of acquisition of the sub-subsidiary as 31 December 1984, the date the *main* group acquires the subsidiary. In this example, reserves of the sub-subsidiary at acquisition for main group purposes would be taken as £400,000. This approach is pragmatic and simple and adopted later in this section. Strictly however, sub-subsidiary profits between the date of acquisition by the subgroup and the main group should be treated as a non-distributable reserve. In Table 8.5 the following entry would be made:

	Consolidated reserves	Capital reserve	Goodwill
Transfer of pre-acquisition profits of *group* to capital reserve 42% × (400,000 − 200,000)	84,000	(84,000)	

	Investment	Share capital	Share premium	Goodwill	Consolidated reserves	Minority interests
Top Dog	2,500	(1,000)	(1,500)		(2,500)	
Upper Cruft (70:30):						
Subgroup investment	490					210
Pre-acquisition (700 + 800 + 1,000)				(1,750)		(750)
Post-acquisition (1,500 − 1,000)					(350)	(150)
Underdog (42 (70 × 60)/58):						
Pre-acquisition (150 + 250 + 400)				(336)		(464)
Post-acquisition (600 − 400)					(84)	(116)
Cancellation:						
Main group investment	(2,500)			2,500		
Subgroup investment (70%)	(490)			490		
Consolidated balances	—	(1,000)	(1,500)	904	(2,934)	(1,270)

Table 8.5   Simultaneous approach (vertical groups) cancellation table

The reason why the short-cut approach is not strictly correct is because the investment market value is measured at 31 December 1982, whereas the sub-subsidiary joined the main group on 31 December 1984, hence they are measured at two different dates and so should not be compared. Also SSAP 22 has more stringent requirements for capital reserves on acquisition (which *must* be credited directly to reserves) than for positive goodwill (which *may* be debited directly to reserves). The short-cut approach aggregates this capital reserve with main group goodwill at acquisition.

Exercise

8.2   Consider the balance sheets (£ million) of Bourgeoisie plc, Prole Ltd and Outcaste Ltd at 30 June 1986:

	Bourgeoisie	Prole	Outcaste
Assets	4,600	190	300
Investment in Prole	200		
Investment in Outcaste		160	
Liabilities	(2,000)	(70)	(100)
Share capital	(400)	(60)	(50)
Share premium	(900)	(100)	(80)
Retained earnings	(1,500)	(120)	(70)

Bourgeoisie acquired a 75 per cent interest in Prole on 31 October 1983, when the retained earnings of Prole were £40 million. Prole acquired its 80 per cent interest in Outcaste on 31 March 1985, when Outcaste's retained earnings were £50 million.

Required

(a)   Produce a cancellation table for Bourgeoisie group at 30 June 1986.
(b)   Interpret the composition of the balances for consolidated reserves, goodwill and minority interests.
(c)   Explain how the cancellation table in (a) above would be changed if Prole had acquired its stake on 31 March 1981 when Outcaste's reserves were £50 million. Reserves of Outcaste on 31 October 1983 had been £60 million.

Mixed groups – direct and indirect shareholdings in sub-subsidiaries

Consider where the group has the following structure:

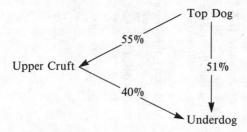

Now Top Dog has a direct and an indirect holding in Underdog. An expanded diagram of the group structure is shown in Figure 8.3.

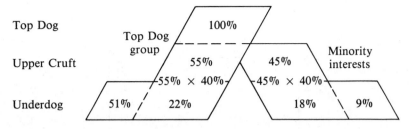

Figure 8.3   Disposition of shareholdings in a mixed group example

Underdog is now a direct subsidiary of Top Dog. However, it is not now a subsidiary of Upper Cruft, therefore no subgroup subconsolidation is required and the simultaneous method is to be used.

Example 8.5   All holdings acquired at same date

Assume the same balance sheets as in Example 8.3 with the changed group structure above, and given the following information. On 31 December 1984, Top Dog acquired a 55 per cent interest in Upper Cruft for £1,600 and a 51 per cent interest in Underdog for £900, when their reserves were respectively £1,000 and £300. On the same date Upper Cruft acquired a 40 per cent interest in Underdog for £700.

All holdings now were acquired on the same date. Consider the computation of direct and indirect holdings of Top Dog:

Holding in Upper Cruft = 55 per cent
Holding in Underdog   = 51% + (55% × 40%) = 73 per cent

and the simultaneous cancellation table is shown in Table 8.6.

As in the vertical group cancellation table, Upper Cruft's investment is split between investment and minority (now 55%:45%), again implicitly defining goodwill as that belonging to main group shareholders only. Again a simple check on the minority interest is whether it equals 45 per cent of the net assets of Upper Cruft plus 27 per cent of Underdog's, i.e.

$$= 45\% \times (7,300 - 5,000) + 27\% \times (2,000 - 1,000) = 1,305$$

Example 8.6   Holding in sub-subsidiary acquired later

If the piecemeal acquisition section has not been covered, this section can be ignored without loss of continuity. Suppose now that Upper Cruft acquired its 40 per cent interest in Underdog on 31 December 1985 for £600, when Underdog's reserves were £400 (i.e. later than the acquisition of Upper Cruft – in Example 8.5 the date was 31 December 1984, and reserves £300).

Now the sub-subsidiary was acquired piecemeal, effectively 51 per cent on 31 December 1984, and a further 55% × 40% = 22 per cent on 31 December 1985. The multiplicative procedure needs to be combined with the piecemeal technique studied earlier. A piecemeal analysis of the *sub-subsidiary's* equity (similar to in Figure 8.1) is shown in Figure 8.4

	Investment	Share capital	Share premium	Goodwill	Consolidated reserves	Minority interests
Top Dog	1,600	(1,000)	(1,500)		(2,500)	315
Upper Cruft (55:45):						
Subgroup investment	900					
Pre-acquisition (700 + 800 + 1,000)				(1,375)		(1,125)
Post-acquisition (1,500 − 1,000)					(275)	(225)
Underdog (73:27):	385					
Pre-acquisition (150 + 250 + 300)				(511)		(189)
Post-acquisition (600 − 300)					(219)	(81)
Cancellation:						
Main group investment	(2,500)			2,500		
Subgroup investment (55%)	(385)			385		
Consolidated balances	—	(1,000)	(1,500)	999	(2,994)	(1,305)

Table 8.6 Simultaneous approach (mixed groups): cancellation table for single date acquisition

Time period	Slices of Underdog equity		Analysis of equity slices		
			51%	22%	27%
			purchase	purchase	minority
Equity to 31/12/84	(150 + 250 + 300)	= 700	357	154	189
Retained earnings 12/84–12/85	(400 − 300)	= 100	51	22	27
Retained earnings 12/85–12/86	(600 − 400)	= 200	102	44	54
Total equity at 31/12/86	(150 + 250 + 600)	= 1,000	510	220	270

Figure 8.4   Mixed groups piecemeal acquisition – analysis of sub-subsidiary equity

The shaded area represents pre-acquisition equity, and its tiered appearance illustrates the piecemeal approach to the calculation of goodwill and consolidated reserves. The simultaneous cancellation table is shown in Table 8.7, based on Figure 8.4. The minority interest is the same as in the previous case as the change in acquisition dates affects the pre-/post-acquisition split, but does not affect the minority interest.

Subsidiary stake in sub-subsidiary prior to joining group

The principle here is no different from the previous section in that pragmatically the date of acquisition is usually taken as that when the main group comes into being. Similar comments apply. The analysis of holdings chronologically can become quite complex if the holding company and subsidiary are both acquiring piecemeal holdings, but this is not considered further here.

Exercises

8.3   Consider the balance sheets in Exercise 8.2, except that the group structure is now as follows.

Bourgeoisie acquired a 60 per cent interest in Prole for £170 million, and a 10 per cent interest in Outcaste for £30 million on 31 October 1983, when the reserves of the latter two companies were respectively £40 million and £20 million. Prole acquired an 80 per cent interest in Outcaste on the same date for £160 million.

Required
(a)   Produce a cancellation table for the main group at 30 June 1986.
(b)   Interpret the composition of the balances thus computed. Ignore the subsequent write-off of goodwill.

8.4   Carry out the calculations using the assumptions in 8.3, except that Prole acquired its 80 per cent interest at 31 March 1985, when Outcaste's reserves were £50 million.

	Proportions pre/post/mino.	Investment	Share capital	Share premium	Goodwill	Consolidated reserves	Minority interests
Top Dog		1,600	(1,000)	(1,500)		(2,500)	315
		900					
Upper Cruft (55:45):							
Subgroup investment		385					
To 12/84 (700 + 800 + 1,000)					(1,375)		(1,125)
To 12/86 (1,500 − 1,000)						(275)	(225)
Underdog:							
To 12/84 (150 + 250 + 300)	0/73/27				(511)*		(189)
To 12/85 (400 − 300)	22/51/27				(22)	(51)	(27)
To 12/86 (600 − 400)	73/0/27					(146)†	(54)
Cancellation:							
Main group investment		(2,500)			2,500		
Subgroup investment (55%)		(385)			385		
Consolidated balances		—	(1,000)	(1,500)	977	(2,972)	(1,305)

Note: * = 357 + 154   † = 102 + 44

Table 8.7 Simultaneous approach (mixed groups): cancellation table for piecemeal acquisition

8.5 Ditto except that Bourgeoisie's 10 per cent interest had instead been purchased on 31 October 1985 for £30 million, when the reserves of Outcaste were £55 million.

Cross-holdings – the case of bilateral holdings between subsidiaries

This section can be omitted without loss of continuity. Sometimes one group company acquires holdings in another which already holds its shares, creating *reciprocal* or *bilateral* holdings. Section 23 of the Companies Act 1985 prohibits a company being a member of its *holding company* unless the holding was acquired before 1 July 1948. Shaw (1973, p. 238) interprets the corresponding section in earlier Acts as requiring the subsidiary to dispose of any shares it may have held in its holding company prior to acquisition. However, there is nothing to prevent cross-holdings between subsidiaries where neither is the holding company of the other. In the author's experience such holdings are rare in the UK, though extremely common in certain other countries (see McKinnon, 1984, on Japan). This section is based on Brault (1979).

Example 8.7   Cross-holdings between subsidiaries

Suppose the mixed group case is modified slightly so that at its acquisition, Underdog already held a 10 per cent interest in Upper Cruft. Apart from this *bilateral* holding, the group structure is the same:

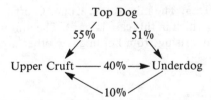

Expressing group relationships using linear equations

In this situation simple multiplication to calculate main group proportionate holdings does not work. Instead a simultaneous linear equations approach is used here, applied first to the mixed group case used in Example 8.5 without (the upward 10 per cent) cross-holdings. The following equations express group *proportional* holdings in this example (where TD, UC, and UD refer respectively to Top Dog, Upper Cruft and Underdog):

$$TD = 1.0$$
$$UC = 0.55TD$$
$$UD = 0.51TD + 0.40UC$$

Substituting the first into the second and the second into the third, we get the proportions used in the simultaneous approach cancellation table.

$$TD = 1.0$$
$$UC = 0.55$$
$$UD = 0.73$$

In the more complex cross-holdings case, the simultaneous equations approach gives more insight. The group relationships are expressed:

$$TD = 1.0$$
$$UC = \quad 0.55TD + \qquad\qquad 0.10UD$$
$$UD = \quad 0.51TD + 0.40UC$$

Upper Cruft is now owned 55 per cent 'downwards' and 10 per cent 'upwards'. Solving these equations by substitution, we get:

$$TD = 1.0$$
$$UC = 0.626$$
$$UD = 0.760$$

So in the simultaneous cancellation table the proportions used for Upper Cruft would be 62.6 per cent for majority and $(100 - 62.6) = 37.4$ per cent for the minority, and for Underdog 76.0 per cent and 24.0 per cent respectively.

Minority interests – complementary equations

The holding company proportions can be checked using complementary equations for minority interests. Consider first the simple mixed group example. Minority holdings in the Top Dog group are expressed by:

$$TD = 0.00$$
$$UC = 0.45 + 0.55TD$$
$$UD = 0.09 + 0.51TD + 0.40UC$$

i.e. there is no minority interest in Top Dog. The minority in Upper Cruft is 45 per cent plus any arising from Top Dog (which in this case is zero). The minority in Underdog is 9 per cent direct plus any arising from holdings by other group companies. Solving these equations, we get:

$$TD = 0.00$$
$$UC = 0.45$$
$$UD = 0.09 + 0.40 \times 0.55 = 0.27$$

These equations show minority proportions, also disclosing the direct minority in Underdog and the indirect minority (22 per cent) arising from subgroup holdings. It is possible to use the equations to determine subgroup holdings alone. For this see Brault (1979).

In the cross-holdings case, the minority structure is expressed:

$$TD = 0.00$$
$$UC = 0.35 + 0.55TD \qquad\qquad\qquad +0.10UD$$
$$UD = 0.09 + 0.51TD + 0.40UC$$

The minority in Upper Cruft is 35 per cent $(100\% - 55\% - 10\%)$ held directly, and indirectly, via Top Dog (55 per cent) and Underdog (10 per cent). Solutions are:

TD = 0.000
UC = 0.374
UD = 0.240

consistent with the original solutions. There are other ways of setting up cross-holding equations (see for example Shaw, 1973, ch. 13), but Brault's (1979) approach has been used here as the simplest way of representing the group holding structure. In larger and more complex groups, such equation systems can be handled by matrix inversion computer routines (see for example Griffin, Williams and Larson, 1980, pp. 455–8). In piecemeal acquisitions, a set of equations is formulated and solved at each ownership change to evaluate holdings, and the techniques discussed earlier in the chapter can be used.

Exercises

8.6   For Exercise 8.3
(a)   Formulate a set of simultaneous linear equations for holdings in the Bourgeoisie group. Solve them and compare solutions with 8.3.
(b)   Formulate complementary equations for minority interests and verify the solutions with part (a).
8.7   Formulate a set of simultaneous equations for following structure. Bourgeoisie holds a 60 per cent interest in Prole and a 65 per cent interest in Outcaste. Prole holds a 30 per cent interest in Outcaste. Outcaste holds a 25 per cent interest in Prole. Formulate and solve complementary equations for minorities.

Acquisition of other classes of equity/liabilities

Sometimes the subsidiary has different classes of equity or liabilities and this affects the computation of goodwill and minority interests. Consider the following balance sheets at 31 March 1987:

	Daddy plc	Sonny Ltd
Assets	400,000	380,000
Investment in Sonny	190,000	—
10 per cent debentures of Sonny	30,000	(60,000)
Other liabilities	(200,000)	(100,000)
Ordinary share capital	(80,000)	(40,000)
Share premium	(150,000)	(60,000)
Preference share capital	—	(25,000)
Retained earnings	(190,000)	(95,000)

On 31 March 1985, Daddy acquired 80 per cent of the ordinary share capital of Sonny, 60 per cent of its preference share capital and 50 per cent of its debentures for £220,000 when Sonny's retained earnings were £80,000. The consideration comprised £190,000 for the ordinary and preference shares and £30,000 for debentures.

Share component

Assuming the preference share dividends were not in arrears, retained earnings here are attributable to the ordinary shares. Thus, the investment is to be cancelled against 80 per cent of the ordinary share capital, share premium and retained earnings at acquisition, and against 60 per cent of the preference share capital. Note Sonny is a subsidiary of Daddy since the proportion of its *equity* owned is:

$$((80\% \times 40{,}000) + (60\% \times 25{,}000))/(40{,}000 + 25{,}000) = 72.3\%$$

Debenture component

The debenture as a long-term debtor in the holding company balance sheet is an intercompany balance to be cancelled on consolidation. The debentures owned by outsiders are liabilities in the *consolidated* balance sheet and *not* a part of minority interests. The holding company's portion of interest paid by the subsidiary would be cancelled against interest received by the holding company, and the remainder (to outsiders) included as a part of consolidated interest payable (not minority interests). The effects of these entries are shown in the following cancellation table.

	Invest ment	Share cap.	Share prem.	Consol. RE	Goodwill	Minor. int.	Debentures
Daddy	190	(80)	(150)	(190)			30
Sonny:							
Pre-acq. – ord. (80:20)					(144)	(36)	
Pre-acq. – pref. (60:40)					(15)	(10)	
Post-acq. (80:20)				(12)		(3)	
Other balances							(60)
Cancellation	(190)				190		
Consolidated	—	(80)	(150)	(202)	31	(49)	(30)

In this example it has been assumed for simplicity that the market value of debentures was equal to face value at acquisition. This would normally be unusual. Strictly, under SSAP 14 liabilities should be revalued at acquisition. In the USA, the revalued amount would be the present value at the market rate of interest *at the date of acquisition* for a similar loan with the same contracted interest payments plus repayment of principal. Possibly the amount paid at acquisition would be a starting point in determining this. The consolidated loan charges would then include the interest payments plus an annual adjustment (akin to depreciation) to charge over the life of the loan part of the 'revaluation excess', or interest charges would be determined by normal discounting principles. For further discussion see Holgate (1986b) who notes that a more common UK practice is to continue to record the debentures at nominal/face amount.

If the preference dividends were in arrears, part of pre-acquisition retained earnings would relate to the preference shares and be split 60:40, the balance being split 80:20. For a further discussion of the complexities arising from more complex financial instruments (e.g. convertible debentures or participating preference shares) see Shaw (1973, ch. 6). In the consolidated profit and loss account, preference dividends are dealt with in a similar manner to ordinary dividends and minority interests include a preference share component, the remaining balance being split according to ordinary share ownership.

Exercise

8.8 Consider the following balance sheets of Geared plc and Cog Ltd at 31 December 1986 (in £000):

	Geared	Cog
Assets	1,540	730
Investment in Cog	210	
8 per cent debentures of Cog	50	(100)
Liabilities	(400)	(200)
Ordinary share capital	(200)	(75)
Preference share capital	(100)	(40)
Share premium	(150)	(90)
Retained earnings	(950)	(225)

On 28 February 1983, Geared plc purchased 70 per cent of Cog's ordinary share capital, 90 per cent of its preference share capital, and 50 per cent of its debentures, all for £260,000. At that date, retained earnings of Cog were £55,000 of which £10,000 represented arrears to preference shareholders. There have been no issues of shares by Cog since that date.

Required Prepare a cancellation table for the Geared group at 31 December 1986, commenting on your breakdown of Cog's equity and the treatment of the debentures.

CONSOLIDATIONS IN PRACTICE

In this book (as in most accounting texts and examination questions) balance sheet consolidations are calculated from scratch. However, consolidations in practice are usually updates of the previous period's calculations. The first part of this section shows how this updating is handled. The second and major part considers how computer packages are used to aid data collection and the consolidation process itself.

The updating form of cancellation table

Example 8.8 shows consolidation as an *updating* of the previous year's calculations.

Example 8.8   Consolidation as updating

Consider the following details relating to acquisitions by Holding Co. over three years ended 31 December 1986:

31 December 1984 Acquired an 80 per cent stake in Subsidiary 1
31 December 1985 Issued shares to increase group working capital
30 June 1986   Acquired a 60 per cent stake in Subsidiary 2 for shares

The equity sections of the three companies for this period were as follows (asset and liability balances are not shown, and at each date are added item by item if there are no alignment adjustments).

	Holding company			Subsidiary 1			Subsidiary 2	
	12/84	12/85	12/86	12/84	12/85	12/86	6/86	12/86
Investment	1,000	1,000	1,400	—	—	—	—	—
Share capital	(500)	(700)	(975)	(200)	(200)	(200)	(100)	(100)
Share premium	(400)	(800)	(925)	(300)	(300)	(300)	(200)	(200)
Retained earnings	(300)	(500)	(800)	(400)	(450)	(500)	(300)	(500)

Table 8.8 shows the cancellation table for the above transactions laid out *in sequential form*, showing the update each year.

Each year's update in consolidated retained earnings corresponds to the total of the year's consolidated profit and loss account. If (as in Chapter 5) an extended cancellation table is necessary to incorporate other assets and liabilities requiring adjustment, the columns in the 'extension' section are attached afresh each year on to the *ongoing* core comprising share capital, premium, consolidated reserves, goodwill and minority interests. In the extended table, only the core is *updated*.

Complete disposals of subsidiaries can be handled by removing all the consolidated balances in the table at the date of disposal, plus the investment. As discussed on page 138, the consolidated retained earnings of the subsidiary plus consolidated gain or loss on disposal will automatically be included when the holding company's reserve movement is included for the year. Piecemeal acquisitions by existing subsidiaries will involve a transfer from minority interests to pre-acquisition profits (i.e. the goodwill column). These aspects and partial disposals are not discussed further here.

Exercise

8.9 Consider the following details relating to acquisitions by Big Brother plc over three years ended 30 September 1986.

30 September 1984 Acquired a 60 per cent stake in Subsidiary 1
31 August 1985   Acquired a 75 per cent stake in Subsidiary 2
30 June 1986   Share issue for cash by Big Brother

The equity sections of the three companies at the relevant dates were

	Big Brother			Subsidiary 1			Subsidiary 2		
	9/84	9/85	9/86	9/84	9/85	9/86	8/85	9/85	9/86
Investment	800	1,700	1,700	—	—	—			
Share capital	(600)	(700)	(975)	(150)	(150)	(150)	(200)	(200)	(200)
Share premium	(500)	(800)	(925)	(250)	(250)	(250)	(350)	(350)	(350)
Retained earnings	(400)	(500)	(800)	(550)	(650)	(850)	(450)	(500)	(600)

	Investment	Share capital	Share premium	Goodwill	Consolidated ret. earnings	Minority interests
31 Dec. 1984:						
Holding Co.	1,000	(500)	(400)		(300)	
Subsidiary 1:						
Pre-acquisition				(720)		(180)
Cancellation Subsidiary 1	(1,000)			1,000		
Subtotal Dec. 1985	—	(500)	(400)	280	(300)	(180)
31 Dec. 1985 update:						
Holding Co.:						
Retained for year					(200)	
Share issue*		(200)	(400)			
Subsidiary 1:						
Retained for year					(40)	(10)
Subtotal Dec. 1985	—	(700)	(800)	280	(540)	(190)
31 Dec. 1986 update:						
Holding Co.:						
Retained for year					(300)	
Share issue for	400	(275)	(125)			
Subsidiary 2 (30 June)						
Subsidiary 1:						
Retained for year					(40)	(10)
Subsidiary 2:						
Pre-acquisition				(360)		(240)
Retained since 30 June					(120)	(80)
Cancellation	(400)			400		
Subsidiary 2						
Subtotal Dec. 1986	—	(975)	(925)	320	(1,000)	(520)

* Note – Other side of the double entry is to Dr. cash, not in table.

Table 8.8 Sequential form of cancellation table showing updating

Required Prepare a consolidation cancellation table showing the initital consolidation at 30 September 1984 and the *updates* for each year to 30 September 1986.

Using computer packages to carry out consolidations

In practice a major problem area is concerned with the logistics of preparing group accounts. For example, Taylor (1984) cites about 140 management reporting entities in the Plessey group which collapse into about 80 entities for statutory reporting purposes, using 19 different currencies. In 1985 ICI plc had 418 subsidiaries using 56 currencies. Such consolidations would be virtually impossible without the use of proprietary or custom-built computer packages, many of which combine statutory consolidations with management reporting, and some of which run on microcomputers. Advantages include speed and accuracy, especially with the increasing disclosures and cross-checking required by the Companies Act and SSAPs. ICI, for example, requires the equivalent of over one hundred pages of detailed reporting forms from each subsidiary in compiling its annual report.

Computer package features

Most modern packages allow data input direct to screen via terminals, allowing easy verification and validation. Errors are quickly identified and exception reports automatically produced. Security of data is ensured by 'passwords' which allow only authorized users to access the package and its information. Password systems often differentiate between levels of access allowed, for example, from inputting and viewing own subsidiary data up to amending, viewing and receiving monitoring reports on the whole consolidation. Some systems allow subsidiaries themselves to input and prevalidate their initial data via remote terminals (even in other countries) which is transmitted electronically to head office.

Packages are usually 'menu'-driven, the screen displaying a list of options. An initial menu might offer the options of viewing raw data or company master files, displaying validation errors on input, displaying or inputting consolidation adjustments, disclosing details of intercompany balances, performing consolidations or subconsolidations (for statutory or management purposes), or analysing the data (e.g. ratios). Accessing options is usually arranged hierarchically. When an option is selected, usually another submenu based on the option selected is displayed to prompt the user. For example, the selection of the consolidate option will provide a submenu requiring the user to state which companies or subgroup and which financial statements he wishes to consolidate. This may access a lower level submenu which might list the codes of various subsidiaries or subgroups. Once the option is fully specified, the package will extract relevant data from the master file, current consolidation adjustments, etc. and perform the consolidation.

A computerized system can carry out 'draft' subconsolidations quickly and effectively even before all consolidated information is agreed, enabling management to review the overall picture at a very early stage whilst the data capture is still in process. The program can also display the current status of the consolidation, e.g. subsidiaries still to submit data, consolidation or company adjustments currently included, errors as yet uncorrected, and the extent of disagreements in intercompany balances. Foreign currency translations also can be easily carried out.

Many packages allow instantaneous analysis of the consolidated data (e.g. comparisons with previous years' or budgeted figures, producing ratio analyses for individual companies, subgroups or the whole group, or producing graphical plots). Segmental data can also be easily produced. The choice between packages often depends on their analytical and report generating capabilities, as well as their speed, computational efficiency and cost. Often statutory reporting is integrated with management reporting and the consolidation is a by-product. However, some companies use microcomputer packages purely for statutory purposes because of the detail required to meet institutional requirements.

Example 8.9 Use of computer packages

Figure 8.5 shows the screen menus for a hypothetical computer package. After logging in with the password (only known to the authorized user), the information on screen 1 appears. The user decides which option he requires. Here he wishes to consolidate the South East Asian Electronics subgroup. He inputs 'e' signifying the 'consolidate' option.

Screen 2 discloses a submenu for the consolidation option. He inputs 'ee' indicating that he wishes to consolidate all the financial statements for the subgroup. Automatically screen 2 scrolls onwards to ask the level of consolidation required. He inputs 'eg', indicating 'subgroup'. The subgroups (prespecified earlier) appear on screen 3. He inputs 'egd' which indicates the South East Asian Electronics subgroup. The computer will then probably provide further screens, e.g. asking if he needs a print-out, and/or giving him a status report of the included information. Menu-driven packages allow new users to use the package easily, saving considerable time in searching manuals for relevant codes. Often regular users are given the option to bypass the menus.

The effect of group structure

Pedley (1985) proposes a set of dimensions to provide a guide in the choice of a suitable system, shown in Table 8.9.

At one end of the spectrum is a centrally organized, wholly owned group, in which there is scope for the use of uniform formats and policies, and where it is easy to specify standardized analyses and consolidation adjustments. In such circumstances it may be possible to key in information at remote terminals and to transmit standardized management reports back to subsidiaries. At the other end of the spectrum is the partially owned 'subsidiary'-based financial conglomerate in which only limited information in differing formats is received from 'investments'. In this case computerization is harder and it may be difficult to issue standard reporting forms to subsidiaries for statutory accounts purposes.

In the middle, a majority owned group may have subsidiaries in differing commercial areas, environments and reporting systems. Here it may be difficult and even undesirable to impose centralized policies, formats and processing. Management reports might be produced in differing styles, and head office extracts relevant information from these differing formats. Standardized reporting may only be used for statutory purposes, and the consolidation package may not include remote data capture possible in the centralized case. These caricatures are useful to exhibit differences between typical group structures.

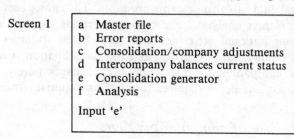

Screen 1
```
a   Master file
b   Error reports
c   Consolidation/company adjustments
d   Intercompany balances current status
e   Consolidation generator
f   Analysis

Input 'e'
```

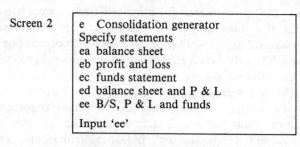

Screen 2
```
e   Consolidation generator
Specify statements
ea  balance sheet
eb  profit and loss
ec  funds statement
ed  balance sheet and P & L
ee  B/S, P & L and funds

Input 'ee'
```

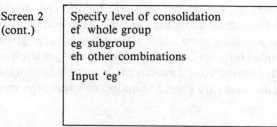

Screen 2 (cont.)
```
Specify level of consolidation
ef  whole group
eg  subgroup
eh  other combinations

Input 'eg'
```

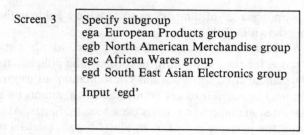

Screen 3
```
Specify subgroup
ega European Products group
egb North American Merchandise group
egc African Wares group
egd South East Asian Electronics group

Input 'egd'
```

Figure 8.5   Screen menus for hypothetical package

| Management style | Exercise of control | |
	Typical % shareholding in group companies	Business sector
Centralized	100	Products
Management	40–100	Services
Investment	10–50	Financial

Table 8.9   Group structures and the choice of consolidation package
Source: Pedley (1985), *Accountancy*, June, p. 121.

Setting up a computerized system

The effort and time involved vary according to the complexity of the group, whether management reporting is to be integrated with statutory reporting, and the extent to which suitable 'off the shelf' packages are available. Whitehouse (1984) commented that the Dowty group took eight weeks from ordering their standard package to live running. Initially the computerized system is often run in parallel with its manual counterpart. Designing reporting forms for subsidiaries is a complex task. These need to be very detailed due to reporting requirements, and also may be used for management reporting. ICI plc receives on average about two thousand lines of information per subsidiary. Within the package itself the basic reporting structure of the group is formulated, and also the normal subconsolidations required, together with those for segmental and management reporting purposes.

Various checks need to be built in, not only total and 'hash' total checks for input validation, but also cross-referencing checks (e.g. that the 'movements in fixed assets' ties up with comparative balance sheets, with the profit and loss account, the funds statement and the notes). The ICI management and financial reporting suite contains over 2,500 such checks, including whether or not a revenue or expense item has been correctly entered as a debit or credit. Often validation against such checks takes longer than the consolidation itself. However, it was stressed by one finance director interviewed by the author that it is most important that the initial data is very carefully checked and screened. It takes an incredible time to locate errors if 'dirty' data is accepted into the consolidation system. In addition the impact of the system on the audit trail needs to be considered and auditors consulted before it goes 'live'.

Instruction manuals for subsidiaries must be written. Realistic reporting timetables need to be assessed, especially in large groups where the preparation and audit of subsidiaries' accounts, the consolidation and its audit have a time-scale of two months or less. Potential problems with foreign subsidiaries need to be foreseen early. The behavioural impact of the computerized system is a major consideration, since a very different mode of working is involved – to a much tighter time-scale in both submitting data and interacting with the package to produce management reports. Once the basic set-up is complete, it is comparatively easy to accommodate, e.g. changes in group structure each year. It can take literally five minutes to set up the master file for a new subsidiary (if you know the passwords!). Computerized systems have a high 'front end' cost but are easy to maintain and use.

Specific examples

Taylor (1984) discusses the issues involved for Plessey in setting up a centralized system integrated with management reporting, opting for computerized data capture and validation on subsidiaries' microcomputers, and electronic transmission to the networked head office minicomputer. Subsidiaries could generate their own information, and also have performance analyses, etc. transmitted back from head office. Taylor observes that statutory accounts preparation was considerably speeded up and detailed Companies Act formats easily incorporated.

Because ICI has over four hundred subsidiaries operating in a vast range of environments, it receives data in a variety of ways, some electronically transmitted, some via telex and some hard copy by post. A head office team handles the custom-designed consolidation system which is integrated with management reporting. ICI staggers its information collection to schedule an inherently lumpy process into a smooth flow for subsidiaries and head office – a major operation in itself for such a large group.

As far as possible, subsidiaries are encouraged to prevalidate data prior to electronic transmission. The transmitted data is processed at head office on a large mainframe computer used solely for consolidation purposes, thus increasing security. Hard copy of the transmitted statutory accounts data is returned by head office to subsidiaries for audit.

The data is subjected to further validation before foreign currency translation and consolidation. As further data is received, the cycle repeats itself until all the data is received and pronounced 'clean'. Monitoring the state of completion of the process is a major task. Each computer cycle takes hours (mainly for validation reasons) and the whole process takes days. Financial statements are produced as well as numerous analyses and quarterly management reports. The programs are designed to be as efficient computationally as possible and to leave a sound audit trail (all alterations being clearly delineated).

Discussion question

8.10 Headache Group has ten subsidiaries and two associated companies. Of the subsidiaries, five operate in the pharmaceutical sector (in the UK (two), Germany, France and India), three as retail chemists (in the UK, France and Germany), one owning a fast-food chain in the USA, and one as a finance subsidiary for the whole group. The associated companies are based in the UK and Australia respectively.

Required You are asked to write a report to advise the board of directors of the Headache Group on factors to be considered in deciding whether or not to computerize the group consolidation, which at present takes two accountants three man-weeks each to complete after statutory accounts have been received from the group companies.

SUMMARY

Technical problems occur where holdings arise from serial transactions (*piecemeal* acquisitions and disposals), whether the date of acquisition should be taken as a single date or a series of dates. Problems occur when a transaction causes the holding to cross the *three tiers* of measurement and disclosure. More complex group structures arise where subsidiaries hold shares in sub-subsidiaries (*vertical* groups), where in addition the holding company holds shares in sub-subsidiaries (*mixed* groups), or where subsidiaries hold bilateral holdings in each other (*cross*-holdings). Controversy arises over whether consolidated accounts for the ultimate group should include all goodwill arising within the group, or just that attributable to ultimate holding company shareholders. Acquisition of different classes of equity was discussed.

In practice the cancellation table is updated each year. Many of the main problems are *logistical* – how to collect data in vast group structures, how to process the data and produce a massive consolidation to a tight schedule. The use of computers has revolutionized the consolidation scene over a short period. Some groups use them for data collection and transmission in addition to consolidation. Initial set-up times are significant, but the use of computer packages in this area has become a necessity for multinational groups because of the increasing complexity of the environment, reporting requirements and the increasing pressure from electronically based capital markets for timely information.

FURTHER READING

Brault, R. (1979) A simple approach to complex consolidations, *CA Magazine,* April 1979, pp. 52–4.

Shaw, J. (ed.) (1973) *Bogie on Group Accounts* (3rd edn), especially chs. 6, 8, and 10, Jordans, Bristol.

Wilkins, R. M. (1979) *Group Accounts: The fundamental principles, form and content* (2nd edn), especially chs. 5, 6 and 9, Institute of Chartered Accountants in England and Wales, London.

9 Foreign Currency Translation

This chapter focuses on the translation of foreign currency *financial statements*. Translation of *transactions* is dealt with only to develop concepts for statement translation. The topic is very important, generating vigorous debate (in conditions under which one favoured approach produces a gain, the other favoured approach usually produces a loss!), spawning numerous empirical studies, and exposing raw nerves underlying consolidation and the historical cost basis. It also provides an interesting application of funds flow concepts. It has assumed growing importance in economic terms, with the vigorous expansion of multinational companies and the decision of the major trading nations to let their exchange rates 'float' freely since 1971. Thus, both the number of companies affected and the size and variability of reported exchange gains and losses have mushroomed.

After looking at basic concepts, translation of financial statements is considered using a numerical case. SSAP 20 is then reviewed, and the translation debate considered from both conceptual and political dimensions.

BASIC CONCEPTS

Foreign currency exposure

This section distinguishes economic and accounting exposure. Note that 'conversion' of foreign currency balances means physically changing one currency into another. 'Translation' means restating a balance in one currency into another, with no actual currency swop taking place.

Economic exposure

In business finance, assets are valued in terms of the net present value of *future* cash flows. If these are denominated in a foreign currency, then their sterling amount will be affected by exchange movements, i.e. they (and the investment) are *exposed* to changes in current and future exchange rates (unless there are compensating changes in interest rates or risk). Such exposure is termed 'economic' exposure.

Accounting exposure

This relates to exchange gains or losses arising from translation of balances or flows resulting from *past* transactions. Whether or not an item is exposed in an *accounting* sense is a matter of definition. Accounting exposure may or may not be correlated with economic exposure, since they measure different things. For each balance sheet item, there are two accepted translation rates; the *current* rate (i.e. the rate at the date of the financial statements), or the *historical* rate (i.e. the rate at the date of the original transaction). As will be shown below, items exhibit accounting exposure if they are translated at the current rate, but not if translated at the historical rate.

Example 9.1   Accounting exposure

	Exchange rate (Marks per £)
1 January 1986	4.1
31 December 1986	3.7

Suppose I purchase 100 marks' worth of stock on 1 January 1986 and hold them throughout the year. Consider the following calculations:

Date	Current rate	Historical rate
1 January 1986	100/4.1 = £24.39	100/4.1 = £24.39
31 December 1986	100/3.7 = £27.03	100/4.1 = £24.39
Difference	£2.64	Nil

The rate at original acquisition of the stock was 4.1 marks to the £ (at the beginning of the year). Under the historical rate approach, the rate remains unchanged at the year-end and so there is no change in the translated balance. However, the *current* rate changes over the year and consequently the current rate translated balance changes. There is a 'gain' of £2.64 because the mark has strengthened against the £. This *accounting* exposure (only using the *current* rate) arose from translating a *past* transaction. Accounting exposure when translating *individual* assets and liabilities at the *current* rate is summarized in Table 9.1.

Type of balance	Overseas currency Stronger (+)	Weaker (−)
Asset (+)	+	−
Liability (−)	−	+

Key + = Exchange gain   − = Exchange loss

Table 9.1   Exposure of individual assets/liabilities to exchange rate fluctuations

For example, when the overseas currency weakens (i.e. more marks to the £ at the year-end than at the beginning), liabilities translated at current rate will show an exchange gain. The amount to be paid at the year-end in sterling will be less than at the beginning, so the debtor firm will show a gain. This can be deduced by the algebra of signs, viz. a liability ($-$) when the overseas currency weakens ($-$) gives $- \times - = +$, hence an exchange gain ($+$). These basic principles apply to all statement translation approaches.

Foreign currency transactions

The translation of foreign currency *financial statements*, requires a basic understanding of the fundamentals of translating *transactions*.

Example 9.2　Translating transactions

A fixed asset is purchased on credit by a UK company for 2,000 marks when the exchange rate is 4.1 marks to the £. Three months later, the debt is paid when the exchange rate is 3.9 marks to the £. Consider the following calculations and how to account for the transaction.

Cost of fixed asset in £ at date of purchase = 2,000/4.1 = £488
Payment for asset in £ three months later   = 2,000/3.9 = £513
Difference   = £25

At the date of purchase
The journal entry would be:

    Fixed asset　　Dr. £488
    Creditors　　　　　　　Cr. £488

Subsequent to the date of purchase
The problem is how to account for the £25 difference arising between the times of purchase and payment. One alternative, the 'one transaction approach', adjusts the original cost of the asset to the price actually paid. The other, 'the two transaction approach', assumes there are two transactions here, a purchase (operating) transaction *and* a financing transaction. The fixed asset cost should remain unchanged and the difference on settlement be shown separately as an exchange loss (a financing expense). Both would show settlement of creditors as:

    Creditors　　　　Dr. £513
    Cash　　　　　　　　　Cr. £513

but would differ as to the disposition of the £25 difference now existing on creditors as a result of the transaction:

One transaction approach

Fixed asset　Dr. £25
Creditors　　　　　Cr. £25

Two transaction approach

Exchange loss (P & L)　Dr. £25
Creditors　　　　　　　　　　Cr. £25

Thus, the one transaction approach shows the cost of the fixed assets as £513, whereas the two transaction approach shows a cost of £488 and separately an exchange loss of £25.

What is the real cost under historical cost accounting? Objections to the one transaction approach might be that such a cost includes events *subsequent* to the original transaction (e.g. runs on the pound!) contrary to the spirit of historical cost. In comparison, bad debts write-offs are disclosed separately in the profit and loss account not as an adjustment to sales, akin to a two transaction approach, the sale and the subsequent adjustment.

It is possible to argue a solution midway between the one and two transaction approaches, that the true cost is the amount *expected* to be paid at settlement, but *estimated* at the original transaction date, to be estimated, for example, using the three months forward rate which is not affected by subsequent events. However, both UK and US accounting standards recommend the *two* transaction approach for *transactions*. This forms the basis of the temporal approach to translating *statements* discussed later. The treatment of forward exchange contracts is not discussed in this book.

Transactions not yet settled
Usually the rate at the date of the current financial statements is used as the best estimate of the settlement rate. A further adjustment is then made at settlement. For example, if the financial statement date was two months after the original transaction, and the exchange rate then was 4.0 marks to the £, the estimated payment would be 2,000/4.0 = £500. The two transaction approach would result in the following:

Exchange loss (P & L)	Dr. £12	
Creditors		Cr. £12

the remaining £13 (i.e. £513 − £500) being adjusted in the next period.

Exercise

9.1 How would the following be disclosed under (a) the one transaction approach, and (b) the two transaction approach?

A fixed asset was purchased on 1 January 1987 for 5,000 marks, the account being settled on 28 February. The exchange rate at 1 January was 2.3 marks to the £, and at 28 February 2.0 marks to the £. The asset has a life of ten years with no scrap value and is to be depreciated using the straight line method.

FOREIGN CURRENCY FINANCIAL STATEMENTS

In consolidated accounts, gains and losses on foreign exchange arise from both translation of *transactions* (of the parent and subsidiaries) *and* the translation of the foreign currency *statements* (of overseas subsidiaries). These two sources could in principle be disclosed separately. The translation of statements can be viewed as a three-stage process as shown in Table 9.2. Stage 2 is the main focus of this chapter. It is important to grasp clearly the order and significance of the three stages.

Stage 1	Completion of local currency financial statements of each group company. Foreign currency *transactions* of each company are translated using two transaction approach.
Stage 2	Translation of each foreign subsidiary's local currency *statements* into the reporting currency of the parent.
Stage 3	Consolidation of the group financial statements, all of which are now expressed in sterling.

Table 9.2   Consolidation of foreign currency statements as a three-stage process

Approaches to translating balance sheets

Many of the controversies in translation arise from the use of historical cost accounting. Since it is the main focus of external financial reporting in the UK for the foreseeable future, the approaches are studied in this context. Under current cost accounting the two main translation approaches described later give the same solution, and many of the problems disappear.

Under historical cost, the alternative approaches can be viewed merely as different *definitions* of which assets and liabilities should be translated at the current rate, and which at the historical rate. These are shown in Table 9.3. 'C' means the balance is translated at the current rate, and 'H' at the historical rate. The 'Net amounts exposed' section shows which items in *aggregate* are exposed in an accounting sense (i.e. translated at the current rate).

Balance sheet item	Translation approach			
	Current Non-current	Monetary Non-monetary	Temporal	Closing rate
Cash, debtors and creditors	C	C	C	C
Stocks and short-term investments:				
– at cost	C	H	H	C
– at NRV	C	H	C	C
Fixed assets	H	H	H	C
Long-term debt	H	C	C	C
Net amounts exposed	Current assets less current liabilities	Monetary assets less monetary liabilities	Current *dated* assets less current *dated* liabilities	Total assets less total liabilities

Table 9.3   Exchange rates used to translate balance sheet items

Long-term debt is a monetary, non-current asset, stated under historical cost at the amount to be repaid. Hence, the current/non-current approach (C–NC) translates it at the historical rate, monetary/non-monetary (M–NM) and temporal at the current rate, and the closing rate approach (CR) at the current rate. Stocks at cost are current, non-monetary assets, stated at historical acquisition cost. However, stocks at NRV are stated at current market price and so for the temporal approach are deemed 'current dated' and translated at the current rate, even though non-monetary.

Table 9.4 is the direct analogue of Table 9.1, but now *net aggregate* balances are exposed, not individual ones. Comparing the two is helpful to get an intuitive idea of exposure under each method. In most firms, current assets exceed current liabilities, and total assets total liabilities, so the net aggregate exposed under the C–NC and closing rate approaches tends to be *asset* balances. The converse applies under the temporal and M–NM approaches because of the inclusion of long-term loans in the exposed aggregate, which usually exceeds the amount of short-term net monetary assets and other net current dated assets giving a net *liability* balance in aggregate.

Thus, the aggregate exposed under the temporal approach is termed net current dated *liabilities*. 'Current dated' refers to the 'datedness' of balances and is not the same as 'current' as in current assets. Analogous to Table 9.1, if the net *aggregate* exposed is an asset balance and the overseas currency is strengthening, the end-of-year translated sterling amount will be greater than at the start and an exchange gain from accounting exposure will be disclosed. For a net liability balance under the same circumstances a loss will be shown, and vice versa if the overseas currency is weakening. Again, gains and losses can be deduced by the algebra of signs. These intuitive results form an important building block for understanding the translation process.

Exercises

9.2 The exchange rates versus the pound for the marc and the frank at the beginning and end of the first three months of 1987 were as follows:

	Marc	*Frank*
1 January 1987	2.5	1.8
31 March 1987	2.7	1.7

Evaluate which of the four translation approaches discussed above will show a gain and which a loss if:
(a) the balance sheets are denominated in marcs;
(b) if they are denominated in franks.
Give an intuitive explanation of your results.

9.3 The gobbledegook/non-gobbledegook (G–NG) approach translates fixed assets and current liabilities at the current rate and all other assets and liabilities at the historical rate. Discuss its properties. (This fictitious approach is used merely as a skills exercise.)

	Closing rate	Approach		
		Current/non-current	Monetary/non-monetary	Temporal
Assets and liabilities exposed	Total assets less liabilities	Currents assets less liabilities	Monetary assets less liabilities	Current *dated* assets less liabilities
Usual net aggregate balance	Asset(+)	Asset(+)	Liability(−)	Liability(−)
Gain or loss when overseas currency is getting:				
− stronger(+)	+	+	−	−
− weaker(−)	−	−	+	+

Key + = Exchange gain　　− = Exchange loss

Table 9.4　Accounting exposure of net aggregates to exchange rate fluctuations

The historical context

According to Nobes (1980) the closing rate was the first method to be widely used. Earlier in the century exchange rates were fixed between major trading nations, and the dollar and pound tended to strengthen against less developed countries' currencies. Thus, the conservative closing rate approach was in keeping with the spirit of the period. Between the world wars exchange rates tended to fluctuate gently around 'norms'. It was argued that non-current items should be translated at the historical rate as exchange rate changes were likely to reverse and average out over the life of the asset or liability. Such reversals did not necessarily take place in the short term. Hence the current/non-current method became more common.

However, this approach was overtaken both by economic events and by conceptual shortcomings. Many countries decided to allow exchange rates to track underlying economic changes more closely, which meant that long-term reversals were less probable. Objections too, were raised to the somewhat arbitrary and ill-defined nature of the term 'working capital'. The literature gradually started to explore the monetary/non-monetary approach. In parallel, a similar classification was made in general price level accounting (CPP), vigorously debated at the same time in the 1950s.

The basic difference between the C–NC approach and the M–NM approach is in the treatment of stocks (a current but non-monetary asset) and long-term liabilities (non-current but monetary liabilities). The C–NC and closing rate approaches show an asset aggregate as 'exposed', whereas the M–NM approach shows a liability aggregate. Often then, the M–NM approach showed a gain when the C–NC and closing rate showed a loss, and vice versa if the exchange rate reversed. For the first time it was possible to show more 'favourable' results by choosing the 'right' translation approach, creating a more political environment. As the dollar weakened in the 1970s, proponents of the M–NM approach were forced to seek to justify their method. The definition of a 'monetary' asset was as ambiguous as for a 'current' asset. For example, how were short-term marketable investments or stocks at NRV to be classified? The temporal approach can be seen as an attempt to modify and to enhance the theoretical respectability of the monetary/non-monetary approach.

The closing rate has been a continuing contender, mainly through its simplicity. Whilst the USA trod the temporal path in the 1970s, followed by Canada (even though an official Canadian research study in 1972 recommended the closing rate), the UK mainly stuck to the closing rate. However, this approach did not have a respectable theoretical framework developed until the end of the 1970s. Then it swept aside the temporal approach, relegating its use to limited, specific circumstances.

The temporal approach

First discussed by Lorensen (1972) in an AICPA research study, it proposes an ingenious solution to the translation problem, similar to the monetary/non-monetary approach. Lorensen's contribution was to give a convincing theoretical rationale and to show that the same rationale could be extended to valuation bases other than historical cost. Assets and liabilities are translated according to their datedness. Balances at historical acquisition prices are translated at historical rate (e.g. fixed assets). Balances at 'current' prices (e.g. debtors and creditors) are translated at current rate. Under current cost accounting, all balances are 'current' dated and thus translated at the current rate.

Under the temporal approach, the group is conceived of as a single entity, a direct extension of the parent. Transactions of foreign subsidiaries are treated *as if* they were direct transactions of the parent, using the familiar two transaction approach described earlier. The parent's currency is taken as the unit of measurement. When a foreign subsidiary purchases a fixed asset in its local currency, financed by a local currency loan, the transaction is treated *as if* it were a direct transaction of the parent. The fixed asset is recorded at the *historical* rate at the purchase date, and is not subsequently adjusted. The loan (an unsettled currency amount) is translated at the current rate of exchange in any financial statements until settlement. Any gain or loss on translation is taken to the *profit and loss account.*

The temporal approach adds the extra assumption, '*as if* they were transactions of the parent' (notionally converting pounds into currency and back to carry out the subsidiary's transactions), to the two transaction approach. Key ideas are single functional currency (the parent's) and the group as a single unified entity for transaction purposes, a direct extension of the parent (see Revsine, 1984, for a numerical example of this). It is argued that the temporal method is internally consistent with historical cost accounting, and this will be discussed later.

The closing rate approach

This approach has many different justifications, many of which are discussed later. Only the 'net investment' rationale is discussed here. Now the group is not viewed as a unified entity transacting in the parent's currency, but as a series of net investments in *autonomous* subsidiaries transacting in *local* currencies in their differing environments. The US standard FAS 52 characterizes such a group as having multiple functional currencies. The temporal approach implicitly assumes a single functional currency, the parent's.

From this perspective, to treat each subsidiary's transactions as if transactions of the parent is misleading. It is argued that as the *net investment* is exposed, all of a subsidiary's assets and liabilities should be translated at the current rate. Since assets and liabilities are purchased, financed and used in the same environment, they will tend to hedge each other. Supporters argue that it is nonsense to show gains or losses arising on, say, liabilities, whilst not showing similar effects on corresponding fixed assets. It is argued that gains and losses on translation under the closing rate approach correlate better with true economic exposure than the temporal approach, as net investments correspond more closely in sign to present values than net current dated liabilities do. Further, since all balances are translated at the same rate, subsidiaries' balance sheet relationships are preserved in group accounts. These arguments are examined later.

Example 9.3   A case study – Aufwiedersehen GmbH

This numerical example clarifies ideas discussed so far, and introduces the technique of foreign currency translation.

Aufwiedersehen GmbH, set up on 1 January 1976, is the 75 per cent owned subsidiary of Goodbuy plc, acquired on 31 December 1985 for £70,000. Its year-end is 31 December. Recent financial statements (DM000) are:

Balance sheets

	1985	1986		1985	1986
Fixed assets	500	600	Share capital and premium	100	100
Stocks	200	250	Reserves	250	350
Cash	100	200	Long-term loan	300	300
			Creditors	150	300
	800	1,050		800	1,050

Profit and loss account – year ended 31 December 1986 (DM000)

Sales	1,000
COGS	(700)
Decpreciation	(100)
Other expenses	(100)
Net profit	100

Further information:
1. All sales were for cash.
2. Fixed assets are at historical cost less depreciation. Opening fixed assets were purchased when the subsidiary was set up in 1976. £200,000 were purchased on 31 August 1986. No depreciation is provided in the year of purchase.
3. Stocks are valued on a FIFO basis, representing at 31 December 1985 and 1986 about four months' purchases. All purchases are on credit.
4. The long-term loan was raised in marks in 1976, repayable at par in 1995. It carries no interest, being an investment incentive from the local government.
5. Exchange rates – marks to the £:

1 January 1976	4.6	30 June 1986	4.0
31 August 1985	4.3	31 August 1986	3.9
31 October 1985	4.2	31 October 1986	3.8
31 December 1985	4.1	31 December 1986	3.7

Translating balance sheets

Opening balance sheet
Under the closing rate, all balances are translated at 4.1, the current rate at 31 December 1985. Under the temporal approach, all current dated items are translated at 4.1 (the current rate) whereas stocks and fixed assets are translated at their acquisition rate. Here stocks represent four months' purchases, so their average purchase date is taken as two months prior to the balance sheet date. Share capital and reserves are a residual figure under both approaches.

Description	Temporal approach		Closing rate	
	Rate	*£ balance*	*Rate*	*£ balance*
Fixed assets	4.6	108,696	4.1	121,952
Stocks	4.2	47,619	4.1	48,780
Cash	4.1	24,390	4.1	24,390
		180,705		195,122
Share capital and reserves	Residual	70,949	Residual	85,366
Long-term liabilities	4.1	73,171	4.1	73,171
Creditors	4.1	36,585	4.1	36,585
		180,705		195,122

Closing balance sheet
The current rate is 3.7 and the same assumption is made about stocks. Under the temporal approach, opening fixed assets of DM500,000 were translated at 4.6, the historical rate. DM200,000 were purchased when the rate was 3.9. DM100,000 of depreciation (on 'old' (4.6) fixed assets) can be deduced by differencing these and the closing balance (DM600,000), which is thus at a composite amount, DM400,000 at 4.6 and DM200,000 at 3.9. This illustrates the greater record-keeping complexity necessitated by this approach to keep track of original datedness of historical dated assets bought *and* sold, causing extra compliance costs.

Description	Temporal		Closing rate	
	Rate	*£ balance*	*Rate*	*£ balance*
Fixed assets	400 @ 4.6	138,239	3.7	162,162
	200 @ 3.9			
Stocks	3.8	65,789	3.7	67,568
Cash	3.7	54,054	3.7	54,054
		258,082		283,784
Share capital and reserves	Residual	95,920	Residual	121,622
Long-term liabilities	3.7	81,081	3.7	81,081
Creditors	3.7	81,081	3.7	81,081
		258,082		283,784

Translating income statements
The choice of rates in the profit and loss account is less well defined. Current UK practice, based on the requirements of SSAP 20 is shown in Table 9.5. The standard allows either of two possible rates under the closing rate approach, reflecting conflicting rationales for this approach, discussed later.

Translation approach	Rates(s)
Closing rate	All items at closing rate (i.e. 3.7)
	or
	All items at average rate for period.
Temporal	Most items at transaction date giving rise to them (usually approximated by the average rate). Historical rates to be used where the expenses and revenues relate to assets and liabilities translated themselves at historical rates.

Table 9.5   Profit and loss translation rates

Profit and loss account

Briggs (1986) quoted statistics compiled by Philips and Drew at the end of November 1985 which showed that of 170 UK companies using the closing rate approach 59 per cent chose the year-end rate and 32 per cent the average rate, and noted a trend towards adopting the latter (which has been chosen here). The temporal approach requires historical rates for cost of sales and depreciation, since their asset counterparts are at such rates, and transaction date rates for the rest (taken as the average rate for the period, 4.0, the rate at 30 June 1986, assuming all transactions have taken place at an even rate). The historical rate for cost of goods sold is approximated by using historical rates for opening (4.2) and closing (3.8) stocks and the average rate (4.0) for purchases.

Description	Temporal approach		Closing rate approach	
	Rate	£ balance	Rate	£ balance
Sales	4.0	250,000	4.0	250,000
Cost of sales:				
Opening stock	200 @ 4.2⎫			
Purchases	750 @ 4.0⎬	(169,330)	4.0	(175,000)
Closing stock	(250) @ 3.8⎭			
Depreciation	4.6	(21,739)	4.0	(25,000)
Other expenses	4.0	(25,000)	4.0	(25,000)
Translated P & L amount		33,931		25,000

Determining the gain or loss on exposure by differencing

Gains or losses on exposure are found by taking the difference between the *change* in translated balance sheet equity figures and the translated profit figure. Later the reasons why such differences correspond to gains or losses will be explained. The tendency of one method to show a gain whilst the other shows a loss is illustrated here.

	Temporal		Closing rate
Translated profit	33,931		25,000
Equity change (95,920 − 70,949) =	24,971	(121,622 − 85,366) =	36,256
Difference – Translation loss =	(8,960)	Translation gain =	11,256

Exercise

9.4   Pizza Cayka Spa is an 80 per cent Latin subsidiary of Gobbledegook plc, a fast-food chain, acquired when its retained earnings were 3,000 maracas. The 31 December draft balance sheets of both companies are:

	Gobbledegook (£)		Pizza Cayka (maracas)	
	1985	1986	1985	1986
Fixed assets (net)	100,000	120,000	8,000	10,000
Investment in PC	3,000	3,000		
Stocks (cost)	31,000	36,000	3,800	4,800
Debtors	20,000	25,000	1,800	3,000
Cash	10,000	5,000	600	1,000
Share capital	(30,000)	(30,000)	(2,000)	(2,000)
Other reserves	(20,000)	(20,000)	(3,000)	(3,000)
Retained earnings	(44,000)	(49,000)	(4,700)	(6,800)
Long-term loan	(50,000)	(70,000)	(2,100)	(4,000)
Creditors	(20,000)	(20,000)	(2,400)	(3,000)

Profit and loss accounts for the year ended 31 December 1986 were:

	Gobbledegook (£)		Pizza Cayka	
	£	£	maracas	maracas
Sales		150,000		112,000
Opening stock	31,000		3,800	
Purchases	130,000		108,000	
Closing stock	(36,000)		(4,800)	
Cost of sales		(125,000)		(107,000)
Expenses		(10,000)		(1,900)
Depreciation		(10,000)		(1,000)
Net income		5,000		2,100

Further information:
1. There were no fixed asset disposals during the year. Depreciation is calculated on opening fixed assets.
2. Exchange rates to the £:

Opening fixed assets and subsidiary acquisition	5 maracas
Opening stock	4 maracas
Closing rate 31 December 1985	3 maracas
Closing stock and year's transactions	2 maracas
Closing rate 31 December 1986	1 maraca

Required
(a) Translate the opening and closing balance sheets and the profit and loss account of Pizza Cayka under both approaches.
(b) By differencing, calculate the gain or loss on translation under closing rate and temporal approaches.
(c) Using the ideas already discussed, try to explain why the gain or loss has arisen under each approach.

Understanding and calculating the gain or loss on exposure

This section deepens earlier discussions by allowing the amount exposed to change over the year. In order to do this it is necessary to produce statements showing *changes* in exposure under the approaches. These are central to understanding foreign currency translation. The funds flow matrix (discussed in Chapter 7) is used for this, and also diagrams to show how gain and loss calculations correspond to intuitive ideas of exposure. If Chapter 7 has not been studied, it is helpful to read the first section, 'Interrelationships between financial statements', and steps in constructing a matrix covered in Example 7.2 before going on.

Temporal approach

'Current dated' items are exposed. Thus, in order to see how this aggregate *changes*, a funds flow statement of such items is needed, and so a funds flow matrix is now prepared (Table 9.6). As shown in Chapter 7, items included in the fund (here net current dated liabilities (NCDL)) are aggregated in the first column. Here they are cash, creditors and long-term loans, since there are no debtors or stocks at NRV. Opening NCDL is:

Cash 100,000 + Creditors (150,000) + Loans (300,000) = (350,000) credit

Similarly from the closing balance sheet, closing NCDL is (400,000) marks. Ignore the bold numbers which are used in a later part of the chapter.

Purchases is deduced by differencing. It is the relevant flow relating to merchandise under the temporal approach rather than COGS (totally external to items comprising NCDL) or payments to creditors (totally internal).

Closing rate approach

Table 9.7 shows the condensed matrix for the closing rate method. Since all items are exposed, it only has two columns. Again ignore bold figures, used later in the chapter. The condensed matrix for the current/non-current approach (not shown here) is the usual working capital matrix.

The following flow statements are extracted by listing the first columns of Tables 9.6 and 9.7. Comparing respective flows line by line shows the closing rate approach has a wider exposure definition.

Flow statements of exposed items

Temporal			*Closing rate*		
Opening NCDL		(350) Cr.	Opening net assets		350 Dr.
Change over year:			Change over year:		
Sales	1,000		Sales	1,000	
Purchases	(750)		COGS	(700)	
Other expenses	(100)		Other expenses	(100)	
	150				
Fixed asset purchase	(200)		Depreciation	(100)	
		(50)			100
Closing NCDL		(400) Cr.	Closing net assets		450 Dr.

Details	Exposed items		Non-exposed items				Residual	
	Net current dated liabilities		Stock		Net fixed assets		Share capital and reserves	
Opening balance sheet	(350)	4.1	200	4.2	500	4.6	(350)	*
1. Reconstruct P & L:								
Sales	1,000	4.0					(1,000)	4.0
COGS			(700)	*			700	*
Depreciation					(100)	4.6	100	4.6
Other expenses	(100)	4.0					100	4.0
2. From notes:								
Fixed asset purchase	(200)	3.9			200	3.9		
3. Differencing:								
Purchases	(750)	4.0	750	4.0				
Closing balance sheet	(400)	3.7	250	3.8	600	*	(450)	*

Table 9.6   Temporal condensed matrix

Details	Exposed items Net assets		Residual Share capital and reserves	
Opening balance sheet	350	4.1	(350)	4.1
1. Reconstruct P & L:				
Sales	1,000	4.0	(1,000)	4.0
COGS	(700)	4.0	700	4.0
Depreciation	(100)	4.0	100	4.0
Other expenses	(100)	4.0	100	4.0
2. From notes:	—			
3. Differencing:	—			
Closing balance sheet	450	3.7	(450)	3.7

Table 9.7   Closing rate condensed matrix

Exercises

9.5   Prepare a condensed matrix under the current/non-current approach for the Aufwiedersehen case (Example 9.3) and a flow statement of exposed items. Compare the statement with the two statements above.

9.6   Using the matrix, prepare flow statements of exposed items under the temporal and closing rate approaches for the Pizza Cayka example in Exercise 9.4.

The time pattern of exposure

Under the temporal approach, the amount exposed increases from a credit balance of DM350,000 to DM400,000, and under closing rate the debit of DM350,000 increases to DM450,000. The top half of Figure 9.1 shows amounts exposed and periods of exposure under both approaches. Operating transactions are assumed to take place half-way through the year. Under the closing rate method, DM350,000 is exposed for six months until the operating transactions (£100,000 in aggregate), then the net balance is exposed for six months more. The temporal approach is similar except the fixed asset purchase specifically occurs in August, then the residual balance is exposed for a further four months.

The information is recast in *incremental* form in the bottom half of Figure 9.1. The total areas are the same but have been divided up differently. So under the closing rate approach, the opening balance of DM350,000 is treated as exposed for the whole year, and the *increment* of DM100,000 is treated as exposed for six months. This produces the same net effect (area) as the top half of the figure. Under the temporal approach, the three rectangles in the top half are redefined into three *incremental* rectangles having the same area. Here the two unshaded rectangles *less* the shaded one show the amount exposed. Incremental exposure is *reduced* by operating transactions.

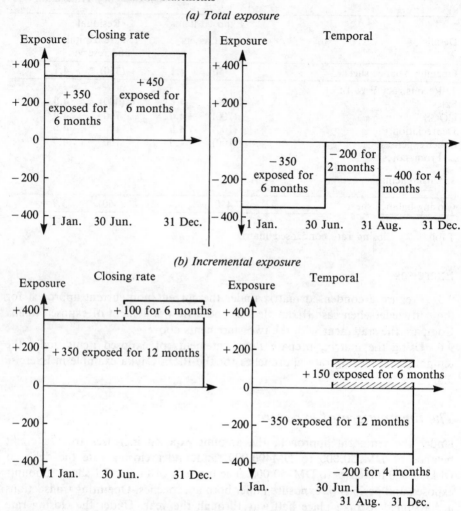

Figure 9.1   Amounts exposed under different translation approaches

The calculation of exchange gain/loss

In this simple example it is easy to demonstrate the link between intuitive notions of exposure and the calculation of exchange gain or loss. The temporal approach is used for illustration here because it more clearly shows the principles involved (e.g. in Table 9.8), leaving the reader to calculate the simpler closing rate amounts.

With more complex transactions or irregular exchange rate patterns, one could treat each (e.g. sales) transaction individually, using the transaction date exchange rate. As an approximation one might use, e.g. quarterly averages. Cost and ease of calculation need to be balanced against increased accuracy (see Taylor, 1984, pp. 19–20). A more formal calculation of exposure gain or loss can be made using the flow statements discussed earlier. Only the closing rate is shown here.

	Date of exposure	Amount	Exchange rate change		Exposure effect
Total amounts exposed	1 Jan. 1986 to 30 June 1986	− 350	$\times$	$\dfrac{1}{4.0} - \dfrac{1}{4.1}$	=	(2,134)
	30 June 1986 to 31 Aug. 1986	− 200	$\times$	$\dfrac{1}{3.9} - \dfrac{1}{4.0}$	=	(1,282)
	31 Aug. 1986 to 31 Dec. 1986	− 400	$\times$	$\dfrac{1}{3.7} - \dfrac{1}{3.9}$	=	(5,544)
						(8,960)
Incremental amounts exposed	1 Jan. 1986 to 31 Dec. 1986	− 350	$\times$	$\dfrac{1}{3.7} - \dfrac{1}{4.1}$	=	(9,229)
	30 June 1986 to 31 Dec. 1986	+ 150	$\times$	$\dfrac{1}{3.7} - \dfrac{1}{4.0}$	=	3,041
	31 Aug. 1986 to 31 Dec. 1986	− 200	$\times$	$\dfrac{1}{3.7} - \dfrac{1}{3.9}$	=	(2,772)
						(8,960)

Table 9.8   Calculation of exchange gain or loss from exposure pattern

Translated flow statements of exposed items – closing rate approach

	Marks	Marks	Rate	Sterling
Opening net assets		350,000	@ 4.1	85,366
Sales	1,000,000			
COGS	(700,000)			
Depreciation	(100,000)			
Other expenses	(100,000)			
		100,000	@ 4.0	25,000
Closing net assets at input rates				110,366
Closing net assets at closing rates		450,000	@ 3.7	121,622
Exchange gain				11,256

Integrating the separate parts – the matrix approach

The funds flow matrix is extremely useful to show how the pieces of the translation process fit together in overview form. Tables 9.6 and 9.7, discussed earlier, show temporal and closing rate matrices respectively. In Table 9.6, the bold figures by the side of each flow indicate the exchange rate used to translate that flow. An asterisk (*) indicates the translated amount is determined by differencing the other translated items in the row or column concerned (e.g. equity is a residual item). The same procedure is used in Table 9.7. Table 9.9 shows the results of this translation (by dividing the marks figure in Tables 9.6 and 9.7 by its attached exchange rate, or by differencing). Again here an asterisk indicates differencing.

In Table 9.9 the subtotal of the translated opening balance sheet and translated transactions is computed (denoted 'converted balances at "input" rates'), and the difference between this and the translated closing balance sheet reveals gain or loss on exposure under each approach. The matrices in marks and in sterling provide a complete, clear summary of the translation data and resulting four financial statements:
1. Translated opening (top line) and closing (bottom line) balance sheets.
2. The translated profit and loss account including gain or loss on translation (right-hand column).
3. The translated flow statement of exposed items. Disclosure of this is not required by SSAP 20. It shows why the gain or loss on exposure arose (left-hand column) and completes the translation process.

Exercises

9.7 Prepare diagrams to show exposure patterns and incremental exposure:
(a) For the Pizza Cayka example (Exercise 9.6), temporal approach.
(b) For the Pizza Cayka example (Exercise 9.6), closing rate approach, and compare the patterns of exposure
(c) For the Aufwiedersehen example (Exercise 9.5), current/non-current approach.

Temporal approach Details	Exposed Net current dated liabilities	Stock	Non-exposed Net fixed assets	Residual Share capital and reserves
Opening balance sheet	(85,366)	47,619	108,696	(70,949)
1. Reconstruct P & L:				
Sales	250,000			(250,000)
COGS		(169,330)*		169,330*
Depreciation			(21,739)	21,739
Other expenses	(25,000)			25,000
2. From notes:				
Fixed asset purchase	(51,282)		51,282	
3. Differencing:				
Purchases	(187,500)	187,500		
Subtotal: converted balances at 'input' rates	(99,148)	65,789	138,239	(104,880)
Exchange loss (difference)	(8,960)			8,960
Closing balances – temporal	(108,108)	65,789	138,239	(95,920)

Closing rate Details	Exposed items Net assets	Residual SC and res.
Opening balance sheet	85,366	(85,366)
1. Reconstruct P & L:		
Sales	250,000	(250,000)
COGS	(175,000)	175,000
Depreciation	(25,000)	25,000
Other expenses	(25,000)	25,000
2/3. Notes/differencing:		
—		
Subtotal: converted balances at 'input' rates	110,366	(110,366)
Exchange gain (difference)	11,256	(11,256)
Closing balances – closing rate	121,622	(121,622)

Table 9.9   Translated condensed matrices – Aufwiedersehen GmbH

9.8   For any of the above parts of 9.7 you have tackled, calculate the gain or loss on exposure and show how it relates to the intuitive notions in the diagram.

9.9   *An overview of the whole process*

In any or all of the following three cases:

(a)   for the Pizza Cayka example, closing rate approach;
(b)   ditto, for the temporal approach;
(c)   for Aufwiedersehen, current/non-current approach,

undertake the following:

(i)   Produce a condensed matrix (using solutions to Exercises 9.5 and 9.6).
(ii)   Insert the relevant exchange rates to produce a *translation* matrix.
(iii)   Translate each item to produce a *translated* matrix.
(iv)   Prepare the four financial statements – the opening and closing balance sheets, the profit and loss account and the flow statement (translated) of exposed items – to show how the gain or loss on exposure arose. Many of these have been produced as a result of earlier exercises, so you will just need to check your translated matrix with your former solutions and prepare remaining statements. Focus on the *interrelationships* among the different statements.

Consolidation using the translated statements

As outlined in Table 9.2, this is stage 3 of the process. Stages 1 and 2 comprise translation of transactions within individual foreign currency statements, then translation of the statements themselves into the reporting currency. Using data from Example 9.3, the following table analyses Aufwiedersehen's equity in *marks* as a prelude to preparing cancellation tables in sterling under the two approaches:

	Majority (75%)	Minority (25%)	Total
Share capital and premium	75,000	25,000	100,000
Reserves to acquisition	187,500	62,500	250,000
Pre-acquisition equity	262,500	87,500	350,000
Reserves since acquisition	75,000	25,000	100,000
Total equity at 31 December 1986	337,500	112,500	450,000

Closing rate approach

Closing equity can be taken directly from the closing balance sheet, translated at current rate, i.e. DM450,000/3.7 = £121,622. A more difficult question is at what rate do we translate equity at acquisition into sterling, the current rate (3.7) or that at acquisition (4.1)? Such a choice merely affects the split between pre- and post-acquisition amounts, since the total is as above. Post-acquisition amounts are merely the residual between closing and pre-acquisition amounts, and so are determined by our choice.

If the historical rate is used, pre-acquisition entry is fixed in sterling in all future translated financial statements. Thus goodwill is fixed at acquisition.

Effectively post-acquisition equity includes an 'update' of pre-acquisition equity from historical to current rate. If the current rate is used, then pre-acquisition equity is retranslated each year at the then current rate. Hence its sterling amount and consequently goodwill will be recalculated each year, allowing goodwill to be affected by events subsequent to acquisition. However, other balances are retranslated each year at the current rate in a similar fashion, so this may not be a conclusive opposing argument.

Conventional practice uses the *historical* rate. Later it will be shown that the choice is linked to the rationale used for the closing rate approach. The following table shows the subsidiary's equity breakdown in *sterling*, using the *historical* rate for pre-acquisition equity:

	Rate	Majority	Minority	Total
Share capital	4.1	18,293	6,097	24,390
Reserves to acquisition	4.1	45,732	15,244	60,976
Pre-acquisition equity	4.1	64,025	21,341	85,366
Reserves since acquisition (residual)		27,192	9,064	36,256
Total equity at 31 December 1986	3.7	91,217	30,405	121,622

and the consequent cancellation table would be:

Details	Investment	Goodwill	Consolidated reserves	Minority interests
Goodbuy:				
Investment	70,000			
Aufwiedersehen:				
Share capital		(18,293)		(6,097)
Pre-acq. reserves		(45,732)		(15,244)
Post-acq. reserves			(27,192)	(9,064)
Cancellation	(70,000)	70,000		
Consolidated amounts	—	5,975	(27,192)	(30,405)

Temporal approach

Here there is not the same ambiguity. Goodwill is not a current dated asset, and so historical rates are used in its computation. The breakdown of the subsidiary's equity in *sterling* is as follows:

	Rate	Majority	Minority	Total
Share capital and pre-acquisition reserves (i.e. pre-acq. equity)	*	53,211	17,738	70,949
Reserves since acquisition	*	18,728	6,243	24,971
Total equity at 31 December 1986	*	71,939	23,981	95,920

The rate of exchange (*) used to translate equity is a composite figure, a residual, dependent on rates used for the other assets and liabilities. The 'total' amounts can be checked against the translated opening and closing balance sheets in Example 9.3. The cancellation table under the temporal approach then becomes:

Details	Investment	Goodwill	Consolidated reserves	Minority interests
Goodbuy:				
Investment	70,000			
Aufwiedersehen:				
Share capital and				
pre-acq. reserves		(53,211)		(17,738)
Post-acq. reserves			(18,728)	(6,243)
Cancellation	(70,000)	70,000		
Consolidated amounts	—	16,789	(18,728)	(23,981)

Exercises

9.10 In the Pizza Cayka example (Exercise 9.4), analyse translated equity in sterling under the closing rate approach, using the historical rate to translate pre-acquisition equity.

9.11 Prepare a set of consolidated accounts for the Gobbledegook group assuming the closing rate is used for Pizza Cayka.

9.12 Ditto assuming the temporal approach is used, and that the translated equity in sterling at acquisition was £1,700.

SSAP 20, 'FOREIGN CURRENCY TRANSLATION' – AN ANALYSIS

SSAP 20, issued in 1983, resulted from three exposure drafts: ED 16, which merely required *disclosure* of the accounting basis followed without specifying a particular approach; ED 21, in 1980, allowed either temporal or closing rate approaches; ED 27, the basis for SSAP 20 later in 1980 which supported the closing rate, allowing the temporal approach in limited circumstances. The ICAEW 'Survey of Published Accounts' showed over 80 per cent of UK companies using the closing rate method in the three years prior to SSAP 20.

In the USA the FASB issued FAS No. 8 in 1975, requiring the temporal method. This was subject to heavy criticism that temporal gains or losses did not correlate with economic exposure and that it caused management to make non-optimal economic decisions to obtain 'acceptable' accounting results. ED 21's tolerance was probably an expedient to cater for UK practice, but allowed UK based companies not to conflict with FAS No. 8. FAS No. 52, issued in 1981, favoured the closing rate approach, superseding FAS No. 8. ED 27's stronger line probably was affected by the US changes. SSAP 20 broadly aligns UK and USA requirements.

Foreign currency transactions

SSAP 20 requires that a subsidiary should translate foreign currency transactions (at the 'individual company stage') using the *two transactions perspective* before submitting its local currency *statements* for translation.

Foreign currency financial statements

The closing rate/net investment method is required unless (paragraph 55) 'the trade of the foreign enterprise is more dependent on the economic environment of the investing company's currency than its own reporting currency' when the temporal method should be used. Once the environmental conditions are decided only one treatment is allowed: under a unified, single currency structure use the temporal method; under a multi-currency, multi-environment structure use the closing rate. SSAP 20 illustrates conditions for the temporal method – e.g. for selling agencies, parts of vertically integrated operations, tax haven operations, etc. The usual currency of operations, the currency to which the operation is exposed, the extent of dependence and the extent of remittability of cash flows are all relevant. However, it is clear that the closing rate approach will predominate.

FAS 52 conceptualizes similar recommendations using the 'functional currency' concept, defined as the currency of the primary economic environment within which the entity operates, 'normally that is, the currency of the environment in which the entity generates and expends cash'. The temporal approach is allowed only where the functional currency of the foreign enterprise is the parent's, and the closing rate where the functional currency is that of the place of location (called in SSAP 20 the 'local currency'). FAS No. 52 terms the temporal approach 'remeasurement' and the closing rate 'translation'. The temporal approach implies a single functional currency for the group, the parent's, whereas the closing rate approach recognizes multiple functional currencies. Under SSAP 20, finding the extent of dependence is analogous to identifying the functional currency of the subsidiary.

Accounting treatment of gains and losses

Diverse treatments have developed over the years, including:
(a) immediate write-off to the profit and loss account;
(b) deferral and gradual amortization to the profit and loss account;
(c) transfer direct to reserves (possibly with reinstatement to the profit and loss account when the investment in the foreign subsidiary is sold);
(d) non-symmetrical treatment using a combination of (a)–(c), e.g. immediate write-off of losses, deferral and amortization of gains.

Deferral and amortization is not allowed in the UK and USA, though the Canadian standard allows deferral of gains and losses on loans. Supporting arguments for this treatment include that companies forecast currency movements in transacting loans and so foreseen movements should be viewed as interest adjustments over the life of the loan. How to prevent management manipulation in separating foreseen versus unforeseen movements is a problem. The technical release on publication of SSAP 20 argues that a symmetrical treatment of gains and losses is necessary to show a true and fair view, and that gains on long-term monetary items dealt with in the profit and loss account of *companies* should be regarded as *unrealized* for distribution purposes.

Temporal supporters recommend gains and losses on statement translation are taken to the profit and loss account (treatment (a)), whereas net investment supporters advocate reserves (treatment (c)). Transaction gains or losses are non-controversial. The differing underlying rationales account for these views. The temporal approach regards statement gains or losses akin to transaction ones ('as if' the parent's) through the profit and loss account, the net investment approach as akin to revaluations of the net investment. Under Companies Act requirements revaluations of fixed assets are taken direct to reserves. Further, to preserve a local currency perspective, it is argued that statement gains and losses should be excluded from the sterling statements, since they do not appear in the local currency ones. SSAP 20 follows these intuitions, as shown in Table 9.10.

	Translation approach	Disposition of gains and losses
Transactions	Two-transaction	Profit and loss
Financial statements	Temporal	Profit and loss
	Closing rate	Reserves

Table 9.10   SSAP 20 requirements on disposition of gains and losses

The cover concept: hedging net investments

SSAP 20's differing locations for transaction and statement gains and losses cause problems for linked transactions where hedging is involved (i.e. matching foreign assets and liabilities so that gains and losses offset). Suppose a parent finances a net investment in an overseas subsidiary by raising a long-term loan in the same currency. *Statement* gains or losses from the net investment (closing rate) would be taken to reserves whereas (the parent's) *transaction* gains or losses on the loan would be taken to profit and loss. A single decision shows gains and losses of approximately the same size in different locations. It is argued that the net position is what is really exposed.

To counteract this, SSAP 20 allows gains or losses on loans used to finance overseas subsidiaries translated under the closing rate to be offset as reserve movements against gains or losses on linked 'net investments' to the extent of exchange differences arising on the latter. There are minimal qualifying requirements. The currency of the loan does not have to be the same as for the net investment (unlike ED 27 which did require this, as does FAS No. 52). Presumably this aims to prevent accounting treatments artificially affecting managements' hedging decisions in a non-optimal way. Further, the aggregate of foreign currency borrowings available for offset should not exceed the total cash expected to be generated by the relevant net investments.

Disclosure

SSAP 20's disclosure requirements are selective. Two quantitative areas are focused on, the net movement on reserves arising from exchange differences, and the treatment of the group's foreign currency net borrowing. The latter requires disclosure of the amounts dealt with in the profit and loss account and separately in reserves under the 'cover' provisions discussed above. A note is required on translation methods used, and on treatment of exchange differences though, as Patterson (1986) shows, companies often only reproduce sections of SSAP 20.

SSAP 20's disclosure requirements compare unfavourably with those of FAS No. 52 which require a detailed analysis of reserve movements caused by exchange differences (e.g. showing effects of hedges, intercompany balances, taxation and sales or disposals) and details of *transaction* gains and losses. SSAP 20 does not require disclosure of the *total* profit and loss account amount. The technical release with SSAP 20 argues such total disclosure is not necessarily helpful because exchange differences cannot be viewed separately from a company's total pricing policy (prices possibly including an element for foreseen exchange movements). Further, a small net amount may disguise large offsetting movements. However, such arguments seem to support greater disclosure rather than none(!). The RTZ Group (quoted by Patterson, 1986) provides a good example of a (voluntary) review of the impact of exchange movements on its results.

THE TRANSLATION DEBATE

This section provides a brief overview of the diverse arguments at the heart of the translation debate which takes place on a number of different levels simultaneously, often with a 'hidden agenda' – writers do not define the problem clearly or state what their assumptions and objectives are. Conclusions often differ because the area examined differs.

SSAP 20 seems to relate the choice of approach to economic 'reality', dependent subsidiaries being translated under the temporal approach and autonomous subsidiaries under the closing rate approach. However, the fact that the approaches have been around for some time before 'plausible' rationales were developed should cause some reflection. Maybe SSAP 20's solution is acceptable, but the mere claim that 'it reflects reality well' can hardly in itself provide sufficient justification for its acceptance. Some argue that the proposals are the outcome of a *political* process rather than one of better measurement.

As in Chapter 3, two levels of debate are examined: first in terms of the functional objectives underlying consolidation of foreign subsidiaries; and, second, in terms of the correct characterization of the standard-setting environment itself.

Functional objectives for accounting for foreign subsidiaries

SSAP 20 (paragraph 2) characterizes the objectives of translation as:

> The translation of foreign currency transactions and financial statements should produce results which are generally compatible with the effects of rate changes on a company's cash flows and its equity and should ensure that the financial statements present a true and fair view of the results of management actions. Consolidated

statements should reflect the financial results and relationships as measured in the foreign currency financial statements prior to translation.

Such objectives are consistent with the closing rate approach. FAS No. 8, the earlier US standard, stated the objectives thus:

> For the purpose of preparing an enterprise's financial statements, the objective of translation is to measure and express (a) in dollars and (b) in conformity with US generally accepted accounting principles (GAAP) the assets, liabilities, revenues, or expenses that are measured or denominated in foreign currency.

which is consistent with the temporal approach! So, which is correct?

Consider now a range of functional objectives proposed for translation, and the extent to which the approaches satisfy them.

To preserve the integrity of the historical cost accounting basis

The temporal approach scores highly. It 'remeasures' foreign currency balances into the reporting currency so as to preserve their 'datedness'. But, for example, should debtors be stated at a *current* or a *future* amount (in which case a forward exchange rate would be more appropriate)? Lorensen (1972) concluded the former. Fortunately, Henning, Piggott and Scott (1978), based on efficient markets empirical research found that current rates of exchange can be used in both cases since the present rate of exchange is an unbiased estimate of future rates (see Nobes, 1980, p. 425).

Some argue that using the closing rate on historical balances approximates current values. However, if the above objective is *accepted*, this can be criticized on the grounds that multiplying a historical dated balance by a current exchange rate produces a meaningless figure, neither a historical cost nor a current value.

Since the temporal approach was largely developed to preserve the integrity of differing valuation systems, it is not surprising that it comes out well here. It ensures no changes in underlying measurement principles. So under current cost accounting all balances would be translated at the current rate. Temporal supporters argue price level adjustments are best dealt with directly, rather than approximated in the translation process.

To be consistent with various consolidation objectives

A commonly stated objective is to present the statements of a group as if they are of a single economic entity. One could argue that the temporal approach is consistent with this. However, as Walker (1978a, pp. 267–79) points out, this objective is not the only possible one and does not itself completely explain conventional practice. Other objectives cited by him include amplifying holding company statements, or presenting the results of holding companies in a different form – each leading to different solutions.

The net investment rationale implicitly challenges the single entity argument. However, its critics argue that if the group does not have a unified quality, line by line consolidation is not appropriate and the equity approach should be used

(Walker's (1978a) amplification objective?). Is there therefore a case for not consolidating most foreign subsidiaries (see Nobes, 1986b, p. 33)? SSAP 14's criteria for non-consolidation include *either* a lack of effective control or dissimilar activities. Foreign subsidiaries sit uneasily at the margin of both.

How dissimilar does dissimilar have to be? What of subsidiaries selling the same product, but in very different environments with different financial structures (e.g. in Germany and Japan most financing is done by banks rather than by the stock market), different business customs, different management structures and different currencies? Does the net investment rationale itself imply significant dissimilarity? It is difficult to assess at what point 'effective' control is lost. A nationalistic local management and/or restrictions on the employment of overseas personnel (e.g. in Nigeria in certain strategic industries) might cause difficulties.

One possibility is the German solution of only consolidating domestic subsidiaries. SSAPs 14 and 20's solutions are pragmatic, defining a spectrum of alternatives. At one end is the dependent foreign subsidiary (temporal). At the other end is the completely autonomous subsidiary selling dissimilar goods in a very different environment (closing rate). Both are fully consolidated. Extreme 'ugly ducklings' are singled out by SSAP 14's exclusion requirements. But there are other possibilities – geographical subconsolidations for autonomous foreign subsidiary groupings, or equity accounting for such subsidiaries with supplemental information. A discussion on the objectives of consolidation is notably lacking in UK standards.

To provide information compatible with economic exposure

It has been argued that closing rate gains and losses correlate much more closely with economic exposure, greatly assisting prediction, e.g. when the foreign currency strengthens, the temporal approach shows a loss, whereas future currency flows have increased in value (i.e. a gain).

However, Nobes (1980) questions whether the main purpose of historical cost accounts is to aid prediction. Also, such correlations may not be high if exchange rate movements between countries are offset by countervailing interest rate movements, causing the interest rate/exchange rate effect to cancel out in the present value calculation. This cancelling effect will not be reflected in accounting figures which are not discounted. Further, it is an empirical question whether adding loosely correlated figures leads to a *total* correlated with anything!

To preserve relationships from the original currency statements

This rationale, cited by SSAP 20, is different from the net investment one. It requires that currency relationships (e.g. the ratio of opening to closing stocks) remain constant in translated figures. Patterson (1986) calls this viewpoint (which is used to justify the closing rate in the profit and loss account) the removal of 'distortion' in translating statements. Strictly though, to achieve this objective if exchange rates change, *all* comparative figures and transactions would be *re*translated each year at the *current* closing rate. Hence sterling comparatives would be different (updated) from the previous year's statements. Pre-acquisition equity would be updated each year and so goodwill would be similarly recalculated.

Whether aggregating such relationship-preserving balances produces a consolidated total that has meaning in terms of historical costs or any other measurement basis is doubtful. As Patz (1977) comments, on translation the place and time dimensions of balances can easily be confounded so that consolidated statements lose much meaning.

Under the *net investment rationale*, comparatives are not updated, and an *average* rate (as an approximation to transaction rates) is used in the profit and loss account, since the change in the net investment is exposed from transaction dates to the year-end. SSAP 20 ambiguously states both rationales and allows *either* average rate or closing rate for the income statement, but ignores comparatives. FAS No. 52 allows only the average rate (as did ED 27).

To choose a measurement unit with desirable properties

None of the general rationales specifies which of multiple exchange rates to use, e.g. buying or selling rates, dividend remittance rates, official versus free market rates, concessionary rates for foreign investment. FAS No. 8 (temporal approach) recommended the dividend rate, which seems inconsistent with translating the subsidiary's transactions as if those of the parent, which would seem to require the historical buying rate for stocks and fixed assets, but the current selling rate for debtors (currency to be received). SSAP 20 recommends the mean of buying and selling spot rates under closing rate. FAS No. 52 diverges in requiring the dividend remittance rate for the closing rate approach if there are no unusual circumstances.

Patz (1977) criticizes the unquestioned use of exchange rates for translation, arguing that their movements often reflect short-term volatility and only import–export trading, not economy-wide purchasing power. Where subsidiaries are autonomous enterprises, he argues for the use of purchasing power ratios, reflecting relative prices for goods within the two economies as a whole, rather than exchange rates. Arguments in favour of purchasing power parities question the measuring unit and so are more readily associated with the price level accounting debate. They have not been influential in practice and so are not examined further here (see Nobes, 1980).

The interaction of translation with price level accounting is an important one. The closing rate is sometimes viewed as a crude adjustment of historical cost balances. As long as translation objectives are not agreed and historical cost is uneasily adhered to, there is an uncomfortable relationship. This is particularly evident when rapid price level changes interact with translation, resulting in conflicting recommendations by SSAP 20 and FAS No. 52 on translating statements of subsidiaries in highly inflationary economies. Using current exchange rates, vast changes in exchange rates often reflect rapid price increases. SSAP 20 requires statements 'to be adjusted where possible to reflect current price levels before [translation]' (paragraph 26). FAS No. 52 requires the temporal approach for such subsidiaries. Both attempt to remove unacceptable 'distortions' in different ways. The reader is referred, for example, to Nobes (1986, pp. 67–9) for further discussion. Under current cost accounting such problems do not arise as both approaches reduce to the same (i.e. closing rate) solution. A further brief discussion of price level accounting and consolidation is made in Chapter 11.

SSAP 20 illustrates a compromise rationalizable from many angles but not completely consistent with any one, suggesting that selection of approach and objectives is based on something other than 'correctness' of particular technical objectives. It is to this that we now turn.

The wider context

Having examined theoretical objectives in the previous section, this section examines research which considers the political and economic environment within which the debate is situated, to gain a greater understanding of its nature.

The political–economic consequences dimension

As outlined in Chapter 3, some writers see the real debate as centred in the behavioural dimension rather than the conceptual one. Watts and Zimmerman (1979) (see pages 63–4) argue that, in a regulated economy, accounting theories are primarily produced in response to vested interests' demands, not because they better represent reality (a 'market for excuses'). Theories justify practice rather than leading it. Financial reporting is viewed in an agency-theoretic framework (see Jensen and Meckling, 1976), in which conflicts of interest exist between owners, managers, etc. Accounting information is part of a negotiated monitoring package between relevant parties to reduce distrust, and hence 'costs'. Each party tries to get the best deal from this negotiated package.

From this perspective, it is not unlikely that a consistent strengthening or weakening of home currencies over the period affected the debate. Sceptics argue that the choice of approach was dictated by the desire to show gains, or at very least to keep losses out of the profit and loss account. This is difficult to evaluate because of long lead times in generating accounting standards, complicated by the fact that the temporal approach affects the profit and loss account, whereas the closing rate approach places differences in reserves. Certainly in the UK a generally declining pound since the start of the 1970s is consistent with it allowing closing rate when the US favoured the temporal method.

In the USA the debate has proved a major area for 'market for excuses' based empirical research, which focuses on characteristics of groups lobbying over the introduction of standards, or choosing to switch from temporal to closing rate between FAS No. 8 and FAS No. 52, when voluntary choice was given prior to the regime of the new standard.

Griffin (1982) and Kelly (1985) examined characteristics of lobbiers over FAS

No. 8. Griffin found they experienced greater swings in pre-tax earnings due to foreign currency accounting rules than non-lobbiers. Kelly found them to have a greater proportion of foreign sales. She also found differences between lobbiers over implementation difficulties and those due to the income effect, but found gearing was not significant in either category, whereas Griffin found a small leverage effect. Both found lobbiers tended to be larger. Griffin (1983) examined whether factors influencing managers' welfare affected their lobbying over FAS No. 52. His multiple discriminant model gave only modest improvement in predicting management behaviour over more naïve models.

Gray (1984), in a survey analysis of firms during the period of free choice between FAS No. 8 and FAS No. 52, found strong evidence that firms chose the alternative which increased their profits or did not reduce their earnings per share. Ayres (1986) assumed that the change to FAS No. 52 would increase reported earnings for most firms. Within this, he hypothesized that (in a 'market for excuses'/agency framework) more management-controlled firms would have an incentive to change to report a better picture of their performance; that because of political exposure, larger firms tend to adopt income-reducing accounting methods; and to increase earnings firms with poorer prior performance and closer to debt and dividend constraints would tend to be early adopters. Using multivariate logistic analysis, he cited evidence to support his hypotheses.

This area of research widens the dimensions of the translation debate, suggesting new avenues of inquiry. In the author's view, much of the work is really of an exploratory rather than a confirmatory nature since the framework is still rather vague in providing operational measures of 'vested interests', etc., and some of the proxy measures used to 'test' hypotheses are rather imprecise. It will take consistent replication using a variety of approaches to ensure that results are not dependent upon models and assumptions.

Efficient markets research

US sources (e.g. Cooper, Fraser and Richards, 1978) suggest that companies changed their foreign currency management practices in response to FAS No. 8, suggesting that managements behaved as if the accounting numbers themselves had real significance. Whether these changes were purely cosmetic and whether investors were fooled is now examined. As discussed in Chapter 3, efficient markets research suggests the market can see through 'cosmetic' changes in accounting numbers, reacting only to those changes which have a real impact on future cash flows, *if* it has enough information to form a judgement. Investors are sophisticated enough to move figures themselves. Also, smoothing income may be counter-productive if the underlying economic process is volatile. Investors would be better served by greater disclosure. However, even this has costs, the social elements of which are implicitly ignored in efficient markets tests.

Dukes (1978) found in 479 multinationals that their share returns were not significantly different from similar domestic companies over the period of issue and implementation of FAS No. 8. Further, companies who changed translation policy as a result of FAS No. 8 did not have significantly different share price behaviour from those not changing.

Because FAS No. 8 routed all translation gains and losses through the profit and loss account, Makins (1982) examined whether the consequent extra volatility of reported earnings affected cost of capital. Did a (presumed) cosmetic change cause a real economic effect? he found the accounting change had little impact overall, but in the short term certain larger firms whose income statements were significantly altered were adversely affected. However, sensitivity in testing is difficult to achieve because of the complexity of holding other factors constant over the period of the test. Hines's (1984) cautions in interpreting such results (page 65) should be remembered here.

It is extremely difficult in practice for investors or analysts to distinguish between cosmetic and real economic changes. For example, multinational groups are not required to analyse exposure in each currency separately, so it is very difficult to see through total figures on change in method. Castanias and Griffin (1986) found, based on published analysts' forecasts, that during FAS No. 52's adoption and implementation, the dispersion of such forecasts increased, and they were revised proportionately more than at other times, and suggested a complex new standard can materially affect perceptions of uncertainty.

O'Keefe and Soloman (1985) found (confirming earlier studies) that managements disbelieve the 'efficient markets' hypothesis – but they comment that it may be in managements' interest to profess disbelief and lobby for a change which may benefit them personally, whilst really accepting the hypothesis. In an agency framework, sophisticated investors would discount share prices to counteract such management behaviour, imposing agency costs on firms (wheels within wheels!)

The 'context' research discussed above certainly suggests that it is naïve to look for a theoretically 'correct' solution. Understanding the context helps one make sense of the range of rationales and positions. However, it still may be true that certain solutions are more generally acceptable than others and these may reflect an aspiration towards 'good' accounting. The reader is left to form her or his own judgement.

Discussion questions

9.13 Explain in your own words the rationales for the closing rate and temporal approaches. Which do you find more convincing? Give reasons.

9.14 Explain the 'cover' concept in SSAP 20, discussing the consequent accounting treatment.

9.15 'If the assumptions about the nature of a group under the net investment rationale (closing rate) are realistic, it makes more sense to exclude foreign subsidiaries from the consolidation and to provide alternative information.'

Required Evaluate this statement, discussing possibilities for the accounting treatment and alternative disclosures for excluded foreign subsidiaries.

9.16   To what extent are group accounts consistent with the idea of a group as a single unified entity? (Note – issues other than foreign currency translation may be considered here.)

SUMMARY

A key concept is that of *exposure* to currency fluctuations. The main focus is on *accounting* exposure arising from the *translation* of results of *past* transactions. Translation of *transactions* is based on the *one* transaction approach (where original balances are updated on settlement) or the *two* transactions approach (where the transaction is broken down into the purchase element and financing element). SSAP 20 requires the two transactions approach.

Four approaches were discussed for the translation of *financial statements*; temporal, closing rate, current/non-current and monetary/non-monetary. The closing rate and to a lesser extent the temporal approaches form the basis of SSAP 20. The translation of balance sheets, income statements, and the flow statement of exposed items was examined, the last showing intuitively how the gain or loss arose, linking more complex calculations with the accounting exposure concept. The matrix provides an *integrating framework* for translation, one part of a *three-stage* process – translation of *transactions* within foreign currency statements, translation of *statements*, and *consolidation* of translated statements.

SSAP 20 was examined and contrasted with FAS No. 52. The criteria for deciding whether to use closing rate or temporal approaches, the treatment of gains or losses and their *disposition* in the profit and loss account or reserves, and provisions relating to *cover* (hedging) of net investments and *disclosure* were discussed. Finally the 'translation debate' was considered, first at the level of the *technical objectives* of translation and consolidation and, second, in terms of its wider economic and political context.

FURTHER READING

In practice and techniques

Accounting Standards Committee (1983) *SSAP 20 – Foreign Currency Translation*, ASC, London.
Financial Accounting Standards Board (1982) *FAS No. 52 – Foreign Currency Translation*, FASB, Connecticut.
Patterson, R. (1986) Foreign currency translation, in L. Skerratt and D. Tonkin (eds.) *Financial Reporting 1985/6*, pp. 53–72, Institute of Chartered Accountants in England and Wales, London.
Taylor, P. A. (1985) The foreign currency translation process: a matrix funds flow analysis, *British Accounting Review*, Vol. 17, No. 1 (Spring), pp. 3–22.

Overviews

Flower, J. (1985) Foreign currency translation, in C. W. Nobes and R. H. Parker (eds.) *Comparative International Accounting* (2nd edn), ch. 12, Philip Alan, Oxford.

Nobes, C. W. (1980) A review of the translation debate, *Accounting and Business Research*, Autumn 1980, pp. 421–31.

Wider debate

Zeff, S. A. (1978) The rise of 'economic consequences', *Journal of Accountancy*, Vol. 146, December, pp. 152–63.

10 Segment Reporting and Disaggregation

The last twenty years have evidenced greatly increasing corporate diversification, across business sectors and continents. The advent of portfolio theory has shown how diversification reduces total risk, particularly where combining firms exhibit quite different but complementary risk characteristics. In a 'perfect' world, portfolio-based market theories imply that investors can carry out such diversification, and that it is unnecessary for companies to do so. In a world with transaction costs, imperfect information and managers eyeing job security in an increasingly complex and uncertain environment, corporate diversification to reduce volatility is hardly surprising.

However, such strategies cause potential information problems when they result in the increasing size of corporate groupings. The amount of information available to users decreases as formerly individual results are consumed into consolidated aggregates. Often these mask very disparate components resulting from the diversification process itself. It is argued that complex groups should provide disaggregated information to assist prediction and assessment. Efficient markets research suggests investors are sophisticated, and that finer breakdowns can reduce risk and aid accurate pricing. Empirical work in this area is examined later (for a review of this literature see Dyckman and Morse, 1986, or Keane, 1980). This increasing call for *segment reporting* has also been fuelled by developments in capital markets and information technology.

Segmental information is usually disclosed in addition to consolidated information, though some authors suggest that such disclosures might be an alternative. The idea of alternative formats to consolidated information is not new. The Companies Act 1948 allowed directors to present alternatives to consolidation (e.g. subconsolidations for parts of the group, or separate financial statements or notes for each subsidiary). This Act also allowed exemptions from inclusion in group accounts where 'the business of the holding company and subsidiary are so different that they cannot reasonably be treated as a single undertaking'.

These might be seen as rudimentary attempts to tackle the averaging problem discussed in Chapter 5. The first direct requirement for segmental information in the UK came in the 1967 Companies Act. The directors' report was required to contain segmental details of turnover and profit before tax, where a company (or group) 'has carried on business of two or more classes'. In the USA the SEC required 'line of business' information by 1970. In 1976 FAS No. 14 considerably expanded US segmental disclosures and far outstrips anything in the UK. Indeed, current UK requirements are weaker than those of the international accounting standard, IAS No. 14 published in 1981. A working party has been set up by the Accounting Standards Committee, with the intention of producing an exposure draft in the first half of 1987 and a standard in 1988.

Consolidation aggregates the accounts of *legal entities*. Segment reporting disaggregates this consolidated information over *economic units*, called 'segments'. These often differ from legal structures in a group since, for example, a subsidiary may be involved in a number of lines of business, or a single geographical location may include a number of legally separate subsidiaries. Accepting for the moment the need for segmental information (discussed later), the main problems arising are segment identification and segment disclosure and measurement. It is to these matters that we now turn.

SEGMENT IDENTIFICATION

There are many possible bases for identifying segments. Emmanuel and Gray (1978) cite as possibilities dissaggregation by:
(a)   industry and product line;
(b)   actual organizational lines;
(c)   geographical areas;
(d)   classes of customers/markets.
Miller and Scott (1980) in a useful review, cite alternative categories.

According to Emmanuel and Gray (1978), a key determinant is that of differing degrees of risk. Here the focus is mainly on use by investors but, elsewhere, Gray (1981) has argued that employees may also be interested in segmental information (e.g. on a plant level). Governments too may have an interest in such areas as monitoring price controls.

As elsewhere in group accounting, the choice between alternatives involves trade-offs between objectivity/hardness, comparability, and relevance. For example, should segment identification be managerially determined or determined according to externally verifiable criteria? The former relates to how management sees and manages the firm but may obscure comparability *between* firms, as management structures differ. The latter (e.g. dissecting by the Standard Industrial Classification) facilitates cross-sectional comparisons across firms and in principle is less open to manipulation, but may bear no relationship to organizational structure. Also, the SIC is not specifically designed for this purpose.

The United Kingdom

The Companies Act 1985 requires two fundamental classifications; by classes of business and by geographical location. It allows managerial discretion and gives no guidance on segment materiality. The Stock Exchange gives minimal guidance on materiality for geographical segments only. A segmental analysis of sales is required if foreign operations in total exceed 10 per cent of consolidated revenues. Segments should be analysed by continent unless 50 per cent or more of total foreign operations relate to a single continent when a further analysis by country is required. A broad geographical analysis giving percentages is sufficient. No accounting standards or exposure drafts exist in this area as yet.

The United States of America

The US standard FAS No. 14, 'Financial reporting for segments of a business enterprise', again incorporates managerial discretion into segment identification. It identifies the same two fundamental classifications for segment identification, industry (lines of business) and geographic area. *Management* determines the basis of segmentation subject to *quantitative* constraints on segment materiality, with a suggestion that profit centres within the entity are a useful starting point. It also requires somewhat less detail about sales to major customers.

The FASB concluded that cross-sectional comparability was not as important to analysts as economic relevance, that managerial determination would still allow comparisons *over time* for the firm itself. However, it is still possible that the two basic classifications above may not correspond to actual organizational structure, and an artificial template is being imposed on the firm *before* managerial discretion is exercised.

The US segment materiality criteria have two main aims. The first is to ensure all significant segments are reported. The second is to ensure that there is not a large unclassified 'other' section. FAS No. 14 defines 'significance' of reportable segments as 10 per cent or more of total revenues (including intra-group sales), or of total operating profits or losses, or of total identifiable assets. A second test requires that the combined sales of all reportable segments thus determined must amount to at least 75 per cent of total external group sales, otherwise more segments must be identified up to a maximum of ten for normal purposes. Materiality criteria for geographical segments are similarly comprehensive though slightly different. Surprisingly however, in a survey Gray and Radebaugh (1984) found that UK based multinationals disclosed significantly more geographical segments than their US counterparts, although the amount of information disclosed about each segment was less.

Emmanuel and Gray (1978) criticize the US proposal for allowing too much managerial discretion in the determination of segments. Instead, for industry segments they suggest an alternative in which the firm's organizational structure is first matched to an SIC (three-digit) level of classification. Management can then depart from such a starting point only by demonstrating that it is inappropriate (the study suggesting criteria for this) or by showing a greater level of disaggregation. The authors suggest this will ensure a greater comparability in disaggregation, and will also allow disclosures to be reasonably consistent with the firm's organizational structure.

SEGMENTAL DISCLOSURE AND MEASUREMENT

Disclosures for each segment

It has been widely argued that availability of segmental information improves performance evaluation of complex entities by allowing finer monitoring, possibly also reducing agency costs (see Jensen and Meckling, 1976). Disclosure possibilities range from minimal details about turnover and profits after tax to full subconsolidations for each segment. However, if the quantity of such information is too great, costs will exceed benefits in terms of preparation and data irrelevance, resulting in superfluity or, even worse, information overload (see, for example, Foster, 1986, pp. 35–6). Little is known about user needs here.

Such a trade-off is difficult to evaluate in a welfare sense since costs tend to fall on parties other than beneficiaries. Beneficiaries may include prospective investors and governmental agencies, whereas the costs may be borne largely by the current shareholders. Benston (1984) found that governmental agencies in the USA tended to underestimate preparation costs of segmental information. Potentially such 'costs' also include competitive damage caused by information disclosure. An early survey in the USA by Backer and McFarland (1968) (reported in Miller and Scott, 1980, p. 9) found twenty-eight executives opposed extra disclosure on these grounds, whereas fifteen found such arguments spurious, commenting that competitors already knew more about margins, etc. than was disclosed in published segmental reports!

The United Kingdom

In the UK and the US, disclosures tend to be greater for industry segments than for geographical ones. The Companies Act 1985 tends towards minimal requirements – for classes of business, turnover and profit before tax; for geographical segments, only turnover. Directors are allowed *not* to disclose such information if *they* consider it to be seriously prejudicial to group interests provided the fact of non-disclosure is noted. The Stock Exchange has a further requirement for listed companies – geographical *profit* disclosure – but *only* for segments whose ratio of profit to turnover is substantially out of line with the rest of the group – disclosure by exception.

The 1985/6 Survey of Published Accounts indicates that over the last two years only 4 per cent of large listed companies did not provide some segmental information, whereas the figures were 15 per cent and 45 per cent for medium listed and large unlisted companies. Unfortunately the Survey does not indicate whether non-publication was because of homogeneity of business or whether the Companies Act exemption was used. Prima facie it seems that where Stock Exchange requirements do not apply, there is a worrying lack of disclosure. Over 85 per cent of large listed companies/groups provided segmental turnover figures for both classifications, and profit by industry segment, but only 55 per cent showed segmental profits geographically.

Certain companies integrate class of business and geographical disclosures into a matrix format. Table 10.1 shows the 1985 disclosure by Cadbury Schweppes plc (previous year also being given in the original). Such a matrix format gives a more detailed breakdown compared to conventional disclosures which effectively give only the marginal totals of such a matrix (i.e. the left-hand column totals and subtotals in Table 10.1). For example, it is possible under this matrix format to assess the differential contributions, structures and changes in, say, the confectionery segment across different continents. However, such inferences would be limited to the extent that allocations are included in such figures (see later). In the UK there is no requirement to disclose accounting policies relating to such allocations. Operating assets are disclosed in excess of current UK requirements, though again there is no requirement in the UK which defines how operating assets are to be determined or even that the basis of measurement must be disclosed.

1985	Total	United Kingdom	Europe	North America	Australia	Africa, Asia and New Zealand
Sales:						
Confectionery	769.6	375.3	53.4	189.1	87.8	64.0
Drinks	668.8	231.9	166.0	168.8	91.2	10.9
Beverages and foods	377.5	286.1	33.8	—	38.7	18.9
Health and hygiene	57.9	57.9	—	—	—	—
	1,873.8	951.2	253.2	357.9	217.7	93.8
Trading profit:						
Confectionery	55.6	40.9	4.3	(6.8)	10.6	6.6
Drinks	42.8	16.9	14.0	1.2	7.9	2.8
Beverages and foods	13.7	6.9	2.3	—	2.6	1.9
Health and hygiene	0.9	0.9	—	—	—	—
	113.0	65.6	20.6	(5.6)	21.1	11.3
Operating assets:						
Confectionery	387.1	166.2	19.5	138.6	26.2	36.6
Drinks	276.2	103.4	47.8	84.3	35.5	5.2
Beverages and foods	94.4	69.7	7.5	—	11.3	5.9
Health and hygiene	17.3	17.3	—	—	—	—
	775.0	356.6	74.8	222.9	73.0	47.7

Table 10.1   Cadbury Schweppes Group – sales, trading profit and operating assets analysis for 52 weeks ended 28 December 1985 (£ million)

The United States of America

FAS No. 14 disclosure requirements go far beyond the minimal requirements in the UK. For reportable industry segments it requires:

1. Turnover/sales:
   (a) sales external to the group;
   (b) intersegment (intra-group) sales or transfers, *and* the basis for accounting for such sales and transfers.
2. Profit and loss information:
   (c) operating profit or loss;
   (d) details of unusual or infrequently occurring items included therein (here it refers to abnormal rather than extraordinary items since operating profit is *before* extraordinary items);
   (e) total segmental depreciation expense, etc.
3. Asset information:
   (f) identifiable assets (not liabilities, which are deemed to be difficult to segmentalize, financing often being handled on a group basis);
   (g) capital expenditures.
4. Other disclosures:
   (h) accounting policies relating to segmental information where these are not disclosed elsewhere;
   (i) certain information about investments accounted for under the equity method as opposed to consolidation;
   (j) a *reconciliation* of revenues, operating profits and identifiable assets, etc. to consolidated amounts.

The requirements for geographical areas are slightly less comprehensive, in that abnormal items, depreciation, capital expenditures and accounting policies are not required, but are still far in excess of UK requirements. Compared to the UK, additional requirements exist for assets employed and purchased, for breakdowns of profit information, for accounting policies and for reconciliations. US requirements provide key statistics rather than full subconsolidations. They further require information about export sales and sales to major customers.

Gray and Radebaugh (1984), in their survey based on 1979 data, found that around one-third of thirty-five UK multinationals surveyed provided voluntary information related to assets, new investments and employees, but practically none disclosed intra-group sales.

International pronouncements

IAS No. 14, 'Reporting financial information by segment', calls for the disclosure of identifiable assets by both industry and geographical segments, as well as the basis for determination of intersegment revenues. However, it has not been adopted in the UK. The OECD and UN have published recommendations in the area which in certain respects go beyond the USA, requiring employee details and, in the former case, capital expenditure by geographical area, but these are unlikely to have a major impact in the UK in the near future.

ICI plc, a large UK multinational quoted on international stock exchanges, adopts most FAS No. 14 requirements, and is used in Table 10.2 as an illustration of its features. In certain respects it goes beyond US requirements in providing a geographic analysis of turnover not only by location of company, but also by

Industry segments

The table below sets out information, on a worldwide basis, for each of the Group's industry segments. The Group's policy is to transfer products internally at external market prices.

	Total assets less current liabilities		Turnover		Profit	
	1985 £m	1984 £m	1985 £m	1984 £m	1985 £m	1984 £m
Consumer and speciality products	1,369	1,286	2,984	2,404	373	302
Industrial products	2,640	3,001	4,998	4,775	282	346
Agriculture	1,132	896	1,995	1,828	181	218
Oil and gas	130	159	1,107	1,349	59	109
Miscellaneous			175	156	—	9
			11,259	10,512	895	984
Net operating assets	5,271	5,342				
Intersegment eliminations			(534)	(603)	1	(1)
Non-operating and miscellaneous assets	443	908				
	5,714	6,250	10,725	9,909	896	983
Royalty income and government grants					82	80
Trading profit					978	1,063
Share of profits less losses of related companies and amounts written off investments					56	71
Net interest payable					(122)	(100)
Profit on ordinary activities before taxation					912	1,034

Non-operating and miscellaneous assets include investments in related and other companies, current asset investments and short-term deposits and cash, less short-term borrowings.

	Capital expenditure		Depreciation	
	1985 £m	1984 £m	1985 £m	1984 £m
Consumer and speciality products	134	84	80	67
Industrial products	259	182	258	257
Agriculture	145	116	66	57
Oil and gas	43	31	56	48
Miscellaneous	53	28	14	11
	634	441	474	440

Table 10.2   ICI Group: Segment information – year ended 31 December 1985

Geographic areas

The information opposite is reanalysed in the table below by geographic area. The figures for each geographic area show the net operating assets owned by and the turnover and profits made by companies located in that area; export sales and related profits are included in the areas from which those sales were made.

	Net operating assets		Turnover		Profit	
	1985 £m	1984 £m	1985 £m	1984 £m	1985 £m	1984 £m
United Kingdom						
– Home sales			2,999	3,120		
– Export sales			2,998	2,835		
	2,598	2,574	5,997	5,955	394	578
Continental Western Europe	597	574	2,065	1,798	76	66
The Americas	1,221	1,158	2,427	2,001	270	214
Australasia, Japan and the Far East	704	836	1,584	1,419	104	105
Other countries including Indian subcontinent	151	200	456	397	52	43
	5,271	5,342	12,529	11,570	896	1,006
Inter-area eliminations			(1,804)	(1,661)	—	(23)
			10,725	9,909	896	983
Royalty income and government grants					82	80
Trading profit					978	1,063

Turnover in each geographic market in which customers are located	1985 £m	1984 £m
Chemicals:		
United Kingdom	2,433	2,346
Continental Western Europe	2,160	1,891
The Americas	2,539	2,111
Australasia, Japan and the Far East	1,805	1,613
Other countries including Indian subcontinent	922	859
	9,859	8,820
Oil	866	1,089
Total turnover	10,725	9,909

Employees Average number of people employed by the Group	1985	1984
United Kingdom	57,200	58,600
Continental Western Europe	14,600	13,200
The Americas	20,400	17,200
Australasia, Japan and the Far East	13,600	13,700
Other countries including Indian subcontinent	12,800	12,900
Total employees	118,600	115,600

Table 10.2 (continued)

location of customer, and also a geographical employee analysis. Note that segmental information is reconciled to trading profit rather than operating profit (see later), which includes more allocated amounts.

From such segmental information it is possible to make rough calculations for and comparisons between each industry segment – of, for example profit/turnover ratios or the extent of capital investment – though geographical analyses of industry segments are not possible in this non-matrix format. Further, as stated earlier, since segments are determined by management, whilst it may be possible to compare segmental information over time for a single group, it is difficult to compare, say, ICI's segmental information with other multinational chemical groups since its internal basis of segmentation may be legitimately (under, say, FAS No. 14) quite different.

Measurement issues – the allocation problem

Measurement and disclosure issues are closely intertwined. It is usually not possible to provide meaningful information finer than the level of disaggregation used internally by the group. Otherwise the quality of disaggregated information becomes suspect as a result of arbitrary allocation procedures. This is particularly true in terms of segment *profit* measures. The 'allocation problem' (discussed in Chapter 4) bites here, especially where for reasons discussed below, management treats certain 'segments' as cost centres rather than profit centres.

As Thomas (1975) points out, the interaction effect causes allocations of costs to be incorrigible (i.e. arbitrary). Interdependent companies produce a greater output in tandem than independently. Such increments from interactions of production factors do not belong to any particular factor since they result entirely from *inter*action. Gray (1981) considers the main problem area to be in vertically integrated firms where there are no intermediate market prices for the transferred product (e.g. semi-assembled car chasses), or with horizontally integrated firms having great interdependencies. The group as a unity produces an amount of profit, but it is impossible to state unambiguously the proportion each segment contributes. The problem with segmental reporting criteria is that they impose a standard template on all groups, treating all segments as profit centres, which may not be how management evaluates segments internally.

The allocation problem is present in most groups to some degree and is potentially an extremely serious one for segmental reporting. Because of its existence, it is relatively easy for management to choose 'fair and reasonable' bases for allocation to enhance or mask underlying segmental profit information as desired.

Example 10.1   The allocation problem

The Fudge Group has the following internal segmental information (in £ million) for the year ended 31 March 1987:

	X	Y	Z
Turnover	500	5,000	2,000
Traceable profit	150	200	600
Net assets	120	120	1,200

Management is concerned that the traceable results show the group as too dependent on segment Z, and wish not to emphasize its success. In published accounts, head office costs of £450 million are to be allocated. Possible allocation bases have been proposed as (i) equally between segments, (ii) turnover and (iii) assets employed.

Required Assess the effects of these allocation bases on reported segmental profits. Assume no intersegment trading.

Allocation basis	Proportions			Allocated costs			Reported profits*		
	X	Y	Z	X	Y	Z	X	Y	Z
Equally	⅓	⅓	⅓	150	150	150	—	50	450
Turnover	500:5,000:2,000			30	300	120	120	(100)	480
Assets employed	120:120:1,200			37	38	375	113	162	225

*Note** reported profits = traceable profits − allocated costs.

Management decided to select basis (iii) since the relative strength of segment Z was de-emphasized. Under US disclosure requirements, each segment would need to be disclosed under this basis as each is more than 10 per cent of either turnover, profits (reported), or net assets of combined segments (though under equal allocation, X would not need to be separately disclosed as it does not satisfy these tests). Note, however, the US definition of reportable segmental profit is different from the basis used in this simplistic example and is discussed below.

The United Kingdom

No guidance over measurement is given in the UK, allowing management virtually unlimited freedom to allocate common costs and define segmental profits as they choose, the bases not being subject to disclosure or audit. This is a very unsatisfactory state of affairs.

The United States of America

FAS No. 14 evidences considerable compromise in this area. Its original exposure draft proposed that segment contribution *and* segment operating profit be disclosed for each segment. Segment contribution was defined as segment revenues less variable expenses and *traceable* expenses. Segment operating profit was defined as segment contribution less non-traceable common operating expenses, allocated on a 'reasonable' basis.

However, FAS No. 14 dropped the contribution disclosure requirement for reasons including the fact that such disclosures might not be comparable or meaningful between enterprises. They might differ purely according to the sophistication of enterprises' internal record-keeping systems. Some argued also that the location where a cost was incurred should not determine its inclusion or otherwise in an accounting measure. This illustrates clearly a problem of published financial reporting – if a general purpose statement is required, a template has to be designed for all enterprises, and its degree of fit may vary considerably given the variety of firms and accounting systems.

Operating profit was defined as prior to interest expense (since financing arrangements vary so much between groups, some being organized centrally – the amount financed by the segment may be therefore an arbitrary figure and non-controllable by it), general corporate expenses, minority interests and extraordinary items. However, it does include common operating expenses (which are to be allocated on a 'reasonable' basis) and unusual or infrequently occurring items which are to be separately disclosed. Obvious excesses as in the previous simplistic example, where 'general corporate expenses' have also been allocated would be checked, but there is still scope for variations in allocations.

Maybe this is a reasonable general purpose compromise, though Walker (1968) considers that such allocation-ridden figures are not useful. It is probably fair to say that for interdependent groups segmental information is pretty useless as the whole cannot meaningfully be split. However, for separable groups (e.g. financial conglomerates) the consolidated 'average' is itself a cocktail, and one needs to study the segmental information. This area is a very useful case study in the trade-offs in producing acceptable general purpose external statements. It cautions extreme care in interpreting group accounts and illustrates how the complexity of enterprises is not always adequately represented in fixed accounting procedures and requirements. It is difficult to evaluate the potential costs and benefits of changes to current requirements.

THE USEFULNESS OF SEGMENTAL INFORMATION

A number of studies have examined the desirability and impact of segmental reporting. For example, Ronen and Livnat (1981) examined whether segmental reporting should be mandatory rather than voluntary. Their theoretical analysis provided some support for mandatory reporting, which they proved to have a tendency to clarify signals produced by voluntary reporting. Prior to SEC mandatory requirements, it was impossible for users to assess whether non-disclosure was because of poor results, or because directors assessed that *private* costs to them exceeded private benefits (e.g. in disclosing more than competitors). Mandatory disclosures overcome this ambiguity allowing *social* costs and benefits to be considered. A number of other theoretical arguments have already been discussed.

Empirical research in this area falls into three main categories; survey research, forecasting studies, and market reaction tests. Most is predominantly US based, examining a particular period around 1970 when SEC requirements changed a voluntary disclosure situation to a mandatory one, prior to FAS No. 14. Tests examine industry segments only. Results are interesting, but care is necessary in extrapolating results to a UK environment. What follows is illustrative rather than exhaustive.

Survey-based research

Surveys generally supported segmental disclosure. Backer and McFarland (1968) (*before* segmental disclosures were required) found many business executives were worried by potential competitive harm resulting from increased disclosure. However, when the FASB itself conducted a survey in 1974 (four years *after* the SEC made line of business disclosures mandatory), executives from twenty-five out of thirty companies considered that such disclosures were useful to sophisticated users. Unsurprisingly, they were opposed to *further* extensions and audit attestation, both of which were imposed by FAS No. 14 in 1976! Baldwin (1984) cites a Financial Analysts Foundation survey that segmental data in the USA is widely *used*.

Forecasting accounting measures

Predictive ability tests tended to pre-date market reaction studies. A number of different methodologies indicate that, particularly in the USA, whilst segmental sales data is useful, the *incremental* effect of segmental profit data is somewhat open to question.

Kinney (1971) and Collins (1976) used *mechanical prediction models* to predict consolidated profits. Segmental sales was found useful, but incremental information about segmental earnings did not appreciably increase predictive performance. Replicating these studies in the UK, Emmanuel and Pick (1980) found similar results but no support for any incremental profits effect. Such studies are joint tests of the data *and* the models chosen, so care is needed in interpretation of results.

Silhan (1982, 1983), using actual company data from 1967–77, *simulated mergers* between independent, single product firms, to generate a series of 'conglomerates'. The original company data then provided segmental information for each 'conglomerate' to test forecasting models. The approach allows control and flexibility in the construction of segmental data, avoiding the allocation problem since the 'conglomerates' are independent. His results confirmed those of the predictive studies, that incremental segmental *profit* data did not improve forecasts. However, in the very short term, he found that quarterly profit data could marginally help forecasters, particularly in smaller conglomerates. However, in practice most groups do not possess such a 'pure' structure, and so it is possible that the simulated groups might be somewhat artificial. The usefulness of Silhan's work is in its reinforcement power.

A number of researchers tried to isolate *mathematically* the conditions under which disaggregation is helpful. For example, Barnea and Lakonishok (1980) found that disaggregated data is not always helpful, the outcome depending on the correlations within the segmental data and between forecasting errors. Allocation procedures were found to reduce the usefulness of segmental data.

Hopwood, Newbold and Silhan (1982) only found segmental information to be useful if the profit series for each segment was generated by a different process, or when the results of some segments led or lagged other segments.

In the former case, disaggregation separated and clarified differing underlying signals masked by aggregation. In the second, knowledge of a *lead indicator* would help the forecasting of other segments' results. They found no evidence of these conditions in the actual companies Silhan (1982) used for his studies. Ang (1979) also isolated conditions under which simple components forecasts may not outperform aggregate ones. These analyses are interesting in that they show that disaggregation is not universally helpful in forecasting.

Baldwin (1984) assessed over the same period whether there was an increase in accuracy in *investment analysts' published forecasts*. Whereas the studies cited above examined whether users *should* be able to improve their forecasts, this study examines whether they did in fact improve them. His study deepened earlier work by Barefield and Comiskey (1975). He compared forecast improvements for three groups of firms; multisegment firms which started to produce segmental reports only after the SEC requirement, multisegment firms which produced reports before and after, and single-segment firms which did not produce such information at all. He found that whilst an overall decrease in analysts' forecast errors was found for all three, the most significant change was where firms produced segment disclosures for the first time. Thus, he argued that mandatory introduction of segmental reporting did help analysts in forecasting.

Market reaction studies

All the forecasting studies focus on *inputs* to user decision models. The market reaction studies focus nearer to the end result of prediction, the market effect. The main hypothesis tested has been that the publication of segmental information reduces the market's perception of risk. Some early studies (e.g. Kochanek, 1974) examined price variability. Later studies examined the effect on the companies' *beta* or market risk, using standard capital asset pricing model (CAPM) methodology.

Kochanek (1974) found that firms making voluntary disclosures reduced their share price variability. Horowitz and Kolodny (1977) did not find evidence of a reduction in market risk or of a price reaction to firms disclosing segmental information. However, Collins and Simonds (1979) using different, more sophisticated methodology concluded that market risk was reduced by such disclosures. Dhaliwal, Spicer and Vickrey (1979) implicitly supported these conclusions, finding a reduction in the cost of equity capital for firms disclosing segmental profit information for the first time. Other studies have examined the role of segmental information in conjunction with other information sources, but these are difficult to interpret unambiguously in the present context.

Overall, the evidence favours the production of segmental information, but there are questions against the usefulness of segmental profit information (possibly as a result of allocation procedures).

Exercises

10.1   The Automotive Group has the following structure across industries and countries:

	Germany	France	Australia
Heavy engineering – car bodies	•		•
Car assembly	•	•	
Motoring retail discount shops		•	•

In Germany, transfers from 'heavy engineering' to 'car assembly' are at cost plus 10 per cent, whereas transfers to the rest of the group are at cost plus 25 per cent. There is no external market for unassembled car chasses. German subsidiaries are heavily loan-financed and also have high short-term financing. Australian subsidiaries are 51 per cent owned and equity financed. In France, the discount shops also do car repair work. Group directors are proposing to disclose two segments geographically, Europe and the Rest of the World, and three 'line of business' segments.

Required
(a)   What disclosures per segment would you recommend?
(b)   Using deductions from the above information, discuss any limitations of the proposed segmental disclosures of the Automotive Group.
(c)   Assess the extent to which a matrix format disclosure would improve the quality of segmental reporting in this case.

10.2   Assess the extent to which segmental reports increase the information content of the standard consolidated financial reporting package. Use the Cadbury Schweppes or ICI examples (Tables 10.1 and 10.2) for illustrative purposes.

10.3   What are the likely economic consequences of segmental reporting (a) on individual groups of companies, (b) from a market or societal point of view? Are there likely to be any conflicts between these perspectives and, if so, discuss.

10.4   Compare and contrast the nature of information disclosed by:
(a)   consolidated financial statements;
(b)   holding company financial statements;
(c)   segmental reporting.

SUMMARY

Consolidation aggregates statements of *legal entities*. The growth in number of business combinations and their degree of diversification has the potential of masking and reducing the amount of information available. Segmental reporting disaggregates into *economic units*. Issues which arise concern segment *identification*, *disclosure* and *measurement*.

Both UK and US requirements require *identification* both industrially (lines of business) and geographically. Within these classifications, both the UK and the USA allow managerial discretion in defining segments, as opposed to externally verifiable criteria. The US standard sets detailed quantitative materiality criteria limiting such discretion, whereas in the UK such criteria are limited to Stock Exchange criteria for listed companies relating to geographical segments. US criteria attempt to ensure that all significant segments are included, and disclosures cover substantially all consolidated amounts.

Segmental *disclosure* requirements in the UK fall short of both international and US ones. Turnover and profits are required for classes of business, and only turnover for the geographical classification. If they consider it seriously prejudicial, directors are allowed not to disclose segmental information. The Stock Exchange requires listed companies to disclose geographical profits only if they are 'abnormal'. In the USA, turnover, profits, identifiable assets and a reconcilation to consolidated amounts are required for both classifications. For industrial segments details of certain profit and loss elements and capital expenditures are required. Some companies in the UK voluntarily use a matrix format. The *allocation* problem haunts segmental measurement. No guidance is given over measurement in the UK, but the US requires *operating* profit to be disclosed, which includes some non-traceable (allocated) expenses. Segmental accounting policies must be disclosed in the USA.

Empirical studies include surveys, predictive ability and market reaction studies. They indicate that segmental reporting is asked for and used, though there is conflict over the amount needed. Studies (including the techniques of mechanical forecasting models and simulated mergers) indicate that segmental sales are useful for forecasting consolidated earnings, but there is some doubt over the incremental effect of segmental profit figures. Generally segmental information seems to affect the market's perception of risk.

FURTHER READING

Financial Accounting Standards Board (1976) *FAS No. 14 – 'Financial Reporting for Segments of a Business Enterprise'*, FASB, Connecticut.

Gray, S. J. (1981) Segmental or disaggregated financial statements, in T. A. Lee (ed.) *Developments in Financial Reporting*, ch. 2, Philip Alan, Oxford.

Miller, M. C. (1980) *Financial Reporting by Segments*, Discussion Paper No. 4, Australian Accounting Research Foundation, Melbourne.

Thomas, A. (1975) The FASB and the allocation fallacy, *Journal of Accountancy*, November, pp. 65–8.

11   Issues and Reflections

Since consolidation was first practised at the turn of the century, the corporate scene has become infinitely more complex, particularly in terms of environmental diversity, sophistication of capital markets and the time-scale for preparation and use of accounts. This chapter tries to draw together and reflect on themes discussed in the book, more often suggesting questions than providing answers.

DESIGNING AN ACCOUNTING TEMPLATE FOR GROUPS OF COMPANIES

A major problem is in designing a common template to fit extremely diverse situations. A common criticism of consolidated financial reporting is that the techniques are far too simplistic and legalistic to reflect the underlying complexity, and are very similar to those adopted fifty years ago, despite the drastic changes that have occurred. As shown earlier, in heterogeneous groups consolidation may be misleading, and in highly integrated groups disaggregation may be meaningless. Is it appropriate to have a single template for all group structures or to define when particular accounting treatments are appropriate (e.g. combinations, tiers of disclosure, reportable segments and foreign currency translation)?

Contingency theory in management accounting suggests diverse internal reporting systems and definitions for firms in different environments and with different structures. However, the constraints and criteria for internal and external reporting differ. In external reporting, greater emphasis is placed on comparability of format, since analysts need to process vast amounts of corporate data. Further, under agency theory, external monitoring may be more difficult than within the firm itself. The former requires clearly defined and non-manipulable measures. This countervailing demand for a common template has its price, of peculiar results in marginal cases.

Particular counter-examples showing peculiarities in treatments (e.g. over vendor placings, manipulation of disclosure by changing marginal shareholdings at the cost/equity/consolidation boundaries) are not themselves sufficient to dismiss current practice as sub-optimal. It is possible that overall benefits from comparability and simplicity of format outweigh peculiarities resulting from imposing such a comparatively simple template. In a conflictual environment it is difficult to design improvements unambiguously because of difficulty in assessing trade-offs between the parties involved. Gerboth (1972) suggests a 'muddling through' approach of step by step experimentation, making small changes at the margin, observing their impact, then taking the next small step and seeing how the dust settles. He suggests this approach overcomes the need for comprehensive and all-inclusive theories. Other than by this approach, it is difficult to assess whether a more 'relevant' template tailored to specific situations would better serve users and increase social welfare.

SUBSTANCE OVER FORM

The phrase 'substance over form' is the US equivalent of a 'true and fair view', but in many ways is more expressive – that the real economic substance of a transaction should be reported, rather than its narrow legal form. As a criterion in UK group accounts, its application is somewhat mixed. In some areas, e.g. in the associated company definition, it prevails, 'significant influence' being the root definition, supported by a rebuttable quantitative fallback based on greater than 20 per cent ownership or not. Also, in accounting for business combinations, SSAP 23 counsels that the legal structures used to effect a combination (a new holding company, or simple investment holding) should itself not affect the accounting approach adopted (paragraph 24).

However, in other areas such application is notably missing. For example, the Companies Act definition of a subsidiary is narrowly legalistic (*de jure*), and for example control of subsidiaries by contractual devices without membership of a company (see pages 18–19) or through other means is not at present considered in defining group membership, though the 'true and fair' requirement provides some amelioration, as will be discussed later. The interpretation UK law will give to the 'control contract' clause in the Seventh Directive definition (see pages 20–21) may have an effect here.

Another example where 'substance over form' does not apply is that of 'vendor rights' and 'vendor placings' in defining a merger. The case of a holding company issuing shares for cash, and then buying out subsidiary shareholders, seems little different in substance from it swapping shares and arranging for the subsidiary's shareholders' holdings of its shares to be placed for cash. Holgate (1986, p. 25) argues that there is a difference in that the merger definition is based on whether or not material resources leave the group, not continuity of ownership rights, and that in the latter case, from the time the *holding company* acquires the shares, no resources leave the group as they do in the former case. However, this seems to be rather casuistic, and in the author's view contrary to 'substance over form' in any reasonable sense.

It seems rather serious that such a minor premeditated change in the form of a transaction can cause such a disparity in accounting treatment, and is probably the first 'breach in the dyke' which may later cause the ASC to follow its US counterpart in considering anti-avoidance legislation. A further example is that of British Syphon Industries (reported in *Accountancy,* July 1986, p. 31) which reduced its holding in Marshall's Universal, selling the shares to its financial advisers (!) the day before making an offer, which then (and only then) satisfied SSAP 23's criteria for merger accounting (see pages 51–2).

The issue of 'substance over form' (true and fair view) has become highly contentious in the wake of the *Argyll* case, discussed in Chapter 2. For example, *Technical Release 603,* 'Off-balance-sheet finance and window dressing', issued in 1985 by the Technical Committee of the Institute of Chartered Accountants in England and Wales (ICAEW, 1985) examines this issue within the context of the *Argyll* decision and subsequent DTI interpretation. It recommends that

> the economic substance of . . . transactions [involving schemes to keep some financing off the balance sheet (off-balance-sheet finance), or transactions whose purpose is to give a misleading impression of financial position (window dressing)] should be considered rather than their mere legal form when determining their true nature and thus the appropriate accounting treatment. Where items are included in the accounts on the basis of the substance of the transactions concerned and this is different from their legal form, the notes . . . should disclose the legal form . . . and amounts.

However, it recommends that in rare cases where such accounting would cause non-compliance with Companies Act provisions, the true and fair view requirements should be satisfied by adequate disclosure, possibly by providing pro forma accounts (which would cover the *Argyll* case situation).

However, in their response the Law Society (1986) suggested that such recommendations go too far, and indeed that they may be contrary to the law. They distinguish amongst other things between 'misleading' window dressing and other off-balance-sheet financing, in the latter case where it is considered that mere compliance with the law will result in inadequate information. In this latter case (amongst others), they consider that the recommendations above which require a changed accounting basis, are contrary to section 228 of the Companies Act (discussed in Chapter 2), which allows departure from the Act's provisions *only* if the provision of *additional* information to that of compliance is not sufficient to disclose a true and fair view.

So the debate hinges on an interpretation of the law. For what range of transactions can the 'true and fair' requirements *only* be properly satisfied by restating the transactions to reflect 'substance over form' (i.e. whether notes alone can adequately compensate for what is deemed to be a fundamentally wrong accounting presentation), a wide spectrum or a narrow one, and what form can this additional information take? At the limit of this debate is the Digilog-type case discussed in Chapter 2 where control of a 'subsidiary' was exercised without membership or majority ownership, deliberately to avoid legal group membership and consolidation (see pages 20–1). All are agreed at the very least extra disclosure should be provided if the 'subsidiary' is material. In practice this would probably not be as pro forma accounts, as this would obviate managements' purpose! However, *TR 603* gives an example of a similar non-subsidiary dependent company as an illustration of off-balance-sheet financing, where assets and liabilities are transferred to such a 'controlled' company to avoid their consolidation. In its arguments it leaves no doubt where its sentiments lean – towards economic substance unless it is contrary to the law. However, it does not specifically express an opinion whether a restatement of the accounts in a Digilog-type case would be legal.

There are certainly powerful arguments against such treatment as the DTI has observed that the 'true and fair' requirement covers only matters to be included in the accounts and does not override the subsidiaries to be consolidated. However, it could be argued that the treatment is an inclusion of *assets and liabilities* under the *de facto* economic control of the holding company as a result of a financing arrangement, rather than the consolidation of a 'subsidiary'. A distinguishing feature from the *Argyll* case might be that control over the assets is exercisable at the balance sheet date, whereas in the latter it was acquired only subsequent to the year-end (see SSAP 17).

It is understandable that accountants would like freedom of interpretation, whereas lawyers would like certainty of interpretation. However, if *TR 603*'s interpretation is reasonable, questions need to be raised as to how far such principles of 'substance over form' should apply. If they apply to off-balance-sheet financing and window dressing, why should they not have more general application in accounting standards – and if so, what of schemes (e.g. vendor rights and vendor placings) to manipulate treatments in accounting for business combinations? The whole area is a Pandora's box which needs to be opened and debated against a background of the incorporation of EEC Directives into UK law, with their characteristic legalistic ambience.

Efficient markets research suggests that, in the specific context of off-balance-sheet financing and window dressing, the form of presentation may be irrelevant if investors can reconcile one treatment to the other. However, it has been the author's experience that where the aim of management is to manipulate presentation in some way, alternative disclosures are seldom as comprehensive. Further, such reconciliations may not be possible in all the cases of substance over form discussed above and, in addition, efficient markets research does not consider wider users of accounts.

In the author's view, it would be a pity if narrow legalistic concepts stifle the relevance of accounting information, though it is not difficult to understand why auditors and lawyers might have vested interests in such legalistic criteria. As a possible first step, in *Technical Release 606* (ICAEW, 1986, p. 2) the Technical Committee of the English Institute comment that 'the ASC will, in reviewing SSAP 2, be considering giving guidance on when the substance of a transaction or arrangement rather than simply its legal form, should be reflected in financial statements'. Hopefully this will be the start of a process which may possibly require further government action as well as an examination of existing accounting standards to bring it to a satisfactory conclusion. It is interesting that in the taxation case *Furniss* v. *Dawson* (1984) the House of Lords dealt a blow to artificial anti-avoidance taxation schemes. Whether this reflects an attitude of wider application one can only speculate.

CONSOLIDATED ACCOUNTS AND PREDICTIVE ABILITY

A variety of group accounting treatments arise from the conflict between published accounts as stewardship reports on past performance, and as bases for future predictions. Snavely (1975) supports merger accounting over acquisition accounting on the grounds of better trend reporting (see page 62). Supporters of the closing rate translation approach argue in terms of better predictive ability (see page 263). In recording acquisitions and disposals of subsidiaries in the consolidated profit and loss account, many argue for presentations which aid prediction (e.g. in the year of acquisition to report, under acquisition accounting, revenues and expenses for the whole year less a pre-acquisition deduction, and in the year of disposal to treat the subsidiary under the equity approach – so that it is easily separable). Others argue that the actual status of the subsidiary should be reported (part-year revenues and expenses on acquisitions, and component revenues and expenses to the date of disposal), reflecting the stewardship viewpoint – what actually happened. The plethora of treatments and proposals reflects confusion over purpose and is unlikely to be resolved until this issue is clarified.

THE STATUS OF CONSOLIDATED EQUITY

Problems in the interpretation of consolidated assets and liabilities and minority interests have been considered in Chapters 4 and 5. However, consolidated equity itself is a complex aggregation of figures and adjustments. Consider, for example, a group which has the following categories in its *consolidated* reserves. What can be said about the meaning of its individual consolidated equity components?

> Share capital
> Share premium
> Merger reserve
> Revaluation reserves
> Other reserves
> Profit and loss

Effects of discretionary dispositions of cancellations and write-offs

A number of extremely large items affect consolidated 'reserves' which do not affect individual company reserves. These include the cancellation processes under merger and acquisition accounting, write-offs of *consolidated* goodwill (which is likely to be larger in most groups than any other form of goodwill), and exchange differences under the closing rate approach in translating subsidiaries' financial statements. Because of their potential size and the discretion given to management over their disposition within reserves, interpretation of the components within consolidated equity and hence comparison between groups is very difficult. Little guidance is given by accounting standards over the choice of which equity components these items are to be cancelled/attributed against.

Under the closing rate approach (see Chapter 7), companies usually make write-offs of exchange differences against retained earnings or revaluation reserves. The latter treatment is presumably justified on the grounds that gains or losses are akin to revaluation adjustments, rather than write-offs against such reserves (see page 260).[1] Under the rare circumstances in which the temporal approach is used, the disposition is against profit and loss (retained earnings).

As outlined in Chapter 4, goodwill has a more chequered disposition. If immediate write-off is chosen, Wilkins (1986) comments that in practice most groups have written it off against 'retained earnings'. Others use 'other reserves', and yet others entitled to merger relief but choosing acquisition accounting in their group accounts, have written it off against the consequent 'merger reserve' (see pages 96–7). A few have used 'revaluation reserves'. However, the DTI has indicated (DTI, 1985) that it feels the restricted uses of revaluation reserves and share premium accounts for *individual* companies under the Companies Act preclude their being used in this way in consolidated accounts too (under section 62 of Schedule 4 which requires consolidated accounts to comply as far as is practicable with individual company requirements). However, a few companies have been given necessary court approval under the Act to use the share premium account for writing off goodwill. So goodwill under immediate write-off finds a variety of homes!

The options potentially available under merger cancellation are wide too. Any excess nominal value of shares issued over shares acquired is required under SSAP 23 to be cancelled against 'reserves', without specifying which. In Chapter 3 it was argued that all the reserves of the subsidiary (including share capital and revaluation reserves) seem to be available for such cancellation (pages 41–2) and possibly the reserves of the holding company too (pages 43–4). The case was distinguished from goodwill on the grounds that the merger cancellation has no counterpart in individual company accounts whereas goodwill does (hence it is argued that section 62 does not apply). The legitimacy of cancellation practices seems to rest on what (if any) was the generally accepted method of merger accounting (which is open to debate as it is not yet well established in the UK). Holgate (1986b, p. 18) makes the interesting point that in considering the availability of reserves, if a subsidiary converted its own share premium into share capital by a bonus issue immediately prior to the merger (an *allowable* use of the share premium account), this would enter the merger cancellation process in determining the excess nominal amount itself (and hence would thus implicitly be 'available').

The merger cancellation approach adopted in the book is to utilize the most 'restricted' reserves first, then the next most, down to retained earnings. However, there is no requirement for a group to adopt this scheme. Indeed Holgate (1986b) points out that even if retained earnings are used for the cancellation of the entirety of any excess nominal value, it will have no effect on distributable profits as *companies*, not groups, make distributions. The effects of both alternatives of treating only the subsidiary's reserves and alternatively combined reserves of holding company and subsidiary as available for merger cancellation were illustrated numerically. If the latter were deemed correct, then under certain circumstances some excess nominal value could conceivably be cancelled against the *holding company's* share premium, in which case it could be possible for consolidated share premium to be less than holding company share premium. Is this reasonable from an accounting viewpoint?

In terms of the functional objectives of merger accounting, it may be so, as from the group's point of view too much share capital has been issued to preserve perfect additivity in combined balance sheet relationships, and so *group* share premium (its nearest 'relative') has been reduced slightly to redress the balance, preserving the additivity of less restricted reserves and retained earnings. Under acquisition accounting such a reduction would not make sense as the analogy used for the group balance sheet is *as if* the subsidiary had been purchased as component assets, liabilities and goodwill. In this case share capital and share premium intuitively should be the same as the holding company's, but this analogy does *not* describe the intuitive nature of a 'merger'. However, many object to these 'intuitive' rationalizations, suggesting that choices are better evaluated in terms of behavioural/political consequences (see pages 63–4). Utilizing *combined* reserves in the cancellation process may be a somewhat risky interpretation for companies to follow, open to some debate.

Because of such discretionary powers in locating these large magnitude items, the meaning of the residual figures within each reserve category is difficult to ascertain. Hendricksen (1982, pp. 464–8) comments that in an individual company there is some conflict as to whether equity components should or do show where an entity's capital came from, the intended disposition of such capital or restrictions on disposition of it, concluding that none of these viewpoints satisfactorily explains current practice. Certainly in consolidated financial statements such niceties are probably trivial in comparison to the discretionary powers discussed above. Rosenfield (in Rosenfield and Rubin, 1986) makes a seemingly radical proposal that consolidated equity (including minority interests) should be disclosed merely as a single item, not broken down into components. He argues that rights to distributions, restrictions, etc. should be included as narrative notes and no attempt should be made to include such matters in the consolidated balance sheet. Maybe this view is not as extreme as it seems at first sight!

Consolidated reserves and distributability

Under UK law, companies make distributions and not groups. Quite correctly, group accounting standards clearly state this. Historically, however, one reason for preparing group accounts was to overcome problems of manipulation of holding company profits using dividend policies of subsidiaries (see Chapter 1). A common assumption was that in some sense this expansion of holding company accounts showed *potential* distributability of holding company funds. For example Campbell and Patient (1985, p. 36) suggest that 'the consolidated realised reserve [could] give an approximate indication of the potential distibution . . . if all the subsidiaries were to pay up their realized profits by way of dividends to the holding company'. To what extent is this viewpoint reasonable?

Walker (1976, pp. 84–100) shows by counter-example that consolidated income is not necessarily a good predictor of actual holding company profits or distributions. In specific cases this is not surprising because (at least in the short term) it is possible to manipulate dividend distributions to massage holding company income – which is one reason why group accounts were produced in the first place! An example is where the subsidiary never pays dividends – but what of *potential* distributability?

There are features of consolidated accounts which minimize their usefulness in assessing *potential* distributability. These include:

1. Consolidated goodwill does not arise in the individual accounts of subsidiaries, and so distributions from subsidiaries are in principle possible in excess of consolidated retained earnings by amounts of goodwill written off against such reserves, and also in the consolidated profit and loss account. Further, directors have discretion over which class of reserves is affected.

2. Under merger accounting a company has discretion as to which reserves at acquisition it wishes to remove on cancellation if nominal amount issued is greater than that amount acquired. Even if a company cancels excess nominal amounts entirely against retained earnings rather than share premium or revaluation reserves it has no effect on distributable profits. But does this remove information content of the resulting figures?

3. It is not obvious that all reserves in consolidated accounts are easily remittable, particularly from foreign subsidiaries (which in a perverse way is a counter-argument for returning to holding company accounts for these subsidiaries, where only remitted profits are disclosed!). Also, the interpretation of closing rate converted revenues and expenses, and reserve balances makes the interpretation of consolidated equity difficult (see Chapter 9).

4. Under Companies Act changes, whether or not a holding company can treat distributions of profits from its subsidiary as a part of its distributable income is now viewed solely through holding company eyes (i.e. on whether or not there is a diminution in value of its investment (see pages 105–8), and is completely disconnected from the situation under earlier Acts of looking beyond to the group accounts situation, the pre-/post-acquisition split in subsidiary profits. Thus certain pre-acquisition profits excluded from consolidation under acquisition accounting may be potentially distributable by the holding company, and certain profits consolidated under merger accounting may not be so potentially distributable.

Holgate (1986a, pp. 23–4) points out that writing off large amounts against *consolidated* profits does not affect distributability since the realized/unrealized distinction only applies to individual companies and not to group accounts. However, he observes that consolidated profit (retained earnings) is sometimes (mistakenly) viewed as the total of realized profits in the group, which as can be seen above is not usually true. To what extent are investors/other users fooled by this?

A key question is whether consolidated equity has information content or not, whether it is *used* to determine potentially distributable profits or not, and further whether it is *potentially* useful if accounting standards made dispositions of write-offs and cancellations more comparable. It is also feasible that the above discussion is irrelevant because users do not consider that the division of consolidated reserves has any real economic impact, or users have enough information to reconcile alternative treatments and so see through such cosmetic tinkering around (see the discussions on the 'efficient markets' hypothesis in Chapters 3 and 9). Further empirical research is needed to see whether there is a real problem here or not.

Nobes (1986b, p. 10) observes some UK groups providing voluntarily, as a note, disclosure of distributable reserves of the *holding company*. He suggests it would be useful for groups to disclose 'what was easily obtainable and could become distributable', which could include the aggregate profit of holding company and UK subsidiaries together with remitted profits of foreign subsidiaries. Certainly at present these amounts, and indeed any meaningful figures at all, are difficult to discern from consolidated accounts. It should be pointed out that, in practice and in finance theory, the relationship between distribution policy and reported profits, consolidated or otherwise, may be somewhat tenuous, and it may be that 'distributable profits' in an accounting sense *might* merely provide some lower end protection for creditors. However, further discussion of such issues is beyond the scope of this text.

PRICE LEVEL ACCOUNTING AND CONSOLIDATION

The text has deliberately focused on consolidation/group accounting under historical cost accounting, since this is the system in general use. The main impact of price level accounting, and particularly current value/cost accounting is where measurement problems coincide with those of aggregation, e.g. accounting for business combinations and foreign currency translation. The discussion below gives simple examples of the effects of using current cost accounting in these areas, which is mainly to reduce or remove differences between alternative approaches.

Accounting for business combinations

Ketz (1984) argues that the main problem in accounting for business combinations is that of asset valuation. He uses a simple example to illustrate the effects of different price level accounting systems under acquisition and merger accounting. In particular, differential write-offs for depreciation and cost of goods sold under both approaches would be eliminated, but the effects of the different cancellation approaches would still apply. The elimination of intra-group stock profits, etc. would be based on replacement costs, and the current operating profit element of the selling company and the holding gains of the receiving company would be eliminated, the latter to be replaced (using a consolidation adjustment) by holding gains to the *group* on those goods. Minority interests would include operating profits and holding gains.

Foreign currency translation

The debate would be greatly simplified under current cost accounting because the temporal approach (based on the 'datedness' of balances) would give the same result as the closing rate approach. Indeed it has been suggested that use of the closing rate approach under historical cost is a crude attempt to 'adjust' for price level changes.

Under current purchasing power accounting, the choice is whether to restate for the subsidiary's local inflation and then translate at the closing rate (restate–translate), or to translate balances at the historical rate and then restate for holding company, home country inflation (translate–restate). Nobes (1986b, pp. 34–5), in his review of the literature, comments that proponents of the former argue it is better for comparisons of performance and in an economic sense, whereas he argues the latter is backed by sounder arguments from an accounting theory point of view since, as generally used, CPP is a historical cost based system. The debate (for which the reader is referred to Nobes, 1986b) is somewhat analogous to the temporal/closing rate debate. It is not examined further here.

THE ROLE OF THEORY

Consolidated reporting provides an interesting case study of wider issues in financial reporting. Approaches to choosing between alternatives are deeply affected by one's perception of the overall financial accounting standard-setting process. Differing perceptions as to the way forward include:

1. Trying to *assess user needs* and thence deduce theories and reporting alternatives to satisfy these. Very little work has been done in this area (see Walker, 1978a). This 'idealistic' approach (e.g. ASSC, *The Corporate Report,* 1975) has been largely abandoned since the late 1970s. Later academic research has focused on the inherently political nature of the reporting process. In such an environment, characterized by conflicts of interests, it is difficult to evaluate 'improvement'.
2. *Formulating* possible *functional/technical objectives* for consolidated reporting and examining the consistency of technical alternatives with these – a much more limited framework than 1. The study by Walker (1978a) in its examination of the objectives for consolidated reporting and their implication for group definition, etc. (pages 21–2) is an example of this approach, which has also been adopted in many of the chapters of this book (e.g. foreign currency translation).
3. Starting with existing accounting techniques, deducing functional objectives which would be consistent with them to *rationalize* and to provide order in current practice. One could argue that Baxter and Spinney (1975) is an example of this approach, though they may consider their approach is more accurately classified under 2. Sometimes it is not easy to distinguish 2 from 3, since the interplay between functional objectives and technical alternatives is

an interactive one. Strictly 2 is a process of *deduction* from 'theory', whilst 3 is a process of *rationalization* from practice.

4. Accept the fact that progress in improving consolidation concepts is a very amorphous and ambiguous concept since techniques are chosen to meet individuals' own ends and so-called theories are merely rationalizations to provide excuses for these vested interests. Watts and Zimmerman (1979) in particular emphasize this viewpoint, whereby choices are evaluated in terms of their behavioural and political consequences.

Chapters of this book have tried to achieve a balance between the last three perspectives for many of the issues in consolidated reporting. The author's belief is that none of them alone is sufficient to explain consolidated reporting. In particular, 2 and 3 provide a route map through complex technical calculations, and at least allow a more mature understanding of the consolidation process and the consequences of choices. Further, even in a political environment they clarify the ground of debate and provide a 'data bank' or information resource for informed argument. Perhaps each of the four approaches forms a facet of a whole view rather than being complete in itself.

THE ROLE OF EMPIRICAL RESEARCH

The environment in which group accounting takes place is extremely complex. Controlled experimentation is rarely possible except in highly artificial contexts. Statistical studies generally have to take data as given and to deduce 'stories'/relationships from it. Most of the work examined in the book involves testing comparatively simple hypotheses, using simplified models and assumptions (e.g about investor behaviour and making statistical assumptions of linearity), necessarily ignoring much complexity to make problems tractable. Conclusions therefore at best suggest directions, and often are amended considerably when another non-overlapping data set is tested or when the statistical approach or the models used are revised.

With these caveats, empirical research in the area has sometimes proved an antidote to extravagant claims by theorists. Surveys confirm the desirability of, e.g. segment disclosures, and often show that many theoretical debates are not viewed as crucial by market makers. Particularly, efficient markets research and market reaction studies in a variety of areas (e.g. in acquisition and merger accounting and foreign currency translation) have suggested that investors can potentially see through cosmetic changes, though the extent of this is somewhat unexplored. Some authors (e.g. Hines, 1984, see page 65) caution against reading too much into such results, on the grounds that the methodology is not sensitive enough to pick up reactions that do occur. Market reaction studies suggest that segmental reporting may reduce market perceptions of risk (see Dyckman and Morse, 1986, for a review of the impact of efficient markets research on accounting in general). Predictive ability research in segmental reporting suggests there is a limit to the amount of useful disclosures.

A developing area discussed earlier is that of examining the political/economic context of group accounting, e.g. in deducing the economic consequences of differing approaches on different parties, the effects of different corporate structures, or in assessing likely reactions of particular pressure groups to proposals. Another is in examining the properties of aggregation/disaggregation itself, either mathematically or by computer simulation – e.g. Silhan's work (1976), discussed in Chapter 10. It is difficult for theoretical approaches to deal with multiple dimensions of consolidated statements simultaneously, and simulation offers assistance in this regard. However, it is not easy to generalize situation-specific results. Possibly the use of simulation could be extended to other areas in group accounting, e.g. foreign currency translation, and accounting for business combinations.

The differing empirical studies and approaches can be viewed as pieces of a jigsaw. What is impressive is not the bright colours on particular pieces, but the extent to which the different pieces fit together over differing approaches, time periods, and countries – the extent to which they give a consistent overall picture. A great weakness of empirical research in the area to date has been a lack of repetition and reinforcement of studies, which therefore provide not enough evidence of sensitivity of results to changes in assumptions, periods, models or countries. Particularly there is a relative paucity of replication of US work in the UK.

Empirical research does not in itself provide policy recommendations in that it does not directly address welfare trade-offs. For example, efficient markets research implicitly considers investors. Even if there is a reaction (and potential benefits for investors), the methodology does not consider the costs of producing such information, which may fall on different parties from those who derive the benefits (see for example May and Sundem, 1976).

FUTURE DEVELOPMENTS IN THE UNITED KINGDOM

Changes in UK requirements on group accounting will result from the incorporation of the EEC Seventh Directive into UK law in approximately three to four years' time. This will (as discussed in Chapters 2 and 3) affect the definition of a group, the definition of a merger, and at a later date extend the exemption from producing consolidated accounts, if the minority agrees, to greater than 90 per cent owned subsidiaries. Another development is a likely standard on segmental reporting, and a working party has been set up by the Accounting Standards Committee to produce an exposure draft in 1987. Preceding the issue of an exposure draft, a consultative paper (ASC, 1987) was issued in January 1987, indicating proposals to move much closer to the US position (see Chapter 10). The paper did not propose quantitative constraints on segment identification, nor that operating profits should necessarily be measured *prior* to allocating central administration costs, nor that exceptional items per segment should be disclosed, unlike FAS No. 14. However, the paper encourages the use of the matrix format and more detailed geographical disclosures. It will be interesting to see how far a future exposure draft will be influenced by the comprehensive requirements of the USA. Funds statements are at present the subject of a major research project commissioned by the Director of Research of the Institute of Chartered Accountants in England and Wales, and it is probable that there will be changes in SSAP 10, when it comes up for revision as part of the ASC's ongoing review of existing standards. This review will be particularly relevant in the light of the fairly dramatic changes exposed in the USA.

Another important theme only given cursory coverage in the text is the extent to which UK standards on group accounts have been influenced or are likely to be influenced by the USA. This is not a simple matter to evaluate, but there is evidence of the UK taking a fairly independent line, particularly with respect to merger definition and the treatment of goodwill (possibly because of the impending impact of European law), although each standard allows options to comply with US requirements. In other areas the similarities (e.g. in the definition of associated companies) are more marked. It seems that on many issues (e.g. merger accounting and foreign currency translation) the UK adopts more minimalist attitudes.

In accounting for business combinations it will be interesting to see whether in the medium term UK standards will tighten criteria for the merger accounting option. It seems unlikely that requirements will be issued dealing with group concepts, the treatment of profits on unrealized intra-group transactions, and related issues of minority interests.

NOTES

1. Presumably similar issues arise over the interpretation of Sections 61 and 62 of Schedule 4 as with goodwill and merger cancellation. However, in principle 'net investment' translation adjustments can also arise in the accounts of individual companies (e.g. with autonomous overseas *branches*). Therefore it could be argued that revaluation reserves can only be utilized under the closing rate approach if one considers the gains and losses are *actual* revaluations. This is a debatable point.

FURTHER READING

Dyckman, T. R. and Morse, D. (1986) *Efficient Capital Markets and Accounting: A Critical Analysis* (2nd edn), Prentice Hall, New Jersey.
Holgate, P. (1986) *A Guide to Accounting Standards – SSAP 23 'Accounting for acquisitions and mergers'*, Accountants Digest No. 189, ICAEW, London.
Nobes, C. (1986) *Some practical and theoretical problems of group accounting,* Deloitte, Haskins & Sells, London.
Walker, R. G. (1978) *Consolidated Statements: A History and Analysis*, particularly chs. 15 and 16, Arno Press, New York.
Wilkins, R. M. (1979) *Group Accounts: The Fundamental Principles, Form and Content* (2nd edn), ICAEW, London.

12 Selected Examination Questions

The following have been selected from recent Professional I and II examinations of the Institute of Chartered Accountants in England and Wales (ICAEW), and Papers 2.9 and 3.1 of the Chartered Association of Certified Accountants (CACA). Many involve a combination of techniques discussed in different chapters of the book. Headings give an idea of the technical areas covered. The areas covered are:

12.1   Alternatives for accounting for investments in group companies.
12.2   Consolidated balance sheet.
12.3   Detective work – reconstructing a subsidiary's balance sheet.
12.4   Consolidated profit and loss with associate.
12.5   Vertical group's consolidated balance sheet.
12.6   Vertical group's balance sheet with alignment adjustments.
12.7   Consolidated balance sheet and profit and loss account.
12.8   Merger accounting.
12.9   Foreign currency translation.
12.10   Consolidated funds statement.
12.11–12.14   Various essay questions on the areas above.

12.1 Accounting for investments in group companies

Public consideration has recently been given to the composition of a group for the purpose of presenting the group accounts for a commercial organization. Consider the following data relating to the year ended 31 August 1981 of Octopus Ltd and Uncertain Ltd.

Balance sheet (£000)	Octopus	Uncertain
Issued ordinary share capital	2,000	1,000
Reserves	3,450	2,000
Debentures	2,000	1,500
Current liabilities	4,550	2,500
	12,000	7,000

	Octopus	*Uncertain*
Fixed assets (net)	6,500	4,000
Investment in Uncertain Ltd at cost	2,000	—
Current assets	3,500	3,000
	12,000	7,000

Profit and loss account (£000)

	Octopus	*Uncertain*
Trading profit before tax	1,100	500
Dividend from Uncertain Ltd including tax credit	130	—
Taxation	(630)	(200)
Profit after tax	600	300
Dividends paid	(300)	(200)
Retained	300	100

Octopus Ltd acquired 50 per cent of the ordinary share capital of Uncertain Ltd on 1 September 1980 for £2,000,000 when its reserves were £1,900,000 and sold this holding on 3 September 1981 for £2,050,000.

You are required to:
(a) prepare the 'group' profit and loss account and balance sheet on three bases:
    (i)   when Uncertain Ltd is treated as a subsidiary;
    (ii) when Uncertain is treated as an associated company;
    (iii) when Uncertain is treated as an investment;   (9 marks)
(b) calculate relevant financial ratios from the financial data produced by these three bases;   (4 marks)
(c) comment on the validity of these three alternative bases.   (7 marks)
(Total 20 marks)
(ICAEW, PE II, December 1981)

12.2 Consolidation balance sheet – miscellaneous calculations

On 31 March 1983 the balance sheet of Grasp Ltd showed an issued share capital of 200,000 ordinary shares of £1 each, fully paid, and a balance on revenue reserve of £97,000.

You also receive the following information:
1. On 1 April 1982 Grasp Ltd had purchased 150,000 ordinary shares of 50p each in Palm Ltd for £100,000. Palm Ltd had an issued share capital of 200,000 ordinary shares of 50p each and a balance brought forward on revenue reserve of £30,000 at that time. In the year ended 31 March 1983 Palm Ltd had a profit after taxation of £49,000 out of which provision had been made for a dividend to be paid of 20p per share. The proposed dividend receivable has been included in the profit and loss account of Grasp Ltd.
2. On 1 August 1982 Grasp Ltd had purchased 90,000 ordinary shares of £1 each in Digit Ltd for £20,000. Digit Ltd has an issued share capital of 100,000 ordinary shares of £1 each. On 1 April 1982 there had been a debit balance on

revenue reserve account of £60,000 and during the year ended 31 March 1983 a loss after taxation was incurred of £39,000. Included in the stock of Grasp Ltd on 31 March 1983 was an amount of £6,000 which had been purchased from Digit Ltd at a profit to that company of 25 per cent on selling price. Digit Ltd had purchased plant and machinery from Grasp Ltd for £10,000 on 1 October 1982 and provided depreciation in its accounts on a straight line basis at 25 per cent per annum, which commences in the month of purchase. Grasp Ltd had sold the plant and machinery to Digit Ltd at its normal selling price which gave a profit of 30 per cent on selling price.

3. On 1 January 1983 Grasp Ltd purchased 45,000 shares of 25p each in Wrist Ltd for £30,000. Wrist Ltd has an issued share capital of 100,000 ordinary shares of 25p each. On 1 April 1982 there had been a balance on revenue reserve of £36,000 and in the year ended 31 March 1983 the profit after taxation was £28,000. No dividend was paid or proposed for the year.

You are to assume the profits and losses of Wrist Ltd and Digit Ltd have accrued evenly throughout the year.

You are required to show how the above items would be reflected in the consolidated balance sheet of Grasp Ltd on 31 March 1983, and to provide detailed schedules showing the make-up of the relevant figures.

Note: ignore advance corporation tax. (27 marks)

(ICAEW, PE I, May 1983)

12.3 Detective work – reconstructing the subsidiary's balance sheet

The following accounts are the consolidated balance sheet and parent company balance sheet for Alpha Ltd as at 30 June 1982.

		Consolidated balance sheet £		Parent company £
Ordinary shares		140,000		140,000
Capital reserve		92,400		92,400
Profit and loss account		79,884		35,280
Minority interest		12,320		
		324,604		267,680
Fixed assets:				
Freehold premises		127,400		84,000
Plant and machinery		62,720		50,400
Goodwill		85,680		—
Investment in subsidiary (50,400 shares)				151,200
Current assets:				
Stock	121,604		71,120	
Debtors	70,420		46,760	
Dividends receivable	—		5,040	
Cash at bank	24,360		—	
	216,384		122,920	

	Consolidated balance sheet £	Parent company £
Current liabilities:		
Creditors	128,660	69,720
Corporation tax	27,160	20,720
Bank overdraft	—	39,200
Proposed dividend	11,760	11,200
	167,580	140,840
Working capital	48,804	(17,920)
	324,604	267,680

Notes:
1. There is only one subsidiary company, called Beta Ltd.
2. There are no capital reserves in the subsidiary.
3. Alpha produced stock for sale to the subsidiary at a cost of £3,360 in May 1982. The stock was invoiced to the subsidiary at £4,200 and is still on hand at the subsidiary's warehouse on 30 June 1982. The invoice had not been settled at 30 June 1982.
4. The profit and loss account of the subsidiary had a credit balance of £16,800 at the date of acquisition.
5. There is a right of set-off between overdrafts and bank balances.

Required
(a) Prepare the balance sheet as at 30 June 1982 of the subsidiary company from the information given above.   (20 marks)
(b) Briefly discuss the main reasons for the publication of consolidated accounts.   (5 marks)

(CACA, Paper 2.9(2), June 1982)

12.4 Consolidated profit and loss account with associate

Kale Ltd, Leek Ltd, Neep Ltd and Sage Ltd have issued share capital in ordinary shares of £500,000, £250,000, £200,000 and £100,000 respectively. The summarized profit and loss accounts for the year ended 28 February 1985 are set out as follows:

	Kale Ltd £000	Leek Ltd £000	Neep Ltd £000	Sage Ltd £000
Turnover	15,721	5,488	6,900	6,102
Cost of sales	8,018	3,183	3,795	2,563
Gross profit	7,703	2,305	3,105	3,539
Distribution costs	1,964	622	875	1,135
Administrative expenses	4,584	1,384	1,799	1,696
	(6,548)	(2,006)	(2,674)	(2,831)
Operating profit	1,155	299	431	708

	Kale Ltd £000	Leek Ltd £000	Neep Ltd £000	Sage Ltd £000
Operating profit b/f	1,155	299	431	708
Dividends from group and associated companies	429			
	1,584	299	431	708
Tax on profit on ordinary activities	504	112	148	257
Profit for the financial year	1,080	187	283	451
Dividend paid and proposed	500	180	150	250
Retained profit for the year	580	7	133	201
Retained profits 1 March 1984	3,216	175	197	463
Retained profits 28 Feb 1985	3,796	182	330	664

You obtain the following information:
1. The par values of the ordinary shares are as follows: Kale Ltd – £1; Leek Ltd – 25p; Neep Ltd – 50p; and Sage Ltd – £1.
2. Kale Ltd acquired 800,000 shares in Leek Ltd on 1 March 1980 when there was a debit balance of £15,000 on the profit and loss account of Leek Ltd.
3. On 1 April 1984, Kale acquired 90,000 shares in Sage Ltd whose profits accrue evenly throughout the year.
4. Kale Ltd acquired 160,000 shares in Neep Ltd on 1 March 1984. Neep Ltd was incorporated and first commenced to trade on 1 March 1983.
5. Kale Ltd purchases goods for resale from Neep Ltd and on 28 February 1985 held a stock of those goods amounting to £222,435. Neep Ltd manufactures only one product and has a standard selling price to all customers.

Requirement
Prepare a consolidated profit and loss account of Kale Ltd and its subsidiaries, incorporating the results of the associated company, for the year ended 28 February 1985, together with your consolidation schedules.   (28 marks)
Note: ignore advance corporation tax.   (ICAEW, PE I, May 1985)

12.5 Vertical groups with piecemeal acquisition

As at 30 June 1985 the draft balance sheets of three companies showed the following position:

	Rock Ltd £	King Ltd £	Chair Ltd £
Fixed assets	135,000	60,000	70,000
Investments at cost	160,000	150,000	10,000
	295,000	210,000	80,000
Current assets:			
Stock	55,240	36,840	61,760
Debtors	110,070	69,120	93,880
Balances at bank	131,290	16,540	52,610
	296,600	122,500	208,250

	Rock Ltd £	King Ltd £	Chair Ltd £
Less current liabilities:			
Creditors	112,060	73,130	78,190
Taxation	30,000	—	22,000
Proposed dividends	100,000	60,000	40,000
	242,060	133,130	140,190
Net current assets/(liabilities)	54,540	(10,630)	68,060
	349,540	199,370	148,060
Financed by:			
Issued ordinary shares of £1 each	200,000	150,000	80,000
Capital reserve	50,000	—	23,000
Revenue reserve	99,540	49,370	45,060
	349,540	199,370	148,060

You also obtain the following information:
1. King Ltd acquired 68,000 shares in Chair Ltd at £2.20 per share in 1981 when the balance on capital reserve was £15,000 and on revenue reserve £30,500.
2. Rock Ltd purchased 80,000 shares in King Ltd in 1982 when the balance on the consolidated revenue reserve was £40,000. Rock Ltd purchased a further 40,000 shares in King Ltd in 1983 when the balance on the consolidated revenue reserve was £45,000. At both dates the balance on the capital reserve in Chair Ltd was £23,000. Rock Ltd held no other investments at 30 June 1985.
3. Proposed dividends from subsidiary companies are included in the figure for debtors in the accounts of the parent companies.

Requirement
Prepare the consolidated balance sheet of Rock Ltd and its subsidiaries on 30 June 1985, together with the consolidation schedules.   (26 marks)

(ICAEW, PE I, November 1985)

12.6 Vertical groups with alignment adjustments

On 1 April 1981 Machinery Ltd bought 80 per cent of the ordinary share capital of Components Ltd and on 1 April 1983 Machinery Ltd was itself taken over by Sales Ltd who purchased 75 per cent of the oridinary shares in Machinery Ltd. The balance sheets of the three companies at 31 October 1985 prepared for internal use showed the following position:

	Sales Ltd £	Sales Ltd £	Machinery Ltd £	Machinery Ltd £	Components Ltd £	Components Ltd £
Fixed assets:						
Freehold land at cost		89,000		30,000		65,000
Buildings at cost	100,000		120,000		40,000	
Less accumulated depreciation	36,000		40,000		16,400	
		64,000		80,000		23,600
Plant and equipment at cost	102,900		170,000		92,000	
Less accumulated depreciation	69,900		86,000		48,200	
		33,000		84,000		43,800
		186,000		194,000		132,400
Investments:						
Shares in Machinery at cost		135,000				
Shares in Components at cost				96,000		
Current assets:						
Stocks	108,500		75,500		68,400	
Debtors	196,700		124,800		83,500	
Cash at bank	25,200		—		25,400	
		330,400		200,300		177,300
		651,400		490,300		309,700
Current liabilities:						
Creditors	160,000		152,700		59,200	
Bank overdraft	—		37,400		—	
Corporation tax	57,400		47,200		24,500	
Proposed dividends	80,000		48,000		12,000	
		297,400		285,300		95,700
		354,000		205,000		214,000
Ordinary shares		200,000		120,000		100,000
10% preference shares		—		—		40,000
Revenue reserves		154,000		85,000		74,000
		354,000		205,000		214,000

Additional information:
1. All ordinary shares are £1 each, fully paid.
2. Preference shares in Components Ltd are 50p each, fully paid.
3. Proposed dividends in Components are: on ordinary shares – £10,000; on preference shares – £2,000.
4. Proposed dividends receivable by Sales Ltd and Machinery Ltd are included in debtors.
5. All creditors are payable within one year.

6. Items purchased by Machinery Ltd from Components Ltd and remaining in stock at 31 October 1985 amounted to £25,000. The profit element is 20 per cent of the selling price for Components Ltd.

7. Depreciation policy for the group is to provide for:
   (a) buildings – at the rate of 2 per cent on cost each year;
   (b) plant and equipment – at the rate of 10 per cent on cost each year including full provision in the year of acquisition.
   These policies are applied by all members of the group.

   Included in the plant and machinery of Components Ltd is a machine purchased from the manufacturers, Machinery Ltd, on 1 January 1984 for £10,000. Machinery Ltd recorded a profit of £2,000 on the sale of the machine.

8. Intra-group balances are included in debtors and creditors respectively and are as follows:

			£
Sales Ltd	Creditors – Machinery Ltd		45,600
	– Components Ltd		28,900
Machinery Ltd	Debtors	– Sales Ltd	56,900
Components Ltd	Debtors	– Sales Ltd	28,900

9. A cheque drawn by Sales Ltd for £11,300 on 28 October 1985 was received by Machinery Ltd on 3 November 1985.

10. At 1 April 1981 reserves in Machinery Ltd were £28,000 and in Components Ltd £20,000. At 1 April 1983 the figures were £40,000 and £60,000 respectively.

Required
Prepare a group balance sheet at 31 October 1985 for Sales Ltd and its subsidiaries complying, so far as the information will allow, with the accounting requirements of the Companies Acts.   (40 marks)

(CACA, Paper 2.9(2), December 1985)

12.7 Combined consolidated balance sheet and profit and loss account

(This question requires a knowledge of mixed groups for the technique of calculating indirect shareholding proportions in Pepper (as discussed in Chapter 8).)

Summarized accounts for three private companies are given below:

Summarized balance sheets on 30 June 1986 (£000)

	Cruet Ltd	Salt Ltd	Pepper Ltd
Goodwill	—	—	160
Tangible fixed assets	2,675	1,925	1,180
Investments (note 2)	1,980	60	—
Intercompany loans	100	—	(100)
Net current assets (liabilities)	930	1,743	(620)
Loans from third parties	(500)	—	—
	5,185	3,728	620

	Cruet Ltd	Salt Ltd	Pepper Ltd
Ordinary shares of £1 each	3,000	1,000	400
Preference shares of £1 each	1,000	1,200	—
Reserves	1,185	1,528	220
	5,185	3,728	620

Summarized profit and loss accounts for the year to 30 June 1986 (£000)

	Cruet Ltd	Salt Ltd	Pepper Ltd
Profit after taxation	600	360	200
Extraordinary items	(100)	40	—
	500	400	200
Preference dividends – paid	(30)	(30)	—
– payable	(30)	(30)	—
Ordinary dividends – paid	(100)	(60)	(40)
– payable	(200)	(80)	(80)
Retained for year	140	200	80
Reserves brought forward	1,045	1,328	140
Reserves carried forward	1,185	1,528	220

The following additional information is given:
1. All shares are fully paid. Preference shares carry a vote only when their dividends are in arrears. The preference dividends are payable on 1 January and 1 July each year.
2. Investments comprise:

	Cost £000
Cruet Ltd:	
900,000 ordinary shares in Salt Ltd	1,500
400,000 preference shares in Salt Ltd	400
46,000 ordinary shares in Pepper Ltd	80
	1,980
Salt Ltd:	
60,000 ordinary shares in Pepper Ltd	60

Cruet exercises a significant influence over Salt Ltd and Pepper Ltd.
3. When Cruet acquired its investment in Salt and Pepper during 1983 those companies had reserves of £400,000 and £100,000 respectively. Salt acquired its holding on the incorporation of Pepper in 1980. Fair values should be assumed to be balance sheet values in 1983 other than for Salt's investment in Pepper.
4. The summarized profit and loss accounts include only those dividends which have been received. No accruals or provisions which may be required have been made for dividends receivable.

Requirement
Prepare a summarized consolidated balance sheet and summarized profit and loss account with full workings and supporting schedules, showing clearly

consolidation adjustments, movements in reserves, minority interests and the carrying value of investments.   (25 marks)
Note: ignore taxation.   (ICAEW, PE II, July 1986)

12.8 Merger accounting

Consolidated Furniture Group plc wishes to adopt the . . . merger accounting principles . . . [as in SSAP 23], 'Accounting for acquisitions and mergers', in respect of its combination with Tables & Chairs Ltd on 30 September 1983.

On 1 August 1983 Consolidated Furniture Group plc acquired 5 per cent of the issued share capital of Tables & Chairs Ltd for a consideration of 80,000 shares of 25p each at an agreed value of 125p each.

The terms of the merger on 30 September 1983, which were accepted by all shareholders and declared unconditional on the same day, were that for every 8 shares held in Tables & Chairs Ltd, a holder received 20 shares of 25p each at an agreed value of 135p each in Consolidated Furniture Group plc plus £3 nominal of 13 per cent unsecured loan stock 2002.

All the shares issued were credited as fully paid and ranked *pari passu* with existing shares in issue except that those issued on 30 September 1983 were not to rank for the final dividend in respect of the year ended 30 November 1983.

The draft summarized balance sheet and profit and loss account of the companies for the year ended 30 November 1983, the accounting reference date for Consolidated Furniture Group plc, were:

Balance sheet (£000)

	Consolidated Furniture Group plc	Tables & Chairs Ltd
Fixed assets	4,563	3,092
Goodwill at cost	—	800
Investments	175	—
Current assets	2,369	3,626
Current liabilities	(2,286)	(4,207)
	4,821	3,311
Share capital	3,000	1,600
Reserves	1,821	1,711
	4,821	3,311

Profit and loss account (£000)

Turnover	36,873	25,003
Profit before tax	1,151	127
Taxation	260	—
Profit after tax	891	127
Dividends paid	288	—
Profits retained	603	127

Additional information is given as follows:

1. The reserves of Consolidated Furniture Group plc at 30 November 1983 consisted of a share premium account of £140,000 and revenue reserves of £1,681,000. The reserves in Tables & Chairs Ltd are undistributed revenue reserves.

2. The issue of the shares made on 1 August 1983 is reflected in the draft financial statements.

3. It is the policy of Consolidated Furniture Group plc to write off goodwill in equal instalments over five years.

4. It is considered that the market value of the 13 per cent loan stock issued is par.

5. The share capitals of the companies are:

   Consolidated Furniture Group plc – ordinary 25p each
   Tables & Chairs Ltd   – ordinary £1 each

6. The directors of Consolidated Furniture Group plc resolve to propose a final dividend of 1p per share. This is not yet reflected in the draft financial statements.

You are required to:

(a) prepare a consolidated balance sheet and profit and loss account, in summary form, of Consolidated Furniture Group plc at 30 November 1983;   (14 marks)

(b) give the revised analysis of reserves of Consolidated Furniture Group plc at 30 November 1983 suitable for inclusion in the published financial statements;   (5 marks)

(c) comment whether you consider merger accounting to be appropriate in the above example giving an indication of advantages which may arise.   (5 marks)

Note: make calculations to nearest £000 and ignore the costs of the merger and advance corporation tax.   (24 marks)

(ICAEW, PE II, December 1983)

12.9 Foreign currency translation

(Though this is the translation of the accounts of a branch rather than a subsidiary, the principles are almost identical. Just remember that the branch account in head office records must equal the head office account in the branch's records.)

Set out below are the balances as on 30 June 1985 in the books of Box Ltd, incorporated in England, and Carton, its unincorporated branch in West Germany. Carton manufactures parts mainly for Box Ltd which are shipped direct to England.

	Box Ltd £	Carton DM
Share capital	(12,000)	—
Share premium account	(2,000)	—
Profit and loss account	(12,280)	—
Head office account	(22,600)	93,420
Fixed assets – cost	24,000	141,710
Depreciation on fixed assets	(12,800)	(63,720)
Stock	37,220	14,930
Debtors	37,000	890
Cash	960	2,960
Current liabilities	(14,880)	(12,680)
Loan from US bank	—	(60,000)
Turnover	(308,530)	(275,650)
Overheads	26,420	67,490
Manufacturing cost including wages	259,490	90,650
	—	—

The following information is supplied:
1. The loan was raised by Carton from a US bank on the guarantee of Box Ltd for a total of $22,500 on 1 July 1984.
2. Cash remitted by Box Ltd of £4,300 has not yet been recorded in the books of Carton at 30 June 1985. In addition, goods in transit from Carton invoiced at DM10,000 have not been included in the books or closing stock of Box Ltd. These transactions may be taken as occurring at the year-end.
3. No depreciation has yet been provided by either Box Ltd or Carton. This will be uniformly calculated at the rate of 10 per cent on cost.
4. The fixed assets of Carton were purchased at an average rate of exchange of £1 = DM4.5 before 1 July 1983. Stock was all purchased within four months of the balance sheet date. Closing physical stock amounts to £32,490 for Box Ltd and DM26,710 for Carton.
5. The rates of exchange were:

1 July 1983	£1 = DM4.5	1 July 1984	£1 = DM4.0 = $1.5
28 February 1984	£1 = DM4.3	28 February 1985	£1 = DM3.6
30 April 1984	£1 = DM4.2	30 April 1985	£1 = DM3.4
		30 June 1985	£1 = DM3.0 = $1.0

Average year to 30 June 1984   £1 = DM4.4
Average year to 30 June 1985   £1 = DM3.6

Requirements
(a) State briefly the factors which should be taken into account when determining which method of accounting for overseas entities as recommended by SSAP 20 should be applied by Box Ltd.   (5 marks)
(b) Produce the balance sheet on 30 June 1985 of Box Ltd incorporating the German branch   (16 marks)
          (21 marks)

Note: make all calculations to the nearest £ and ignore taxation and the elimination of any inter-branch profit.

(ICAEW, PE II, December 1985)

12.10 Consolidated funds statements

(In general, professional questions on consolidated funds statements have been rather long but simple or abstruse and complex. The following question is not difficult, but in principle requires computation of consolidated opening and closing balance sheets before computing a straightforward funds statement. In an examination this would probably be done by educated guesses of the relevant funds flow items, which either requires a good knowledge of funds statements, or more likely perpetuates its preparation as a quick series of *ad hoc* and ill-understood adjustments to differenced balance sheets!)

The following summarized accounts have been prepared by Furniture Ltd and its subsidiary Chairs Ltd for the years ended 31 May 1979 and 1978.

Balance sheet at 31 May (£000)

	Furniture Ltd		Chairs Ltd	
	1979	1978	1979	1978
Issued ordinary share capital	6,000	4,000	550	500
Issued preference share capital	3,000	3,000	400	400
Retained profits	2,490	2,000	117	100
10% debentures	5,000	4,000	1,000	500
Trade creditors	600	400	300	250
Current taxation	1,695	1,446	127	60
Proposed dividend	600	500	55	—
Overdraft	—	—	1,392	1,304
	19,385	15,346	3,941	3,114
Land and buildings	2,500	2,000	700	600
Plant and machinery	9,500	8,000	1,000	800
Investment in Chairs at cost	440	400	—	—
Stock and work-in-progress	750	600	600	400
Debtors	2,500	2,000	1,500	1,250
ACT recovery	546	497	41	14
Cash and bank balances	3,149	1,849	100	50
	19,385	15,346	3,941	3,114

Profit and loss account for year to 31 May

Trading profit for the year	3,500	3,000	300	150
Debenture interest	500	400	100	50
Taxation (treated as current taxation)	1,400	1,200	100	60
Dividends paid				
– ordinary	300	300	—	—
– preference	210	210	28	28
Dividends proposed, ordinary	600	500	55	—
Retained	490	390	17	12

	Furniture Ltd		Chairs Ltd	
	1979	*1978*	*1979*	*1978*
The trading profit for the year is stated after charging depreciation of	1,000	800	150	100

Furniture Ltd acquired the ordinary shares of Chairs Ltd on two dates; 400,000 of £1 each on 31 January 1970 for £400,000 and 40,000 of £1 each for £40,000 on 31 January 1979 on the occasion of a rights issue to all ordinary shareholders.

Neither company sold any fixed assets during the year.

You are required to:
(a) prepare a consolidated statement of source and application of group funds for the year ended 31 May 1979; and   (19 marks)
(b) state what difference it would make to the statement if Furniture Ltd had acquired its holding of 400,000 ordinary shares on 1 June 1978 instead of on 31 January 1970.   (7 marks)

(26 marks)

(ICAEW, PE II, July 1979)

12.11 In the early days of group accounting (up to about 1929) the consolidation and equity methods were regarded as alternative accounting treatments for investments in subsidiaries and for the profits/losses generated by them. Since then the consolidated method has prevailed in this field.

You are required:
(a) to outline the similarities, and differences, between the two methods;   (5 marks)
(b) to explain the conventional present-day uses of the two methods; and   (5 marks)
(c) to argue for *or* against the general use of the equity method, in accounting for investments in subsidiaries.   (6 marks)

(16 marks)

(CACA, Paper 3.1, December 1983)

12.12 The managing director of Holdings plc is considering with his merchant bankers the mix of consideration in formulating the proposals to make an offer for all the ordinary shares in Sitting Duck plc. He is concerned about the effect on the consolidated accounts of Holdings plc of the various offers the company could make in the light of the principles for accounting for acquisitions and mergers now embodied in SSAP 23, and the two different methods of accounting dependent upon the circumstances of the business combination.

Requirement
Write a report to the managing director stating:
(a) what conditions are required to be met if merger accounting is to be used;   (3 marks)

(b) what are the differences in principle between acquisition accounting and merger accounting;   (3 marks)
(c) how the difference on consolidation is calculated under merger accounting and how it is reflected in the financial statements; and   (3 marks)
(d) the advantages and disadvantages of using each method of accounting so that he can structure the proposed deal using the appropriate method.   (12 marks)
                                                                          (21 marks)
                                                              (ICAEW, PE II, July 1986)

12.13 SSAP 20, 'Foreign currency translation' (1983), constitutes the first definitive statement of practice in this area.

You are required:
(a) to define concisely the two methods of foreign currency translation specified in SSAP 20;   (4 marks)
(b) to explain the precise circumstances in which the use of each method is mandatory under SSAP 20; and   (8 marks)
(c) to justify the treatment prescribed in SSAP 20 for overseas investment financed by overseas borrowing.   (3 marks)
                                                                          (15 marks)
                                                              (CACA, Paper 3.1, June 1984)

12.14 The equity method of valuing certain forms of investment made by one company in another has been in common use since the early 1970s.

Required
(a) Define concisely the term 'equity method' and outline the accounting procedures by which it is applied.   (5 marks)
(b) Describe the present position regarding the use of the method, as referred to in the law and in SSAPs 1 and 14.   (10 marks)
(c) Assess the validity of the equity method as an alternative to other modes of accounting for the relevant investments.   (10 marks)
                                                                          (25 marks)
                                                          (CACA, Paper 3.1, December 1985)

Bibliography

AICPA (1959) *Accounting Research Bulletin No. 51 – Consolidated financial statements*, American Institute of Certified Public Accountants, New York.

AICPA (1970) *Accounting Principles Board Statement No. 4 – Basic concepts and accounting principles underlying financial statements of business enterprises*, AICPA, New York.

AICPA (1970) *Accounting Principles Board Opinion No. 16 – Business combinations*, AICPA, New York.

AICPA (1970) *APB Opinion No. 17 – Intangible assets*, AICPA, New York.

AICPA (1971) *APB Opinion No. 18 – The equity method of accounting for investments in common stock*, AICPA, New York.

AICPA (1971) *APB Opinion No. 19 – Reporting changes in financial position*, AICPA, New York.

ASC (1971) *Statement of Standard Accounting Practice 1 – Accounting for associated companies*, (revised 1982), Accounting Standards Committee, London.

ASC (1971) *SSAP 2 – Disclosure of accounting policies*, ASC, London.

ASC (1974) *SSAP 6 – Extraordinary items and prior year adjustments*, (revised 1986), ASC, London.

ASC (1975) *SSAP 10 – Statements of source and application of funds*, ASC, London.

ASC (1978) *SSAP 14 – Group accounts*, ASC, London.

ASC (1980) *SSAP 17 – Accounting for post-balance-sheet events*, ASC, London.

ASC (1983) *SSAP 20 – Foreign currency translation*, ASC, London.

ASC (1984) *SSAP 22 – Accounting for goodwill*, ASC, London.

ASC (1985) *SSAP 23 – Accounting for acquisitions and mergers*, ASC, London.

ASC (1987) *Segmental reporting – a consultative paper*, ASC, London.

ASSC (1975) *The Corporate Report*, Accounting Standards Steering Committee, London.

Ang, J. S. (1979) Aggregate versus component forecasts of financial statement items, *Review of Business and Economic Research*, Fall 1979, pp. 30–42.

Ayres, F. L. (1986) Characteristics of firms electing early adoption of FAS No. 52, *Journal of Accounting and Economics*, 8 (1986), pp. 143–58.

Backer, M. and McFarland, W. B. (1968) *External Reporting for Segments of a Business*, National Association of Accountants.

Baldwin, B. A. (1984) Segment earnings disclosure and the ability of security analysts to forecast earnings per share, *The Accounting Review*, Vol. LIX, No. 3, pp. 376–89.

Barefield, R. M. and Comiskey, E. E. (1975) Segmental disclosures by diversified firms and security prices: a comment, *The Accounting Review*, Vol. L, No. 4, pp. 818–21.

Barnea, A. and Lakonishok, J. (1980) An analysis of the usefulness of disaggregated accounting data for forecasts of corporate performance, *Decision Sciences*, Vol. 11, January, pp. 17–26.

Barton, A. (1974) Expectations and achievements in income theory, *The Accounting Review*, Vol. XLIX, No. 4, pp. 664–81.

Baxter, G. C. and Spinney, J. C. (1975) A closer look at consolidated financial theory, *CA Magazine*, Part 1, Vol. 106, No. 1, pp. 31–6; Part 2, Vol. 106, No. 2, pp. 31–5.

Benston, G. J. (1984) The costs of complying with a government data collection program: the FTC's line of business report, *Journal of Accounting and Public Policy*, Vol. 3, No. 2, pp. 123–37.

Bird, P. (1982) After Argyll Foods what is a 'true and fair view', *Accountancy*, Vol. 93, No. 1066, pp. 80–1.

Brault, R. (1979) A simple approach to complex consolidations, *CA Magazine*, Vol. 112, No. 4, pp. 52–4.

Briggs, P. (1986) Defining the currency conversion argument, *Accountancy* Age, 27 March, p. 15

Briloff, A. J. (1972) *Unaccountable Accounting*, Harper & Row, New York.

Briloff, A. J. (1976) *More Debits than Credits*, Harper & Row, New York.

Briloff, A. J. (1980) Leveraged Leasco, *Barron's*, October 20, pp. 4–5 and 22.

Campbell, L. G. and Patient, M. L. (1985) *Accounting for Goodwill*, Deloitte, Haskins & Sells, London.

Castanias, R. P. and Griffin, P. A. (1986) The effects of foreign currency translation accounting on security analysts' forecasts, *Managerial and Decision Economics*, Vol. 7, pp. 3–10.

Catlett, G. R. and Olsen, N. O. (1968) *Accounting for Goodwill*, ARS No. 10, American Institute of Certified Public Accountants, New York.

Clarke, F. L. (1978) Patz on parities, exchange rates and translation, *Accounting and Business Research*, Vol. 9, No. 3, p. 75.

Collins, D. W. (1976) Predicting earnings with subentity data: further evidence, *Journal of Accounting Research*, Vol. 14, No. 1, pp. 163–77.

Collins, D. W. and Simonds R. R. (1979) SEC line-of-business disclosure and market risk adjustments, *Journal of Accounting Research*, Vol. 14, No. 2, pp. 352–83.

Cooke, T. E. (1985a) SSAP 22 and 23: do they lack clear objectives?, *Accountancy*, Vol. 96, No. 1104, pp. 101–4.

Cooke, T. E. (1985b) Accounting for goodwill – a review, *The Investment Analyst*, No. 78 (October), pp. 3–7.

Cooke, T. E. (1986) *Mergers and Acquisitions*, Basil Blackwell, Oxford.

Cooper, K., Fraser, D. R. and Richards, R. M. (1978) The impact of SFAS No. 8 on financial management practices, *Financial Executive*, Vol. XLVI, No. 6, pp. 26–31.

Copeland, R. M. and Wojdack, J. F. (1969) Income manipulation and purchase-pooling choice, *Journal of Accounting Research*, Vol. 7, No. 2, pp. 188–95.

Deloitte, Haskins & Sells (1983) *Corporate Structure – subsidiaries or divisions?*, Deloitte, Haskins & Sells, London.

Department of Trade (1982) The true and fair view and group accounts, reprinted in *Accountancy*, Vol. 93, No. 1062, February, p. 11.

Department of Trade (1985) Reply to a letter by P. Rutteman, *Accountancy*, Vol. 96, No. 1100, April, p. 9

Dhaliwal, D. S., Spicer, B. H. and Vickrey, D. (1979) The quality of disclosure and the cost of capital, *Journal of Business Finance & Accounting*, Vol. 6, No. 2, pp. 245–66.

Dukes, R. E. (1978) *An Empirical Investigation of the Effects of [SFAS No. 8] on Security Return Behaviour*, Financial Accounting Standards Board, Connecticut.

Dyckman, T. R. and Morse, D. (1986) *Efficient Capital Markets and Accounting: a critical analysis* (2nd edn), Prentice-Hall, New Jersey.

Edey, H. (1985) SSAP 23 is about recognising business needs, *Accountancy*, Vol. 96, No. 1101, May, pp. 13–14.

Edwards, J. R. and Webb, K. M. (1984) The development of group accounting in the United Kingdom to 1933, *The Accounting Historians Journal*, Vol. 11, No. 1, pp. 31–61.

Eggington, D. (1965) Unrealised profits and consolidated accounts, *Accountancy*, Vol. 76, No. 861, pp. 410–15.

Emmanuel, C. R. and Gray, S. J. (1978) Segmental disclosures by multibusiness multinational companies: a proposal, *Accounting & Business Research*, Vol. 8, No. 31, pp. 169–77.

Emmanuel, C. R. and Pick, R. H. (1980) The predictive ability of UK segment reports, *Journal of Business Finance & Accounting*, Vol. 7, No. 2, pp. 201–18.

FASB (1975) *Financial Accounting Standard No. 8 – Accounting for the translation of foreign currency transactions and foreign currency financial statements*, Financial Accounting Standards Board, Connecticut.

FASB (1976) *FAS No. 14 – Financial reporting for segments of a business enterprise*, FASB, Connecticut.

FASB (1981) *FAS No. 52 – Foreign currency translation*, FASB, Connecticut.

FASB (1986) *Exposure draft – Statement of cash flows*, FASB, Connecticut.

Flower, J. (1985) Foreign currency translation, in C. W. Nobes and R. H. Parker (eds.) *Comparative International Accounting, op. cit.*, ch. 12.

Foster, D. F. (1983) The Seventh Directive – practical implications for the UK, *The Accountant's Magazine*, Vol. LXXXVII, No. 929, November, pp. 429–30.

Foster, G. (1986) *Financial Statement Analysis* (2nd edn), Prentice-Hall, New Jersey.

Foster, W. C. (1974) Illogic of pooling, *Financial Executive*, Vol. XLII, No. 12, December, pp. 16–21.

Gaertner, J. F. (1979) Proposed alternatives for accounting for business combinations – a behavioural study, *Abacus*, Vol. 15, No. 1, pp. 35–47.

Gagnon, J. M. (1971) Purchase/pooling: empirical evidence, *Journal of Accounting Research*, Vol. 9, No. 1, pp. 52–72.

Garnsey, Sir G. (1923) *Holding Companies and their Published Accounts*, Gee & Co., London.

Gerboth, D. L. (1972) 'Muddling through' with the APB, *Journal of Accountancy*, Vol. 133, May, pp. 42–9.

Gray, D. (1984) Corporate preferences for foreign currency accounting standards, *Journal of Accounting Research*, Vol. 22, No. 2 (Autumn), pp. 760–4.

Gray, S. J. (1981) Segmental or disaggregated financial statements, in T. A. Lee (ed.) *Developments in Financial Reporting*, ch. 2, Philip Alan, Oxford.

Gray, S. J. and Radebaugh, L. H. (1984) International segment disclosures by US and UK multinational enterprises: a descriptive study, *Journal of Accounting Research*, Vol. 22, No. 1, pp. 351–60.

Greene, R. (1980) Equity accounting isn't equitable, *Forbes*, March 31, pp. 104–5.

Griffin, C. H., Williams, T. H. and Larson, K. D. (1980) *Advanced Accounting* (4th edn), pp. 455–8, Irwin, Homewood Illinois.

Griffin, P. (1982) Foreign exchange gains and losses: impact on reported earnings, *Abacus*, Vol. 18, No. 1, pp. 50–69.

Griffin, P. (1983) Managerial preferences for FAS No. 52, *Abacus*, Vol. 19, No. 2, pp. 130–8.

Gynther, R. (1969) Some conceptualising on goodwill, *The Accounting Review*, Vol. XLIV, No. 2, pp. 247–55.

Hardcastle, A. and Renshall, M. A. (1985) *Financial Reporting under the Companies Act 1981: Implementation in Practice*, Institute of Chartered Accountants in England and Wales, London.

Heath, L. C. (1977) *Financial Reporting and the Evaluation of Solvency*, Accounting Research Monograph No. 3, American Institute of Certified Public Accountants.

Hendricksen, E. S. (1982) *Accounting Theory* (4th edn), Irwin, Homewood, Illinois.

Henning, C. N., Piggott, W. and Scott, R. H. (1978) *International Financial Management*, McGraw-Hill, New York.

Hines, R. D. (1984) The impact of stock market reaction for financial accounting standard setting, *Accounting and Business Research*, Vol. 15, No. 60, pp. 3–14.

Holgate, P. A. (1986a) *A Guide to Accounting Standards – Accounting for Goodwill*, Accountants Digest No. 178, Institute of Chartered Accountants in England and Wales,

London.

Holgate, P. A. (1986b) *A Guide to Accounting Standards – SSAP 23 'Accounting for acquisitions and mergers'*, Accountants Digest No. 189, Institute of Chartered Accountants in England and Wales, London.

Hong, H., Kaplan, R. S. and Mandelker, G. (1978) Purchase vs pooling: effects on stock prices, *The Accounting Review*, Vol. LIII, No. 1, pp. 31–47.

Hopwood, W. S., Newbold, P. and Silhan, P. A. (1982) The potential for gains in predictive ability through disaggregation: segmented annual earnings, *Journal of Accounting Research*, Vol. 20, No. 2, pp. 724–32.

Horowitz, B. and Kolodny, R. (1977) Line of business reporting and security prices: an analysis of an SEC disclosure rule, *Bell Journal of Economics*, Vol. 8, No. 1, pp. 234–49.

Hughes, H. P. (1982) *Goodwill in Accounting: A History of the Issues and Problems*, Georgia State University.

IASC (1976) *International Accounting Standard No. 3 – Consolidated financial statements*, International Accounting Standards Committee, London.

IASC (1977) *IAS No. 7 – Statement of changes in financial position*, IASC, London.

IASC (1981) *IAS No. 14 – Reporting financial information by segment*, IASC, London.

IASC (1983) *IAS No. 22 – Accounting for business combinations*, IASC, London.

IASC (1986) *IAS No. 25 – Accounting for investments*, IASC, London.

IASC (1986) *IED No. 28 – Accounting for investments in associates and joint ventures* (exposure draft), IASC, London.

ICAEW (1985) Off-balance-sheet finance and window dressing, *Technical Release 603*, Institute of Chartered Accountants in England and Wales, London.

ICAEW (1986) Invitation to comment on TR 603, *Technical Release 606*, ICAEW, London.

Ijiri, Y. (1975) *Theory of Accounting Measurement*, Studies in Accounting Research No. 10, American Accounting Association, Sarasota, Florida.

Jensen, M. C. and Meckling, W. H. (1976) Theory of the firm: managerial behavior, agency costs and ownership structure, *Journal of Financial Economics,* No. 3, pp. 305–60.

Keane, S. M. (1980) *The Efficient Market Hypothesis*, Gee & Co., London.

Kelly, L. (1985) Corporate management lobbying on FAS No. 8: some further evidence, *Journal of Accounting Research*, Vol. 23, No. 2 (Autumn), pp. 619–31.

Ketz, J. E. (1984) Accounting for business combinations in an age of changing prices, *Accounting and Business Research*, Vol. 14, No. 55, pp. 209–16.

Kinney, W. (1971) Predicting earnings: entity versus sub entity data, *Journal of Accounting Research*, Vol. 9, No. 1, pp. 127–36.

Kitchen, J. (1972) The accounts of British holding company groups, *Accounting and Business Research*, Vol. 2, No. 6, pp. 114–36.

Knox, R. W. (1977) *Statements of Source and Application of Funds: A Practical Guide to SSAP 10*, Institute of Chartered Accountants in England and Wales, London.

Kochanek, R. F. (1974) Segmental financial disclosures by diversified firms and security prices, *The Accounting Review*, Vol. XLIX, No. 2, pp. 245–58.

Law Society (1986) Off-balance-sheet finance and window dressing, *Release S105*, Law Society, London.

Lee, T. A. and Tweedie, D. (1977) *The Institutional Investor and the Corporate Report*, Institute of Chartered Accountants in England and Wales, London.

Leo, K. J. (1984) *Accounting for Business Combinations*, Discussion Paper No. 8, Australian Accounting Research Foundation, Melbourne.

Livnat, J. and Sondhi, A. C. (1986) Finance subsidiaries: their formation and consolidation, *Journal of Business Finance & Accounting*, Vol. 13, No. 1, pp. 137–47.

Lorensen, L. (1972) *Reporting foreign operations of US companies in US dollars*, Accounting Research Study No. 12, American Institute of Certified Public Accountants, New York.

Ma, R. and Parker, R. H. (1983) *Consolidation Accounting in Australia: Concepts and Practice*, Longmans, Melbourne.

Makins, J. H. (1982) Measuring the impact of floating rates and FAS No. 8 on costs of capital for multinationals, *Journal of Accounting Research*, Vol. 20 Supplement, pp. 41–68.

Mason, J. (1983) Funds statements: time to end the confusion, *Accountancy*, Vol. 1084, December, pp. 95–9.

May, R. G. and Sundem, G. L. (1976) Research for accounting policy: an overview, *The Accounting Review*, Vol. LI, No. 4, pp. 747–63.

McKinnon, J. L. (1984) Application of Anglo-American principles of consolidation to corporate financial disclosure in Japan, *Abacus*, Vol. 20, No. 1, pp. 16–33.

McKinnon, J. L., Martin, C. A. and Partington, G. H. (1983) Clarifying funds statements – the two-entity test, *Accounting and Finance*, Vol. 23, May, pp. 79–87.

McLean, A. T. (1972) *Accounting for Business Combinations and Goodwill*, Part 3, Institute of Chartered Accountants in Scotland, Edinburgh.

Miller, M. C. (1981) The funds statement debate: a reconsideration of objectives and concepts, *The Chartered Accountant in Australia*, Vol. 52, No. 1, pp. 55–8 (see also comment by Clift in Vol. 53, No. 3).

Miller, M. C. and Scott, M. R. (1980) *Financial Reporting by Segments*, Discussion Paper No. 4, Australian Accounting Research Foundation, Melbourne.

Moonitz, M. (1951) *The Entity Theory of Consolidated Statements*, The Foundation Press, New York.

Most, K. S. (1982) *Accounting Theory* (2nd edn), Grid Publishing Inc., Columbus, Ohio.

Nobes, C. W. (1980) A review of the translation debate, *Accounting and Business Research*, Vol. 10, No. 39, pp. 421–31.

Nobes, C. W. (1986a) Financial reporting by multinational groups: a few of the questions, and fewer answers, in *Symposium on Financial Accounting Research*, School of Financial Studies, University of Glasgow.

Nobes, C. W. (1986b) *Some Practical and Theoretical Problems of Group Accounting*, Deloitte, Haskins & Sells, London.

Nobes, C. W. and Parker, R. H. (eds.) (1985) *Comparative International Accounting* (2nd edn), Philip Alan, Oxford.

O'Keefe, T. B. and Soloman, S. Y. (1985) Do managers believe the efficient market hypothesis?: additional evidence, *Accounting and Business Research*, Vol. 15, No. 58, pp. 67–79.

Parker, R. H. (1977) Concepts of consolidation in the EEC, *Accountancy*, Vol. 89, No. 1014 (February), pp. 72–5.

Parker, R. H. (1983) The Seventh Directive: some first impressions, *The Accountant's Magazine*, Vol. LXXXVII, No. 928, October, pp. 388–91.

Parker, R. H. (1985) Consolidation accounting, in C. W. Nobes and R. H. Parker (eds.) *Comparative International Accounting*, ch. 10, *op. cit.*

Parker, W. M. (1966) Business combinations and accounting valuation, *Journal of Accounting Research*, Vol. 4, No. 2, pp. 149–54.

Patterson, R. (1986) Foreign currency translation, in L. Skerratt and D. Tonkin (eds.) *Financial Reporting 1985/6*, pp. 53–72, Institute of Chartered Accountants in England and Wales, London.

Patz, D. (1977) A price parity theory of translation, *Accounting and Business Research*, Vol. 8, No. 29, pp. 14–24.

Peasnell, K. V. (1977) A note on the discounted present value concept, *The Accounting Review*, Vol. LII, No. 1, pp. 186–9.

Pedley, R. (1985) Group accounting: a helping hand to better management, *Accountancy*, Vol. 96, No. 1101 (May), pp. 121–3.

Rayburn, F. R. (1979) The evolution of pooling of interests accounting: 1945–70, Working Paper No. 18, pp. 288–317, in *Academy of Accounting Historians Working Paper Series*, Vol. 1, Academy of Accounting Historians, Virginia.

Revsine, L. (1984) The rationale underlying the functional currency choice, *The Accounting Review*, Vol. LIX, No. 3, pp. 505–14.

Robb, A. J. (1985) Funds statements and the two-entity test, *Abacus*, Vol. 21, No. 1, pp. 101–8.

Ronen, J. and Livnat, J. (1981) Incentives for segment reporting, *Journal of Accounting Research*, Vol. 19, No. 2, pp. 459–81.

Rosenfield, P. and Rubin, S. (1985) *Consolidation, Translation, and the Equity Method*, Wiley, New York.

Rosenfield, P. and Rubin, S. (1986) Minority interests: opposing views, *Journal of Accountancy*, Vol. 161, March, pp. 78–88.

SEC (1984) In the matter of Coopers & Lybrand and M. Bruce Cohen CPA (*Digilog* case), *Accounting and Auditing Enforcement Release No. 45*, Release No. 21520, Securities and Exchange Commission, New York.

Shaw, J. (1973) *Bogie on Group Accounts*, Jordans, Bristol.

Shaw, J. (1976) Criteria for consolidation, *Accounting & Business Research*, Vol. 6, No. 25, pp. 71–8.

Silhan, P. A. (1982) Simulated mergers of existent autonomous firms: a new approach to segmentation research, *Journal of Accounting Research*, Vol. 20, No. 1, pp. 255–62.

Silhan, P. A. (1983) The effects of segmenting quarterly sales and margins on extrapolative forecasts of conglomerate earnings: extension and replication, *Journal of Accounting Research*, Vol. 21, No. 1, pp. 341–7.

Silhan, P. A. (1984) Company size and the issue of quarterly segment reporting, *Journal of Accounting and Public Policy*, Vol. 3, No. 3, pp. 185–97.

Skerratt, L. and Tonkin, D. (eds.) (1985) *Financial Reporting 1984/5: A Survey of UK Published Accounts*, Institute of Chartered Accountants in England and Wales, London.

Skerratt, L. and Tonkin, D (eds.) (1986) *Financial Reporting 1985/6*, Institute of Chartered Accountants in England and Wales, London.

Snavely, H. J. (1975) Pooling should be mandatory, *CPA Journal*, Vol. XLV, No. 12, pp. 23–6.

Taylor, P. A. (1979a) What are funds flow statements?, *Accountancy*, Vol. 90, No. 1033 (September), pp. 89–92.

Taylor, P. A. (1979b) Published funds statements and SSAP 10, *Accountancy*, Vol. 90, No. 1034 (October), pp. 95–8.

Taylor, P. A. (1985) The foreign currency translation process: a matrix funds flow analysis, *British Accounting Review*, Vol. 17, No. 1, pp. 3–22.

Taylor, T. (1984) NTR puts order into Plessey's far-flung empire, *Accountancy*, Vol. 95, No. 1087, pp. 131–5.

Thomas, A. (1975) The FASB and the allocation fallacy, *Journal of Accountancy*, Vol. 140, November, pp. 65–8.

Topple, B. (1979a) Goodwill on consolidation, *Accountancy*, Vol. 90, No. 1026, pp. 114–20.

Topple, B. (1979b) Consolidated accounts: questions of control, *Accountancy*, Vol. 90, No. 1029, pp. 123–9.

Tweedie, D. (1981) *The Institutional Investor and Financial Information*, Institute of Chartered Accountants in England and Wales, London.

Walker, R. G. (1968) Disclosure by diversified companies, *Abacus*, Vol. 4, No. 1, pp. 27–38.

Walker, R. G. (1976) An evaluation of the information conveyed by consolidated financial statements, *Abacus*, Vol. 12, No. 2, pp. 77–115.

Walker, R. G. (1978a) *Consolidated Statements: A History and Analysis*, Arno Press, New York.

Walker, R. G. (1978b) International accounting compromises: the case of consolidation accounting, *Abacus*, Vol. 14, No. 2, pp. 97–117.

Watts, R. L. and Zimmerman, J. L. (1979) The demand for and supply of accounting theories: the market for excuses, *The Accounting Review*, Vol. LIV, No, 2, pp. 273–305.

Whitehouse, I. (1984) Group accounts: Croda and Dowty tame a monster, *Accountancy*, Vol. 95, No. 1092, pp. 106–8.

Whittaker, J. and Cooke, T. E. (1983) Accounting for goodwill and business combinations: has the ASC got it right?, *Accountants' Magazine*, Vol. LXXXVII, No. 919, pp. 18–21.

Wilkins, R. M. (1979) *Group Accounts* (2nd edn), Institute of Chartered Accountants in England and Wales, London.

Wilkins R. M. (1986) Takeovers, in L. Skerratt and D. Tonkin (eds.) *Financial Reporting 1985/6*, Institute of Chartered Accountants in England and Wales, London.

Willott, R. (1985) *Current Accounting Law and Practice 1985*, Quinta Publishing, London.

Woolf, E. (1985) Goodwill: SSAP 22 the best answer?, *Accountancy*, Vol. 96, No. 1101 (May), pp. 119–21.

Wyatt, A. R. (1963) *A Critical Study of Accounting for Business Combinations*, Accounting Research Study No. 5, Accounting Principles Board, New York.

Wyatt, A. R. (1983) Efficient market theory: its impact on accounting, *Journal of Accountancy*, Vol. 155, February, pp. 56–62, 65.

Zeff, S. A. (1978) The rise of 'economic consequences', *Journal of Accountancy*, Vol. 146, December, pp. 152–63.

Author Index

Subject Index